Stanley L. McMichael
and
Paul T. O'Keefe

LEASES

PERCENTAGE, SHORT
and LONG TERM

Sixth Edition

Englewood Cliffs, N.J.
PRENTICE-HALL, INC.

Prentice-Hall International, Inc., *London*
Prentice-Hall of Australia, Pty., Ltd. *Sydney*
Prentice-Hall of Canada, Ltd., *Toronto*
Prentice-Hall of India Private Ltd., *New Delhi*
Prentice-Hall of Japan, *Tokyo*

Fourth Printing . . . . . April, 1980

Library of Congress Cataloging in Publication Data

McMichael, Stanley L
  Leases; percentage, short and long term.

  First published in 1921 under title: Long
term land leaseholds.
    1. Leases—United States. I. O'Keefe, Paul T.
II. Title.
KF590.M3 1974   346'.73'04346   73-15969
ISBN 0-13-527309-9

This publication is designed to provide accurate and
authoritative information in regard to the subject
matter covered. It is sold with the understanding that
the publisher is not engaged in rendering legal, accounting, or other professional service. If legal advice or
other expert assistance is required, the services of
a competent professional person should be sought.

*. . . From the Declaration of Principles jointly adopted
by a Committee of the American Bar Association
and a Committee of Publishers and Associations.*

ABOUT THE AUTHORS:

STANLEY L. McMICHAEL was one of the nation's
foremost authors and experts in the real estate field
with over forty years experience. His twenty-one
classics include "McMichael's Appraising Manual,"
"How to Finance Real Estate," and "How to Operate
a Real Estate Business."

PAUL T. O'KEEFE is presently associated with James
Felt-Hubert & Hubert Inc., specialists in consultant,
appraisal, management and brokerage work. A recognized authority in the field, Mr. O'Keefe's background
includes the buying, selling, managing, leasing, ex-
changing and appraising of all types of real estate
throughout the country. He has made appraisals
for the City of New York, the State of New York,
and for various urban renewal agencies. He also
acts as consultant to nation-wide banking interests.
From 1958 to 1961 Mr. O'Keefe took leave of
absence from his business career to act as Deputy
Mayor of New York City and subsequently became
its Commissioner of Real Estate. He is a member of
the Real Estate Board of New York, the American
Institute of Real Estate Appraising, and the New York
Appraisal Society.

Table of Contents

1. Origin of Leasing **1**

In early Greece · In early Rome · In early England · In America · The short-term lease · The percentage lease

2. Definitions **6**

3. Essential Features and Characteristics of Leases . . . **10**

Names of lessor and lessee · The demise or letting · The recitals or description · The habendum-duration of the lease · The reddendum or rental · Covenants

4. Short-Term Leases **20**

Short-term leases dominate the market · Lease should be written · Lessor-lessee relationship · General rules for short-term leases · Lease forms · Need for legal counsel

5. General Considerations in Short-Term Leases . . . **24**

Dwellings · Apartments · Stores · Office buildings · Loft buildings, manufacturing buildings, storage space

6. Percentage Leases **32**

Development of the percentage lease · Kinds of percentage lease · Advantages and disadvantages of percentage leases · Where should percentage lease be made? · What kind of business should operate under a percentage lease? · What are tenant qualifications?

v

7. Percentage Leases, Minimum Rental and Percentage Rate   40

Minimum rental · Should the minimum rental be equivalent to fixed rental value? · Percentage rates · Percentage tables · Table of percentage rates

8. Percentage Lease Accounting Provisions .   .   .   48

Definition of sales · Right to inspect lessee's books · Reporting sales-settling accounts

9. Special Provisions in Percentage Leases .   .   .   56

Name under which business is to be conducted · Prior possession · Continued occupancy · Manner of conducting business · Restriction against other outlets · Tenant advertising · Sub-leasing · Exclusives · Differential between wholesale and retail sales · Percentage differentials for varying types of merchandise · Off premises sales · Allowance to tenant for capital improvements · Recapture clauses

10. Concessions or Leased Departments   65

Reasons for leasing department · Departments most commonly leased · Rentals · Location · Term of lease · Nature of operation · Store name, advertising and promotion · Fixtures · Employees · Store customs · Delivery service · Sales receipts · Taxes and insurance · Default

11. Shopping Center Lease   71

Types of shopping centers · Characteristics of shopping centers · Influence of shopping center characteristics on leases

12. Chain Stores   84

Postwar development in chain stores · Extent of chain store operations today · History of chain store operations · Methods of operation · Chain store operations in the real estate field · The real estate broker in chain store lease · Chain store leases

13. Long-Term Leases 92

What is a long-term lease? · Utilization of long-term leases · Classification of long-term leases · Long-term leases on land · Long-term leases on land and improvements

14. Sales and Leaseback 105

The lessor in sale-leaseback transactions · The lessee in sale-leaseback transactions · Advantages and disadvantages of sale-leaseback transactions · Sale-leaseback vs. mortgage financing · Fixing the sales prices and rental terms · Option to repurchase · Type of property

15. Valuation of Leaseholds 115

The "open market" concept should prevail · What creates leasehold value · What limits leasehold value · Theory of leasehold valuation

16. Financing Leaseholds 126

Leasehold financing · Mortgaging the fee · When is leasehold mortgagable? · Value · Investment by lessee · Sale and financing of subordinate lease interests

17. Income Tax Laws and Leases 133

Changes in laws and regulations · Summary of basic principles of taxation · Income and expense in tax computations · Considerations of the owner-lessor · Considerations of the lessee

18. Drawing the Lease: The Lawyer and the Broker . . . 143

Standardized leases · Standard forms not always adaptable · Chain store lease forms · The lawyer · Letter of intent—agreement to make lease · Re-negotiating the deal

SPECIMEN LEASES

Percentage Leases **151**

      Percentage Store Leases, 151
      Percentage Lease Evolved in Chicago, 157
      Percentage Lease Used in Knoxville, 168
      Chain Store Percentage Lease, 171
      Los Angeles Percentage Lease, 179
      Shopping Center Lease, 187
      Concession Lease, 210
      News Stand Percentage Lease, 222

Short-Term Leases **225**

      Office Lease, 225
      Lease in New Office Building, 235
      Apartment Lease, 268
      Lease for Furnished House or Apartment, 272
      Theater Lease, 274
      Lease on Manufacturing Space, 277
      Loft Lease, 284
      Farm Lease, 293
      One Family House Lease, 295
      Gas Station Lease, 296
      Billboard and Sign Lease, 298
      Oil Well Lease (Short Form), 300
      Oil Well Lease, 301
      Lease for Drilling for Oil and Gas, 304
      A Short Form of a House Lease, 307

Long-Term Leases (Over 25 Years) **309**

      Commitment to Purchase in Sale-Leaseback
         Transaction, 309
      Lease Used in Sale-Leaseback Transaction, 310
      Forty-Year Lease to the Woolworth Company, 323
      Ninety-Nine Year Lease, 329
      "Short Form" of Ninety-Nine Year Lease, 339
      Building Agreement, 347
      Lease of Air Rights, 355

Miscellaneous Leases and Forms **384**

    Short Form Lease, For Purpose of Recording, 384
    Extension of Lease, 385
    Form for Collecting Lease Renewals, 385
    Option to Rent Chain Store Property, 386
    Method for Renewing Industrial Lease, 386
    Waiver of Priority, 387
    Chattel Mortgage Clause, 388
    Assignment of Lease and Leasehold Estate, 389
    Lease Permitting Purchase by Amortization Process, 390
    Amortized Lease Agreement, 400
    Agreement to Make a Long-Term Lease, 404
    Agreement to Make a Long-Term Lease, 407
    Agreement to Sell a Leasehold Interest, 409
    Mortgage Deed, 411
    Check Sheet Containing Items to Consider in Creating,
        Selling, or Appraising Long-Term Leases, 416

Index **435**

Preface

Since the publication of the earlier edition of this book there have been many significant changes in leasing techniques throughout the United States. There have been five principal causes: the continuing expansion of chain store systems; the development of large scale shopping centers; the growing acceptance of the sale-leaseback as a means of achieving 100 per cent financing; the impact of Federal income tax law and regulations on lease transactions; and the wider use of the long-term ground lease as a financing device.

These changes have made it necessary to alter the text of the previous editions. Most of the chapters have been subject to substantial revision. In the work of revision I have eliminated extraneous material not directly affecting lease transactions. It might be noted that in this text I have not considered condominiums or cooperatives except in those uncommon instances when condominiums and cooperatives are tied in with lease transactions.

The condominium itself is essentially not a lease. It is a series of purchases within a development with the individual purchaser receiving title to the portion that he occupies. The condominium units which are individually owned can, of course, themselves be leased but under normal leasing procedures.

In the case of the cooperative, the owner is generally a corporation who sells participating stock in the property. The cooperator, in consideration of the purchase of his stock interest, is entitled to have a proprietary lease on one of the units in the cooperative. This may be residential, commercial or industrial. The cooperator-lessee also has the right to sublet under his proprietary lease but normal leasing procedures are followed in these transactions.

There is one significant adjustment in leasing procedures—the inclusion of escalation clauses in commercial property leases—which require the tenant to pay a proportionate share of increased real estate taxes and operating charges. This is necessary and equitable in an expanding economy.

In the preparation of this text I am indebted to many individuals, to professional and non-professional organizations for their valued assistance and advice. Their names are too numerous to mention but my gratitude must be noted.

PAUL T. O'KEEFE

CHAPTER 1

Origin of Leasing

Origin of the practice of leasing for terms of years is shrouded in antiquity. It had been engaged in for hundreds of years, even before the time of Christ. In subsequent years it has been followed in countries all over the world.

The methods differ widely in detail but are essentially the same. The premises described in the written document are simply rented for a stated consideration. The owner is known as the *lessor* and the tenant as the *lessee*.

IN EARLY GREECE

Leases in perpetuity were granted by the Athenian government upon mines owned by the state. A certain sum in cash was paid at the outset as security and the annual rental fixed at 4 per cent of the profits (a form of percentage lease). The lessee could sell his lease or borrow money on it (a form of leasehold financing). Gold mines in Thasos and silver mines in Laurium were held in this way. Perpetual leaseholds on arable land in Attica were mentioned, in lists of property, by Grecian orators as early as 500 B.C.

IN EARLY ROME

The history of leasing as followed in Rome is vague, but there is little doubt that the rulers of the early empire exercised absolute control over all the land and apportioned it out among a favored few, who became the overlords of their time and generation.

Having large areas of land which they were not able to cultivate or realize a profit from, they devised a rental or leasing system which has its counterpart today in modern long-term leases. This type of early lease was called an "emphyteusis." The grantee was called the "emphyteuta" and did not become actual owner of the property, but simply had the right of possession under certain stipulated conditions.

Those conditions conferred a perpetual right upon him and his heirs to possession of the land in consideration of a fixed annual payment, but he was not entitled to abandon it, nor was he able to free himself of his obligations without his lord's consent. The latter was entitled to hold the grant forfeited if the tenant fell three years in arrears in his rent (in church lands for two years), or if the land taxes were in arrears for a similar period. Provision was also made that he could not alienate (transfer) the land or assign or sublease the premises without the lord's consent.

If the alienation was by sale, the tenant was required to state the price fixed, so as to give the lord his statutory right of buying it in at the same price. All conditions having been met, and the lord's consent having been acquired, the tenant then had the right to proceed by paying a 2 per cent commission to the lord on the consideration involved. These early lords, therefore, were the first to collect commissions on the transfer of real estate.

IN EARLY ENGLAND

It was doubtless from this early source that land leases came into existence in England. The feudal or baronial system as practiced in England was patterned after the Roman one. English kings claimed the ownership of all the land in their kingdom, and the laws of Great Britain recognize even today no absolute private ownership in land.

Early English barons, like the earlier Roman lords, fell back upon the system of renting or leasing their properties, and it was in England that the system of long-term land leases was refined and practiced widely. Today many British families in the nobility have extensive holdings in the business centers of large cities. The Duke of Westminster, for example, possesses large areas of business property in the city of London under long-term leases, some of which have entered upon for successive terms of 99 years each.

Prior to the reigns of Henry VII and Henry VIII, leases were not given the same legal recognition as today. They were easily voided; the lessee was often dispossessed and awarded only a nominal sum for the value of his improvements, and that sum could only be collected after suit had been instituted, the case tried, and the verdict rendered in his favor. Acts were passed during the reigns of Henry VII and Henry VIII enabling the tenant to retain or recover possession of leased land. From that time on the making of long-term leases flourished in England and leases became a matter of valuable possession.

English leases were made earlier than the reign of William the Conqueror. Some years ago a report was published that a lease for 999 years executed in London had expired and heirs of the original lessee were again granted possession of the premises.

Lord Coke, who lived in the reign of Queen Elizabeth, in his writings on the subject of leases, suggested that a lease for 1,000 years might on its face suggest fraud; it is thought that to avoid such a contingency the lessors of those early days set upon 999 years as the extreme limit for the life of the lease. Such leases, in any event, were made at that time.

England, in following its practice of leasing land for long periods, has handed down many of the peculiarities of the present system. Modern demands and conditions, however, have resulted in the introduction of new features in different parts of the country; the result is a decided lack of uniformity.

IN AMERICA

Leasing for terms of years, particularly long terms, was first introduced into this country about the year 1700 in the cities of Baltimore and Philadelphia, settled largely by English colonists. In New York, settled by Hollanders, leasing was not known until a much later date.

Laws in different states of the Union frequently limit the term for which leases, particularly on agricultural land, may be made. This was evidently done to prevent the setting up of landlordism of a baronial type. It is well for one to become thoroughly familiar with the laws governing the state in which one lives; but beyond such specific state regulations, the principles of making leases are practically the same throughout the entire country.

Modern long-term building leases, such as are used extensively in large American cities, came into general use from 1870 to 1880 and differed from earlier land leases, inasmuch as the lessee obligated himself to improve the leased property with suitable buildings within a given period, thereby enhancing it in value. These more modern leases also required the lessee to furnish bond that he would not only pay his rent promptly, but also would live up to his building covenant when the time came due for its enforcement.

The 99-Year Lease

Just why leases came to be made for a period of 99 years is uncertain. Matthew Bacon, author of "A Treatise on Leases and Terms for Years" published in London, England, in 1798, explains in various parts of his book that the 99-year period represents three lives, but Bacon does not indicate why such a term was selected as the length of time a lease was to prevail. It is supposed by some that there was an English common law which prevented a lessor from granting a lease for 100 years and that it was therefore made for a somewhat briefer period, but no real evidence has ever been found to substantiate this theory.

Utilization of the 99-year lease as a medium for the development of modern American cities flourished during the early part of this century. In more recent years, and particularly since World War II, long term leases were made to developers who generally have shorter terms with renewal options extending the actual lease to 99 years or even a longer period. Such leases have been used principally in cases where the tenant is making a substantial improvement, such as a new office building. The original period of the lease would probably be co-terminus with the real estate financing. The renewal options generally carry a provision for land reappraisal which might produce higher rentals during the option periods, but would stipulate that the rent in no circumstances would be lower than during the initial lease term.

The practice of leasing has done much to build up American communities, whether in the form of percentage leases to chain stores or the utilization of valuable sites for building projects; with the landlord contributing his land for a rental consideration and the tenant providing a building capable of earning a good return upon its production cost.

The Short-Term Lease

Short-term leases, ranging in terms from one to twenty years, have been used for centuries on all types of properties, single family houses, multi-tenanted apartment houses, store buildings, industrial properties, etc.

The Percentage Lease

The modern percentage lease came into existence about 1915. Since that time it has been used extensively in the leasing of store properties, particularly those located in the centers of real estate business activity.

CHAPTER 2

Definitions

Lease: A contract transferring the right to the possession and enjoyment of real estate for a definite period of time.

Lessor: the owner—one who lets the property.

Lessee: the tenant.

Rent—Rental: the consideration paid by the lessee for the possession and use of the property.

Covenants: clauses in the lease which define the rights and obligations of lessor and lessee.

Term—Lease Term: the specified duration of the lease, i.e., "the lease has a term of 10 years." When used in the plural, this word has a different meaning; it is then usually synonymous with "covenants," i.e., "the terms of the lease provide that the tenant must maintain the property in good condition and make all interior repairs."

Leasehold—Leasehold estate: the lessee's interest in the property created by the lease. The full designation for this interest is "leasehold estate" but it is commonly referred to as a leasehold.

Sublessor—Sublessee—Sublease: sometimes a tenant is permitted to lease his interest to a third party. The original lessee thereby becomes a *sublessor*. The new tenant is the *sublessee*. The new agreement between sublessor and sublessee is a *sublease*.

Prime Tenant: when one or more subleases have been made on a property, the original lessee is sometimes referred to as the prime tenant.

Sandwich Lease: intermediary instrument in three or more leases on the same property, i.e., A leases to B, B subleases to C, C subleases to D; the agreement between B and C would be called a "sandwich lease."

Tenancy at Will—Month-to-Month Tenancy: lease agreement cancellable by either party on short notice—usually 30, 60 or 90 days.

Long-Term Lease—Short-Term Lease: there is no clear understanding as to what is a short-term lease and what is a long-term lease. By common usage, people in the real estate business have come to regard a long-term lease as one for a period of 21 years or more. Throughout this book we will generally use the expression "long-term lease" in this accepted sense.

"Short-term lease," on the other hand, has various relative connotations. Leases on one family dwellings and apartment houses are made customarily for a one-, two- or three-year term. It would be misleading to refer to a ten-year lease on such a property as a "short-term lease."

On the other hand, the purchase lease transaction entered into by insurance companies and business or industrial concerns usually involve a lease term of at least 21 years. A ten-year lease in such a transaction would be considered a short-term lease.

The principal fallacy in lease terminology is the assumption that short-term and long-term leases collectively constitute an all-inclusive classification. Actually there are intermediate-term leases that properly could be called neither short-term nor long-term. These would include a great many of the everyday commercial leases that are made for ten to fifteen year periods.

No nomenclature has been developed for this type of lease. In this text, we will generally consider them in the short-term category because their covenants will be more closely akin to the covenants of a short-term than a long-term lease.

If any lease for less than 21 years is referred to as a long-term lease, it will be with the qualification that it pertains to the type of property involved—for instance, a ten-year lease (supra) on a one family dwelling.

Percentage Lease: a lease wherein the tenant is required to pay as rental a specified percentage of the gross income from sales made upon the premises.

Net Lease: a lease in which the tenant pays all or a substantial part of cost of operating and maintenance. There are various expressions used in the real estate business to describe the many variations in net lease transactions. For instance, if a lease provides for the tenant to pay *all* operating expenses, maintenance costs, insurance, real estate taxes, etc., it might be referred to as "100% net" or "net-net." If the lease provides for the tenant to maintain and operate the premises only, it might be referred to as "net-excepting for taxes, insurance and outside repairs."

Net Rental: rental paid under a net lease agreement.

Gross Lease: the antonym of net lease. One in which the owner pays taxes, insurance, maintenance, operating expense, etc. The gross lease today is confined largely to apartments and older commercial buildings. In other commercial properties there is generally a negotiated sharing of the cost of operation.

Escalation clause: a lease covenant providing for the tenant to pay any increase in taxes and/or operating expense above the amounts prevailing at the time of the execution of the lease agreement. The usual escalation clause also provides for a decrease in rental if there is a decline in real estate taxes or operating expenses.

Primary and Secondary Rentals: a lease covenant under which a rental is divided into two categories. The primary rental is a fixed amount usually based upon a definite percentage of property value as established at the time of the execution of the lease agreement. The secondary rental, which would be prorated according to the space which a tenant might occupy in a building, covers the expense of taxes, repairs and insurance, water, heat, etc. The secondary rental agreement achieves the same result as an escalator clause.

Short-Form Lease: when either of the parties wishes to record a lease agreement but does not want the rentals and covenants

exposed to the public eye, a short-form document is sometimes used which recites the fact that a lease has been made
between the parties covering certain premises for a specified
term. It would then stipulate somewhat as follows: "This lease
has been made upon the rents, terms, covenants and conditions
contained in a certain collateral agreement or lease between
the parties hereto and bearing even date herewith."

Assignment: an instrument by which a lessee transfers his interest
to a third party. For all practical purposes, an assignment is
synonymous with a sublease.

Extension: an agreement by which a lease is made effective for an
additional period of time beyond its expiration date—usually
synonymous with renewal.

Renewal Option: a lease covenant giving the lessee the right to
extend the lease for an additional period of years on specified
terms.

Security: a sum of money, or equivalent, deposited by the lessee
with the lessor or a trustee, as guarantee for performance under
the lease terms.

Concession: an allowance, usually in the form of rent abatement,
made to the lessee by the lessor. Concessions are made for a
variety of reasons—to induce a tenant to sign a lease; as consideration of additional expenses of the tenant, as, for example,
moving expenses, rental obligations on lease of premises which
tenant is vacating, and so on.

Bonus: generally refers to payment made by lessee to the lessor as
additional consideration.

CHAPTER 3

Essential Features and Characteristics of Leases

A lease is a binding contract between owner and tenant under which the tenant secures the possession and profits of land and/or improvements in exchange for a rental or consideration. Because it is a binding contract, neither owner nor tenant should enter into such an agreement without the advice of legal counsel.

All leases have seven essential parts:

1. Names of lessor and lessee.
2. The demise, or letting of the premises.
3. Recitals, covering the description of the property and how title is held.
4. The habendum, defining the beginning and the term of the letting.
5. The reddendum, or terms of rental (amount of rent—method of payment).
6. Signatures and acknowledgments.
7. The covenants and conditions under which the tenant or lessee holds occupancy.

In most leases, the first six of these essential features can be included in a few short paragraphs but many pages may be required for the covenants, particularly on long term leases.

NAMES OF LESSOR AND LESSEE

This indenture made the .. day of ...... between ...... party of the first part, hereinafter called the "lessor" and the .... Company, a duly organized and existing corporation, having an office and place of business at .... City of .... State of ...., party of the second part, hereinafter called the lessee...........

The foregoing is a standard opening clause in a lease agreement setting forth the names of the parties to the lease. It is important that the lessor's name be exactly the same as it is in the deed or other instrument under which the lessor has title or possession of the property.

Leases can be made generally speaking by any person capable of making a contract. A lease by or to an infant is voidable at his option. A guardian is necessary in such cases to bind an infant. The making of a lease by a married woman is governed by the statute in each state controlling her right to make contracts. In most states, equal rights are granted with the husband. In dealing with an insane person or incompetent, the transaction must be through a guardian or a committee. Leases by corporations must be made by duly authorized officials.

THE DEMISE OR LETTING

The lessor has agreed to let and hereby does let and demise to the lessee, and the lessee has agreed to take and hereby does take from the lessor.

The foregoing simple clauses which usually precede a description of the leased premises are characteristic of the legal phraseology used in demising or actual granting of lease rights.

THE RECITALS OR DESCRIPTION

The identification of the leased premises can be done briefly— that is by street number, or by a full legal description of the property. In many short-term leases for periods of say five years or less, the parties may be satisfied with the simpler methods of identification.

The recital clause might read:

. . . grade floor store and basement of building at 780 Main Street, City of . . . . State of . . . .

But as the lease term increases, and the commitments of lessor and lessee become correspondingly more serious, the tendency is to describe the property by metes and bounds, or as it is described in the registered deed.

When both land and building are leased, a description of the building in general terms is often desirable, but the lease of the land will carry the right of possession of the buildings located on it, unless expressly excepted.

THE HABENDUM—DURATION OF THE LEASE

This lease is for a term of .. years commencing on the .. day of . . . . . . 19 .. and ending on the .. day of . . . . . . 19 ..

These sentences describe the term during which the lease is effective. It is not necessary that the lease be executed on the day on which it becomes effective. It may be executed six months or a year in advance of the effective date.

It is important to remember that a lessor cannot convey use of the premises for a longer period than he himself controls the property. For instance, a life tenant as lessor might make a lease agreement for ten years, but such an agreement would be automatically cancelled on his death. If a lessee is subletting, he cannot make a lease agreement beyond the term of the original lease.

THE REDDENDUM OR RENTAL

This lease is made for and in consideration of an annual rental of $ . . . ., payable . . . . The first payment shall be due on . . . . . . at . . . . . The succeeding payments shall be due on the .. day of each and every succeeding . . . . at . . . . Lessor may from time to time designate other places for the payment of the rent by written notice to lessee.

The method of payment of the rental is usually a matter of agreement. In most residential and commercial properties rental is paid monthly. In some large properties and particularly those under a net lease for a long period of years, rental may be paid quarter annually, semi-annually or even annually.

COVENANTS

As noted previously, the lease is a binding contract between owner and tenant under which the tenant secures the possession and profits of land and improvements in exchange for a rental or consideration. Expressed or implied in the agreement is the requirement that the tenant will give the property adequate care and maintenance.

Lease covenants therefore have to do with one of the following fundamentals:

1. The tenant's obligation to pay rent.
2. The tenant's right to possession and quiet enjoyment.
3. The tenant's obligation to maintain and care for the property.

Covenants may be simply expressed. In the next chapter we quote the covenant section from an Arlington, Virginia, lease, containing only four sentences. But in most leases, covenants are more specific, more detailed, and may contain a number of clauses covering each of the three fundamental elements.

Some of the most detailed leases are those used in the New York City area. Any normal contingency that might arise between landlord and tenant is covered by the various forms used by the Real Estate Board of New York. The most comprehensive of the New York Board's forms is its standard office lease which we have used as a basic reference in this chapter, although we have also had reference to leases on other types of properties. (The actual lease form will be found in the Appendix at page 235.)

The Tenant's Obligation to Pay Rent

The reddendum simply states that the tenant will pay the rent in equal monthly payments (or at other regular intervals, most leases being on a monthly basis). Rental is invariably paid in advance. Lease covenants pertaining to the tenant's obligation to pay rent might cover the following matters:

> Bills and Notices
> Default
> Bankruptcy
> Utility charges
> Taxes—Insurance
> Security

BILLS—NOTICES

In most rental properties, it is customary but not obligatory for the landlord to send a rent bill at the beginning of the month. A lease covenant may state that the bill can be delivered to the tenant personally, sent by registered mail, or left for him at the premises.

DEFAULT—REMEDIES OF LANDLORD

If the tenant defaults in the payment of rent, the landlord may repossess the premises (by evicting the tenant if necessary), or may sue the tenant, or both.

The landlord may then lease the property to a new tenant and hold the defaulting tenant liable for any loss of rent because of such reletting, and for any costs incidental to the reletting, such as attorney's fees, brokerage, advertising, etc.

BANKRUPTCY

The New York Real Estate Board form provides that if a bankruptcy proceeding affecting a tenant is not discharged within 30 days, or if the tenant assigns for the benefit of creditors, the landlord has the option of cancelling the lease.

UTILITY CHARGES

Some leases provide for utilities, such as electricity, to be provided to the tenant at the owner's expense. Others may require the tenant to pay these charges directly (if submetering is legal). Still other leases may require the tenant to reimburse the landlord for electric and water charges. Such reimbursement will generally be provided for in the monthly rental bill.

TAXES—INSURANCE

Net leases usually require that the tenant pay real estate taxes and building insurance. Real estate taxes are customarily classified as "additional rent." Insurance, in these cases, is classified as a tenant expense.

SECURITY

If the tenant makes a security deposit with the landlord, the landlord generally has the right to retain this money in the event of a rental default. Deposit is usually returned at the end of the lease term or applied to the final rental payment(s).

The Tenant's Right to Possession and Quiet Enjoyment

In consideration for the rental paid the landlord guarantees to the tenant, the use, possession and quiet enjoyment of the premises. Lease covenants pertaining to these tenant rights might cover the following:

> Use
> Compliance with Statutes
> Fire Insurance
> Property Loss, Damage, Fire Loss
> Building Services
> Access
> Assignment—Mortgaging
> Eminent Domain
> Failure to Give Possession

USE

The use to which the premises will be put is defined in the lease. The definitions may be general such as "residence for occupancy by one family." In other cases the use may be more closely circumscribed, particularly in retail stores where the owner will want to limit or eliminate competition between adjoining tenants.

COMPLIANCE WITH STATUTES

The tenant will agree to comply with any local, state, or federal laws, rules, or regulations covering the use or the occupancy of the property. In New York, for instance, there is a prohibition against the tenant cleaning windows in "violation of Section 202 of the Labor Law." This clause pertains to the use of safety devices for outside cleaning of windows.

FIRE INSURANCE

The tenant will agree to comply with regulations of the Fire Underwriters and not to use the premises or commit any act that might cause the fire insurance rates to increase.

PROPERTY LOSS, DAMAGE, FIRE LOSS

Covenants on fire loss, damage, property restoration, etc., may be the subject of protracted negotiations. A covenant may be included in the lease holding the landlord harmless for any property loss, damage by fire or personal injuries occurring in the premises unless caused by the landlord's neglect.

If the premises are damaged by fire or other cause for which the tenant is not responsible, the landlord may repair the damage and make a rent allowance to the tenant for the period during which the repairs are being made. If the damage is caused by the tenant, the landlord may make the repairs without a rent abatement and will retain the right for further action against the tenant. The landlord usually reserves the right to terminate the lease if the property is rendered uninhabitable by fire.

BUILDING SERVICES

If building service such as heat, elevator services, air conditioning, etc., are to be furnished to the tenant by the landlord, they are usually specified in detail, both as to the nature of the service and as to the manner and frequency of performance.

ACCESS

The landlord is usually given the right of access to make any necessary structural or mechanical repairs. He is often given the right of access to show the property to prospective new tenants if the lease is expiring or if there is likelihood of the present tenant moving.

ASSIGNMENT—MORTGAGING

If the tenant is given any right to assign or sublet the premises or to mortgage his leasehold interest, it should be carefully set forth in a lease covenant. Most leases specifically prohibit lease assignments without the owner's consent.

The prospect of a lessee securing a mortgage on a short-term lease is so remote that short-term documents are usually silent on this point.

EMINENT DOMAIN

Most leases drawn today carry an eminent domain clause extinguishing the rights of the lessee if the property is taken in condemnation proceedings.

Although the chance that a specific property may be taken by the municipality, state or Federal government is remote, there have been in the past many litigated actions arising out of lessee's claims for a portion of the condemnation award.

Under most jurisdictions the maximum that can be awarded for a piece of property is its fair and reasonable market value. If, therefore, the lessee has any claim, it would be asserted against the owner's interest. If a piece of property is adjudged to be worth $50,-000 in a condemnation proceeding, any value assigned to the leasehold interest is deducted from the $50,000.

Lessees today will generally consent to the inclusion of the eminent domain clause unless the lessee has made substantial improvements to the property. In such a case he might expect the owner to indemnify him for the reasonable value of these improvements at the time of condemnation.

FAILURE TO GIVE POSSESSION

Occasionally a landlord is unable to give possession of the premises on the date specified: (1) because the building may not have been completed, (2) because he has been unable to gain possession from the previous tenant or (3) because repairs or remodeling may not have been completed.

Leases may contain a covenant holding the landlord harmless for this inability to give possession and at the same time not releasing the tenant from his obligation to take the property. Rent, of course, would not commence until possession had been given. In many leases on new office buildings an outside limit is set as a possession date. If the owner is unable to deliver possession by this date, the tenant may have the right of cancellation.

In many leases on new buildings the owner assumes the tenant's obligation under his old lease. This is particularly true where an owner is desirable of securing a particular tenant. In some cases the tenant may have as much as three or four years of an unexpired lease term in his present quarters. In an active rental market an owner of a new building may feel that he is taking a relatively small risk in assuming such an obligation because the leasehold interest thus acquired can probably be disposed of at little or no loss.

The Tenant's Obligation to Maintain and Care for the Property

As noted before, the tenant's obligation to maintain and care for the interior of the property may be a total one or a partial one but only in long-term net leases does the tenant customarily take care of the exterior of the building.

There should be a clear-cut understanding as to: (a) what the tenant is required to do, (b) what the landlord is required to do, and (c) what the tenant is prohibited from doing.

The tenant's obligations might be covered by covenants pertaining to the following:

> Alterations
> Repairs
> Care of Public Areas
> End of Lease Term

ALTERATIONS

Alterations are made generally only with the landlord's consent. If the alterations constitute an addition to the structure, they automatically become the property of the landlord. The landlord, however, in consenting to a tenant's alteration program, may require removal of the alterations at the expiration of the lease and the restoration of the property to its original condition.

In our chapter on shopping centers (Chapter 11), we discuss an alteration program which may be made by the tenant and for which he will be reimbursed in installments by the owner. The reimbursement may also take the form of rent allowances.

In the preceding chapter, we discussed alteration programs in new office buildings where the tenant receives a partial reimbursement from the owner.

The general pattern however, is for the cost of alteration to be borne completely by the tenant, particularly in short-term leases.

REPAIRS

The tenant will be required to maintain the property in a good state of repair, both as to structural and mechanical building details, unless the lease specifies that all or part of this work is to be performed by the landlord.

If the tenant fails in the maintenance that he is required to do by the lease, the landlord may have the option of doing the work and making a proper charge to the tenant.

CARE OF PUBLIC AREAS

The tenant will usually be required to keep public areas, such as halls, free from obstruction. Cleaning of this space is frequently an obligation of the landlord.

END OF TERM

At the end of the lease term the tenant will usually be required to return the property to the landlord in as good condition as he received it, except for ordinary wear and tear. He will be required to remove all debris and obstructions. In describing the condition at the expiration of the lease, the term "broom clean" is customarily used.

CHAPTER 4

Short-Term Leases

Leases are alike in principle, except with respect to length of tenure. They may be for one year or in perpetuity. The rights and privileges are usually the same, although when the term is longer, greater care is taken in drawing the covenants. For leases drawn for one year, the tenant's obligation to maintain the property in good repair may be covered by a single sentence. When a lease is drawn for long period of years, it must be borne in mind that the document may be reviewed a generation hence by persons who had nothing to do with the original agreement, and it would therefore be important to leave as little as possible to the imagination.

SHORT-TERM LEASES DOMINATE THE MARKET

By far the greater number of leases on real property are short-term agreements. It is safe to say that more than 90 per cent are for a period of ten years or less. Although it may be true that the long-term lease, because of the financial commitments involved, may be more profitable to the broker, it is nevertheless a fact that the broker's day-in-and-day-out experience in leasing is with the run-of-the-mill short-term agreements covering houses, apartments, stores, and offices. Short-term leases are also used on a variety of other properties, such as markets; theatres; factories; vacant land;

oil-gas and mineral rights; railroads; concession rights of various sorts; sign and billboard privileges; docks and piers; landing fields for airplanes; gasoline stations; pipe lines for oil, gas or water; poles for electric wires; sidewalk and window displays, and so on.

LEASE SHOULD BE WRITTEN

It is customary to have a lease, even for the shortest term, in writing; but in many parts of the United States a verbal or oral lease for one year is binding in law. Proper proof of the oral agreement is necessary. Most states require that all leases for a term longer than three years be written and properly witnessed.

LESSOR-LESSEE RELATIONSHIP

In a long-term lease, a lessor is turning over the use and occupancy of his property to the lessee for a period of years. The lessee truly becomes a partner of the lessor in the property. The term "leasehold estate," which technically can be applied to *any* lessee's interest, is customarily used only to describe the interest of the long-term lessee. The owner or lessor, therefore, in a long-term agreement, usually examines into the character and financial standing of the lessee much more painstakingly than he would if the lease were being drawn for only a few years.

In a short-term lease, the "partnership" element is usually lacking. Dealing is more at arm's length. The lessor has two principal concerns: to see that his rent is paid, and to see that the lessee keeps the property in good condition. This is why the average short-term lease appears to be such a unilateral agreement. Tenants often comment on the apparently one-sided aspect of these leases. Actually, the lease *should be* one-sided, because in the run-of-the-mill lease transaction, the principal thing that the tenant expects is peaceful possession. Except for those cases in office buildings and apartments where tenants are provided with building services, the tenant's rights can be covered by a simple clause. On the other hand, the landlord has a valuable asset to protect. He wants to make certain that the tenant will not only do nothing to injure the property, but will keep it in good condition and will return it to him in as good condition as it was at the outset of the lease—allowing, that is, for normal depreciation.

In some cases, landlords are willing to use a short form lease in which the tenant's obligations are set forth simply and in general language. On the other hand, most landlords will insist on a lease that is reasonably specific when it comes to defining the obligations and duties of the tenant in maintaining the property. These matters are more fully discussed in Chapters 3 and 5.

GENERAL RULES FOR SHORT-TERM LEASES

Under most leases—long-term or short-term—the tenant maintains the property. In the case of short-term leases on certain types of multi-tenanted city properties, such as apartment houses, office buildings, loft buildings and some store buildings, maintenance may be supplied by the owner. Maintenance might be confined to providing heat, or it might, as in the case of certain office buildings, include heating, lighting, cleaning, and periodic decorating. In the case of single tenant occupancy, maintenance by the owner is usually limited to exterior or structural repairs.

Taxes, Insurance and Other Maintenance Costs

Real estate taxes and building insurance are customarily paid by the owner under short-term leases. As the lease term increases, the percentage of cases in which the tenant assumes the burden of paying taxes and building insurance increases also. Where the tenant takes care of maintenance and pays taxes and insurance, the lease is called a "net lease." Relatively few net leases are drawn for periods of less than ten years.

In some short-term leases, particularly where the lease period exceeds five years, an escalation clause is included which provides that the tenant will pay for any increase in taxes above the amount paid during the first year of the lease. In some cases the escalation clause covers increase in operating expenses as well. In multi-tenanted properties, the escalation clause is usually established on a pro-rata basis. If the tenant's space has a value equivalent to 5 per cent of the total rental value of the property, he then is obligated to pay 5 per cent of any real estate tax increase. Increase in maintenance costs will usually be pro-rated according to space occupied by the tenant.

Assigning or Subletting

The tenant's right to sublet or assign is strictly limited in short-term leases. In many cases it is completely withheld. If the right to sublet is granted, it is invariably limited to a subletting "with the consent of the lessor."

Improvements Made by Tenant

In more than 95 per cent of short-term leases, interior improvements to the property are made at the expense of the tenant and customarily he must secure the consent of the owner before making such improvements. Improvements of a structural nature become the property of the owner at the expiration of the lease, unless otherwise specified in the lease agreement. Trade fixtures are usually considered the property of the tenant. Short-term leases rarely, if ever, give the tenant the right to remove structural improvements.

LEASE FORMS

In most areas, lease forms covering the standard types of property are available at stationers or printers. Throughout the United States there is a growing tendency for local real estate boards to have lease forms approved, oftentimes prepared by the board's legal counsel. Many of these boards leave space on the lease document for imprinting the broker's name.

In using these standard forms, it is important to remember that state laws vary regarding the rights and duties of lessors and lessees, so that the use of such forms should always be confined to the state in which the form originated.

NEED FOR LEGAL COUNSEL

In any event, lease forms should be used with the utmost care. If substantial changes are to be made in phraseology, or if covenants are to be added or eliminated, it is a wise precaution to do so only with an attorney's advice. Most assuredly, a layman should never attempt to draft a lease agreement himself.

CHAPTER 5

General Considerations in Short-Term Leases

Although it is true that any type of property may be leased, the average real estate man's experience in this field will be limited to the standard types of properties—dwellings, apartment houses, office buildings, store buildings, loft or storage and manufacturing buildings. Sometimes a single property can be used for more than one of these purposes. Frequently an office building or an apartment building has stores on the grade floor level and in many instances, too, a single tenant will make diversified use of leased property. A manufacturing concern, for instance, may conduct a retail store in the manufacturing building; a doctor may occupy an apartment for professional offices as well as for residential use.

In this chapter we propose to treat of the general considerations affecting leases on these standard types of property.

DWELLINGS

It is likely that more leases are closed on one family dwellings than on any type of property, despite the fact that the one family dwelling is seldom constructed for the purpose of leasing. In some of the more heavily settled areas of the country, particularly where there is an industrial concentration, we occasionally find single family homes built to rent. But the vast majority have been built for owner occupancy. The fact that they are offered for rent usually represents a change in the living pattern of the owner: he may be moving out of the area temporarily or permanently; he may be buying a larger house; he may find the cost of home ownership too burdensome; his family may have grown up and moved away, and he no longer needs the number of rooms he has; there may be a death in the owner's family, and so on.

Under these circumstances, most owners will want to sell their homes. But situations will arise where an owner may prefer to lease rather than to sell. It may be that he wants to retain ownership for future occupancy by himself or some other member of his family; he may not be satisfied with prices offered in the market; or he may prefer rental income to the lump sum cash payment he would get on a sale.

But whatever the circumstances, the leasing of a one-family dwelling is, in principle, a temporary affair. It is usually a stopover on the road to a property sale. It is so recognized by lessor and lessee.

Although people have oftentimes rented a home for a long period of years in preference to buying, actually most home renters are people who are not in a position to buy. From their point of view too, the rental arrangement is a temporary one. They may be unable to make the necessary cash payment to secure a home in a desired neighborhood; they may be "looking the neighborhood over" before buying; the head of the house may be contemplating a change of employment which would necessitate moving to another area; there may not be any houses available in the immediate area which suit the family's requirements.

Because of these considerations, most dwelling leases are for one year and the lease agreement tends to be simple and uncomplicated.

Tenant's Obligations

The tenant generally will be required to maintain the interior of the property in good repair. He will not be required to make structural or mechanical repairs unless he causes damage to the buildings. For instance, if the furnace goes out of order, the owner is expected to make the repairs unless it can be shown that the damage was caused by the tenant. The tenant will pay for fuel and for lighting. He will usually pay water bills, particularly where water is metered.

If he is going to continue in occupancy for a few years, the owner may agree to absorb the cost of repainting or redecorating, but in most instances, owners will require tenants to take care of all such expenses. This can be readily understood when we realize that the complete repainting of the interior of a seven- or eight-room house might be the equivalent of three or four months' rent. The tenant will be required to turn the property back in good condition at the expiration of the lease.

The Owner's Obligation

The owner's obligation is usually limited to payment of real estate taxes and building insurance and to seeing that the property is kept in a good state of repair. Most leases are silent on the matter of the owner's obligation to make structural or mechanical repairs.

Form of Lease

The one family house lease is the simplest of all lease forms. First, because of the nature of the transaction, and secondly, because the contract is of short duration and it is easy for the landlord to gain possession of the property.

Covenants can be stated generally, as in the following Arlington County, Virginia, dwelling lease.

The said lessor covenants for the lessee quiet enjoyment of the property, and that if the said building shall be destroyed or so injured by fire as to render it untenable, this lease shall be terminated.

The said lessee covenants to pay the rent in the manner above stated; that he will not assign without leave; that he will leave the premises in good repair; that the premises shall not be used during the said term for any other purpose or purposes than those above specified; that all gas and electric bills which shall be unpaid at the termination of the tenancy shall be regarded as so much rent due to the lessor and be recoverable by all the remedies to which he may be entitled for the recovery of the rent hereinbefore reserved; but at the expiration of the said term, to wit, on the .. day of ...... 19 .., without any notice requiring him so to do he will deliver to the lessor, his agents or assigns, quiet and peaceful possession of the said premises. The lessee acknowledges the receipt of .. keys and agrees to return the same, and to replace all glass broken out during his tenancy at the expiration of his lease. Any damages caused by the bursting of water pipes, from failure to turn off the water in cold weather or from stoppage of waterclosets, shall be repaired at the expense of the lessee and the lessee covenants that the lessor may re-enter for default of .. days in the payment of any installment of rent, or for the breach of any covenant herein contained.

APARTMENTS

Although apartments are residential accommodations, there is an essential difference between a lease of a one family dwelling and of an apartment unit, in that the average apartment building has been planned and designed for rental purposes and the owner is, of his own volition, in the business of renting for profit.

In the case of the rented one family dwelling, the owner may regard the lease as a "one shot" operation because he is planning to sell the building eventually. In the typical apartment lease, the owner is aware of the fact that the present tenant is probably not permanent and that other tenants will follow him. Dealings therefore in apartment leases are on a more businesslike basis and particular care is taken in the drafting of covenants relative to the preservation of the property and the use to which the tenant puts the property.

Another consideration in apartment leases is the fact that the building has other tenants whose desire for privacy and peaceful occupancy must be protected. The owner therefore, through covenants, may exercise a reasonable degree.of control over the conduct of his tenants.

Tenant's Obligation

The tenant will be obligated to keep his apartment in good condition but under most leases he will not be required to make any structural or mechanical repairs.

Insofar as day-to-day building maintenance is concerned, there is no uniform practice in apartment leasing. Large city apartment buildings usually provide heat, maintenance of public space, elevator service and periodic redecorating for tenants. Some include electricity and gas in rental. At the other extreme would be the 2-story apartment house—most frequently found in suburban areas —where each apartment unit has its own heating equipment. In the majority of these buildings, the tenant takes care of all of the day-to-day maintenance, including heat. He may even be required to keep the sidewalk in front of his own particular unit clear in winter. The tenant in such an apartment unit is in the same general position as the tenant in a one family dwelling.

Owner's Obligation

The apartment house owner customarily pays for real estate taxes, building insurance and water charges. The services to tenants vary, as noted in the preceding paragraph, depending on the type of building. Most apartment leases call for some form of periodic redecorating. If the lease is silent on the decorating provision, there should at least be an understanding between the owner and tenant as to precisely what the owner will do for the tenant. It is axiomatic, of course, that such work would be reflected in the rental. Many disputes have arisen in the past when a tenant has "assumed" that a landlord would do certain work for him when the lease was silent on the matter of maintenance.

In New York City and other areas, where rent controls have continued, building services are often the subject of dispute and are reviewed by the governmental agency in charge of administering the rent laws. The New York State Rent Commission, for instance, has power to reduce rents where standard services are curtailed or eliminated.

STORES

Store leases will contain the standard clauses on maintenance found in residential leases. The owner usually pays taxes and building insurance, although as the lease term increases there may be a tendency for the owner to insist on a net lease, in which the tenant pays taxes and insurance, particularly where there is single tenant occupancy. Escalation payments for increased real estate taxes are becoming an accepted practice because of the uncertainty of assessments. Tenants cannot reasonably insist on a rental which provides for no increases should there be an increase in the tax levy.

Restrictions on Tenants

Outside of the standard clauses on care, maintenance and peaceful occupancy, there are three matters of primary importance in the average store lease. The first is the use of the premises. The tenant will, in most instances, be limited to a specific use or type of business. If he is selling men's clothing and furnishings, he probably would not be allowed to sell pipes and tobacco. If he is selling ladies' dresses, he might be prohibited from selling perfumes. If he is selling automobile equipment, he might be prohibited from selling television sets. This limitation is essential where the owner has adjacent stores.

In the new shopping centers (Chapter 11), the tenant's retailing activities will be carefully circumscribed. Many shopping center leases have failed of consummation because of these limitations.

Structural Improvements, Fixtures

The second primary consideration is concerned with structural improvements. In the majority of cases, the store owner will turn over the store on an "as is" basis to the tenant who will make the necessary interior alterations. If the tenant is to make the alterations, they must be done subject to the owner's supervision and approval. Any structural additions will become the property of the owner at the end of the lease. Sometimes—particularly in the new shopping centers—a tenant will be partially reimbursed for expenditures on structural additions (Chapter 11). In some cases the owner will make the necessary improvements. Covenants affecting such work must be carefully drawn and carefully worded so that there is no misunderstanding as to: (a) what work is to be done, (b) who pays for it, and (c) who has ultimate title to the structural additions.

The third primary consideration affects trade fixtures. These are the counters, lighting devices, conveyors, and so on, used by the tenant in the operation of his business. They are invariably installed by the tenant at his own expense and are usually removable at the end of the lease term. The installation, however, should be done only with the owner's consent and subject to the owner's supervision, principally so as to avoid any damage to the building structure. If the removal of trade fixtures might cause some damage to the building structure, a covenant might be included in the lease prohibiting their removal at the end of the lease term.

OFFICE BUILDINGS

Rented office space varies widely in character, quality, and in services provided to the tenant. The range is from the small ground floor or second floor office in outlying or suburban sections of metropolitan areas or on secondary business streets of smaller communities, to the large, modern, air conditioned units found in most of our principal cities.

Rents, usually computed on a square foot basis, will vary from less than $2.00 per square foot for some of the older units (where the tenant gets no service from the owner), to $9.00 and $10.00 per square foot for the prime space in newer buildings in New York, Chicago, Los Angeles, and a few other cities.

The older units with cheaper rents are no different than store properties. The tenant takes the property in its existing condition. He makes necessary repairs and alterations. He takes care of his own cleaning. He may or may not supply heat. The owner collects the rent and pays taxes and building insurance.

On the other hand, the leasing of large office units, particularly in new buildings, can be complicated. It usually necessitates supplementary agreements and covenants not found in any standard lease form. This point can best be illustrated by taking a typical case.

The AAA corporation becomes interested in renting an entire floor in a new air conditioned office building. The floor has a net rentable area of 50,000 square feet, and a lease is to be made at $400,000 per annum for ten years.

Owner's Obligation

The owner agrees to give the tenant the space, and to supply air conditioning with the tenant paying electrical charges. The owner agrees to keep the air conditioning in good repair and to repaint the premises every three years. Improvements to the space might be made by the owner at the owner's expense as follows: asphalt tile floors throughout; a specified amount of linear feet of interior partitioning of standard type; hung ceilings with standard fluorescent lighting fixtures; a specified number of electrical floor outlets; plastered walls, painted in the color selected by the tenant, and so on. Nightly cleaning service will be supplied by the owner: windows will be cleaned at specified intervals; air conditioning will be operated during business hours; regular elevator service will be furnished during business hours; tenant will have access to the building on a 24-hour basis.

Tenant's Work

The AAA corporation will not occupy the space as finished by the owner. There probably will be changes in such things as partitioning, floor covering, lighting fixtures, wall finish, and so on, to suit the tenant's particular requirements. The practice is that these changes will be made by the owner or tenant at the tenant's expense, but an allowance will be made by the owner to the tenant for the cost of the improvements that the owner had agreed to furnish. For instance, if the owner had agreed to install 1,000 feet of gypsum block partitioning and the tenant wishes to have movable steel partitioning which would be more costly, the owner will allow the tenant the cost of gypsum block partitioning with the tenant bearing the differential in cost. The specific allowance to be made by the owner in these cases is a matter of negotiation between tenant and owner.

The Escalation Clause

Another important feature of most leases in new office buildings is the escalation clause, which provides that the tenant will pay his pro-rata share not only of increased real estate taxes, but also of operating and maintenance costs. Few tenants object to the tax escalation clause, but many object to the clause for operating expenses, claiming, among other reasons, that it is difficult to determine what are legitimate increased costs. In some cases tenants have consented to pay a pro-rata share of any increase in labor costs which are determinable.

In these agreements, the tenant's share of increased expense is usually determined by the ratio between the space which he occupies and the total rentable area in the building. The clause also provides that the tenant would be given an allowance if any of these costs decrease.

LOFT BUILDINGS, MANUFACTURING BUILDINGS, STORAGE SPACE

Leases on buildings in the manufacturing category are relatively simple because the tenant is required to maintain his own space, and the complicated clauses pertaining to the owner's obligation to provide building services are therefore eliminated. In the case of multi-tenanted buildings, the owner will usually supply heat and elevator service, but all costs for such items as cleaning, decorating, electricity, are paid for by the tenant. In the case of a single occupancy building, the owner customarily provides nothing beyond structural maintenance and repairs. He will, of course, excepting where the lease is on a net basis, pay real estate taxes and building insurance.

CHAPTER 6

Percentage Leases

A percentage lease is an instrument wherein it is agreed that the tenant shall pay as rent a stipulated percentage of gross dollar volume of sales of merchandise and/or services.

DEVELOPMENT OF THE PERCENTAGE LEASE

While the development, refinement, and intensive use of the percentage lease has been accomplished during the past 35 years, and more particularly in the post World War II period, the economic forces that have made this type of instrument a logical one for renting business properties have been gathering force since the beginning of the century.

Slowly but steadily the small or moderate sized retail operator has been giving way to the chain store operator. The neighborhood grocer and butcher have been replaced by the super market, and an increasingly larger percentage of retail business is moving from local stores to central business districts and to urban and suburban shopping centers. New marketing techniques have been developed. Gross business has increased, but in many instances profit margins have decreased. Competition has put a premium on location.

The owners of centrally located retail properties came to the realization that such properties could, *solely by virtue of specific locations,* create a valuable estate for a lessee unlike the estate which would be created for the lessee in another type of property, such as an apartment house or an office building.

An apartment house tenant, for instance, might find a particular neighborhood or a particular area convenient for residential purposes. But given a reasonably broad selection of apartments of similar size within that area, he can usually live as efficiently and as happily in one apartment as in the other. Apartments within a given building might vary in price because of light, air, exposure, and so on. But, except for these characteristics, it is difficult to conceive of any particular benefit that might inure to an apartment house tenant because he happens to be at number 28 Broadway instead of in an identical building at number 58 Broadway. Similarly, a business corporation, a law firm, an insurance firm, or some such typical occupant in an office building, might find that its business requirements make it necessary that the office be located in a certain section of the business district. But it would be difficult to conceive that an attorney's total fees would increase by 50 per cent solely because he happened to be located on a particular floor in a particular building.

On the other hand, the tenant with goods to sell—the retail operator—finds location an increasingly dominant factor in the conduct of his business. Not only is a good location essential to the initial success of the retailer's business, but of itself, it is a factor in the development of his business potential. True, the tenant, in order to realize his potential, will have to conduct his business intelligently and aggressively. The location will not of itself make a successful operator out of an inept businessman. But the astute and aggressive businessman who properly exploits his location can develop a volume of business in one location that he might not achieve in any other spot. It is not unreasonable therefore that a property owner should expect to share proportionately the earnings which his property has helped to create.

In rare instances only can a retail operator pick out a general area and say *"any place* within this area will suit my purpose." (As a matter of fact, experienced real estate men realize that there can be as much as a 25 per cent to 50 per cent differential in sales potential between the opposite sides of the same street.)

Lease Term

Another factor that has contributed to the development of the percentage lease has been the insistence of retail operators on longer leases. In the 1920 era, many leases of retail properties were written for three or five years, whereas today the ten-year lease is probably the most common. Many tenants require a longer lease with renewal privileges because they have made a heavy financial investment in the property.

When leases are drawn for 10 or 15 year terms, owners of retail properties will insist on a percentage clause as a safeguard against inflation. The percentage lease is, from the owner's point of view, an insurance against the hazards of renewal options.

Strangely enough, the percentage lease or percentage rental was first given widespread use in Depression days as a device for the protection of tenants. At that time, many merchants were weighed down by high rents and declining business. They sought some compromise in their lease agreements which might be based on business volume. Many owners agreed readily to this form of recasting the lease agreement because they viewed it as a necessary device to keep a good tenant in business.

Today, the percentage lease is a standard real estate instrument in most retail areas.

KINDS OF PERCENTAGE LEASE

The Building Managers Association of Chicago gives the following classifications of percentage leases.

1. A lease requiring a specific percentage of gross sales as rental with a guaranteed minimum.
2. A lease requiring a specific percentage of gross sales as rental with no guaranteed minimum.
3. A lease, as in Number 2, but with a minimum established after a fixed period of time and based on a percentage of the average rental developed during the "no minimum period."
4. A lease designating the rental as a percentage of profits.

Type Number 1 is the most common and probably the most equitable form of percentage lease, provided that the minimum rental is established on a reasonable basis. If the landlord requires the minimum rental equivalent to the figure that he might obtain if the property were leased at a fixed rental, the deal would be one-sided in the landlord's favor. He is taking no chances because his minimum rental is 100 per cent of the recognized fair rental value. On the other hand, if he asks a minimum rental sufficient to pay carrying charges and a moderate return on his investment, he will encounter much less opposition on the part of the tenant. As a matter of fact, most tenants who would accept a percentage lease deal are sufficiently aware of market conditions and values to insist on a reasonable minimum rental arrangement. In the post-war era, many tenants, because of their desire to secure new outlets, have paid both high minimum rentals and high percentage rates. This, in our opinion, is a temporary market phenomenon that has tended to disappear as an adequate supply of good retail locations has become available.

The second type of percentage lease on which no minimum guarantee is obtained, and type Number 3 where there is no initial minimum rental, are usually found in locations which are not sufficiently well established as retail areas to command a minimum rental. This type of lease is also used to attract the "hard to get" tenants. The owner may compensate for the "no minimum" arrangement by securing a slightly higher percentage clause than would obtain if there were a minimum.

Such a lease has its obvious drawbacks. The most serious is the difficulty of securing adequate mortgage financing. Many of the larger mortgage lenders have indicated an unwillingness to predicate a loan on property with straight percentage leases on anything other than a most *conservative* basis. As a matter of fact, we know of lenders who will refuse to make a mortgage loan unless the leases contain guaranteed minimums.

The fourth type of lease in which the landlord collects a part of the profits as rental is rarely used. It actually takes the form of a partnership between the landlord and the tenant. Some attorneys have maintained that the landlord can be held responsible for the debts of the tenant should the tenant fail. The well-drawn percentage lease, on the other hand, will state specifically that there is no partnership between landlord and tenant.

It is clear, too, that accounting problems might arise in the determination of what constitutes a profit. Such problems would not occur where the rental is determined by a percentage of gross sales.

ADVANTAGES AND DISADVANTAGES OF PERCENTAGE LEASES

1. The percentage lease is a means of reconciling differences of opinion between landlord and tenant as to rental value.

2. The percentage lease, with a properly drawn minimum clause, is a stabilizing device.

3. It is in accordance with sound economic theory in that the tenant pays for what he gets. He is buying the services that the property is capable of rendering for a term of years. If the property is productive, his rental increases. If it is not productive, he is committed only for the minimum rental.

4. The percentage lease possesses advantages to the tenant wherever future sales volume is uncertain by reason of (a) the undeveloped character of the locality; (b) the danger of excessive competition; (c) other adverse factors which can neither be foreseen nor forestalled.

5. A percentage lease is likewise favorable to the tenant in cases where the "mark up" is necessarily small and rigid control of every item of expense is essential to protect net profit.

6. The percentage lease is undesirable from the tenant's point of view if the minimum rental is equivalent to the fixed rental that the owner could obtain for the property.

7. The percentage lease offers no advantage to a tenant who is able to estimate sales with any degree of accuracy and who is interested only in prime rated locations. In such cases, the ratio of rent to sales may reasonably be expected to diminish from year to year if the lease calls for a straight rental, whereas a percentage lease would surrender that advantage to the owner. This explains why a few selected retail or chain store tenants, dominant in their own field and desirable as tenants from the owner's point of view, have refused to make percentage leases. The number of such tenants is constantly diminishing.

8. If the minimum rental is low, the owner places his earning potential almost solely in the hands of the tenant. If the tenant is an aggressive merchandiser who will utilize the property to its full extent, the owner's income will go up. If the reverse is true, his income will decline. Because of this, most percentage leases contain clauses which to some extent guarantee the proper operation of the tenant's business. These clauses are discussed in Chapter 9.

WHERE SHOULD PERCENTAGE LEASES BE MADE?

1. The percentage lease generally is most adaptable to properties in *prime* retail areas, urban or suburban. Within the prime areas, specific locations are referred to as "100%," "90%," "80%," etc. In a central business district of a community there is usually only one "100% location," invariably at the principal business intersection. The four corners of such an intersection will be graded according to desirability for retail use. Two of the corners might be "100%," and the other two "90%."

Any properties within the "retail rating" area are susceptible to percentage leases.

2. Retail properties outside prime areas may be susceptible to percentage leases where special value may attach to the retail location by virtue of its immediate surroundings. Typical of this category would be stores or concessions in large office buildings or apartment houses.

3. Shopping centers. Practically all shopping center leases are on a percentage basis. The principal exceptions would be professional offices or government agencies (such as branch post offices).

As indicated previously, a few chain store organizations which may be highly desirable from the owner's point of view, have consistently refused to enter into percentage leases. Some tenants in this category may be desirable from the owner's point of view because of their prestige. They may be responsible for the owner securing more favorable financing. They may also attract other tenants.

4. The percentage lease is not appropriate in small neighborhood stores where leases would customarily be made for three or five years. Most owners of this type of property would prefer a fixed rental and shopkeepers would probably be unable to render satisfactory accounting of sales. Also, the shortness of the term may offset many of the advantages of the percentage lease where it is generally expected that sales volume will increase as time goes by.

WHAT KIND OF A BUSINESS SHOULD OPERATE
UNDER A PERCENTAGE LEASE?

We have indicated in the preceding discussion that percentage leases are most successfully used in retail areas and that, as a matter of fact, their use is confined largely to these areas. It follows therefore that a retail business is the type of operation to which the principles of the percentage lease are most applicable.

An organization operating exclusively as a wholesale distributor or jobber should not be expected to pay on a percentage basis. Some percentage lease tenants may, however, operate partly on a wholesale as well as on a retail basis. In this case a different percentage arrangement would apply to the revenue derived from wholesale operations.

Professional tenants, those who sell services rather than goods, and business tenants on the upper floors of office buildings, are almost universally excluded from percentage arrangements. There are exceptions to this. For instance, many beauty parlors or barber shops have percentage leases.

In recent years in the New York City area, some stock exchange houses have paid percentage rentals calculated not on the volume of business done by the particular brokerage house but on the volume of business done for a specified period on the New York Stock Exchange.

WHAT ARE TENANT QUALIFICATIONS?

One of the leading Chicago brokers has rated tenants on the basis of their desirability as follows:

1. Highly responsible business organizations (many of which are chain stores) whose merchandising methods have been proven sound and whose accounting systems and business veracity may be depended upon.
2. Local merchants or small chains whose dependability has been proven by successful operation over a period of years in the same district wherein the new space is situated, or in a similar district.
3. All other merchants, including those of poor financial standing or unfavorable records, those starting business on a "shoestring," and the downright "fly by nighters."

It has been the writer's experience that there can be exceptions to the third classification. The most noteworthy example is that of the two highly competent, aggressive young men, leaving managerial positions in a large chain store organization and starting in business for themselves on limited capital. They proved to be excellent tenants.

According to another mid-western broker, the landlord should inquire into the following matters which pertain to the character and business operation of the tenant:

1. How much business can be expected of the applicant?
2. Is he an aggressive advertiser?
3. Is his past record of performance good?
4. Does he own other stores nearby which might share business on the advertising he does?
5. What kind of goods will he sell and will they be priced to move readily in a competitive market?
6. Is this a one man business which might suffer if the owner became ill or died?
7. Will this tenant put the property to its highest and best use?
8. Does the acceptance of this tenant involve radical changes in a property involving a considerable expense? If so, who will pay for these changes?
9. Is the tenant willing to accept a recapture clause in his lease?

CHAPTER 7

Percentage Leases, Minimum Rental and Percentage Rate

MINIMUM RENTAL

There are different schools of thought as to the proper standards for determining the minimum or guaranteed rental in a percentage lease deal. It is difficult to set forth any absolute rules because these rules could not be considered applicable to all properties.

For instance, it has been stated many times that the minimum rental should be sufficient to pay carrying charges such as taxes and insurance and to give the owner a reasonable return on his investment. The rental might be determined readily where there is a single tenancy property—provided that there would be an agreement on what *constitutes* a *reasonable return.*

There would be comparatively less difficulty in the case of shopping centers where there is a single owner and where minimum rentals can be pro-rated on a square foot basis, or established with some variation according to location within the center. But this rule could not be readily applied in the case of a top-grade retail store in an office building, a situation that we find prevalent in many central business districts of our major cities, because of the impractical aspect of allocating a portion of the owner's investment to the store space and also because of the difficulty of apportioning real estate taxes and other carrying charges to the store space as opposed to the office space.

On such an office property it would probably be best to use the front foot or square foot rental prevailing in the area as a guide. Conversely, the application of any front foot or square foot rental to shopping center properties would be impractical, because the shopping center is a self-contained unit and could be compared only with other shopping centers. It would be readily recognized that comparison between shopping centers would have little validity.

In other words, one set of criteria would be used in central district multi-tenanted properties. Another set of criteria would be used in the case of single tenant properties or in shopping centers.

SHOULD THE MINIMUM RENTAL BE EQUIVALENT TO FIXED RENTAL VALUE?

It has been contended by some owners that the minimum rental should be the same as the owner could obtain from a tenant on a fixed rental agreement with no percentage clause. Tenants will maintain that such a proposition is a one-sided deal (unfair to the tenant), and that the minimum should be less than the fixed rental value.

Again, it is difficult to generalize because there are many specialized situations, but it is our opinion that as a rule *there should be a moderate spread between the fixed rental value and the minimum guaranteed rental.*

Let us recite an example of what we mean. Assume that there is a store in a central business district, 60 x 100, and that it can be established that the prevailing rate for such property on a fixed rental deal would be $600 per front foot or $36,000 per annum. Let it also be assumed that the tenant negotiating for the space is in a business which would normally pay a 7% percentage. Let it finally be assumed that the tenant can reasonably be expected to achieve a minimum $400,000 sales volume. If he has a reasonably successful year, his volume will reach $500,000, and if he has a banner year, he might get as high as $700,000. On a 7% basis, his rents would be, on the three assumptions of volume, $28,000; $35,000;

$49,000. In our opinion, a minimum guaranteed rental of about $30,000 would be equitable.

On the other hand, the tenant might want such a property very badly because of its particular location, and would be willing to pay a premium in the form of a higher guarantee. As we have said, specialized situations might arise which would make any rule inoperative.

In shopping centers, where practically all leases are on a percentage basis, it can be assumed that if the owner were to rent all of the stores on a fixed rental basis, he would require higher amounts than he obtains under his minimum guarantees.

It must be remembered, of course, that the average tenant in a percentage lease deal, is well able to negotiate for himself. In the vast majority of situations, after a deal has been "traded out," the end result will be an equitable lease.

There are other factors that can affect the minimum guarantee as well as the percentage rate. There would be such matters as the owner's investment in the tenant's space, i.e., if the fixtures are already installed and are the property of the owner; or if the owner installs fixtures for the tenant; or if an allowance is made to the tenant to complete the exterior of the property in accordance with his own design; or if an allowance is made to the tenant to install air conditioning ducts in accordance with the tenant's plan, etc.

PERCENTAGE RATES

Prevailing rates in percentage leases might seem to have a mystifying, if not unexplainable, aspect—namely, the wide variation in percentages for different types of businesses. Let us suppose that in (or fairly close to) a business center of a good sized city we have among other stores, a department store, a men's clothing and furnishing store, a women's dress shop, a popular priced jewelry store, a "quality" food store, a super market, and a parking lot. If all these businesses were operated on percentage leases, we might find that the department store pays 2 per cent; the men's clothing and furnishing store 7 per cent; the women's dress shop 6 per cent; the "quality" food store 5 per cent; the super market 1½ per cent; the parking lot 50 per cent.

If we were given information on the gross revenue of each of these tenants in order to determine the actual rentals being paid, we would find that the differential, if the rental were broken down to a square foot or front foot basis, would not be as great as the percentage differential. But it might still be wide, and it would be wider than the differential that would prevail if these properties were rented or leased on a fixed rental basis.

Tenant's Ability to Pay—"Mark up"

It should be borne in mind that under a percentage lease we add to the factor of real estate value the factor of what the tenant is able to pay. But what the tenant is able to pay depends in large measure on how much money the tenant makes. We can therefore assert that *the basic determinant of a proper percentage rate* is the tenant's "mark up" or margin of profit. It is common knowledge that the super market and the department store operate on a narrow margin of profit. The costume jewelry store might have a 100 per cent margin of profit.

The parking lot operator has no inventory. Usually his only expenses are for insurance and payroll. The operator of a large city parking lot might have a total revenue of $50,000 per annum with only a $10,000 outlay for employees and insurance. If his lease calls for a 50 per cent rental, he still has an extremely profitable operation.

There are many other contributing factors in establishing the percentage rate. The factors are numerous and so variable that it would be impossible to set forth any system of computation by which we could arrive at a proper percentage rate for a hypothetical situation.

We do know, however, that there are pretty well established ranges of percentage rates for specified businesses. For instance, for a popular priced women's dress shop in good retail locations, the percentage range might be from 5 per cent to 8 per cent. This would mean that under the most adverse conditions, if the tenant is willing to accept the store, he can *afford* to pay 5 per cent and that under no circumstances could a tenant in this line of business afford to pay more than 8 per cent; whether he will pay 5 per cent, 6 per cent, 7 per cent or 8 per cent will depend on a number of considerations. These same considerations would generally apply in determining the precise percentage for other types of retail operators. Among these considerations are:

1. Size of the city or the community. Larger cities will generally produce a larger sales volume than moderate sized cities. If the retailer can see a greater volume of business, he may be willing to pay a higher percentage because his cost of doing business should decrease relatively as his sales volume increases.

2. The economic characteristics of the city or community. Certain types of business, such as an exclusive specialty shop, might prosper in a high income community only. A popular priced dress shop will generally be most successful in a moderate income community.

3. A specific location may be best adaptable to a specific type of business. There are certain types of stores that can operate successfully only if they are at, or very close to, the 100 per cent retail location. Other stores may not require immediate adjacency to the 100 per cent location but may be satisfied with a 70 per cent or 80 per cent location, provided that there is substantial pedestrian traffic. Another store may prefer a location where pedestrian traffic is predominantly female. Other stores may want to be adjacent to a large department store.

4. A retailer in a highly competitive line of business may pay a higher percentage, if he can be assured that a location is relatively free from competition. Shopping center owners can give this assurance better than the owners of downtown business properties.

5. Physical adaptability of the store to the business. The size, shape, and frontage of the store can affect a tenant's business and correspondingly can affect the percentage he is willing to pay. Some tenants might want as much window display space as possible; to others this might not be an important consideration. To one tenant, basement space may be usable only for storage, to others it might be highly productive sales space. One tenant may require high ceilings, another may want as much natural light as possible.

Almost two decades ago, the Brownlow Realty Organization of Knoxville, Tennessee made the following pertinent observations about percentage leases. It is interesting to note that most of these opinions still hold true.

> As regards the determining of the proper percentage rate, one opens a veritable Pandora's box. Some lines of retailing have excessive competition. Chain drug stores are an outstanding illustration. Through excessive competition, they have placed their business on a basis where they simply cannot pay the per-

centage rates which will produce the same rent in many 100 per cent locations that other types of business will do. The drug business is extra hazardous for a landlord in that new near-by competition can sometimes reduce percentage returns by as much as 50 per cent.

One extra women's dress shop or shoe store in a neighborhood will often lower the percentage returns from competing businesses to some extent, but nothing like a drug store will do. The same is true of some grocery stores.

The question "How much percentage can a certain type of business afford to pay?" is not the same as "What percentage can a landlord afford to rent at?" I know of a situation where an outlet of one of the leading men's shoe chains in the United States is returning the poorest percentage in that line in the city in which it is located. As a chain store leasing broker, interested in advancing the interests of both landlord and tenant, I am willing for other towns to get the tenants who don't produce the proper volume under percentage leases. Most of the confusion under such lease rates is due to failure to distinguish between the two questions propounded above. If all landlords acted on this difference, the low rent producers, through failure to get locations, would be compelled to establish higher mark-ups where they could afford to pay a percentage which would produce a rental commensurate with the value of the property to *other types of tenants*. Experience on the part of the leasing broker plus complete knowledge of local conditions must be the foundation of any successful leasing business.

The foregoing is of general application throughout the country, but nearly every city and certain sections of the business centers within individual cities are subject to special conditions. For instance, at one time, when the women's dress shop business was being overdone all over the country, it became a wise policy to refuse any more tenants of this kind and even to get rid of some whose leases were expiring. The result was that this type of tenant later produced the highest rentals under percentage leases of any type of retailer. One of our best tenants in this line, who pays our standard 8 per cent gross on sales, a composite figure arrived at where the tenant handles not only dresses but suits, millinery, and smallwear, has had a 3 per cent lease for the past twelve years in a neighboring city of the same type as we have in our city, which I believe he would not have renewed if it had not been for a recent boom in the women's apparel business. His 8 per cent with us has been highly profitable and his 3 per cent lease in the other city has not been. This difference is due entirely to failure in the other city to control excessive competition or, to put it another way, lack of intelligent management.

PERCENTAGE TABLES

The tables that follow cover many types of businesses and were compiled by and are used here by permission of the National Institute of Real Estate Brokers, affiliated with the National Association of Real Estate Boards. It is merely suggestive of the rates used in leases that were negotiated in many small and large cities during the 12-month period preceding the survey that resulted in the issuance of the table. Such a compilation is merely a guide to the selecting of the proper rate. A table such as this is never static. The ranges suggested here are extreme.

TABLE OF PERCENTAGE RATES

The National Institute of Real Estate Brokers of the National Association of Real Estate Boards publishes annually a comprehensive study of percentage lease rates. Other local and regional real estate organizations have published similar rate schedules although none of them are as complete as that published by the Institute. It is interesting to note that there is little variance in the rates shown by the Institute and by other organizations. The list we have published is substantially the same as that published in the Institute report.

The Institute's study covers rates charged in regional shopping centers, local centers, outlying shopping districts, downtown commercial areas, etc. It also shows rates paid by national chains, local chains, and independent operators. For full information on this all important subject we suggest that a copy of the report be obtained from the Institute, 155 E. Superior St., Chicago, Ill. 60611. Cost is $15.

The appended list does not show the full range of rates on all types of properties. The "normal" range only is shown:

Type of Store	Range in % Rate	Type of Store	Range in % Rate
Automobile Accessories	3 to 4	Camera-Photography Stores.	6 to 10
Automobile Dealers	3	Candy Stores	6 to 10
Bakeries	5 to 7	Children's Clothing	5 to 8
Barber Shops ....,....	8 to 10	Cocktail Bars—Taverns	8 to 10
Beauty Shops	8 to 10	Delicatessen	5 to 6
Book and Stationery Stores	5 to 8	Department Stores	2 to 3
Bowling Alleys	8 to 10	Discount Stores	1 to 2½

Type of Store	Range in % Rate	Type of Store	Range in % Rate
Drapery	4 to 5	Luggage Stores	6 to 8
	2 to 4 (Chain)	Men's Apparel	4 to 6
		Men's Furnishings	6 to 8
Drug Stores	3 to 5 (Individual)	Millinery	10 to 12
		Music—Musical Instruments	4 to 6
		Office Supplies	5 to 6
Dry Cleaning & Laundry	6 to 8	Optical Stores	8 to 10
Dry Cleaning & Laundry (Coin Operated)	8 to 10	Paint—Wallpaper	4 to 6
		Parking Lots (Attended)	40 to 50
Family Apparel	5 to 6	Parking Lots (Non-Attended)	50 to 60
Florists	8 to 10	Photography Shops	5 to 8
Florists (Garden Supply)	6 to 8	Restaurants	6 to 8
Furniture Stores	4 to 5	Sewing Machine Stores	4 to 5
Furriers	6 to 8	Shoe Repair	8 to 10
Gifts Shops	8 to 10	Sport Goods	4 to 6
Hardware Stores	4 to 6	Supermarkets	1½ to 2
Hosiery—Lingerie	6 to 8	Variety Stores	2½ to 4
Household Appliances—Radios—T.V.	3 to 5	Women's Apparel	5 to 8
Jewelry Stores	7 to 10	Women's—Children's Furnishings	6 to 8
Liquor Stores (Package)	4 to 6		

Percentage Lease
Accounting Provisions

If an owner is selective in choosing the tenant with whom he will make a percentage lease, there will be little fear of dishonest practice on the part of the lessee when it comes to the settlement of his accounts and the determination of what rental is due the lessor.

There are many stories being told which illustrate how a dishonest tenant *might* operate in order to cheat the owner even though such practices are definitely the exception. There is the story of the tenant with two stores; one highly successful and on a percentage lease; the other doing a very disappointing volume of business but on a fixed rental. The tenant was making weekly reports to the owner and before the end of each week he merely switched cash registers between the two stores.

In another case it was reported that a tenant had four retail outlets, one of them on a percentage lease, the other three on fixed rentals. He arranged it so that all returned merchandise was directed to the percentage lease store, thus reducing its sales volume.

Despite the fact that more than 99 per cent of tenants would cause an owner few worries on the matter of dishonesty, it is nevertheless essential that the fiscal relationship between owner and tenant should be clearly defined in a percentage lease.

The following matters should be carefully covered in the lease agreement:

1. The definition of *gross* sales, or *gross* receipts against which the specified percentage rate is charged.

2. That the lessee should keep proper accounts and that his books should be available to the lessor for inspection.

3. That sales volume be reported periodically to the lessor by the lessee (usually monthly, sometimes more frequently).

4. That financial accounts be adjusted periodically by the payment of excess rentals. This would usually be done on a quarterly or an annual basis.

The following excerpt from a lease used by the Brownlow Realty Organization of Knoxville, Tennessee covers all of these four points briefly.

> In addition to the rentals mentioned, lessee shall, on or before the 10th days of January, April, July and October, beginning with the 10th day of October, 1945, and ending with the 10th day of July, 1950, pay to lessors a sum of money equivalent to 8 per cent of the amount of the gross sales made in and from the leased premises by lessee, its subtenants and concessionaires, during the three preceding calendar months in excess of $23,-812.50. The term *gross sales*, as herein used, shall include the aggregate volume of all sales of merchandise and services made in and from the leased premises, whether for cash or on a charge basis, paid or unpaid, collected or uncollected, less all credits for returned merchandise, merchandise trade-ins, exchanges, refunds, allowances and any retail sales tax imposed by any governmental authority which is legally paid by the purchaser and for which lessee merely acts as a collection agency.

DEFINITION OF SALES

Following are sample clauses used in different percentage leases in defining sales, gross sales or gross receipts.

1. The term *gross sales* as herein used shall be held to include the sales price of all merchandise of every sort whatsoever sold, and the charges for all services performed for which charge is made by the lessee or by other person, persons or corporation selling merchandise or performing service of any sort in, upon, or from any part of the said demised premises, and shall include merchandise sold or services performed either for cash or for credit, regardless of collections in the case of the latter, but shall exclude merchandise so purchased which is returned

by the purchaser and accepted by the lessee, and all allowances made by the lessee to its customers.

2. The term *gross receipts* as used herein shall include: (1) the selling price of all merchandise sold whether for cash or on credit and in case of sales on credit, whether payment is actually made or not; provided, however, that the selling price of all merchandise returned by the customer to the lessee and accepted by it shall be excluded; and (2) the charges made by the lessee, or by anyone on its behalf, for the rendition to its customers of services of any kind whatsoever.

3. The term *gross sales* as used herein shall include: (1) the selling price of all merchandise sold, whether for cash or on credit and in case of sales on credit whether payment is actually made or not; provided, however, that the selling price of all merchandise returned by the customer to the lessees and accepted by them shall be excluded; and (2) the charges made by the lessees, or by anyone on their behalf for the rendition to their customers of services of any kind whatsoever.

It is expressly understood in this connection that all orders taken in the herein demised premises, whether the merchandise is delivered from the premises or not, shall be included in the gross sales of this store; and it is further understood that any merchandise delivered from the herein demised premises (excepting return merchandise), whether it be delivered to a customer or to another place of business conducted by the lessee provided such place of business be within the state of Pennsylvania, shall also be considered gross sales for the purpose of computing said rental.

4. The term *sales* as used in this lease shall be deemed to mean the aggregate amount of the gross selling price of all merchandise sold in, on, or from the demised premises, whether by the tenant or any of its concessionaires or licensees and whether for cash or on credit, and shall include all interest and carrying charges, if any, on sales made on credit and all service charges (other than service charges in connection with the .... of merchandise sold in, on, or from the demised premises, which shall be excluded) and shall not include any of the following:

    a. Sales on credit to the extent that such sales are charged off as losses or bad debts (which shall be deducted in the year in which the same are charged off by the tenant, provided, however, if such sales so charged off shall later be collected during the term hereof, they shall be included as sales in the year when collected to the extent collected);

    b. Merchandise returned for which cash has been refunded or credited;

    c. Merchandise given away;

    d. Merchandise exchanged;

    e. Any sums or credit received in settlement of claims for loss or damage to merchandise;

    f. The amount of any discounts allowed on the sale of any article of merchandise;

g. Merchandise transferred to other stores of tenant or returned to tenant's factory, or to manufacturers or jobbers;

h. Amounts received by the tenant from any concessionaire or licensee as rent or advance rent or bonus or other payment for such concession or license;

i. Any taxes levied upon the sale or purchase of merchandise by tenant; or

j. Sales tax or other taxes upon or based upon the sale or sales price of merchandise and which must be paid by tenant or collected from its customers, whether or not the same may be commonly known as *sales tax*. all of which such taxes referred to in the aforesaid items (*i*) and (*j*) are to be excluded, regardless of whether imposed by any existing or future laws or ordinances of any municipal, state, or federal authority or other taxing authority. Merchandise, bonds, or gift certificates or the like redeemed at the demised premises, no matter where purchased, shall be included in *sales*, and merchandise bonds or gift certificates or the like purchased in or at the demised premises but not redeemed in or at the demised premises shall not be so included.

RIGHT TO INSPECT LESSEE'S BOOKS

The following clauses pertain to the keeping of accounts by the lessee and the lessor's right of inspecting the lessee's books:

1. The lessee further covenants that it will keep separate and accurate records of the gross sales covering all business done or transacted in, upon or from said demised premises, and that it will give to the lessor the right at any and all reasonable times to inspect said records. Said lessor shall be given access at any and all reasonable times to any other books or records that may be necessary to enable it to make a full and proper audit of the gross income of all business done in, upon or from said demised premises.

2. The lessee further covenants that for the purpose of ascertaining the amount payable as additional rent for any year as hereinabove provided, it will keep at the premises herein demised, books which shall show daily sales made by the lessee in, on, or from the demised premises and further agrees to deliver to the lessor monthly statements of the total sales made in, on or from said premises, sworn by the Secretary of the lessee and to furnish lessor with duplicate statements of account of the annual audit of all such sales, or, at the election of the lessor, to give the lessor access to such books, accounts, records and reports of receipts kept in or upon the premises herein demised as show the daily sales in such business by lessee and to permit lessor to have an audit made thereof by accountants appointed by the lessor. If such audit reveals error as result of which the lessor has been paid less than the amount to which it is entitled, then the expense of such audit shall be borne by

the lessee, otherwise it will be borne by the lessor. If the lessor is not satisfied with any daily, weekly, annual or other statement rendered to it by the lessee, it shall within ten (10) days of the receipt of such statement give notice in writing to the lessee of its dissatisfaction. Unless within ten (10) days of the receipt of such notice, the lessee shall have satisfied the lessor as to such statement, the lessor shall be entitled to an audit of the books and accounts of the lessee to be made by the lessor's accountants and at the joint expense of the lessor and lessee. The result of such audit shall be final and binding upon both parties.

3. The lessee agrees to keep such records and figures of accounting as conform with the requirements of good accounting, and as has been customary in its own business. The lessor shall have the right at all reasonable times to have their own personal representative examine such records and figures of accounts of the lessee in order to determine the correct amount or amounts due to the lessor. Any expense arising out of this audit shall be borne by the lessor.

4. Tenant covenants that for the purpose of ascertaining the amount payable as such additional rent for each lease year, it will keep full and complete records and books of account, showing all sales in, on or from the demised premises to enable landlord to ascertain the additional rental due it hereunder and will keep said records and books of account on file for a period of not less than twelve (12) months after the close of each lease year.

REPORTING SALES—SETTLING ACCOUNTS

The following clauses have to do with the reporting of sales and the settling of accounts.

1. On or before the twentieth day of each month during the term of this lease, commencing with the second month thereof, the lessee shall deliver to the lessor a correct statement of the gross sales of all business done in, upon or from said demised premises during the next preceding month as shown by the lessee's records. In addition to such monthly statements, the lessee shall on the 1st day of February in each year during the term of this lease, and upon the expiration of the lease, render to the lessor a certified public accountant's statement showing the total gross sales of all business done in, upon or from said demised premises for the year ending the 31st day of December preceding, or for such fractional part of a yearly period as occurs at the beginning and expiration of this lease. If the lessor is not satisfied with any monthly, annual or other statement thus submitted, then the lessor shall give notice to the lessee of such dissatisfaction within thirty (30) days after receipt of the statement complained of. Unless within ten (10) days after the receipt by the lessee of such notice of dissatisfaction, the lessee shall satisfy the lessor with respect to such statement thus complained of, then the lessor shall have the privilege of having an audit made of the account

books and records pertaining to the aforesaid business of the lessee. Such audit shall be made by certified public accountants in good standing to be selected by the lessor, which accountants shall work in conjunction with like accountants selected by the lessee. The expense of such audit shall be borne jointly by the lessor and the lessee, and the lessee shall render all possible assistance to such accountants and shall give them access to all books of accounts and other records that may be necessary to enable such accountants to make a full and complete audit of all gross income of all business done in, upon or from said demised premises.

2. Lessee shall keep separate sales checks on which shall be recorded each sale made in, upon or from the demised premises and shall, at the end of each and every business day, mail to the lessor, at the place herein provided for the payment of rent, a report of daily gross sales of merchandise and/or the performance of any service for any customer or patron for compensation in, upon or from the demised premises, and also mail to the lessor, on or before the 10th day of each month, a copy of lessee's bank statement showing deposits of all proceeds of daily sales during the next preceding month; and shall also keep separate, complete and accurate records and books of account showing all business of every kind, nature or description done or transacted in, upon or from the demised premises. As soon as practicable after the close of the lessee's fiscal year, they shall mail to the lessor, at the place herein provided for the payment of rent, a certified copy of an annual audit by a certified public accountant of the books of account regarding all business transactions in, upon, or from the demised premises. The lessor shall have the right at all reasonable times to enter upon the demised premises and examine and inspect the sales checks, records and books of account of the lessee and to make copies and excerpts therefrom, and to do anything that may be necessary to enable the lessor to make a full, proper and complete audit of all business done or transactions made in, upon or from the demised premises. Nothing herein contained, however, shall require lessee to preserve the sales checks during each fiscal year of the lease for a period longer than sixty days after certified audit for such fiscal year is mailed to lessor.

(The above requires daily reporting of sales, an unusual arrangement.)

3. At the end of each annual period of the term of this lease, the amount of gross sales during each calendar year shall be computed at 6 per cent of the amount of gross sales, during such calendar year, and if the amount of gross sales for the preceding calendar year, computed at 6 per cent shall be greater than the minimum guaranteed rental paid by the lessee during that year, then the lessee shall pay to the lessor on January 15th of each and every year during the term of this lease the difference between the minimum guaranteed rental paid and the computed rental of 6 per cent on the annual gross sales for the preceding calendar year. All settlements made on January 15th of each year shall be based on gross sales computation made by the lessee. The lessee further agrees that on or before April 15th of each year, to furnish to the lessor a certified statement by .... or other auditors of similar stand-

ing, of the amount of the gross sales in, out, through, or from the demised premises for the preceding calendar year, as used in computing the lessee's total sales in the regular annual report as rendered by the auditors for the lessee, and should there be any variation between the computation submitted by the lessee in the gross sales figures, and that of ...., a further adjustment will be effected, based on the certificate of the lessee's auditors. The lessee further agrees to furnish the lessor current monthly reports of sales in or from the demised premises for the preceding calendar month.

4. As a further consideration lessee shall, on or before the 10th day of each month, beginning with the 10th day of August, 19.., and ending with the 10th day of July, 19. , certify to lessors, over the signature of some responsible officer of lessee, on behalf of lessee, the total gross sales for the preceding calendar month, made by lessee, its subtenants and concessionaires, in the within leased premises. This certificate shall give the above-mentioned information broken down into the various departments operating in the within leased premises and shall clearly show all amounts deducted as sales taxes. Lessee agrees to keep an accurate record of its sales in the leased premises, which records, as well as all other accounts, books and papers referring to such sales, shall be available and open to the inspection of lessors and their duly authorized representatives at reasonable intervals and times.

5. Tenant covenants and agrees on or before the twentieth day of each month during the term hereof, and on or before the twentieth day of the month next succeeding the termination of this lease, to furnish to landlord a full statement of the sales in the demised premises during the previous month. Not later than thirty days after the close of each lease year of the term, tenant shall furnish to the landlord a certified copy of an auditor's report of tenant's sales for such year, said audit to be made by a reputable firm of independent certified public accountants who may be the certified public accountants for the tenant. Any amount of additional rent for such year shall be due to landlord simultaneously with the furnishing of such statement, and tenant covenants and agrees to pay the same accordingly.

6. Tenant shall permit landlord or its representatives, annually, to inspect the above-mentioned records and books of account relating to sales made in, on or from the demised premises, for the purpose of examination and verification of the aforementioned annual reports, provided such inspection shall be made within sixty days after delivery of such respective reports and shall be limited to the period covered by each such respective report, except as hereinafter provided. Each such annual report shall become final and binding upon the landlord and the tenant unless, within sixty days after the furnishing thereof, the landlord shall submit to the tenant a statement of any errors therein. In the event, however, the landlord shall have failed to inspect said records and books of account as herein provided and, thereafter, upon the inspection of such records and books of account in respect of a subsequent year, shall ascertain that the report rendered for such subsequent year was incorrect to the extent

of not less than the sum of ...... Dollars ($....) of additional rent, anything hereinbefore contained notwithstanding, the landlord shall have the right to inspect the said records and books of account for all prior years subsequent to the date of the last inspection, and to be paid any proper adjustment in respect of the additional rent which may be due for any such prior year which may be shown upon or as a result of any such inspection to the extent that same shall not become uncollectible as the result of any applicable Statute of Limitations. In the event that as a result of any claim made by the landlord upon the tenant for additional rent tenant shall pay such additional rent under protest, such payment shall be without prejudice to the right of the tenant to recover back the amount of such payment to the extent that the same is unwarranted and was not due from tenant to landlord; provided that any action or proceeding therefor shall be commenced by tenant within sixty days after such payment.

CHAPTER 9

Special Provisions in Percentage Leases

The quasi-partnership between owner and tenant arising out of the percentage lease transaction makes it advisable at times that certain clauses be included in the lease defining more clearly the owner-tenant relationship and safeguarding the interests of both parties under the percentage arrangement.

The owner, in a fixed rental transaction to a responsible tenant is usually satisfied to let the tenant go his own way in the conduct of his business. In a percentage lease deal the owner has a direct interest in the manner in which the tenant operates his business. The tenant on the other hand wants a clear definition of his rights as well as of his obligations.

This chapter discusses typical clauses of this nature sometimes found in percentage leases.

NAME UNDER WHICH BUSINESS IS TO BE CONDUCTED

Merchandising firms and chain store organizations may have subsidiary corporations which engage in the same line of business and which may sell a different type and quality of merchandise from that sold by the parent company. The owner may want to guard against the occupancy of the premises by such a tenant. The following clause has been used in percentage leases to cover this eventuality.

Tenant agrees, upon becoming entitled to possession of the demised premises, as herein provided, to install promptly and thereafter operate and maintain throughout the term of this Lease a women's retail ready-to-wear store which is comparable to that conducted or maintained by Tenant at other locations throughout the United States in its "Lessee" stores, so far as the demised premises are adaptable therefor, and at which store Tenant will offer for sale a complete line of all grades of women's ready-to-wear garments sold by Tenant and known as "Lessee." Tenant agrees to operate its store in the demised premises under the trade name "Lessee," provided that if at any time Tenant shall be prohibited or prevented from using said trade name by causes beyond its control, then the Tenant may operate such store under such other trade name as a majority of the other stores of Tenant in the metropolitan district. It is further agreed that if in two successive years falling within the term of this Lease, commencing on (May 1st) and ending on the next succeeding (30) of (April), the gross sales and business transacted by Tenant and Tenant's licensees, if any, shall be less than $154,300 in each of such two successive years, then Tenant may, upon the expiration of such two successive years, change its trade name "Lessee" to the trade name "Second" or to any other name which Tenant may select, provided said name is satisfactory to Lessor.

PRIOR POSSESSION

When a new store building or shopping center is being constructed, leases are usually executed well in advance of the date of completion. The lease becames effective and occupancy is set for a time when it is anticipated that the building will be finished. In some cases a tenant may be willing to accept occupancy of his quarters before the effective date of the lease if the building is completed or even to accept occupancy if that portion of the building which he is to occupy has been completed but the balance is uncompleted. The tenant would usually be willing to pay a straight percentage rental during this period but would want to be excused from the minimum guarantee provision.

In the event tenant takes possession of said premises prior to completion of same and transacts business therein, tenant shall pay to the lessor as rental for said premises from the date tenant begins transaction of business until April 30, 19.., an amount equal to seven per cent (7%) of all sales and business transacted in said premises during said period but shall not be obligated to pay to lessor minimum rental as stipulated here until May 1, 19... It is understood and agreed, however, that all of the provisions contained in this lease governing percentage rental shall apply and govern the percentage rental for said period.

CONTINUED OCCUPANCY

If it is assumed that the minimum guaranteed rental is less than the fixed rental value of the property, it is clear that the owner might suffer a loss if the tenant discontinues the operation of the store and continues to pay only the minimum guarantee. To guard against this eventuality, there is sometimes included in percentage lease agreements, a clause providing for the payment of a penalty over and above the minimum guarantee.

Lessee covenants to, and it is of the essence of this lease that the lessee shall, continuously and uninterruptedly during the term of this lease, occupy and use the premises for the purpose hereinabove specified, except while premises are untenantable by reason of fire or other unavoidable casualty, and in this connection it is agreed that in case of breach of this covenant the lessee shall in addition to the rental hereinabove provided for, pay to the lessor monthly a sum equal to 25 per cent of the monthly rental stipulated herein for each and every month during which the premises are not so continuously and uninterruptedly used and occupied, as liquidated damages for the lessee's breach of covenant, it being recognized by the parties that the exact amount of damages to the lessor on account of such breach cannot be accurately ascertained. This provision shall, however, in no wise abridge or affect any other right or remedy which the lessor may have on account of or in connection with the lessee's breach of this covenant.

MANNER OF CONDUCTING BUSINESS

The owner wants to make certain that the tenant conducts his business on a proper competitive level with other firms or organizations in the same business. He wants to make certain that the business shall be conducted actively during the entire term of the lease, that the tenant shall keep a proper stock of merchandise and that his store hours shall be the same as those of other competing organizations.

Excepting as is herein otherwise provided, the lessees shall open their business in the demised premises at the beginning of the term of this lease, and diligently conduct such business during the entire term hereof;

they shall maintain upon said demised premises a substantial stock of merchandise and a reasonable number of employees for such purpose, and keep the demised premises open for business during the hours of each business day generally observed by the merchants in the vicinity of the demised premises, excepting when prevented from so doing by any casualty, strike, lockout, act of God, or other cause beyond the control of the lessees, and excepting in case of death of any of the members of the firm, officers of the corporation, lessees herein, or of the death of the manager of the store, and excepting also legal holidays and holidays not established by law, but generally observed by the merchants or any association of merchants in the vicinity of the demised premises.

RESTRICTION AGAINST OTHER OUTLETS

A clause common to all types of commercial leases is one prohibiting the lessee from opening up or operating a competitive store within a given radius or distance of the leased premises. It is clear that this type of clause is more important in a percentage lease than in a fixed rental lease.

Lessees agree that they will not, directly or indirectly, engage in or become interested in any business for the sale at retail of men's and boy's clothing, hats and caps, or any of such articles within a radius of two miles, less two city blocks, from the demised premises during such time as this lease shall be in force and effect.

TENANT ADVERTISING

The importance of tenant advertising is pointed up quite clearly by the Store Leasing Committee of the Building Managers Association of Chicago: "Merchandising according to present interpretation should mean the use of all appropriate media to stimulate the sale of a commodity or service. Visual media—such as newspapers, magazines, television—where a product warrants it, are as necessary to the operation of a retail business as window and store display. Most areas have an established potential sales volume, which requires continued effort by all situated therein to maintain. Many business sections have lost the ground and some have even become extinct because some few merchants have attempted to save on advertising dollars at the expense of themselves, the area, and others."

Despite the importance of advertising there has been a growing disinclination to use a clause in leases specifying the volume of advertising that the tenant must do because:

1. If the tenant is selling a product that warrants media advertising, he will be as aware of its necessity to his business operation as is the owner of the property. To such a tenant an advertising clause is unnecessary and needlessly restrictive.
2. If the tenant is a small operator he might be unwilling to commit himself to a fixed promotional expense.
3. In the case of a chain store tenant it would be extremely difficult to make a satisfactory allocation of advertising expense to its various branches.

SUB-LEASING

The percentage lease should, of course, provide for the owner's permission in any form of subletting, particularly if the entire leased premises are to be sublet. Actually, the subletting of the entire premises usually results in a new lease negotiation because the owner will want the same assurances from the new tenant that he had from the original tenant without releasing the original tenant from his obligations under the lease.

Subletting a portion of the leased premises is a much more common practice. It is important to the owner that the sales of these concessionaires be included in the lessee's gross business.

The Tenant shall not have the right to assign the within Lease, nor sublet the demised premises, in whole or in part, without first obtaining the written consent of the Lessor. The Lessor covenants and agrees that it will not unreasonably or arbitrarily withhold such consent. Nothing in this paragraph contained, however, shall prevent the sale on the demised premises of any merchandise which Tenant has the right to sell thereon under the terms of this Lease (with the exception of ladies' dresses, suits and coats which shall be sold by Tenant only) through licensees or concessionaires who conduct their business under Tenant's trade name (and the sales and business of such licensees and concessionaires shall be part of the sales above referred to).

EXCLUSIVES

In the case of a shopping center or where an owner controls a group of contiguous stores, tenants oftentimes require the exclusive right to sell the type of merchandise specified in the lease. This is a matter that should be approached with caution because in some instances, the granting of exclusives is detrimental to the tenant, as well as to the owner. It is, however, justified in many instances and on the owner's part is compensated for, by the "restriction against other out-lets" clause.

Lessor covenants and agrees that so long as this Lease shall be in force the Lessor will not operate or use or permit the operation or use of the premises first hereinabove described, or of any building thereon, except the demised premises, as or for a retail women's ready-to-wear store, and will not operate or use or permit the operation or use of such premises first hereinabove described, with the exception of the demised premises and the easterly portion of the premises first hereinabove described now under lease to Store A, for the sale of women's dresses, coats, suits and skirts, sweaters, blouses, and costume jewelry and intimate wearing apparel (which shall not include shoes and hosiery); provided, however, that no such prohibited operation or use of the premises first hereinabove described, or any building thereon, shall constitute a breach of the foregoing covenants until written notice of such prohibited operation or use is given by Tenant to Lessor, and until the Lessor has had a reasonable time thereafter within which to bring about a termination of such prohibited operation or use, Lessor agreeing that upon such notice, it will promptly take proper steps to remedy said prohibited operation; and provided further that the Tenant hereby acknowledges that it is fully informed that the Lessor is negotiating for a lease of part of the premises first hereinabove described to Second Store, Inc., under a lease which permits said Second Store, Inc., to conduct upon said premises a women's shoe store for the sale of women's shoes and such accessories as are commonly included in other stores now operated by Second Store, Inc., and Tenant further acknowledges that it is fully informed that the Lessor has entered into a lease with Store A, of the premises immediately east and adjoining the store proposed to be leased to Second Store, Inc., which lease permits said A Store to conduct upon said premises a variety store of the type which is at the present time commonly known as (A Dollar Store), and Tenant agrees that the Lessor may at any time operate or use or permit the operation or use of the premises first hereinabove described, or any building thereon, except the demised premises, as or for such a variety store of the type which is at present time commonly known as (A Dollar Store), or for a store for the sale of ladies' shoes and accessories.

DIFFERENTIAL BETWEEN WHOLESALE AND RETAIL SALES

When a lessee engages in a wholesale sales operation as a supplement to his principal business of retail sales, the owner should be compensated, although the percentage would probably not be as high as the percentage that would apply on his retail volume. If the tenant is allowed to conduct a wholesale business the lease should set forth specifically the rates covering both types of operation.

PERCENTAGE DIFFERENTIALS FOR VARYING TYPES OF MERCHANDISE

The Building Managers Association of Chicago points out that "some percentage leases apply to occupancy with multiple lines of business, namely, the principal line of business and other lines incidental thereto. This condition is illustrated by such combinations as:

> Candy store and soda fountain.
> Tobacco of all types and novelties.
> Bottled liquors and bar sales.
> Restaurant and bar or liquor sale.
> Men's suits and haberdashery.
> Women's dresses and accessories.
> Cameras and greeting cards.

The first mentioned represents the principal or authorized line, the second the supplementing line.

Since a different rate of percentage is applicable to the different types of merchandise which fall within rather widely removed categories, it is frequently necessary to provide in the lease for various percentage rates. This procedure necessitates the reporting of the sales volume in each of the categories and a separate computation on each. The minimum rental is then credited against the total of percentage rentals."

OFF PREMISES SALES

The retail store may oftentimes be a headquarters or central point for the generating of sales through direct mail, advertising, etc. These sales are not consummated on the premises. This situation is most frequently found in the branch or suburban store operation of large organizations. The suburban or branch store may not be as fully stocked as the main store. The main store advertises certain lines of merchandise and because of this advertising, inquiries are directed to the suburban store. The suburban store will then have the merchandise shipped direct to the customer from the main store. There can be no set rule for handling this type of sale. Obviously, the owner should be entitled to some compensation under his percentage lease when the store which he has leased is a vehicle for producing the sales volume.

The term "Gross Sales" means the dollar aggregate of the price charged for all goods, wares, merchandise, beverages and food sold, leased or licensed, and all charges for services sold and/or performed, by the Tenant in, at, on or from the Demised Premises, whether made for cash, on credit, or otherwise, and without reserve or deduction for inability or failure to collect (including, but not limited to): (A) sales, leases or licenses of goods, wares, merchandise, beverages, food or services (i) where the orders therefor originated and/or are accepted in, at, on or from the Demised Premises but delivery thereof is made from or at any place other than the Demised Premises, or vice-versa, (ii) made pursuant to mail, telegraphic, telephone or other similar orders received or filled in, at, on or from the Demised Premises or directed thereto.

ALLOWANCE TO TENANT FOR CAPITAL IMPROVEMENTS

The basic principle of most store leases—percentage or fixed rental —is that capital improvements are paid for by the owner while fixtures and most interior fittings are taken care of by the tenant.

Under certain circumstances, the tenant may make some capital improvements which are usually the responsibility of the owner and would be compensated for the cost of these improvements, in one way or another. For instance, in many major shopping centers tenants want to have the exterior or some phases of the interior design treated in accordance with their plans. These improvements may well be considered capital expenditures. Because it is impossible to anticipate tenant requirements in advance of the start of construction, these specialized features cannot be included in the general contract. In such cases, the owner makes the tenant a specific allowance for the completion of his space.

This subject is discussed further in Chapter 11, where typical lease clauses covering tenant's work will be found.

RECAPTURE CLAUSES

Many a landlord would be willing to give a percentage lease to a tenant if he had a method of canceling it when the tenant did not live up to expectations and do the business necessary for the landlord to receive the minimum rent set for the premises. This is exactly what is accomplished by the inclusion of the so-called *recapture* or *cancellation* clause. Although this clause is not extensively used, it is a sure-edged tool to sever the tenant from the location if he does not make good according to the anticipations of the landlord.

In order that the arrangement may not be unfair to the tenant, who may have expended considerable money moving to the location, buying and installing fixtures, carrying on promotional business to get started and obtain volume, the tenant is given the opportunity of paying an excess amount over the percentage actually produced by his business, the excess being sufficient to reimburse the landlord up to the point of the latter's minimum guarantee. By doing this, the tenant is permitted to carry on until (1) he builds up his business to the volume necessary to meet the percentage demand, or (2) decides that he is not in the right business for the location and agrees to surrender his lease and vacate.

Typical wording for a recapture clause for a percentage lease is as follows:

It is further understood and agreed that in the event that during the period from January 1, ... to December 31, ..., the rent realized from the premises herein demised shall be less than ($), then the lessor, if it so elects, may terminate this lease forthwith on the thirtieth day of ...., by serving upon the lessee sixty (60) days' previous written notice of its intention so to do. But the lessee shall have the right, within five (5) days after receipt of such notice, to pay to the lessor, in cash, the difference between the rent paid by the lessee to the lessor, and the said ($); and that such payment by the lessee to the lessor, as herein provided, shall simultaneously cancel said notice of termination and render the same null and void and of no further force or effect.

It is further understood and agreed that in the event said lessee pays up said deficiency as hereinbefore stated, the rental for the last (   ) years of said lease is to be as set forth in Clause No. 1 of said lease; or in the event that the said lessee does not pay up this deficiency in cash, if lessee elects to continue this lease in full force and effect to its expiration on December 31, ..., then the rental to be paid by the lessee to the lessor for the period from (   ) to (   ) shall be a minimum guaranteed annual rental of ($), or ($) per month; plus (   ) per cent of all gross sales in excess of ($) per month.

CHAPTER 10

Concessions or Leased Departments

In certain types of mercantile operations, a portion of the premises owned or leased by the mercantile firm may be leased or subleased to an independent operator on a concession basis.

The practice is most prevalent in department stores, where usually there will be one or more such concessions. The practice is also common in specialty shops where the owner is in, let us say, the ladies' dress business and will lease counters for the sale of hosiery and bags, accessories, etc. Concessionaires also operate in food markets, amusement parks and in other types of business operations.

We are concerned here largely with the prevailing practices in department stores, although the basic principles behind the leasing or subletting of department store space will apply to other types of businesses.

REASONS FOR LEASING DEPARTMENT

The question would naturally be asked "why should a department store lease concession rights to an independent operator?" It has been found that there are three principal reasons for this practice.

1. Personnel difficulty faced by the store in securing the necessary specialized personnel required to operate the department.
2. Disproportionately heavy inventory investment required.
3. Highly specialized style features of merchandise which could result in heavy markdowns.

It should not be inferred from the foregoing that the operators of the leased departments do not find their businesses profitable. As a matter of fact, many of them are highly profitable and pay high square foot rentals to the department stores; but store management knows from experience that these operations, because of their specialized nature, can be more effectively run by other persons.

DEPARTMENTS MOST COMMONLY LEASED

A survey prepared by the Philadelphia Retail Controllers Association for the Controllers Congress of the National Retail Dry Goods Association showed that the ten most commonly leased departments are main floor millinery, beauty salon, photographic studios, sewing machines, lending libraries, watch repair, shoe repair, optical equipment, vacuum cleaners, and basement millinery. Among other departments frequently leased are electrical appliances, radios and televisions, fur and rug storage, shoes, jewelry, automobile accessories, restaurants and lunchrooms, meats, groceries and baked goods, etc.

There is no norm or standard on the number of departments which might be leased in a given store. This will depend on management policy.

A Mercantile Rather Than a Real Estate Transaction

Actually, the dominant features of a lease agreement drawn between a department store owner and a concessionaire are more closely related to the mercantile than to the real estate business. We are devoting a chapter to the subject of this type of lease because it is not uncommon for real estate men to negotiate them. Oftentimes a real estate man is called on by some client in a retail business to negotiate such a lease for him with a department store. The following remarks on special concession lease features should prove helpful.

RENTALS

Invariably, the rental is on a percentage basis; in a number of cases there is a minimum guarantee as well. Rarely will you encounter a straight rental agreement for a concession. When you do, it will usually be on some type of operation which is installed as a convenience to the store management, such as an employees' cafeteria.

The percentage rate is usually higher than would prevail for the same type of business operation conducted in a single store.

Where the prevailing percentage for a particular type of operation in a good retail location would be 10 per cent, we might find the rate for a concession in a department store at 15 per cent to 20 per cent. It is interesting to note that the Controllers Institute calls these payments *commissions* instead of rental.

The reasons for these higher percentages are not difficult to understand. The tenant or concessionaire is customarily furnished, free of charge, with heat, light, janitor and elevator service. He would also have the right to use the rest rooms and toilets provided for the store's employees and ordinarily would be allowed the pro-rated use of display windows.

But, most important of all, he would be operating under the name of the department store. The store therefore gives him the benefit of its prestige and reputation. This, of course, is a valuable asset to the average concessionaire and he is willing to pay a price for it. In addition, the store furnishes him with a made-to-order clientele.

We have not suggested any range of percentages for different types of leased departments, because any such table would be misleading, since there can be a wide range in such percentages depending on considerations such as location within the store, capital investment by the store in fixtures, services furnished free of charge by the store, etc.

LOCATION

The lease agreement should clearly state the location of the leased department within the store. It should also state the number of square feet to be leased.

The store would probably reserve the right to change the location and the space of the leased area to any other part of the store if required by the general conduct of its business. If such removal were required, the store would customarily bear the cost.

TERM OF LEASE

Most such leases are short-term arrangements, usually for one year with automatic renewal provisions. They sometimes provide for short-term (i.e., 30 or 60 day) cancellations.

NATURE OF OPERATION

It is obvious that the lease agreement should carefully state the purpose for which the leased department is to be used. It might also probihit the tenant or lessee from operating a retail establishment or similar leased department within a specified distance from the department store. Since the lessee is operating under the store's name, there would usually be clauses in the lease controlling the supply of merchandise or inventory which the lessee will carry, its quality and price. In other words, the lessee would be required to carry a full and complete line of representative and salable merchandise comparable with the general stock of other merchandise, as to quality and value, carried by the store. The merchandise should be priced competitively with merchandise sold at similar establishments.

STORE NAME, ADVERTISING AND PROMOTION

The tenant's business is usually conducted only in the name of the department store. The right to use the store's name would, of course, terminate with the end of the lease agreement. Advertising in the form of signs, letterheads, business cards done by the lessee would have to have the store's approval. General promotional campaigns conducted by the store would be participated in by the lessee on a pro-rated basis. The lessee would also be required to make a definite agreement as to the amount of newspaper advertising that he would do. This advertising would be done under the store's name and the lessee would receive the benefit of any contract rate for space which had been obtained by the store. The lessee would also have the right to use of window display space at specified times. Usually, the services of the window decorators would be supplied free of charge by the store.

FIXTURES

The installation of furniture, fixtures, and appliances is a matter for negotiation. In most cases they would be installed by the lessee. They would be the lessee's property at the termination of the lease unless their removal might cause damage to store property. In such cases, the lease might provide for the fixtures to revert to the store owner. The maintenance, care, and cleaning of fixtures and appliances is usually the responsibility of the lessee.

EMPLOYEES

Under most such lease agreements the employees of the lessee are hired through the store's employment department. Their salaries, however, are paid by the lessee. This is not only important, but in most cases necessary to proper store management, because it can insure uniform employment practices and may eliminate jurisdictional disputes. Employees normally would be eligible for the store's profit sharing and pension plan and would be entitled to buy merchandise at the same discount rate as other store employees. The lessee would, of course, have an agreement with the store as to starting salaries and increments.

STORE CUSTOMS

The lessee would be required to abide by all regulations covering the hours of opening and closing of the store, observance of holidays and general conduct of the business.

DELIVERY SERVICE

Store would provide the same delivery service as it affords its own customers. Usually this would be billed to the lessee at cost.

SALES RECEIPTS

Sometimes the store has a central point for the receipt of all cash. If this is so, the lessee's sales would clear through this central point. If separate cash registers are maintained in the different departments, the lessee would usually be required to report all sales daily and to deliver sales tickets and proceeds to the store office daily.

TAXES AND INSURANCE

The lessee would be required to pay all municipal, county, state, and federal taxes levied against his merchandise, sales income or equipment. In reference to sales and excise taxes, many stores retain the money collected for such taxes and pay them in the store's own remittance to state and Federal agencies.

The lessee would be required to carry adequate public liability, workmen's compensation and other similar forms of insurance. He would also be expected to carry the necessary burglary, robbery, fire, earthquake, etc. insurance so that the store would be held harmless for any accident occurring on the lessee's space or from any damage caused to his merchandise by fire or other reasons.

DEFAULT

The store would reserve to itself the customary remedies of a lessor in the event of a default on the part of the concessionaire.

CHAPTER 11

Shopping Center Leases

A shopping center is a group of stores, not part of an urban or suburban business district, with central operation, management, control or ownership. In practically all instances the shopping center will have automobile parking facilities adjacent or readily available for customer use. These facilities may be owned and operated by the shopping center management and reserved for the exclusive use of shopping patrons or they may be facilities shared in common with adjacent business or residential properties. They may be privately owned and operated or owned and operated by some public agency.

The shopping center lease is essentially the same as a store lease or a commercial lease. Because of conditions peculiar to shopping centers generally, or to a particular shopping center, the lease may —and probably does—have covenants not found in the average store lease.

The brief discussion of the essential characteristics of shopping centers which follows serves to accentuate their unique features which require special consideration and special covenants in lease agreements.

TYPES OF SHOPPING CENTERS

There is a wide range in the size of shopping centers and in the facilities they offer. They fall into three major classifications:

1. Neighborhood Center

The neighborhood center generally has a supermarket as the key tenant and will cater to a restricted geographical area, usually within a mile of the center. Other tenants might include drug store, hardware store, stationery store, delicatessen, etc. Total rentable store area would probably be less than 25,000 square feet. Total area including parking facilities might be 2 to 5 acres.

2. Intermediate Center

The intermediate center would have a variety store (such as Woolworth, Kresge, etc.) or junior department store (such as J. C. Penney, Sears Roebuck, Korvettes, etc.) or both as the key tenant or tenants. There would be many more auxiliary stores and the center would serve a larger geographical area. Total rentable area might be from 25,000 to 250,000 square feet. Total plottage including shopping facilities might be from 5 to 20 acres.

3. Regional Center

The regional shopping center will have one or more major department stores as key tenants and will offer complete shopping facilities to its trading area which might embrace 75 to 100 square miles.

Total rentable floor space might exceed 1,000,000 square feet. The rentable floor area will probably be air-conditioned and maybe completely covered, including mall areas. Total area of the center, including parking, may be in excess of 100 acres.

Regional centers have been built almost exclusively in the suburban sections of our larger metropolitan areas.

CHARACTERISTICS OF SHOPPING CENTERS

There are four principal points of dissimilarity between a typical shopping center and a central business district. These points, of a physical and economic nature, are usually reflected in the terms and covenants of a shopping center lease. They are:

1. Central facilities and administration, i.e. parking, streets, roads —central management office.
2. The speculative element: the fact that the shopping center is more of an economic unknown quantity than the central business district.

3. The planning element: the fact that type of store, character of tenancy, store size, layout, etc., are matters of preliminary planning.
4. Completion of buildings: the requirement, in many centers, that the tenant is responsible for certain items of building construction as well as the customary items of store fixtures and equipment.

Parking, Streets, Roads, General Administration

The business operation of an individual tenant in a shopping center is practically no different than the operation by the same tenant in a central business district. It is true that if a shopping center is in a suburban area there will be more emphasis on brands of merchandise used by suburban residents—gardening and household equipment, sports clothes, etc.—but merchandising operations, store fixtures, store layouts, credit policies, are essentially the same.

In a shopping center certain necessary physical facilities must be created or maintained by the owner. In a central business district these facilities are available and are therefore, more or less, taken for granted.

PARKING AREA, STREETS, ROADS

If the adjacent parking area is owned by the shopping center management it must be maintained in summer and in winter. No matter whether the shopping center is large or small, maintenance and cleaning of the parking area will be necessary. If the center is open at night, the area will probably be lighted. In many northern areas snow removal is an additional item of expense.

In the larger centers, particularly on peak shopping days, attendants or traffic officers will be required to handle customer parking. Where facilities are provided for thousands of cars, the center will have to have its own maintenance crew to keep the access roads in a state of repair, to keep the parking areas in usable condition, to paint lines and directional signs, and so on.

Most of the larger centers will require private police facilities. If, however, the area is deeded to the local municipality for maintenance and operation as a public facility, traffic control and maintenance of the area become a matter of public expense.

In some fringe suburban areas, municipal officials have agreed to dedicate and maintain parking facilities for shopping center developers or for certain key tenants, particularly department stores. But where a large center is developed in an outlying area, as is the case with most regional shopping centers, the likelihood of municipal operation and maintenance of the parking area is remote.

In addition to the parking facilities and road maintenance, most of the larger centers will have some form of landscaping requiring the constant attention of gardeners and other maintenance men.

GENERAL ADMINISTRATION

The complexity of the operation of the larger shopping center and the extent of its services require a central administrative office which, in addition to rental arrangements, will handle tenant relations, bookkeeping, project supervision, employment, etc.

The Speculative Element

The central business district is an established component of a community's economy. It may be on the downgrade or upgrade, but area trends are reasonably predictable. Most shopping centers must still be considered to be in the experimental stage. The speculative element is present to a more marked degree than in the central district.

In the postwar years local shopping centers have sprung up in profusion seemingly wherever land was available. Thus far the majority of them have been successful. Many have achieved moderate success while some few have been failures. The development of most of the smaller centers was founded on the scantiest research. Tenancy in these centers has definite speculative characteristics. Economic mortality among individual tenants has been relatively high.

In the larger shopping centers, the regional centers in particular, development almost invariably has been preceded by careful and painstaking research, engaged in not only by the shopping center owner but by the major tenants, particularly the department stores. Department stores will frequently use outside consultants of established reputation who will make a thorough and exhaustive economic analysis of the primary and secondary shopping areas, covering population growth, transportation, buying habits, competitive shopping facilities, business potential, etc. Similar studies by the shopping center owners are used as a means of attracting the smaller tenants who cannot afford to make their own studies.

But despite the precautions taken by owner and tenant, the human element is always present so that the conclusions drawn from the studies are not always definitive. Consultants, for instance, may give qualified approval to a location in a growing area where any one of a series of contingencies may arrest the growth trend. The decision as to whether or not to proceed becomes a matter of the owner's judgment, and inevitably, has a speculative element.

In two cases that we know of, the owner's decision to proceed with the shopping center on the basis of a qualified endorsement by economic consultants was more emotional than reasoned. One of the centers proved to be a failure, the other was a borderline case.

Fortunately, these cases are relatively few in the larger centers but it must be conceded that almost any *new* shopping center presents risk elements which are not found in established central business districts. Risk elements are, of course, attributable mostly to the fact that there is no comparable experience in the area on which tenants can estimate their business potential. The estimate of potential must be predicated on a series of data as to population, income, competitive facilities, etc., and on assumptions or conclusions based on these data.

The shopping center is a new economic phenomenon. Researchers are discovering a few things about their operation, about the shopping habits and preferences of customers, for example, that will prove of inestimable value to future developers and will serve to eliminate to a large degree the speculative element that is an inescapable feature of present-day centers.

THE PLANNING ELEMENT

Large shopping centers are usually planned as to the number of stores, the type of stores, size of stores, relative location of stores, and so on.

For instance, in a shopping center with a given number of square feet of rentable area, there may be room for a certain number of ladies' wear or specialty shops, men's clothing or furnishing stores, etc., over and above the space occupied by the department store.

The need for these stores might be based on experience and/or economic analysis. The economic studies might also show that the area in which the center is located badly needs and will support a women's apparel store carrying a certain quality of merchandise within a limited price range, but that it would not support a store carrying a different grade of merchandise at a different price range. As a result of such studies, many shopping center owners have declined seemingly attractive offers from certain tenants on the ground that the merchandise they carry, the prices they charge, or their merchandising methods, etc., would not be acceptable to the residents of the market area.

The net result of careful planning in a well located shopping center therefore, is a carefully controlled policy of tenant selection. The astute owner will seek out certain tenants while at the same time refusing to negotiate with other tenants in the same line of business. He will make concessions to a desirable tenant that he would not make to a tenant who would contribute less to the overall success of the center.

COMPLETION OF BUILDINGS

In some of the larger centers built in the early postwar years, owner-tenant difficulties arose over the quality and design of certain items installed by the owner, such as store fronts, floor, wall and ceiling finishes, electrical outlets. These are matters of building construction and are, therefore, normally supplied to the tenant by the owner. (Trade fixtures and store equipment are supplied by the tenant, while items that are considered part of the "real estate" are furnished by the owner. Certain construction items, such as air conditioning, might be a matter of negotiation as to who does the installing and who pays for it.)

But the difficulties that arose in shopping centers were occasioned by items which would normally and properly be part of the owner's responsibility, both as to installation and financing. Because of these difficulties it has now become the policy in many large shopping centers to have the tenant complete the construction after the building shell has been finished and the utility lines installed. The plans for such work would be approved by the owner, and, in many instances, the tenant would use the owner's general contractor both for purposes of efficiency and economy. This arrangement has a twofold advantage. It gives the tenant full latitude in completing the space according to his own needs, and it reduces the owner's initial capital outlay. The tenant's outlay of funds for this improvement is properly a part of the owner's expense and is provided for either through an immediate cash reimbursement or through a rental allowance.

INFLUENCE OF SHOPPING CENTER CHARACTERISTICS ON LEASES

We saw above that the shopping center differs from a central business district in four major respects: the provision of parking and central administrative facilities; the speculative element arising from the fact that a shopping center is still a new economic phenomenon; the planning element and the practice of having a tenant complete the construction of the individual store units. Each of these points of difference is customarily reflected in a shopping center lease.

Parking—Central Administration

The owner will seek to recover a pro-rated share of the cost of central maintenance, including administrative expense. The items covered are often referred to as "pro-ratables." The expense is usually apportioned on a square foot basis so that the pro-ratable charge of a tenant who occupies 5 per cent of the rentable area of the shopping center, will be 5 per cent of the total of all pro-ratable items.

Heat and air conditioning would not be included in these charges. In some shopping centers both are provided to the tenant. In some, the tenant supplies the heat and installs his own air conditioning unit. In others, the owner may supply the heat and furnish chilled water to the tenants for air conditioning. In one way or another, the heat and air conditioning items will be reflected in the tenant's rental, but in this respect a shopping center lease is no different than the average store lease. Typical clause in shopping center lease covering the pro-ratable items is as follows:

The Tenant agrees to pay to the Landlord a "Common Area charge" with respect to each Lease Fiscal Year as set forth in this Section.

The Common Area charge to be paid by the Tenant for any Lease Fiscal Year shall be the Tenant's pro-rata share of the Landlord's actual gross costs for such Lease Fiscal Year of maintaining and operating the Common Areas (and of affording police and/or fire protection services to the Shopping Center, if and to the extent so provided).

Such Charge for any Lease Fiscal Year shall be paid by the Tenant as follows: The Landlord shall, at or before the start of such Lease Fiscal Year, notify the Tenant of the amount which the Landlord estimates will be the amount thereof for such Lease Fiscal Year, and the Tenant shall pay such amount in equal monthly installments in advance on or before the first day of each month. On or before the September 30 immediately following the end of such Lease Fiscal Year, the Landlord shall deliver to the Tenant a statement, certified to by a certified public accountant, showing the Common Area charges to be paid by the Tenant with respect to such Lease Fiscal Year computed in accordance with the provisions of this Section, the amount thereof theretofore paid by the Tenant during such Lease Fiscal Year, and the amount of the resulting balance due thereon, or over-payment thereof, as the case may be. Appropriate adjustment shall thereupon be made between the parties, on demand, on the basis of such statement. Such statement, so certified, shall be conclusive between the parties.

For the purposes of determining the Common Area charge to be paid by the Tenant for any Lease Fiscal Year, the Tenant's pro-rata share of the Landlord's such gross costs shall be that proportion of the whole which the Floor Space in the Demised Premises bears to all Floor Space occupied during such period in the entire Shopping Center.

Such gross costs of maintenance and operation shall include all costs and expenses of every kind or nature incurred by the Landlord in the operation, maintenance and/or repairing of all the Common Areas (and providing the police and/or fire protection services referred to above, if provided) in a manner deemed by the Landlord to be reasonable and appropriate and for the best interests of the Shopping Center, as determined in accordance with generally accepted accounting principles and allocated to any particular Lease Fiscal Year on the accrual method of accounting. Without otherwise limiting the generality of the foregoing, there shall be included in such gross costs the cost of: premiums with respect to public liability, property damage, compensation and other insurance carried on or with respect to the Common Areas; cleaning; snow and ice removal; landscaping; operation of lighting, loud speaker and music systems; supervising with attendants and employment of other personnel used in such operation, maintenance and repair; taxes on the operation of, or the right to operate, such areas for the intended purposes; repairs, replacements and maintenance not properly chargeable to capital account; procurement of supplies and equipment not properly chargeable to capital account; and other similar costs. There shall, however, be excluded therefrom real property taxes and assessments, depreciation, and matters properly chargeable to capital account. Any revenue derived from charges to the public for the parking of cars in the Shopping Center shall (to the extent, if any, that it exceeds the sum of excise and similar taxes levied on such revenue and depreciation, in accordance with generally accepted accounting principles, on any equipment installed to collect such revenue) first be credited on the gross costs determined with respect to the Common Areas.

In addition to the Common Area charge to be paid by the Tenant with respect to any Lease Fiscal Year the Tenant shall also pay the following, if applicable; if any vehicle of the Tenant or any Concessionaire, or of any of their respective officers, agents or employees, is parked in any part of the Shopping Center other than the employee parking area(s) designated therefor by the Landlord, an amount equal to the daily rate therefor established by the Landlord from time to time (which rate shall not exceed Ten Dollars ($10.00) for each such vehicle for each day, or part thereof, if it is so parked in such other part of the Shopping Center. All amounts due under the provisions of this paragraph shall be payable by the Tenant during the Lease Fiscal Year in question within ten (10) days after demand therefor.

Speculative Element

The elements of speculation peculiar to shopping centers would be reflected in the lease terms. The owner, of course, would strive for a minimum guaranteed rental as an offset against a percentage of sales. The cautious tenant might try to avoid the payment of a minimum guaranty, but if the center is a desirable one and well located he would probably be unable to achieve his objective. As a concession for the elimination of a minimum guarantee or the payment of a lower minimum, the tenant may acquiesce in giving the owner a slightly higher percentage within the range applicable to his particular type of business. For instance, a tenant occupying a central business district store might pay a rental well in excess of $10 per square foot against 7 per cent of gross sales. In a shopping center he might be able to settle at $6.00 per square foot against 8 per cent of sales but the owner might require a slightly higher percentage arrangement.

This custom, of course, does not have universal application. In some of the best located shopping centers where success seemed to be a foregone conclusion, tenants have paid close to the minimum rents that they would pay in the central city district. On the other hand, as the speculative element of a center becomes more apparent, the tenant's resistance to standard rental terms will be more and more reflected in the actual lease agreement.

Planning Element

It is a known fact that there is a marked differential between the square foot rentals that different types of stores can afford to pay. A chain bakery can afford to pay more than a supermarket; a specialty shop more than a department store. Rental that a tenant can afford to pay will be determined by two things: volume of sales in relation to store size and margin of profit.

In the central business districts rental values on a particular street will be established on a front foot or square foot unit that will apply

with minor variations to the entire block. If the 100 per cent location in a given area rents at $1,000 per square foot, then the stores
in the same block may be rented at slightly decreasing front foot
units as they become further removed from the 100 per cent location. These rentals will apply to any type of tenant. You do not,
under normal circumstances, find leases being consummated at $8
per square foot for one tenant and $4 per square foot for a tenant
in an adjoining store. Nor will there be any marked differential between the square foot rentals of small stores and large stores.

In many well planned shopping centers, a different set of standards will prevail. The owner will have his store distribution as to
type of tenancy predetermined. There will be specific locations for
key tenants—the large space users—and adjacent locations for the
secondary and the satellite tenants. A key tenant might occupy
25,000 square feet at grade level with an equivalent amount in basement area. A secondary tenant might occupy 2,500 to 3,000 square
feet. It would not be uncommon for the square foot minimum rental
of the secondary tenant to be substantially higher than that of the
key tenant.

As to actual rentals paid under the percentage clause, the differentials might be even more striking. A well rated department store,
for instance, might pay a percentage of about 2 per cent, and a
sales volume of $150 per square foot would be considered satis-
factory, so that in this circumstance the actual rental paid by the
department store would be $3 per square foot. On the other hand
it would not be uncommon to find smaller stores, such as a delicatessen, stationery store, credit jewelry shop, etc., paying total
rentals in excess of $10 per square foot.

The planning element, therefore, in shopping centers results in a
sliding scale of minimum guaranteed rentals that will bear some
relation to the actual rental which the tenants may pay after the
application of the percentage formula.

Completion of Buildings

The required completion of certain elements of building construction by the tenant requires a cash outlay on the part of the tenant
for which he is entitled to repayment from the owner. As noted
before, this repayment may be on an immediate cash basis, or in the

form of a rent abatement with the latter arrangement preferable to many owners because it reduces his necessary capital outlay.

The items of expense thus underwritten by the tenant are referred to in shopping center parlance as "reimbursables."

A typical covenant providing for such reimbursement by the owner is as follows:

A. PURPOSE:

It is the purpose of this Exhibit to describe the work which is to be Tenant's Work under this lease; to designate which portion of Tenant's Work is to be Tenant's Allowance Work; to establish the standards of work applicable to all Tenant's Work; and to define the method of approval by the Landlord of Tenant's Work.

B. TENANT'S WORK DEFINED:

Tenant's Work is all work required to be done in preparing the Demised Premises so that it may be operated for business with the public (including, without limitation, Tenant's Allowance Work) other than Landlord's Work.

All Tenant's Work is to be designed and performed at the Tenant's cost and expense, subject to the provisions of this lease, after prior approval (in accordance with the Landlord's procedures from time to time in effect) of the plans and specifications therefor by the Landlord in accordance with the provisions hereof.

Tenant's Work shall include, without limitation, the following items:

1. Interior walls, curtain walls, partitions and doors, exclusive of partitions enclosing toilets.
2. Interior painting, papering, and panelling.
3. Floor coverings, whether or not affixed to floors.
4. Exterior and interior store signs.
5. Show window backgrounds, bulkheads, show window floors, show window ceilings and valances.
6. Conversion of service stairs, if any, into customer stairs after the Landlord has constructed the same as part of the Landlord's Work.
7. Providing and installation of all lighting fixtures and electrical equipment for any portion of the Demised Premises, including, without limitation, the store front(s) and/or show windows.
8. Trade fixtures and furnishings.
9. Elevators, escalators, dumbwaiters, conveyors, chutes, vertical lifts, pneumatic tubes and shafts, doors, and other like matters with the Demised Premises, except such as may be furnished by the Landlord as part of the Landlord's Work, if any; and improvement of any thereof so provided by the Landlord after the Landlord has constructed the same.
10. All special plumbing work that may be required or desired by the Tenant due to the nature of the Tenant's business or is otherwise beyond the scope of the Landlord's Work.

11. Electrical power distribution for heating, cooling and ventilation and other special Tenant equipment and apparatus.
12. All water piping, coils, air-handling apparatus, ductwork, controls and other necessary appurtenances to heat, cool and ventilate the Demised Premises.
13. All special heating and ventilating work that may be required or desired by the Tenant due to the nature of his business.
14. All other items of work not specifically listed in Exhibit C as Landlord's Work.

C. TENANT'S ALLOWANCE WORK:

Tenant's Allowance Work is that portion of Tenant's Work described in this Division C.

The Tenant's Allowance Work shall be paid for by the Tenant but, after completion of all thereof in accordance with this Exhibit and compliance with all the other items set forth in this lease, the Landlord shall pay to the Tenant the amount set forth in such Section. The Tenant agrees to perform all the Tenant's Allowance Work and first to obtain therefor the prior approval of the Landlord. Tenant's Allowance Work shall include all the following:

1. Store front(s), including, but not restricted to, entrances.
2. Hung ceilings in the Primary Areas in the Demised Premises.
3. Electrical distribution system for lighting circuits within the Demised Premises, exclusive of store fixtures, signs, intercommunication systems, TV conduits or other comparable installations.
4. Heating and normal code ventilation equipment within the Demised Premises.
5. Plastering of wall space and column space in the Primary Areas in the Demised Premises; provided however, that in no event shall there be included plastering of (i) space on interior walls, curtain walls, partitions or doors, except partitions around toilets provided by the Landlord or (ii) space within the Primary Areas not visible to customers (i.e., panelled, blocked by fixtures, etc.).

D. APPROVAL OF TENANT'S WORK:

All Tenant's Work must, before any work thereon is started, receive the approval of the Landlord. The Tenant shall submit for such approval, to the Landlord through the Landlord's architect (a) detailed plans and specifications for all Tenant's Allowance Work, and also for all other Tenant's Work if and to the extent that such other Tenant's Work will require mechanical or electrical installations which will be connected to utilities furnished by the Landlord or will affect the exterior appearance of the building or its structural, mechanical or electrical components, and (b) preliminary plans and specifications for all other Tenant's Work.

In order to obtain such approval of the Landlord for such work, all such plans and specifications therefore must satisfy each of the following:

1. Comply with all applicable statutes, ordinances, regulations and codes and the requirements of any governmental regulatory body.
2. Coordinate with the time schedule of the general contractor(s) constructing the Shopping Center.
3. Comply with the general character of the Shopping Center.
4. Comply with the standards of the National Board of Fire Underwriters (NBFU), The National Electric Code (NEC), The American Gas Association (AGA) and the American Society of Heating and Air Conditioning Engineers (ASHAE) and the requirements of all public utility companies serving the Shopping Center.

CHAPTER 12

Chain Stores

‖‖‖

A chain store organization is a centrally owned and/or controlled retail merchandising operation with at least two branch outlets. Although such considerations as methods of operation, quality and variety of merchandise, and management policies vary widely, the underlying theory of all chain store operations is that consumer prices can be reduced through volume selling and centralized administration costs. The chain store is one of the most important segments of the commercial leasing market.

POSTWAR DEVELOPMENT IN CHAIN STORES

From 1931 to the end of World War II there was an effective cessation of building activity and of business expansion. Following the end of the war, business organizations found themselves with huge cash surpluses and an unprecedented demand for their products. The chain store organizations were particularly well situated to take advantage of the demand for consumer goods and of the availability of capital.

In their postwar expansion the chains not only decided to open many new outlets but in most instances planned their newer units on a larger and more elaborate scale. Super markets that were formerly satisfied with store units of 40', 50' or 60' frontage, discovered that the *minimum* desirable frontage was 100' and that a store

150' or more in depth was much more efficient for operating purposes than the old standardized unit which was 100' in depth. This expansion in size as well as in number of outlets extended to other types of chain stores, particularly to apparel stores, stores carrying other lines of consumer non-durable goods, and stores carrying consumer durable goods.

In the postwar period the chain stores for the first time began to give serious consideration to the motoring public. They eagerly preempted the good locations in well situated shopping centers. "Drive-ins" of all kinds came into existence, including shoe repair concerns, laundry agencies, food stores, restaurants and banks.

EXTENT OF CHAIN STORE OPERATIONS TODAY

Today there are more than 15,000 chain store organizations in the United States ranging from those with 3 or 4 units up to the largest organization with more than 13,000 units. The net expansion in the postwar period has been tremendous. While new suburban and shopping center locations have been eagerly sought after, there have been relatively few chain store units closed in central business districts. In certain areas, in line with new merchandising policy, two or more smaller units in a given area may have been merged into a single larger unit. In some instances, central city locations have been abandoned when lease terms have expired, but in comparison with the over-all number of operating units, the stores closed are not a significant portion of the total supply.

Today the chain system of operation extends to practically every phase of merchandising—food, clothing, drugs, cosmetics, hardware, household equipment, jewelry, fabrics, millinery, restaurants, etc. Even department stores are gradually being merged into chain operations and today a substantial portion of the major department store units throughout the United States is controlled by six organizations.

HISTORY OF CHAIN STORE OPERATIONS

Chain stores are not an innovation. Indeed, the first chain of record is said to have flourished in China several hundred years before the birth of Christ.

As in many other things, the Japanese imitated the Chinese. In Japan in the year 1643 a chain system was established by the Mitsui mercantile family, which through the years grew great even to the point of including railroads, steamship lines, manufacturing plants, and many banks among its assets.

In America

The first great business enterprise on the North American continent that took the form, more or less, of a mercantile chain was the Hudson's Bay Company, launched in Canada about 1670. It included most of the American continent north of the present Canadian boundary and was originally a series of fur-trading posts. About 1800 it became involved in a great trade war with an independent concern known as the Northwest Company, but some twenty years later peace was declared and a merger effected. This continued until 1859 when the monopoly was terminated by the Dominion of Canada's paying $300,000 and granting about 7,000,000 acres of land in consideration of the company's relinquishing its monopolistic rights. The company, already securely entrenched, continued to be a mighty factor in the supply of goods throughout much of the Canadian territory. Today it maintains a huge department store in Winnipeg and operates scores of trading posts throughout the north country.

In the meantime, about 1850, a small business came into being, conducted by one man, H. W. Carter, who first drove a small wagon throughout the countryside, protecting himself from highwaymen with a shotgun, and selling the kinds of goods that had formerly hung from the shoulders of weary foot peddlers. Carter expanded until he operated a flock of gaudily decorated wagons. His salesmen not only sold at retail to anyone who sought their wares but also supplied small shops and stores throughout the thinly populated territories through which they traveled.

The A & P

In 1859 began the activities of what has become America's largest chain, the Great Atlantic & Pacific Tea Company, popularly known as the A & P. George Gilman, then engaged in the leather business, bought a shipload of tea and opened a small retail store on Vesey Street in Manhattan. Gilman painted the front of his shop a vivid red and forthwith sold out his initial cargo of tea at a dollar a pound.

Restocking, he expanded slowly on wheels, starting with one brightly painted wagon and then another, until a whole fleet of wagons were scurrying about the country selling coffee and tea. Later he began to rent stores and establish outlets throughout the eastern states. This growth has gone on from year to year until now the chain can be found represented in almost every state in the union, with more than 15,000 outlets.

Mail Order Houses

Successfully promoted mail-order businesses have brought into being several important chain merchandising units. In 1872 A. Montgomery Ward and George R. Thorn opened the first mail-order house in Chicago. This was followed in 1893 by the launching of Sears, Roebuck & Company, in the same city. These chains are noted for the successful and large-scale manner in which they continued to expand, even during the depression and war years.

The Variety Stores

The motto "Great oaks from little acorns grow" must have impressed the mind of Frank W. Woolworth, founder of what is now a chain of over 2,000 stores in this country with branches in England, Puerto Rico, and elsewhere. Woolworth was a clerk in a Watertown, N. Y., store, drawing a salary of ten dollars a week, when he became interested in the merchandising theory that goods of a miscellaneous character, mostly small, cheap novelties, placed on a counter by themselves and offered at five and ten cents each, would sell readily. He suggested the idea to his employer and the result was that the newly stocked counter was soon stripped. The idea had been born, had been demonstrated, and had proved a success, and it was not long afterward that Woolworth, borrowing a few hundred dollars to test his faith, went into business for himself in Utica, New York. The store was a success from the first, and it was not long before more outlets were opened and the chain launched upon a successful career that made its creator a multi-millionaire.

The idea of mass distribution of merchandising through chain stores was not long in attracting the attention of shrewd merchants, and shortly after Woolworth made his demonstration a number of chains came into existence which have since grown in size, wealth, and importance. Some of these concerns are: McCrory, founded in 1882; Kroger Grocery Company, 1884; Bohack, 1887; John R. Thompson, 1891; Owl Drug, 1892; Kinney, 1893; Melville Shoes, 1894; the Ginter Company, 1895; Kress, 1896; and Kresge, 1897.

METHODS OF OPERATION

There is an infinite variety to the chain stores' methods of doing business. The simplest method of operation is the store offering for sale its own manufactured product. Typical of these units would be those of the Singer Sewing Machine Company and some of the major tire companies. As a side line the individual units might carry merchandise of another manufacturer that has a subsidiary use to the merchandise being purveyed by the manufacturer-store operator. The stores, however, are primarily outlets for the company's own manufactured product. The company-owned retail outlet effectively eliminates the jobber, retailer and other types of middlemen.

The most complex operation is found in those chain store units offering a wide range of merchandise, little of which is manufactured by the chain organization. Typical of this classification would be food super markets and department stores. Many of the super markets and the chain department stores have their own branded merchandise but this is generally produced by some independent manufacturer or processor and labeled for the chain store organization.

The department store operation is probably the most complex of all chain operations. It is actually a group of semi-independent business enterprises under a single roof and with central managerial control. The department store operation has become so complex at times that it has been found advisable to lease some of its activities to independent concessionaires (Chapter 10).

It is obvious that the chain store organization that does not sell its own manufactured product has a whole complexity of problems not found in, let us say, the Singer Sewing Machine chain store operation. Most of these problems are concerned with buying, warehousing, distributing and marketing.

Strangely enough, the more complex the chain store operation becomes, the more competitive is the field and the lower the margin of profit. Super markets and department stores—admittedly the most complex—also are the most competitive and have the lowest profit margin of any of the retail businesses.

Between these two extremes is the great majority of the chains;

the drug stores, variety stores, shoe stores, ladies' dress shops, men's clothing stores, and so on, with a wide range of problems in buying and merchandising, many of which are common problems and many of which are peculiar to the individual chain.

Chain store organizations have one thing in common—central administration. At the headquarters office, company policies are set and here will be found the managerial controls over the various phases of the store operation. One of the keystones in chain store operation is the matter of store location, which is also a matter of primary concern to the real estate broker. Properly speaking, the only concern a real estate broker should have with the buying, merchandising, warehousing, and other related problems of the chain store organization is when these problems are reflected in the company's real estate operation.

CHAIN STORE OPERATIONS IN THE REAL ESTATE FIELD

Practically all of the chain store organizations have central office control over real estate operations. Many of the larger chains operating on a nationwide basis have district managers who necessarily have a reasonable degree of autonomy—but most of whom operate under procedures and policies established at the main office.

In most cases chain stores are tenants, not owners, of their retail outlets. Some chains may build their own stores but usually will sell them to an investor and lease them back. Because of the competitive nature of the chain store operation, it would be impractical in most instances, for the chains to have capital tied up in real estate ownership, particularly when there is an abundance of real estate investment capital for taking these properties off their hands or for building accommodations to their specifications.

The larger chains have staffs that are constantly on the lookout for new outlets—either for expansion purposes or to replace older outlets which may have lost their desirability. Most of the chain store organizations will make their own studies of an area and of particular locations. They will make their own estimates of sales potential, competitive business, location of other chains, etc. The real estate broker can assume that the successful chain store organization will know pretty well what it wants in the way of real estate accommodation.

It is also important to remember that the individual chains may have developed standardized store units as to over-all dimensions, frontage, depth, storage requirements, selling space, etc. Because the chain store operation is a mass operation and because fixtures may be designed to fit standardized layout, the broker can assume he will meet resistance if he submits a property which deviates in any essential feature from the chain's established standard unit.

THE REAL ESTATE BROKER IN CHAIN STORE LEASE

The soundest advice that can be given to a broker operating in the chain store field is—know your chains.[1] There can be a great deal of waste time and waste motion in submitting properties for the consideration of chain store organizations which will be turned down at first sight.

It is also advisable that the broker know his community because he may be required to answer any one of a variety of questions from a potential chain store lessee. Among the matters he might be questioned on are such things as:

Population
Population trends
Trading area
Population and population trends in trading area
Per capita income
Income trends
Principal industries and businesses
New businesses or industries in area
Why did they come to the area
Businesses or industries that have moved from the area
Why did they leave
Rate of unemployment (trends)
Total retail sales
Retail sales per capita
Trend in retail sales

[1] The "Directory of Leading Chain Stores in the United States," Published by Chain Store Business Guide, Inc., 2 Park Avenue, New York City, is a publication that should be in the hands of every active broker doing chain store business. It contains the names of 7,658 chains in various categories operating more than 214,939 stores. It also contains the street addresses of the principal offices of each of the companies, the names of the responsible officers, and the geographical area in which the particular chain operates.

Department stores—names
Variety stores—names
Outlying shopping centers
Tenants in shopping centers

CHAIN STORE LEASES

Chain store organizations customarily have their own lease forms. Obviously their covenants will be less restrictive on the tenant than those found in the standard forms prepared for or by the various real estate boards. But in most cases they represent a composite of the chain store's leasing experience and of what is acceptable to owners on a nationwide basis.

On the other hand most of the chains are prepared to execute a specialized type of lease agreement different from its standard form —such as a shopping center lease which has been prepared by the shopping center management.

CHAPTER 13

Long-Term Leases

WHAT IS A LONG-TERM LEASE?

In Chapter 2 we explained that the expressions "short term" and "long term" as applied to leases have a relative significance. For purposes of this discussion we are adopting the commonly accepted concept of a long-term lease as one which has an initial term of twenty-one years or more.

Questions are often asked by persons unfamiliar with the intricacies of lease transactions, such as "Why make any distinction between a short-term and a long-term lease? Aren't they basically the same thing—an agreement to acquire the use of property in exchange for rent?"

The answer to this question would have to be a qualified affirmative. The essential features of a lease (Chapter 3) should be found in all lease agreements, short term or long term; and yet as the lease term lengthens the lessee's rights in the property take on an added significance because they closely approach the rights and privileges of an owner. By the same token, his obligations to maintain the property must be more closely defined.

The outstanding characteristic therefore of a long-term lease as opposed to a short-term lease is a more careful delineation—through the medium of lease covenants—of the rights and obligations of lessor and lessee.

For instance, in the short-term Virginia lease (page 295) the covenants as to use, occupancy and maintenance read "The said lessee covenants to pay the rent in the manner above stated; that he will not assign without leave; that he will leave the premises in good repair; that the premises shall not be used during the said term for any purpose or purposes than those above specified."

In a long-term lease the matter of rent payment alone might cover several paragraphs.

21-Year Standard Is Arbitrary

The twenty-one year line of demarcation for a long-term lease is an arbitrary one. If a lease were made for eighteen or nineteen or twenty years, both parties would no doubt exercise the same care and precaution as they would in the execution of a twenty-one-year lease and there probably would be no differences in lease covenants. The reason for the twenty-one-year standard is that through usage in the real estate business, this has become the most common initial period for long-term leases. In other words, the twenty-one-year lease is common, a nineteen- or twenty-year lease is a rarity.

UTILIZATION OF LONG-TERM LEASES

The long-term lease has become an increasingly important instrument of real estate operation in the postwar period. Basically, it is a means of bringing an investor with capital together with a property owner, who for some reason cannot or will not sell, and who by the same token cannot or will not make the necessary capital expenditures for the improvement of his property. Lessors may be individuals, partnerships, private corporations, estates, public or quasi-public corporations, charitable, educational or philanthropic institutions, and so on. Because of the nature of the long-term commitment, few lessees in these transactions are speculators. Most frequently the lessee is an investor or a user.

Tax Consideration

An important contributing factor to the increase in use of the long-term lease in the past few decades has been the growing impact of Federal income taxes—personal and corporate. (Chapter 17.) The Federal tax laws have been indirectly responsible for many transfers of real estate on a long-term-lease basis which would not have been practical on a sale basis because of unfavorable tax impact.

As an Aid to Rental Housing

In the past two decades the long term ground lease has also been widely employed in housing projects where, if properly used, it can be a vehicle for reducing rental charges, because in effect the developer of the project is "borrowing" the value of the land at a moderate interest rate. If the developer owned the land he would, in practically every case, expect a larger return on its value than he pays under the long-term-lease agreement.

To many developers the long-term ground lease—particularly where the leasehold mortgage is insured by the Federal Housing Administration—has provided a desirable avenue of personal investment as noted later in this chapter.

CLASSIFICATION OF LONG-TERM LEASES

There are two methods by which long-term leases may be classified; first, according to property type; second, according to lease terms and renewal provisions.

As to Type of Property

There are two broad subdivisions under this classification:

1. Property on which the lessee agrees to construct a new building.
2. Improved property where the lease contemplates the long-term use of the existing improvements by the lessee without demolition or new construction. The lease may, of course, provide for capital improvements to the existing building by the lessee.

In the postwar years there has been a substantial increase in the number of long-term leases of the second type. The motivating force behind these leases has in many instances been income tax considerations, which have also contributed to the active sales market for income producing real estate.

As to Lease Term and Renewal Provisions

Under this classification long-term leases may be subdivided into three general categories.

a. The flat, straight or ungraded lease, where the rental is a fixed sum each year for the entire term.

b. The graded or step-up lease, where one or more advances in rental are put into effect, the rental then becoming a fixed sum each year for the remainder of the term.

c. The reappraisal or revaluation lease where the property is re-appraised or valued periodically, the lessee being required to pay rental varying with the value of the land. Present day revaluation leases customarily provide only for an *increase* in ground rental at each reappraisal period. In other words, the rental for the preceding lease term is established as a minimum for each succeeding term but this minimum may be increased if the reappraisal so requires.

LONG-TERM LEASES ON LAND

The long-term lease on land—the so-called "ground lease"—is still more widely employed than the long-term lease on both land and improvements. Long-term ground leases can become, and usually are, complicated in their provisions because of the requirement that the lessee shall construct a new improvement.

As noted above, this is a common device by which two forms of capital are brought together, capital in the form of land ownership, and investment capital for putting up the building. From the point of view of landlord and lessee, the long-term ground lease has many advantages, as we shall see later. Almost invariably the long-term ground lease is a net lease under which lessee pays all carrying charges including real estate taxes.

Types of Lessees—Long-Term Ground Lease

The lessee in a long-term ground lease falls into one of four basic categories.

a. An investor who will build and sublet to a single tenant, such as a large commercial or mercantile organization.

b. An investor who will build and sublet to many tenants. A typical lessee in this category would be an office-building developer.

c. A user who will build for his own exclusive occupancy. Typical of this category would be a large commercial or industrial organization constructing a home-office building on the leased land.

d. A user who will occupy a portion of the building and sublet a part of the building to a single tenant or individual tenants. In this category might be a commercial organization constructing an office building on leased land for its own occupancy but also providing additional space for rent to outside tenants. This rented space can serve either as a safeguard against future requirements of the company or as a means of reducing the company's over-all cost of occupancy.

Advantages of Long-Term Ground Leases

TO THE OWNER

1. By leasing property for a long term of years the owner escapes the possible burden of capital gain taxes which might result from a sale of the property.

2. Property with a long-term ground lease is exceptionally desirable in an estate plan.

3. The capital improvement made by the lessee insures the stability of ownership.

4. Leasing to responsible parties for a term of years may enhance the value of the land.

5. It eliminates the problem of reinvestment of funds which might follow the sale of the property.

6. It develops maximum property utilization without any capital investment on the part of the owner.

7. Because of the leasehold improvement, the fee is readily mortgagable; and it is readily salable if the owner decides to put it on the market.

ADVANTAGES TO THE TENANT

1. He makes no cash investment in the land, which presumably is rented to him at a fair figure in consideration of his having improved it with a suitable structure.

2. He is able to secure the use of a well located tract of land by

the expenditure of only enough money for the erection of a building.

3. The businessman is enabled to put his money into his building and to retain that portion which would otherwise go for land for the operation of his business.

4. The ground rental as a business expense is deductible when computing taxable income. The tenant would not have the equivalent tax advantage if he owned the land in fee.

5. If a tenant makes a ground lease at 5 or 6 per cent net on a reasonable appraised valuation, it is the same as borrowing capital (the value of the land) at a lower over-all rate than he could obtain on mortgage financing—and with a more favorable tax impact. In effect, he has 100 per cent financing on the land.

6. While an owner achieves a stability in his investment the lessee would have the right to mortgage his leasehold interest. In many instances mortgage lenders have purchased property and leased it for development purposes. The same lenders have then made leasehold mortgages on the new improvements so that the total financing might be greater than can be achieved under a conventional financial structure.

Developing Long-Term Ground Leases

TYPES OF PROPERTY—BUSINESS OR COMMERCIAL PROPERTY

The majority of long-term ground leases will be in business or commercial areas or in areas suitable for development with multi-family housing projects. As a rule only prime locations are susceptible to leasehold improvements because a lessee would be disinclined to make a substantial investment on land which he does not own, in any other than a well established area. In addition, the likelihood of securing leasehold financing would be diminished if the property were not centrally located.

RESIDENTIAL PROPERTY

In only a few sections of the United States is the ground lease used as an instrument for the development of one-family homes. The custom is most common in Maryland where "ground rent" is a recognized means of acquiring possession of property in urban residential areas. The lessee secures possession of the property for a ninety-nine year term and is thus (subject to his payment of the ground lease) in a position equivalent to fee ownership. Local lending institutions do not hesitate to grant full leasehold financing subject to the prior lien of the ground lease.

There has been a growing use of the long-term ground lease as an effective instrument in the development of large-scale housing projects. Interestingly enough this widespread practice started with projects where the mortgages were insured by the Federal Housing Administration. The origin was through a set of unusual circumstances.

When the original FHA regulations were written, provision was made for the insurance of mortgages in such States as Maryland and Missouri where it is the accepted practice to construct one-family homes on leased land (see above). The regulation provided that mortgages would be insured on "property held in fee simple or under renewable lease for not less than ninety-nine years or under lease with term of not less than fifty years from date of mortgage." *But the regulation did not limit this leasehold provision to the states for which it was specifically intended.*

Astute operators who were engaged in the development of large-scale rental projects in the postwar period discovered that this could be a·device for making a particularly advantageous investment. The site for development would be purchased by the operator in his own name or in the name of a family member or of a dummy corporation. The land would then be leased to the building corporation, which would arrange a leasehold mortgage insured by FHA. This mortgage generally covered the full cost of construction. The fee owner who was in reality the lessor and lessee, under different legal entities, made an investment that took priority over the government-insured mortgage.

It was later discovered when these projects got into operation that the leasehold device could be an effective means of reducing rentals on apartment houses that might be constructed with conventional mortgage financing. This would be true particularly in areas of high land value.

INDUSTRIAL

The long-term ground lease is less frequently used in industrial real estate than in any other type. In the first place, the potential geographic area for an industrial development is usually much wider than it is for business, commercial or multi-family residential development. An owner's refusal to sell a particular piece of industrial land, therefore, would not have the significance to the user that it might have in a business or commercial district. In addition, the advantages to the lessee are substantially diminished because if the lessee is a responsible industrial organization, the sale and leaseback technique would offer more advantages than could be obtained from the construction of an improvement on leased land.

FIXING THE RENT

The first step in fixing the rent on a long-term ground lease is to agree on the value of the land. The value would be as if vacant and unimproved. The second step would be to determine the percentage of value at which the land will be rented. In practically every instance the rental will be net, with the lessee paying all real estate taxes and other charges incidental to the use of the land.

The ground rent usually is the primary lien on the property after real estate taxes. It is therefore important to the lessee to make a detailed financial projection so that he will be reasonably certain that the ground rent will not impose any undue burden on him. In other words, he should be assured that after paying the required ground rent, there will be sufficient income to pay operating expenses, taxes on land and improvements, and to show an adequate return on his capital investment in the leasehold improvement.

Essentially, the approach to valuing land for long-term ground leases is the land residual method. A simple illustration might be as follows:

A developer proposes to put up an office building costing $1,000,-000 on leased land. He estimates that after paying all carrying charges, including estimated real estate taxes, and after making a reserve for loss of rents or vacancies (in some new buildings where all of the space is leased for fifteen years or more to prime tenants, vacancy allowance has been eliminated in estimating net return) there will be $120,000 available for ground rent and for interest and amortization on the cost of the leasehold improvement. Assume that 9 per cent, or $90,000, is considered a reasonable return on the building investment, leaving $30,000 available for the payment of ground rent. This is the dollar sum which the owner can afford to pay in ground rent. It would represent 6 per cent on a land value of $500,000.

During the initial lease term the important thing to the lessee is the dollar amount of the rental—not the rate of return on the assumed capital value. As a matter of fact, in most long term lease agreements, the capital value of the land is not mentioned—only the amount of the rental is cited. But there will be, of course, an oral understanding as to how the rental is computed, i.e., what the land value is and what percentage of land value the rental represents.

The rate of return on land value becomes important to the lessee if the lease has a reappraisal provision wherein it is specified that for the renewal term the rent will not be lower than during the first term but that it may be increased if the reappraisal shows the current rental to be inadequate.

Invariably the reappraisal provision will specify that the renewal rental shall be a certain percentage—say 6 per cent—of appraised valuation. The percentage rate used in the reappraisal will customarily be the same as that used for the initial lease term—even though this percentage is inferred rather than specified where the rental for the initial term is recited.

Taking the example above, the lessee *during the initial term* is concerned only with the fact that he is paying an annual $30,000 ground rent. It does not matter whether it is computed as 5 per cent of $600,000, 6 per cent of $500,0000, or 8 per cent of $375,-000. But during the renewal term the percentage rate assumes primary importance.

The reappraisal provision on long term leases usually calls for representation by lessor and lessee through the medium of appraisers or arbitrators and for the selection of a third party by the two lessor/lessee representatives if they do not agree on a land valuation.

DANGERS OF HIGH GROUND RENTALS

While top-ranking locations have elements of financial advantage to the lessee, it must not be assumed that the lessee can be reckless in paying a premium—via excessive ground rents—for the use of a particular piece of property. The ground rent may be only a small fraction of total property income but it must be remembered that it is a primary lien. The history of the 1930's is fraught with examples of foreclosures and reorganizations of leasehold interests where the lessee's ground rental obligation could not have been justified by any theory of land valuation.

INFLATION AS A THREAT TO LESSOR'S INTEREST

The sharp inflationary trends of the postwar period may cause hesitancy on the part of owners to make a twenty-one-year ground lease even though the renewal rentals are on a reappraisal basis.

In the postwar period, building costs have risen sharply. Rentals —excepting where controls are still in effect—have reflected the inflationary trend. Every active appraiser knows that there has been an upturn in real estate prices and values. An income property appraised in 1959 at $100,000 might very well be appraised at $150,000 or higher ten years later.

For many years it was believed that a land owner would suffer little loss through inflation because of committing himself to a fixed rental for a 21-year period since land values in central city districts had not increased proportionately with general real estate values. This belief was buttressed by the fact that in many central business districts land values had remained reasonably constant over a quarter of a century.

This concept was changed in the 1960s when the general inflationary trends extended into the area of land value. It was heightened to some extent by the scarcity of desirable land in the central cities. Desirable land diminished in quantity because of the growth of undesirable and substandard city areas, thus reducing the proportion of land which might be deemed to have an adaptability for long range development.

This increase in land value extended to suburban areas, although in these areas there has been substantially less land committed to long term leases.

Growing land costs have brought about many long term ground leases where the lessor has guarded against inflation by obtaining a percentage of property rentals with the ground rent as a minimum. In effect, therefore, the ground lease becomes a *long term percentage lease.*

SPECIAL USERS

If a special user, such as a bank or commercial organization, wishes to lease land for its own occupancy without developing maximum land utilization, the ground rental should be predicated on the land's highest and best use.

For instance, a bank might wish to construct a headquarters office on a plot which could be used for a multi-story office building. Total building area occupied by the bank might be 50,000 square feet, whereas a commercial structure with 200,000 square feet might legally be erected. In this case the owner of the land is entitled to, and should get, a rental predicated on a residual land value which assumes construction of the 200,000 square foot building.

SECURITY TO THE LESSOR

In Chapter 5 there are discussions of lease provisions covering the lessor's security. Essentially, the lessor's need for security in a long-term ground lease ends when the leasehold improvement has been completed, although a security deposit of the lessee may be held by the lessor as a reserve against future ground rent payments.

But between the signing of the lease and the completion of the leasehold improvement, the lessor needs legal and/or financial assurance on two principal points. If a property, when leased, is improved with income-producing buildings that must be demolished by the lessee prior to the construction of a new leasehold improvement, there is a period during which the ground owner has a well defined risk because of the demolition of the revenue-producing building or buildings. The second risk occurs during the construction of the new leasehold improvement. The ground owner wants assurance not only that the proper type of building will be erected but that the building will be completed according to plans and specifications. He will not want to assume any contingent obligations to contractors or sub-contractors. Whatever the form of risk the owner can be protected by the lessee giving him a bond of completion or by the deposit of cash or collateral.

If the leasehold improvement is substantial there will be a building agreement (supplementary to the main lease agreement) entered into between lessor and lessee. The building agreement spells out in full detail the type of building to be constructed, the time for beginning and completing construction, and other clauses, all looking toward the protection of the lessor.

Because of its cost, the bond of completion is often eliminated. The lessor should insist that some satisfactory substitute in the form of cash or collateral be posted in lieu of the bond.

DEFAULTS

In the event of default in the payment of ground rent, the lessor has a twofold security. He can repossess the property on a free and clear basis because all other liens are subordinate to his interest. If the leasehold interest has been mortgaged, the mortgage instrument will contain a clause permitting the leasehold mortgagee to cure the lessee's default and to assume the lessee's position.

TERMINATION

When all of the renewal options under a ground lease have terminated, there are three general methods for the disposition of the buildings or improvement:

a. Buildings revert unconditionally to the lessor.
b. Lessor is required to purchase the buildings at their depreciated value. The value is usually determined by appraisal.
c. Lessee has an option to purchase the land at an appraised price.

Since it is assumed that during the term of a sixty-three-year or eighty-four-year ground lease the lessee will have derived every financial advantage that could reasonably be expected from the improvements, it is most common today that the buildings revert unconditionally to the lessor at the expiration of the last renewal term. The third of these methods is the least commonly used.

LONG-TERM LEASES ON LAND AND IMPROVEMENTS

The long-term lease on land and improvements has been growing in favor as an instrument of real estate finance. It is most commonly found in the sale and leaseback field where an investor with funds purchases land and buildings and leases them to the seller at a fixed annual rental, but this type of long-term lease is by no means limited to sale-leaseback transactions.

Straight lease deals for long terms of years have been made on virtually all types of property, but the greatest prevalence has been on special purpose properties or those which present unusual management problems such as hotels, theatres, garages and many of these leases carry some form of a percentage arrangement.

CHAPTER 14

Sale and Leaseback

⎯⎯⎯⎯⎯⎯⎯⎯⎯⎯⎯⎯⎯⎯⎯⎯⎯⎯⎯⎯⎯⎯⎯⎯⎯⎯⎯⎯⎯⎯⎯⎯⎯⎯⎯⎯

The sale and leaseback transaction is a relatively new technique or device in the area of real estate finance. It involves the sale of property at cost or at an established market price with the seller leasing the property from the buyer for a long term of years, usually with renewal options, at an annual rental computed as a fixed percentage of the selling price.

Customarily the annual rental is established at a price that will give the purchaser a fixed annual return on his outstanding investment and will amortize the investment fully over the initial lease term. As a matter of bookkeeping, the owner could use the declining principal balance method of accounting wherein a certain part of the investment is amortized each year. The portion of the rental attributable to interest declines annually, whereas the portion attributable to amortization increases.

Although the "full payout" over the initial lease term is standard procedure, there are other possible variations in the method of establishing rentals. For instance, the lessor may be satisfied with a recapture of part of his investment over the initial lease term. This might be the case in a central business district where it could be reasonably assumed that the land will not depreciate in value over the first term of the lease. Deals have been made where the net rental is made up of interest and amortization on the improvements and interest only on the land.

In a few instances, rentals have been graduated, either upward or downward, during the initial lease term. This device has been used most frequently to suit the financial requirements of the lessee.

In some deals, the lessee might be given an option of renewal after the initial lease term at a substantially reduced rental. If, for instance, a building is sold for $1,000,000 and leased back for a period of 25 years at $94,000 per annum net (sufficient to amortize fully the million dollar investment and pay 8 per cent interest on the declining principal balance) lessee might be given an option to renew for two or three 10-year terms at an annual rental of 5 or 6 per cent of original cost.

The theory behind this type of transaction is that the lessor's investment has been completely recaptured at the end of the original lease term so that while the rental may be reduced it reflects a return on a 100 per cent fully amortized investment.

It must be noted that this type of transaction can be advanced when the real estate market is in a capital surplus position. In a period of normality or capital shortage, the lease which provides for an extension on an appraisal basis (with the original rental as a minimum) is likely to be more common.

THE LESSOR IN SALE-LEASEBACK TRANSACTIONS

The purchaser in a sale-leaseback transaction becomes the lessor. In many cases, this means an institution, organization or group with funds for long-term investment.

Where the lessee is a highly rated company, the purchaser-lessor may be an insurance company or a pension fund. At the present writing, state and Federal regulations make such purchases illegal for mutual savings banks, savings and loan associations, or commercial banks (where the commercial bank is investing its own funds, not trustee funds). Sale-leaseback deals to highly rated companies have also been made, for example, by university endowment funds, religious, charitable and fraternal organizations.

The highly rated companies will be able to lease at a basic interest rate approximating the prime mortgage rate. If a company could borrow mortgage money at 6 per cent interest, it might make a

25-year leaseback deal at 7¾ per cent, which would amortize the investment in the 25-year period and pay 6 per cent interest on the principal balance. These relatively low rates of return effectively discourage most private investors from venturing into this field. However, private investors have engaged in sale-leaseback transactions where the credit rating of the lessee was satisfactory but was not sufficiently high to command the minimum interest rates. In many such cases with the assistance of favorable mortgage financing, investors have realized returns of 10 to 20 per cent on their equity money.

Pension funds, which are a major source of capital for sale-leaseback transactions, fall into three general classifications:

1. The "insured" plan, where the funds are handled by a life insurance company which guarantees a fixed annual return to the fund. The insurance company comingles the pension trust funds with its own money, for investment purposes. If a life insurance company, therefore, administered the affairs of 10 pension trusts it would be impossible for a broker to approach a life insurance company with the proposition that the funds of a *particular pension trust* be invested in a specific sale-leaseback transaction. In this respect, the "insured" pension funds differ from the "trusteed" funds.

2. The "trusteed" funds are mainly administered by commercial banks. Under this plan the trust department of the commercial bank handles the pension fund investment, but all funds are segregated as required by trust laws. Under this type of administration the capital of individual pension funds is available for investment in specific deals.

In a few instances where large sums of money have been involved, banks which administer a number of such funds have allocated participating shares in the over-all transaction to individual pension funds. In most instances, commercial banks have full discretionary powers in the investment of pension fund money. There are cases where fund investment is controlled by the bank, as trustee, and by the fund itself in a joint capacity.

3. Independently administered funds. Some pension funds, particularly larger ones, are self-administered. If contributions to the fund come from the employer only, management of the fund will customarily stay in the employer's hands. In some cases, investment of the fund is controlled by an employer-employee committee. If

the employees make any contribution to the fund, there will probably be employee representation in management on the fund's affairs. The majority of funds today are of the non-contributing type.

THE LESSEE IN SALE-LEASEBACK TRANSACTIONS

The seller in a sale-leaseback transaction becomes the lessee. There are many variations in the possible type of operation but the prime motivation on the part of the lessee is to recapture the capital which he has put into a piece of real estate and at the same time to retain operation of the real estate.

This might mean a business or industrial organization selling a property which it has constructed for its own use. It might be a commercial organization with a headquarters building that can be partially leased to outside interests. This would provide room for future expansion by the commercial organization, if the sub-leases are on relatively short terms. It might also be a profitable venture and would reduce the organization's own cost of occupancy.

In other cases, real estate operators will construct, rent, and operate a property on a normal conventional basis and then engage in a sale-leaseback transaction to recapture the capital outlay presumably for use in extended real estate operations.

The lessee's credit rating is the prime determinant of whether or not a deal can be made. It would be extremely difficult for a company without a satisfactory credit rating to be able to make such a deal even if supported by real estate value because most lessors properly regard the sale-leaseback transaction as a 100 per cent financing device, and they are unwilling to extend this type of financing to a company whose credit is not satisfactory.

ADVANTAGES AND DISADVANTAGES OF
SALE-LEASEBACK TRANSACTIONS

To the Lessor

To the lessor, the advantages and disadvantages are easily analyzed. Funds are invested with reasonable safety for a long term of years. In addition to the security afforded by the tenant's credit rating, there is the additional security of the real estate and the fact that after the expiration of the renewal periods, lessor will have unencumbered ownership of what presumably may be a valuable parcel of real estate.

As noted before, if the tenant's credit is satisfactory but not prime, the interest rate increases, so that whatever risk is inherent in the tenant's credit rating is compensated for by additional return.

On the negative side, there is the fact that purchaser-lessor is committing his funds for long-term investment at a fixed return in an economy that has consistently shown inflationary trends. It is obvious, therefore, that sound investment policy would dictate against committing any large portion of an investor's assets to long-term, fixed-return investments. Investment in sale-leaseback transactions should therefore be a carefully planned feature of portfolio diversification.

To the Lessee

To the lessee the principal advantages are:

1. He has possession of real estate without any capital investment.
2. His annual rental as an expense is totally deductible when computing net income for tax purposes.
3. His leasehold may have substantial value when the option to renew the lease at reduced rentals becomes effective.

The principal disadvantage to the lessee is the surrendering of the ownership of the real estate and of any benefits, taxwise or other, that might arise from real estate ownership.

Although the sale-leaseback is a method of 100 per cent financing and allows a corporation to have full possession of real estate without any capital investment, and without being obliged to show the real estate as a balance sheet item, it must not be assumed it is the end-all and be-all for business, commercial, or industrial organizations that want the long-term use of real estate. Each transaction stands or falls on its own merits. Advantages and disadvantages should be carefully analyzed before any decision is made.

SALE-LEASEBACK vs. MORTGAGE FINANCING

A simple comparison of the financing and tax aspects of the sale-leaseback method of financing as opposed to mortgage financing is appended below.

The comparison is based on the following assumptions:

Commercial organization has constructed a building with

Land Cost	$ 200,000
Building Cost	1,000,000
Total Cost	$1,200,000

Plan 1

Self-liquidating mortgage of $800,000 is available at 6% interest.
Level payments would be $62,560 per annum.
Building has a 50-year useful life.
Straight line depreciation is used.
Corporate taxes at standard rates.

Plan 2

Sale and leaseback deal is available at 6% interest rate for 25 years—7.82% level payments or $93,840 per annum net. Option to renew for 25 years at a reduced rate.

In either case the organization will be required to pay real estate taxes, operating expenses, and to maintain the property. Cash outlay and tax deductions for these items would be the same in both cases.

Under the mortgage plan (Plan 1), mortgage payments would be $62,500 per annum or $1,564,000 for the 25 years. Since the mortgage is self-liquidating, $764,000 of this amount would be interest. The balance would be amortization of the entire principal sum of the mortgage. If we assume the building to be worth $1,000,000 and to have a 50-year useful life, depreciation allowance under the straight line depreciation plan would be $500,000.

Under the sale-leaseback plan (Plan 2), annual net rental would be $93,840; the total for 25 years would be $2,346,000.

	Plan 1 *$800,000 Mortgage* *@ 7.82% Constant*	Plan 2 *Sale @ $1,200,000* *Leaseback @ 7.82%*
Total Cash Outlay to meet financial charges:		
25 year total	$1,564,000	$2,346,000
Total Tax Deduction:		
Plan 1, 52% of interest and depreciation	$ 657,280	
Plan 2, 52% of net rent		$1,219,920
Net Cash Outlay after tax deductions	$ 906,720	$1,126,000
Required Cash investment	$ 400,000	None

The above table shows that the differential in net cash outlay for 25 years is $220,000 less under the mortgage plan, but this requires an initial cash investment of $400,000 which the company would presumably have available for use in its business operation under the sale-leaseback plan.

FIXING THE SALES PRICES AND RENTAL TERMS

Rental

As noted above, the rental is customarily calculated at a rate which will pay out the investment over the initial lease term and will produce a satisfactory interest rate to the purchaser-lessor. The rental therefore will be determined by the interest rate and term of lease (Table on page 114). The interest rate, in turn, will be determined by the current status of the money market and the rating of the tenant.

Sales Price

Under the ideal type of deal the price of the property would be its cost. If it is a new building the purchaser-lessor may require that the cost be audited. It may also be required that the purchase price be supported by an appraisal. The appraisal would have to be justified by standards other than the rental to be paid by the lessee. Although the selling price is frequently a cost figure, there are many instances of sales made at below or above cost.

Initial Lease Term

Sale-leaseback transactions have been made for 10-, 15-, 20-, 25- or 30-year periods, but there is no rule that the initial lease term must be in multiples of 5 years. An 18-year, or 23-, or a 27-year transaction might be arranged. In the majority of transactions the initial lease term has been 20 or 25 years where the tenant's credit has been prime. In instances where the tenant's credit has been satisfactory but not prime, the common range of initial term has been 10 to 20 years.

Basic Interest Rate

The basic interest rate for companies with prime credit has fluctuated in the postwar period. In the late 1940's, at the time of our greatest surplus of investment capital, basic rates were as low as 3½ per cent on 25-year deals. Since then, in periods of capital shortage, the rate has more than doubled. Over the postwar years the norm for such transactions with prime rated companies has been between 4½ and 5½ per cent. If the initial term is decreased, let us say, to 20 years, the rate might go down by a small fraction, say ⅛th of a point. Similarly, the rate might go higher if the initial term is increased.

It is important to keep in mind that the low rates are obtainable only by the best companies. There can be substantial differentials in the over-all net rental charges made to the prime rated companies and to those which may be well regarded but do not have the resources or the earning capacity of the larger companies.

For instance, if a company established for 50 years, with a net worth of $100,000,000 and doing a gross annual business of $150,-000,000, wishes to sell and lease back a new $5,000,000 plant, it might, during a favorable market period, sell the plant at cost and lease it back for 25 years at a 6.74 per cent over-all rate for 25 years (basic interest rate 4½ per cent).

On the other hand, let us take the case of a company with a net worth of $2,000,000 doing a gross annual business of $5,000,000. Assume that the company has been in business for 20 years but in that period its sales and earnings have fluctuated widely. It is currently in a very satisfactory position because of a tremendous backlog of government orders (government work representing 50 per cent of the firm's total business). The company builds a plant for $1,000,000 and wishes to sell it and lease it back.

Where the top-rated company would have no difficulty in securing sale-leaseback money at an over-all rental rate of 6.74 per cent of sales price for a 25-year period, the second company might have to do a lot of "shopping" before finding a buyer. The buyer would probably not be an institution but an investor or real estate operator. Maximum lease terms would probably not exceed 15 years. *Rental might be more than 10 per cent.*

It is interesting to note that in many sale-leaseback transactions with top-rated tenants the basic interest rate for a 25-year deal might be lower than the going rate for prime mortgages on a 15-year term. This condition would obtain only in the case of the highest rated companies. It is an indication that the chief determinant insofar as the purchaser-lessor is concerned is the credit of the company and that the security of the real estate is a secondary consideration.

OPTION TO REPURCHASE

Many of the sale-leaseback transactions made during the early postwar years contained provisions for the seller to repurchase the property at the owner's book value (or at some equivalent figure) after a period of years. Let us say that a property was sold for $1,000,000 and leased back for $67,500 per annum for 25 years. If we assume basic interest to have been 4½%, the purchaser-lessor's investment would be reduced to about $540,000 at the end of 15 years. If this were a typical repurchase deal the seller would have the right to buy the property back at the end of this intermediate term at an equivalent of the $540,000 figure. The Treasury Department effectively stopped this type of transaction by ruling that the sale was not a bona fide sale but merely 100 per cent mortgage financing, and that therefore only the portion of the rental attributable to interest could be deductible when computing net income for tax purposes.

In the case above, total rental payments for 15 years would total slightly over $1,000,000. Of this sum $460,000 would be amortization, so that a disallowance of the amortization payments for income tax purposes would have serious repercussion on the seller.

It is possible to arrange for repurchase options in sale-leaseback transactions, but any relationship of the option price to the lessor's current book value is fraught with danger. *A repurchase option requires expert tax counsel* if it is to be reasonably free of any subsequent unfavorable rulings on the part of the Treasury Department.

TYPE OF PROPERTY

In most cases, the lessee will be a user and the property will be industrial or commercial in character. Top-ranking business and industrial firms have used the sale-leaseback device for headquarters office buildings, manufacturing and distributing centers, divisional offices, storage facilities, and so on. Sale-leaseback has also been used as a financing device on prime income producing properties.

An illustration of an ingenious use of the sale-leaseback device is given below.

A top-grade office building was sold to an investing syndicate for $8,750,000 all cash. Simultaneously, the syndicate sold the building to a life insurance company for $7,500,000 and leased it back for a long term of years at $450,000 per annum net (6 per cent of the $7,500,000 sales price). The lease, which ran for about 30 years, had renewal options at lower rentals. At the time the lease was made, the property was producing about $550,000 net on a free and clear basis. It was also evident that with moderate capital expenditures, with careful management and with an aggressive rental program the net income could be increased.

What this transaction actually boiled down to was this: the syndicate which bought the property for $8,750,000 and sold it to the insurance company for $7,500,000 was paying $1,250,000 for a long-term lease on the property at $450,000 per annum net.

Since the time of the consummation of the sale-leaseback transaction, the net return on the property has increased substantially to the extent that the lessees, even with an additional capital investment of $1,000,000 in building improvements, are earning about 20 per cent on their money.

LEVEL PAYMENTS (IN PERCENTAGE) REQUIRED FOR COMPLETE AMORTIZATION OF LESSOR'S INVESTMENT.

Lease Term in Years	Basic Interest Rate											
	3%	3½%	4%	4½%	5%	5½%	6%	6½%	7%	8%	9%	10%
10	11.72	12.02	12.33	12.64	12.95	13.27	13.59	13.91	14.24	14.90	15.58	16.27
11	10.80	11.11	11.41	11.72	12.04	12.36	12.68	13.01	13.36	14.01	14.69	15.40
12	10.04	10.35	10.66	10.97	11.28	11.60	11.93	12.26	12.59	13.27	13.97	14.68
13	9.40	9.70	10.01	10.33	10.65	10.97	11.30	11.63	11.97	12.65	13.36	14.08
14	8.85	9.16	9.47	9.78	10.10	10.43	10.76	11.09	11.43	12.13	12.84	13.57
15	8.37	8.68	8.99	9.31	9.63	9.96	10.30	10.64	10.98	11.68	12.41	13.15
16	7.96	8.27	8.58	8.90	9.23	9.56	9.90	10.24	10.59	11.30	12.03	12.78
17	7.59	7.90	8.22	8.54	8.87	9.20	9.54	9.89	10.24	10.96	11.70	12.47
18	7.27	7.58	7.90	8.22	8.55	8.89	9.24	9.59	9.94	10.67	11.42	12.19
19	6.98	7.29	7.61	7.94	8.27	8.62	8.96	9.32	9.68	10.41	11.17	11.95
20	6.72	7.04	7.36	7.69	8.02	8.37	8.72	9.08	9.44	10.19	10.95	11.75
21	6.48	6.80	7.13	7.46	7.80	8.15	8.50	8.86	9.23	9.98	10.76	11.56
22	6.27	6.59	6.92	7.25	7.60	7.95	8.30	8.67	9.04	9.80	10.59	11.40
23	6.08	6.40	6.73	7.07	7.41	7.77	8.13	8.50	8.87	9.64	10.44	11.26
24	5.90	6.23	6.56	6.90	7.25	7.60	7.97	8.34	8.72	9.50	10.30	11.13
25	5.74	6.07	6.40	6.74	7.10	7.45	7.82	8.20	8.58	9.37	10.18	11.02
26	5.59	5.92	6.26	6.60	6.96	7.32	7.69	8.07	8.46	9.25	10.07	10.92
27	5.46	5.79	6.12	6.47	6.83	7.20	7.57	7.95	8.34	9.14	9.97	10.83
28	5.33	5.66	6.00	6.35	6.71	7.08	7.46	7.85	8.24	9.05	9.89	10.75
29	5.21	5.54	5.89	6.24	6.61	6.98	7.36	7.75	8.14	8.96	9.81	10.67
30	5.10	5.44	5.78	6.14	6.51	6.88	7.26	7.66	8.06	8.88	9.73	10.61

CHAPTER 15

Valuation of Leaseholds

Leasehold valuation is one of the more complex subjects in the appraisal field. Similarly, the mathematics of leasehold valuation oftentimes becomes involved and complicated. In this chapter, therefore, we will limit ourselves to an explanation of the principles of leasehold valuation and to the application of these principles in typical and relatively uncomplicated cases.

The *lease* is the written instrument binding *lessor* and *lessee* to its terms. The rights in the property created for the lessee by the lease are called a *leasehold* or *leasehold estate* or the *leasehold interest* or the *lessee's interest*. The lessor's interest in the property is the primary interest. The lessee's interest is secondary.

A man who leases a one-family house for one year therefore has a leasehold or a leasehold estate, just as much as the man who holds a ground lease for 99 years on property which he has improved with a million-dollar structure. But, in practice, the terms "leasehold" and "leasehold estate" are seldom used in reference to the rights of a short-term lessee.

THE "OPEN MARKET" CONCEPT SHOULD PREVAIL

The valuation of a lease or of a leasehold should be based on the same principle as the valuation of a fee interest. The ultimate test is market value, using the willing buyer-willing seller theory with all of the appraiser's safeguards against the vagaries of current market price.

A substantial percentage of leases, both short term and long term, may have a definite and readily determinable value *to the lessee* but because of lease restrictions, economic causes or other reasons, the benefits are peculiar to the lessee, cannot be transferred or sold, and therefore have no market value.

In appraisal treatises we often see the terms "value of lessee's interest" and "value of lessor's interest." As used in these texts, the value of the lessee's interest is the value of the leasehold *to the lessee*. It is not an open market value. "Leasehold value" and "value of lessee's interest" are therefore not necessarily synonymous when the latter term is used in reference to a value which attaches only to the lessee as a tenant in possession. This distinction will be discussed at greater length in a later portion of this chapter.

WHAT CREATES LEASEHOLD VALUE

There are two general methods by which leasehold value is created:

(a) By change in market conditions. Leasehold value may be created when the rental value of the property becomes greater than the rent reserved in the lease. There are many limiting factors to this theory of value as will be seen in the next section.

(b) By lessee's capital investment. Leasehold value may be created when the lessee constructs a new leasehold improvement, or when he makes a substantial capital investment in remodeling or adding to an existing structure.

WHAT LIMITS LEASEHOLD VALUE

There are two principal limiting factors to leasehold value:

(a) Lease Covenants. When a leasehold interest is sold, the sublessee acquires the lessee's interest with all of the limitations that may be imposed by the lease covenants. The sublessee does not have the right of negotiation with the original lessor. In other words, he buys a deal that has already been made without his knowledge or consent and which may, in many respects, not suit his type of operation.

The most important covenant is the right of assignment. In the majority of leases there is some restriction placed on this right. If no right of assignment is given to the lessee, then the leasehold is not marketable and accordingly has no market value, even though the rental called for in the lease may be substantially below the true rental value.

Here we have a prime illustration of the distinction that can be drawn between the "value of the lessee's interest" and "the value of the leasehold." Let us assume that a business man rents a property at $10,000 per annum and that there is an unexpired 10-year term of his original 15-year lease. Let us also assume that business conditions in the area have improved to the extent that the rental value of the property has gone up to $20,000. Let it be further assumed that the lessee has no right of assignment or that on any assignment any profit or increased rental must go to the lessor. With such a state of facts, two things would be clear: (1) The lease would have a substantial value to the *lessee;* (2) The leasehold is not marketable and therefore has no market value.

Denial of the right to assign therefore can effectively negate any leasehold value. In like manner, other covenants pertaining to the use and maintenance of the property may also serve to limit it.

(b) Lease Term. The length of the unexpired lease term will obviously affect the valuation of the leasehold interest. If we start with the assumption that the lessee has the right of assignment and that the leasehold has a demonstrable value, it is clear that the value will be greater if the lease has 10 years to run than if it has 5 years to run.

THEORY OF LEASEHOLD VALUATION

The theory of leasehold valuation is well established. It has been developed from the two basic points mentioned above: that leasehold value is created by a change in market conditions or by a capital investment on the part of the lessee.

The techniques of valuation evolving from this theory of valuation are many and varied. As noted at the beginning of this chapter, leasehold valuation is one of the more complicated problems that faces the appraiser. In applying the theory of valuation to specific cases, there are more limitations, qualifications, and exceptions than in any other kind of valuation.

In this chapter we are not concerned with fee values or with the value of the lessor's interest except where the derivation of these values is a necessary step in the valuation of the leasehold interest. If for instance it is established that land leased for 21 years at $6,000 per annum net has a value of $100,000, this fee value is not relevant to our discussions. We are interested in the market value of what the lessee has—the right to use the property for 21 years at a net rental of $6,000 per annum. In subsequent portions of this chapter, the term "lessee's interest" will be used synonymously with "leasehold," which means that we are assuming that the lease is assignable and therefore marketable.

There are two primary theories of leasehold valuation:

Theory 1. *In property where there is no capital investment made by the lessee, the leasehold has value only if the rent reserved in the lease is less than the true economic rental value. The measure of leasehold value is the present-day discounted worth of the sum of the annual differentials for the remaining lease term.*

The discount theory is based on the economic fact that present money, because of its earning potential, commands a premium over future money. $3,312.12 invested today at 8 per cent interest will pay an annuity of $1,000 for four years at the end of which period the capital sum will have been exhausted. The difference between the $4,000 in total annual payments and the $3,312.12 is the discount. Obviously, the discount will vary as the assumed interest rate varies. (See Discount Tables, pages 120 to 123.)

Anyone buying an annuity will discount it for interest as of the date of purchase. The lessee who holds a lease at less than the fair rental value has in effect an annuity (the differential between the fair rental value and the rent reserved in the lease) which stems from his leasehold interest. There is, of course, an assumption that this differential will be maintained during the remainder of the lease term.

Translating the leasehold interest into value is the same as discounting the "annuities" for the balance of the lease. Take as an example the property with an assumed worth of $100,000 and a rental value of $8,000 per annum net (8 per cent of fee value). Let it be further assumed that the property is leased for a term of years, with 15 years remaining, at $6,000 per annum.

The differential between the rental value and the lease rental is $2,000 per annum. This represents the lessee's "annuity" for 15 years. Discounted at 8 per cent interest, the leasehold would be valued at $17,000.

In this same case, if the fee or lessor's interest were appraised, it would suffer a diminution in value because the lease is unfavorable from the lessor's or fee owner's point of view. The same mathematics would apply and a proper valuation of the fee interest would be $100,000 minus $17,000 or $83,000.

Similarly (although the value of the fee is not our primary concern), a lease to a *responsible* tenant at a rental in excess of true rental value might give property a value above the free and clear market value.

If we take the case above of the property valued at $100,000 with a fair rental value of $8,000 and assume it to be rented for $10,000 per annum, it would give the lessor or fee owner an "annuity" of $2,000 over and above the fair rental value predicated, of course, on the tenant's responsibility and ability to pay. In this case, the fee might be valued at $100,000 plus $17,000 or $117,000. The leasehold interest would be valueless.

Active leasing brokers have had experience with many similar situations where the lessee has discovered he has an unfavorable lease and is willing to make a cash settlement for a cancellation.

In many instances, leases have been sold for a substantial sum where there is no differential between the fair rental value of the property and the rent reserved in the lease. This situation occurs most frequently when someone wants to get possession of a particular property or to go into business at a particular location. The price paid for the lease is a premium for possession of the property and has little or nothing to do with the intrinsic value of the leasehold itself.

Theory 2. Where a leasehold improvement has been constructed by a lessee, the chief measure of the value of the leasehold is the benefit to be derived from the improvement during the remainder of the lease term. The benefit may be measured in terms of income or of utility.

This theory goes back to one of the most widely accepted definitions of value "the present worth of future benefits." The "present worth" should, of course, bear some close relationship to the cost of the leasehold improvement. When a lessee constructs a building on leased land, anticipating a certain net return on his investment, and achieves that return, it usually signifies that the value of his

TABLE 1. PRESENT VALUE

(*For Computing Lessor's Interest in Rentals*

This table will be found invaluable in determining today's worth of any saving or increase of income which extends through future years. It shows the present worth of an annually recurring saving or rental or income of $1 per year for any number of years at a given rate of interest. For example, what is the value of an annuity in the form of a leasehold estate to lessor calling for $6,000 annually for 25 years, money being worth 6%? See factor 25 periods, 6%, equals $12.783, which equals the value of $1, multiplied by $6,000 equals $76,698.00. If the rental is payable semiannually, multiply the periods, viz., 25, by 2 and divide the rate by 2, making 50 periods at 3%, which factor is 25.730 multiplied by $3,000 equals $77,199.00. If

Yrs.	1¼%	1½%	1¾%	2%	2¼%	2½%	2¾%	Yrs.
1	.988	.986	.983	.980	.978	.976	.973	1
2	1.963	1.956	1.949	1.942	1.934	1.997	1.920	2
3	2.927	2.912	2.898	2.884	2.870	2.856	2.842	3
4	3.878	3.854	3.831	3.808	3.785	3.762	3.739	4
5	4.818	4.783	4.748	4.713	4.679	4.646	4.613	5
6	5.756	5.697	5.649	5.601	5.554	5.508	5.462	6
7	6.663	6.598	6.535	6.472	6.410	6.349	6.289	7
8	7.568	7.486	7.405	7.325	7.247	7.170	7.094	8
9	8.462	8.360	8.260	8.162	8.066	7.971	7.878	9
10	9.346	9.222	9.101	8.983	8.866	8.752	8.640	10
11	10.218	10.071	9.927	9.787	9.649	9.514	9.382	11
12	11.079	10.907	10.740	10.578	10.415	10.258	10.104	12
13	11.930	11.731	11.538	11.348	11.164	10.983	10.807	13
14	12.771	12.543	12.322	12.106	11.896	11.691	11.491	14
15	13.601	13.343	13.093	12.849	12.612	12.381	12.157	15
16	14.420	14.131	13.850	13.578	13.313	13.055	12.805	16
17	15.230	14.908	14.596	14.292	13.998	13.712	13.436	17
18	16.030	15.673	15.327	14.992	14.668	14.353	14.049	18
19	16.819	16.426	16.046	15.678	15.323	14.979	14.646	19
20	17.599	17.169	16.753	16.351	15.964	15.589	15.227	20
21	18.370	17.900	17.448	17.011	16.590	16.185	15.793	21
22	19.131	18.621	18.130	17.658	17.203	16.765	16.343	22
23	19.882	19 331	18.801	18.292	17.803	17.332	16.879	23
24	20.624	20.030	19.461	18.914	18.399	17.885	17.401	24
25	21.357	20.720	20.109	19.523	18.962	18.424	17.908	25
26	22.081	21.399	20.746	20.121	19.523	18.951	18.402	26
27	22.796	22.068	21.372	20.707	20.071	19.464	18.883	27
28	23.502	22.727	21.987	21 281	20.608	19.965	19.351	28
29	24.200	23.376	22.592	21.844	21.132	20.454	19.806	29
30	24.889	24 016	23.186	22.396	21.645	20.930	20.249	30
31	25.569	24.646	23.770	22.938	22.147	21.395	20.681	31
32	26.241	25.267	24.344	23.468	22.638	21.849	21.100	32
33	26 905	25.879	24.908	23.989	23.117	22.292	21.509	33
34	27.560	26.482	25.462	24.499	23.587	22.724	21.906	34
35	28.208	27.076	26.007	24.999	24.046	23.145	22.293	35
36	28.847	27.661	26.543	25.489	24.495	23.556	22.670	36
37	29.479	28.237	27.069	25 969	24.934	23 957	23.036	37
38	30.102	28.805	27.586	26.441	25.363	24.349	23.393	38
39	30.718	29.365	28.095	26 903	25 783	24.730	23.740	39
40	31 327	29.916	28.594	27.355	26.193	25.103	24.078	40
41	31.928	30.459	29 085	27 799	26.595	25.466	24.407	41
42	32.521	30.994	29 568	28.235	26.988	25.821	24.727	42
43	33.107	31.521	30.042	28.662	27.372	26.168	25.038	43
44	33.686	32 041	30 508	29 080	27.748	26.504	25.341	44
45	34.258	32.552	30.966	29.490	28.115	26.833	25 636	45
46	34.823	33.056	31.416	29.892	28.474	27 154	25.924	46
47	35.381	33 553	31.859	30.287	28.822	27.467	26.203	47
48	35.931	34 043	32.294	30 673	29.170	27.773	26.475	48
49	36 475	34 525	32.721	31.052	29.506	28.071	26.740	49
50	37.013	35.000	33.141	31.424	29.834	28.362	26.098	50

OF $1 PER ANNUM

or Lessee's Profit in a Lease)

the rental is payable quarterly, multiply the periods, viz., 25, by 4 and divide the rate by 4, making 100 periods at 1½%, which factor is 51.6247 multiplied by the quarterly payment of $1,500 equals $77,437.05. It will be observed that the difference between a semiannual and an annual calculation is approximately $492 or ⅝ of 1% in the aggregate amount, while the difference between a quarterly and an annual calculation is about $640, or about ⅝ of 1%. Note that these calculations are for full years commencing on the first day of the year. The present worth of such worth as of a particular day should be taken, plus the intervening interest and payment.

Yrs.	3%	3½%	4%	4½%	5%	5½%	6%	7%	8%	Yrs.
1	.971	.966	.962	.957	.952	.948	.943	.935	.926	1
2	1.913	1.900	1.886	1.873	1.859	1.846	1.833	1.808	1.783	2
3	2.829	2.802	2.775	2.749	2.723	2.698	2.673	2.624	2.577	3
4	3.717	3.673	3.630	3.588	3.546	3.505	3.465	3.387	3.312	4
5	4.580	4.515	4.452	4.390	4.329	4.270	4.212	4.100	3.993	5
6	5.417	5.329	5.242	5.158	5.076	4.996	4.917	4.767	4.623	6
7	6.230	6.115	6.002	5.893	5.786	5.683	5.582	5.389	5.206	7
8	7.020	6.874	6.733	6.596	6.463	6.335	6.210	5.971	5.747	8
9	7.786	7.608	7.435	7.269	7.108	6.952	6.802	6.515	6.247	9
10	8.530	8.317	8.111	7.913	7.722	7.538	7.360	7.024	6.710	10
11	9.253	9.002	8.760	8.529	8.306	8.093	7.887	7.499	7.139	11
12	9.954	9.663	9.385	9.119	8.863	8.619	8.384	7.943	7.536	12
13	10.635	10.303	9.986	9.683	9.394	9.117	8.853	8.358	7.904	13
14	11.296	10.921	10.563	10.223	9.899	9.590	9.295	8.745	8.244	14
15	11.938	11.517	11.118	10.740	10.380	10.038	9.712	9.108	8.559	15
16	12.561	12.094	11.652	11.234	10.838	10.462	10.106	9.447	8.851	16
17	13.166	12.651	12.166	11.707	11.274	10.865	10.477	9.763	9.122	17
18	13.754	13.190	12.659	12.160	11.690	11.246	10.828	10.059	9.372	18
19	14.324	13.710	13.134	12.593	12.085	11.608	11.158	10.336	9.604	19
20	14.877	14.212	13.590	13.008	12.462	11.950	11.470	10.594	9.818	20
21	15.415	14.698	14.029	13.405	12.821	12.275	11.764	10.836	10.017	21
22	15.937	15.167	14.451	13.784	13.163	12.583	12.042	11.061	10.201	22
23	16.444	15.620	14.857	14.148	13.489	12.875	12.303	11.272	10.371	23
24	16.936	16.058	15.247	14.495	13.799	13.152	12.550	11.469	10.529	24
25	17.413	16.482	15.622	14.828	14.094	13.414	12.783	11.654	10.675	25
26	17.877	16.890	15.983	15.147	14.375	13.663	13.003	11.826	10.810	26
27	18.327	17.285	16.330	15.451	14.643	13.898	13.211	11.987	10.935	27
28	18.764	17.667	16.663	15.743	14.898	14.121	13.406	12.137	11.051	28
29	19.188	18.036	16.984	16.022	15.141	14.333	13.591	12.278	11.158	29
30	19.600	18.392	17.292	16.289	15.372	14.534	13.765	12.409	11.258	30
31	20.000	18.736	17.588	16.544	15.593	14.724	13.929	12.532	11.350	31
32	20.389	19.069	17.874	16.789	15.803	14.904	14.084	12.647	11.435	32
33	20.766	19.390	18.148	17.023	16.003	15.075	14.230	12.754	11.514	33
34	21.132	19.701	18.411	17.247	16.193	15.237	14.368	12.854	11.587	34
35	21.487	20.001	18.665	17.461	16.374	15.391	14.498	12.948	11.655	35
36	21.832	20.290	18.908	17.666	16.547	15.536	14.621	13.035	11.717	36
37	22.167	20.571	19.143	17.862	16.711	15.674	14.737	13.117	11.775	37
38	22.492	20.841	19.368	18.050	16.868	15.805	14.846	13.193	11.829	38
39	22.808	21.103	19.584	18.230	17.017	15.929	14.949	13.265	11.879	39
40	23.115	21.355	19.793	18.402	17.159	16.046	15.046	13.332	11.925	40
41	23.412	21.599	19.993	18.566	17.294	16.157	15.138	13.394	11.967	41
42	23.701	21.835	20.186	18.724	17.423	16.263	15.225	13.452	12.007	42
43	23.982	22.063	20.371	18.874	17.546	16.363	15.306	13.507	12.043	43
44	24.254	22.283	20.549	19.018	17.663	16.458	15.383	13.558	12.077	44
45	24.519	22.495	20.720	19.156	17.774	16.548	15.456	13.606	12.108	45
46	24.775	22.701	20.885	19.288	17.880	16.633	15.524	13.650	12.137	46
47	25.025	22.899	21.043	19.415	17.981	16.714	15.589	13.692	12.164	47
48	25.267	23.091	21.195	19.536	18.077	16.790	15.650	13.730	12.189	48
49	25.502	23.277	21.341	19.651	18.169	16.863	15.708	13.677	12.212	49
50	25.730	23.456	21.482	19.762	18.256	16.932	15.762	13.801	12.233	50

PRESENT VALUE

Yrs.	1¼%	1½%	1¾%	2%	2¼%	2½%	2¾%	Yrs
51	37.544	35.468	33.554	31.788	30.156	28.646	27.248	51
52	38.068	35.929	33.960	32.145	30.470	28.923	27.492	52
53	38.585	36.383	34.358	32.495	30.778	29.193	27.729	53
54	39.097	36.830	34.750	32.838	31.078	29.457	27.960	54
55	39.602	37.271	35.135	33.175	31.373	29.714	28.185	55
56	40.100	37.706	35.514	33.505	31.660	29.965	28.404	56
57	40.593	38.134	35.886	33.828	31.942	30.210	28.617	57
58	41.079	38.555	36.252	34.145	32.217	30.448	28.824	58
59	41.560	38.971	36.611	34.456	32.486	30.681	29.026	59
60	42.035	39.380	36.964	34.761	32.749	30.909	29.223	60
61	42.503	39.783	37.311	35.060	33.006	31.130	29.414	61
62	42.966	40.181	37.652	35.353	33.258	31.347	29.600	62
63	43.423	40.572	37.987	35.640	33.504	31.558	29.781	63
64	43.875	40.958	38.317	35.921	33.745	31.764	29.957	64
65	44.321	41.338	38.641	36.197	33.980	31.965	30.128	65
66	44.761	41.712	38.959	36.468	34.211	32.161	30.295	66
67	45.196	42.081	39.272	36.733	34.436	32.352	30.458	67
68	45.626	42.444	39.579	36.994	34.656	32.538	30.616	68
69	46.051	42.802	39.881	37.249	34.871	32.720	30.770	69
70	46.470	43.155	40.178	37.499	35.082	32.898	30.919	70
71	46.834	43.502	40.470	37.744	35.288	33.071	31.065	71
72	47.292	43.845	40.756	37.984	35.490	33.240	31.207	72
73	47.696	44.182	41.038	38.220	35.687	33.405	31.345	73
74	48.095	44.514	41.315	38.451	35.879	33.566	31.479	74
75	48.489	44.842	41.587	38.677	36.068	33.723	31.610	75
76	48.878	45.164	41.855	38.899	36.252	33.876	31.737	76
77	49.262	45.482	42.118	39.117	36.432	34.025	31.861	77
78	49.642	45.795	42.376	39.330	36.609	34.171	31.981	78
79	50.016	46.103	42.630	39.539	36.781	34.313	32.099	79
80	50.387	46.407	42.880	39.744	36.950	34.452	32.213	80
81	50.752	46.707	43.125	39.946	37.115	34.587	32.324	81
82	51.113	47.002	43.366	40.143	37.276	34.719	32.432	82
83	51.470	47.292	43.603	40.336	37.434	34.848	32.537	83
84	51.822	47.579	43.836	40.525	37.588	34.974	32.640	84
85	52.170	47.861	44.065	40.711	37.739	35.096	32.740	85
86	52.514	48.139	44.290	40.893	37.886	35.216	32.836	86
87	52.853	48.412	44.511	41.072	38.031	35.332	32.931	87
88	53.188	48.682	44.728	41.247	38.172	35.446	33.023	88
89	53.519	48.948	44.942	41.419	38.310	35.557	33.112	89
90	53.846	49.210	45.152	41.587	38.445	35.666	33.199	90
91	54.169	49.468	45.358	41.752	38.577	35.771	33.284	91
92	54.488	49.722	45.560	41.914	38.706	35.875	33.366	92
93	54.803	49.972	45.760	42.072	38.832	35.975	33.345	93
94	55.114	50.219	45.955	42.228	38.956	36.073	33.525	94
95	55.421	50.462	46.148	42.380	39.077	36.169	33.601	95
96	55.725	50.702	46.337	42.529	39.195	36.263	33.674	96
97	56.024	50.938	46.523	42.676	39.310	36.354	33.756	97
98	56.320	51.170	46.705	42.819	39.423	36.443	33.816	98
99	56.613	51.399	46.885	42.960	39.534	36.529	33.885	99
100	56.901	51.625	47.061	43.098	39.642	36.614	33.951	100

OF $1 PER ANNUM (Cont.)

Yrs.	3%	3½%	4%	4½%	5%	5½%	6%	7%	8%	Yrs.
51	25.951	23.629	21.617	19.868	18.339	16.997	15.813	13.832	12.253	51
52	26.166	23.796	21.748	19.969	18.418	17.058	15.861	13.862	12.272	52
53	26.375	23.957	21.873	20.066	18.493	17.117	15.907	13.890	12.288	53
54	26.578	24.113	21.993	20.159	18.565	17.173	15.950	13.916	12.304	54
55	26.774	24.264	22.109	20.248	18.633	17.225	15.991	13.940	12.319	55
56	26.965	24.410	22.220	20.333	18.699	17.275	16.029	13.963	12.332	56
57	27.151	24.550	22.327	20.414	18.761	17.332	16.065	13.984	12.344	57
58	27.331	24.686	22.430	20.492	18.820	17.367	16.099	14.003	12.356	58
59	27.506	24.818	22.528	20.567	18.876	17.410	16.131	14.022	12.367	59
60	27.676	24.945	22.623	20.638	18.929	17.450	16.161	14.039	12.377	60
61	27.840	25.067	22.715	20.705	18.980	17.488	16.190	14.055	12.386	61
62	28.000	25.186	22.803	20.772	19.029	17.524	16.217	14.070	12.394	62
63	28.156	25.300	22.887	20.834	19.075	17.558	16.242	14.084	12.402	63
64	28.306	25.411	22.969	20.894	19.119	17.591	16.266	14.098	12.409	64
65	28.453	25.518	23.047	20.951	19.161	17.622	16.289	14.110	12.416	65
66	28.595	25.621	23.122	21.006	19.201	17.651	16.310	14.121	12.422	66
67	28.733	25.721	23.194	21.058	19.239	17.679	16.331	14.132	12.428	67
68	28.867	25.817	23.264	21.108	19.275	17.705	16.350	14.142	12.433	68
69	28.997	25.910	23.330	21.156	19.310	17.730	16.368	14.152	12.438	69
70	29.123	26.000	23.395	21.202	19.343	17.753	16.385	14.160	12.443	70
71	29.246	26.087	23.456	21.246	19.374	17.776	16.401	14.169	12.447	71
72	29.365	26.171	23.516	21.288	19.404	17.797	16.416	14.176	12.451	72
73	29.481	26.253	23.573	21.328	19.432	17.817	16.430	14.183	12.455	73
74	29.592	26.331	23.628	21.367	19.459	17.836	16.443	14.190	12.458	74
75	29.702	26.407	23.680	21.404	19.485	17.854	16.456	14.196	12.461	75
76	29.807	26.480	23.731	21.439	19.509	17.871	16.468	14.202	12.464	76
77	29.910	26.551	23.780	21.473	19.533	17.887	16.479	14.208	12.467	77
78	30.010	26.619	23.827	21.505	19.555	17.903	16.490	14.213	12.469	78
79	30.107	26.685	23.872	21.536	19.576	17.917	16.500	14.218	12.471	79
80	30.201	26.749	23.915	21.565	19.596	17.931	16.509	14.222	12.474	80
81	30.292	26.810	23.957	21.593	19.615	17.944	16.518	14.224	12.476	81
82	30.381	26.870	23.997	21.620	19.634	17.956	16.526	14.228	12.477	82
83	30.466	26.927	24.035	21.646	19.651	17.968	16.534	14.232	12.478	83
84	30.550	26.983	24.072	21.671	19.667	17.979	16.542	14.235	12.480	84
85	30.631	27.037	24.109	21.695	19.684	17.990	16.549	14.238	12.482	85
86	30.710	27.089	24.142	21.717	19.698	18.001	16.555	14.241	12.483	86
87	30.786	27.139	24.175	21.739	19.713	18.010	16.562	14.244	12.484	87
88	30.861	27.187	24.207	21.760	19.726	18.019	16.568	14.247	12.485	88
89	30.933	27.234	24.237	21.780	19.739	18.027	16.573	14.250	12.486	89
90	31.002	27.279	24.267	21.799	19.752	18.035	16.579	14.253	12.488	90
91	31.070	27.323	24.295	21.817	19.764	18.043	16.584	14.255	12.488	91
92	31.136	27.365	24.322	21.834	19.775	18.051	16.588	14.257	12.489	92
93	31.200	27.406	24.348	21.852	19.786	18.058	16.593	14.259	12.490	93
94	31.263	27.445	24.373	21.867	19.796	18.064	16.597	14.261	12.491	94
95	31.323	27.484	24.398	21.883	19.806	18.069	16.601	14.263	12.492	95
96	31.381	27.520	24.420	21.897	19.815	18.075	16.605	14.264	12.492	96
97	31.438	27.556	24.443	21.911	19.823	18.081	16.608	14.265	12.493	97
98	31.494	27.590	24.464	21.924	19.832	18.086	16.611	14.266	12.493	98
99	31.547	27.623	24.485	21.937	19.840	18.091	16.614	14.267	12.493	99
100	31.599	27.655	24.505	21.950	19.848	18.096	16.618	14.269	12.494	100

leasehold interest is at least equivalent to his capital investment in the building. Leasehold value may be greater than the amount of lessee's capital investment, if ground rental is below market value.

For all practical purposes, the value of a long-term leasehold interest derived by discounting the estimated net income flow over the lease term is little different than a straight capitalization of the net income if it is assumed that discount rate and capitalization rate are the same. A property with a net income of $8,000 capitalized at 8 per cent has a fee value of $100,000. An income of $8,000 per annum for forty-two years, discounted at 8 per cent, has a present worth of $96,000. For 63 years it would be $99,200.

Following are a few simple examples of leasehold valuation.

Example 1. Assume that a building had been constructed on leased land and is earning $25,000 per annum net after the payment of ground rent, real estate taxes and all operating expenses. Assume also that the lease has only 10 years to run, at the end of which time the building will revert to the lessor. Also assume that because of the short remaining term in the lease that the money invested in such a leasehold purchase should earn at least 10 per cent (in other words, that the $25,000 per annum income for 10 years should be discounted at 10 per cent) the leasehold value would be:

$25,000 × 6.144 (10 year factor at 10 per cent discount) or $153,600.*

Example 2. Assume that a new building has just been completed on leased land at a cost of $2,000,000 and that on the basis of long-term leases to prime tenants it can be expected to earn $160,000 net per annum after the payment of ground rent, real estate taxes and operating expenses. Let it also be assumed that the lease is for 21 years with two renewal options—a total of 63 years.

Using 8 per cent discount table, the value of the leasehold interest would be:

$160,000 × 12.4092, or $1,985,472, or $2,000,000 in round figures.*

Note: Capitalized at a straight 8 per cent rate, the $160,000 income would have a value of $2,000,000, the cost of the improvement. This illustrates the point that there is little difference between leasehold value arrived at by the discounting process, or fee value arrived at

---

* Using standard annuity tables sometimes referred to as "Present Value of $1. per annum."

by income capitalization when the remaining lease term is 40, 50, 60 years or more.

Example 3. Let us assume the same state of facts as in Example 2 and let it be further assumed that the ground rent is $50,000 per annum, based on a land value of $1,000,000 at 5 per cent. In order to produce a fair return on the building and pay the ground rent, net earnings should be $210,000 after payment of real estate taxes and operating expenses.

Let us assume that the property actually earns $230,000, and that 8 per cent is conceded to be the fair and reasonable return on the building. This would leave $70,000 of the net income available for capitalization into land value. In other words, the ground rent is too low by $20,000. Following the standard appraisal process, however, we would value the land at $1,400,000 but the lessor's interest would be worth only $1,000,000 because it is encumbered with a $50,000 ground lease. In effect the lessee has acquired part of the land value because of his favorable lease. Total leasehold value would therefore be $2,000,000 plus $400,000 or $2,400,000.

If the lease required a reappraisal at the end of the first 21 years, then the lessee's favorable rental would, in theory, continue only for that period. Appraisal would then be made as follows:

Land would be valued at $1,400,000. The fair ground rental would be $70,000 per annum. The actual ground rental is $50,000. The lessee therefore has an "annuity" of $20,000 in the form of additional income which would be paid as ground rent if he did not have his favorable lease. Using a 5 per cent discount factor, lessee's interest in the land would be $256,000. Total leasehold value would be $2,000,000 plus $256,000 or $2,256,000.

CHAPTER 16

Financing Leaseholds

Financing is defined as "providing money for." In real estate this may be done in many ways: by mortgages, bonds, debentures, notes, and so on. The most common instrument of real estate finance is the mortgage, under which the borrower is obligated to repay the loan on a specified schedule with the real estate as security.

Although a sale of property is obviously not *financing*, the typical sale or leaseback transaction under which the seller retains control of the property by taking a lease for a long term of years is for all practical purposes a 100 per cent financing device.

LEASEHOLD FINANCING

Leasehold financing is a borrowing by the lessee, generally through a mortgage, with the lessee's interest as security. A leasehold mortgage is subordinate to the lessor's or fee interest, which in turn may be separately mortgaged or financed. A default of the lessee under a leasehold mortgage therefore does not affect the lessor, except that the holder of the leasehold mortgage may acquire the leasehold interest through foreclosure or other remedial procedures.

On the other hand, a default of the lessee in the payment of his rent to the lessor imperils the rights of the leasehold mortgagee because these rights are secured by a secondary lien and would be wiped out in the event of a foreclosure of a primary lien. For this reason, leasehold mortgagees insist on the right: (1) to cure any default on the part of the lessee in the payment of the primary rent, and (2) to assume the lessee's position under the current lease.

MORTGAGING THE FEE

In some cases where a lessee has agreed to construct a costly improvement, the lessor may permit the mortgaging of his fee interest. But this privilege should not be given to the lessee indiscriminately, because the lessor's rights are thereby merged with those of the lessee. By this action, the lessor in effect gives the lessee equal status in his fee position.

Such a mortgaging is *not leasehold financing*. But because of its direct effect on the lessor-lessee relationship, we are giving general details as to how this type of transaction works. Let us assume that a piece of land is worth $50,000, for which the lessee pays a rental of $3,000 annually (6 per cent net). Plans are made for the construction of a $75,000 building, but the lessee, who is in a retail line of operation, wants to commit as little of his cash as possible to a real estate investment. The lessor has full confidence in the lessee, his business operation, his financial standing. As a result, he merges his interest with that of the lessee for mortgage purposes. The total property value would therefore be $125,000, and the lessee might be able to secure a mortgage for the full cost of building construction, so that he has no cash investment in the real estate. The benefits in such a type of operation are:

1. The lessor leases his land at a valuation which he considers its full worth and draws this rental monthly throughout the term of the lease.
2. He avoids having to pay any excess profit taxes which might have accrued had he sold the land outright at a much higher figure than it cost him.
3. He secures a permanent improvement and a reliable tenant for his premises.
4. He eventually has the building turned over to him or his heirs cost-free so that it can be re-leased to the same or another tenant at terms then considered suitable.
5. He has a tax-free investment, for in most long-term leases the tenant pays all expenses including taxes (except the Federal income tax) on what the landlord receives as rent.

6. The tenant secures the kind of a building improvement he wants on reasonable terms with rental fixed for a long term of years.

The late Clarence M. Lewis of the New York bar, one of the best-versed lawyers on the subject of leaseholds in this country, had the following comments to make about the right of a tenant to mortgage the fee to a property where he is the lessee under a long-term lease.

1. If the lease does not prohibit it, the tenant has the right to mortgage his leasehold interest but not to mortgage the land and the improvement on it. In cases where a tenant hires vacant land or demolishes the existing building and erects a new building, the practice of the landlord granting to the tenant the right to mortgage the fee is becoming more frequent. Of course, when this is done the rights of the landlord must be properly safeguarded, and this can be done in several ways.

2. The landlord should have satisfactory security either by way of cash, securities, or a completion bond for the erection of a new building.

3. In addition, the amount for which the tenant may mortgage the property should be limited to a reasonable percentage of the value of the land and building as appraised by a competent and reliable appraiser, and, in addition, the tenant should be permitted only to secure his loan from a bank, trust company, or other conservative loaning institution so that he will not be in a position to borrow from a reckless lender more than the amount to which he would be entitled from a conservative lender.

4. The right to mortgage the land and building, properly safeguarded, may be beneficial to both the landlord and the tenant. It permits the landlord with vacant or inadequately improved property and with no knowledge of building operations to have his property improved at the expense of the tenant without the use of the capital which would be necessary to erect a new building.

5. The right to mortgage the fee must be properly and adequately safeguarded and the proceeds of the loan applied to the erection of the new building. There are many instances in which leases granting to the tenant the right to mortgage the land as well as the buildings have been made, new buildings erected, and the tenant secured a great increase in his income. Up to the present time I know of no case where the tenant has been given permission to mortgage the fee where there has been any litigation which would seem to indicate that transactions of this kind have been unsuccessful.

WHEN IS A LEASEHOLD MORTGAGABLE

There can be only one estate enjoying the full use of land, but there can be many different interests in land. Any interest in land that may be the subject of sale, grant, or assignment may be mortgaged. Accordingly, there may be a mortgage on a rent, an estate for life, or an estate for years. A leasehold, which is an estate for years, therefore *can* be mortgaged.

Mortgage loans upon land owned in fee without restriction or limitation as a class, are recognized everywhere as excellent security, but loans upon interests in land less than the full fee simple ownership are neither as common nor as well accepted as a basis for credit. In such loans there is a limitation upon the interest of the mortgagor in the property that detracts from the security. Risk of loss to the lender is likewise enhanced. Leaseholds come within this category. There are certain qualities a leasehold must have to constitute an acceptable risk.

VALUE

Our first premise would be that a leasehold is mortgagable only if it has value. (Leasehold valuation is discussed in the preceding chapter.) The value of the leasehold is the difference between its benefits and its burdens. Its benefits are measured in terms of the property's productivity *as real estate*. The burden is the rent specified in the lease agreement.

As a simple illustration, take the case of a tenant having a lifetime lease on a business property at $800 per annum net. If 8 per cent is assumed to be a fair rate of return, then the property has a capitalized value of $10,000, on the basis of the rent paid under the lease agreement. If, on the other hand, the property has a true rental value of $1,000 per annum net, it would have a capitalized value of $12,500, on the basis of the true rental value. In this case, the tenant's leasehold would be worth $2,500, the difference between $10,000 and $12,500.

If the lease were for a short term, let us say five years, the leasehold value would be measured in terms of the present worth of $200 (difference between lease rent of $800 and fair rental value of $1,000) for five years at 6 per cent interest, or $840. In neither case should the tenant's prospective income from his *business operation* conducted in the premises be considered as an element of leasehold value unless the business operation is so well established that it has a definite and direct influence on rental value.

On the other hand, if the actual rental value of the property were $50 per month (the same as the rent provided in the lease) then the leasehold would be valueless. This would hold true even if the tenant had a reasonable anticipation of making money from a business operation conducted on the premises.

In the above illustration the leasehold value, if any, is attributable either to astute negotiation on the part of the lessee or to an increase in rental value after the lease was negotiated. Leasehold value, in other words, was not created by any *capital investment* on the part of the lessee. In such cases, with rare exceptions, institutions are disinclined to make mortgage loans, despite the fact that such leaseholds on prime commercial properties can acquire substantial value in an inflationary period.

INVESTMENT BY LESSEE

In another illustration, an investor leases a tract of land in a central district for a long period of years—say 99 years—at $10,000 per annum net, and agrees to erect a building on the land. Let us assume that 5 per cent is a fair rate of return on the land and 7 per cent on the building, and that the building on completion has an earning potential of $35,000 per annum after paying all operating expenses including ground rent.

The value of the land and building therefore, would be as follows:

Land	$200,000	($10,000 capitalized @ 5%)
Building	500,000	($35,000 capitalized @ 7%)
Total value of property	$700,000	
Lessee's interest (Leasehold value)	$500,000	
Lessor's interest	$200,000	

Leasehold value in this case would be the capitalized value of the improvement and would represent a mortgagable risk to an institution which had the legal power to make such loans.

As a general, but not an ironclad rule, it might be stated that the *leasehold qualifies as a mortgagable risk only if there is a capital investment in the property on the part of the lessee.*

Sometimes leaseholds are sold. Sale of the leasehold would not necessarily affect its eligibility for mortgage purposes. In the foregoing example, let us assume that the lessee on completion of the building sells his leasehold to another investor for $700,000. The sub-lessee or the new owner of the leasehold, we assume, will be satisfied with 5 per cent on his investment, since the property earns only $35,000 per annum. The sub-lessee's leasehold estate is mortgagable but it would be valued for mortgage lending purposes at only $500,000, not the $700,000 that he paid for it.

In those rare cases where leasehold mortgages have been arranged without any capital investment on the part of the lessee, they have occurred when the lessee has a long-term lease on land and improvements and a rental well below stabilized market levels. This excess rental value must be established to the satisfaction of the mortgage lender. The best evidence would be a series of long-term sub-leases to responsible tenants at an aggregate rental well above that paid by the lessee.

If the property is occupied by the lessee who conducts a business on it, excess rental value would have to be established by comparison with adjacent properties of a similar nature or by converting the lessee's business earnings into terms of rental value.

SALE AND FINANCING OF SUBORDINATE LEASE INTERESTS

Any interest in real estate *can* be sold, assigned or mortgaged. In many cases the rights of a holder of an interest in real estate to sell, assign, or mortgage may be limited in the deed, lease, or other instrument through which he holds his interest. Assuming, however, that his rights are not circumscribed by any legal restrictions, there is an infinite variety of ways in which a person may operate in the disposition of a real estate interest. Recently one of our more astute real estate operators worked out a transaction along the following lines:

1. He leased a tract of land for a long period of years with appropriate renewals at an initial ground rent of $300,000 per annum net.
2. On the land he constructed an office building costing between $9,000,000 and $10,000,000.
3. The building was completed under favorable circumstances so that after paying ground rent, real estate taxes and all oper-

ating expenses, his estimated net return was $1,000,000 per annum (this is approximately 10 per cent of cost of leasehold improvement).

4. He sold the leasehold improvement to an insurance company for $8,000,000 and leased it back for the same term of years as his initial ground lease at a rental of $640,000 per annum. The insurance company therefore became the lessee and the developer became the sub-lessee.

5. He then sold his sublease position to a real estate operator for $2,000,000 and again leased the property back from the operator at $240,000 per annum (12 per cent of the cost of the sublease purchase). By this transaction the real estate operator became the sub-lessee and the developer became the sub-sublessee. The net result was that the developer had possession of the property without any cash investment. He had a net return of $120,000 per annum after payment of operating expenses, real estate taxes and rents under the ground lease, sublease and sub-sublease. In addition, his real estate company had a profitable management contract for the operation of the building.

CHAPTER 17

Income Tax Laws and Leases

Every real estate transaction today is affected by the Federal Income Tax Laws. A decision to sell, assign, mortgage or lease a property should therefore be viewed in light of the impact of these laws (and of the administrative rules and regulations which have the same force and effect as law).

The use of the lease as a financing device has become more widespread because under certain circumstances it may have favorable tax implications. The simplest illustration of this fact is the growing popularity of the sale-leaseback transaction under which one of the principal benefits to the lessee is that the rental paid is totally deductible when computing taxable income. The sale-leaseback transaction has, of course, other than tax benefits but in this chapter we will concern ourselves mainly with the application of tax laws to this and other types of lease transactions.

CHANGES IN LAWS AND REGULATIONS

Federal income taxes are levied by the Internal Revenue Service, a branch of the Treasury Department, under authority given to it by the Congress. The laws are supplemented by departmental regulations which, in some cases, have the full force and effect of law.

The laws and regulations are in turn the subject of departmental rulings and interpretations on matters of issue between the taxpayer and the government. These rulings and interpretations are subject to review by the United States Tax Court and courts of superior jurisdiction.

Since the Internal Revenue Code was enacted, there have been many changes in the basic law and in the regulations. There is no doubt that future years will see further changes. Similarly, administrative rulings and interpretations have been set aside or confirmed by the courts in thousands of cases. It is important for the real estate owner to know the current status of law, regulations, and interpretations. For this purpose, he should have recourse to expert tax counsel—either an attorney or certified public accountant experienced in these matters.

SUMMARY OF BASIC PRINCIPLES OF TAXATION

Following is a general summary of applicable laws and regulations in lease transactions.

Owner-Lessor

1. Net income from the operation of real estate is taxable. Rate of taxation depends on the type of ownership, i.e., personal, corporate, etc.
2. Net income is total income less allowable expenses.
3. Allowable expenses would include:
    Depreciation.
    Mortgage interest.
    Real estate taxes (if paid by owner).
    Cost of operation or maintenance (if paid by owner).

Lessee

As a rule, the lessee has no income from the real estate excepting in cases where all or part of the property might be sublet. As a general business expense the lessee may deduct the following when computing taxable income.

    Rentals paid under the lease (business or professional).
    Real estate taxes (if paid by Lessee).
    Cost of operation and maintenance (if paid by Lessee).

Depreciation of Leasehold improvements (if paid for by the Lessee).

Interest on Leasehold mortgage (if any).

Following is a simple example of the general applicability of income tax laws to a standard type of lease transaction:

Assume: Property valued @ $150,000 (land $25,000; building $125,000) is leased to commercial tenant @ $20,000 per annum for 10 years. Lease has a 5-year unexpired term.

Tenant sublets portion of property @ $5,000 per annum.
Tenant maintains property. Annual cost $5,000.
Tenant spent $30,000 in improving interior of property.
Owner pays real estate taxes and insurance. Annual cost $4,500.

Owner purchased property when lease was made at which time remaining useful life of building was estimated at 40 years.

Property was mortgaged for $80,000 at time lease was made with interest at 5 per cent and amortization at 3 per cent per annum.

Lessor's Tax Computation

Income		$20,000
Deductible Expenses		
Real Estate taxes and insurance	$4,500	
Mortgage Interest	3,400	
(5% of principal which would be reduced to $68,000 at end of 5 years)		
Depreciation (straight line)		
2½ of $125,000	3,125	
	11,025	
Net taxable income		$8,975

Lessee's Tax Computation

Income		$ 5,000
Deductions		
Rent	$20,000	
Maintenance Cost	5,000	
Depreciation of leasehold improvements	3,000	
	28,000	
Excess of deductions over income		$23,000

The lessee would therefore have a net deduction of $23,000 attributable to real estate when computing the income tax on his business operation.

INCOME AND EXPENSE IN TAX COMPUTATIONS

Since both lessor and lessee will strive to reduce taxable income to the minimum permissive amount, it is obvious that any legal means by which income can be spread or pro-rated over a period of years would be advantageous. Similarly any means by which money spent on real estate can be immediately deducted, instead of amortized over a period of years, would likewise be advantageous provided, of course, that the business operation is a profitable one.

Because of this natural objective there have been many rulings by the Treasury Department as to how and when income is to be credited and how and when deductions are to be allowed.

CONSIDERATIONS OF THE OWNER-LESSOR

In the preceding paragraphs we outlined briefly and in broadest terms the general principle of tax laws and regulations applying to the lessor-lessee relationship. Appended below is a brief resumé of supplementary laws, regulations, and rulings covering these basic principles.

Rentals and Other Payments Made by Lessee to Lessor

RENTS

Rents are taxable as ordinary income and are to be reported in the year received.

BONUSES

Bonus paid by lessee to lessor is considered ordinary income to be reported in the year received.

ADVANCE RENTALS

Advance rentals are considered ordinary income to be reported in the year received.

SECURITY DEPOSITS

The security deposit is for all practical purposes an advance rental but lessors may defer reporting if the lease provides that the deposit is the lessee's property to be treated by the lessor as a trust fund until a specified release date, and that the deposit is made to secure performance of the lessee's obligations in the lease.

If, on the other hand, the lease provides that the deposit is to be used as rent in discharge of the final payments under the lease, the deposit will be treated as an ordinary advance rental payment and would have to be reported as income in the year in which it is received.

PAYMENT FOR CANCELLATION OF LEASE

If a lessee pays a sum for the privilege of cancelling a lease it must be reported by the lessor as ordinary income in the year of receipt.

Money Spent by the Lessee Pursuant to Lease Requirements

REAL ESTATE TAXES

Technically speaking the real estate taxes paid by a lessee pursuant to lease requirement are considered ordinary income to the lessor. However, this has no effect on his taxable income because he is entitled to a deduction in a similar amount.

IMPROVEMENTS TO PROPERTY

Improvements made by the lessee to an existing building are not included in the lessor's taxable income because the lessor realizes no income when the improvement is made nor does he realize income at the termination of the lease. At the same time the rental value may subsequently increase as a result of the improvement and this, of course, would be reflected in the owner's tax report in later years.

If the lessee is required to make capital improvements to the property and it is clear that his rental has been reduced because of the improvement cost, then the improvement cost might be construed as immediately taxable income to the lessor—as rent paid in kind.

Cost of Operation and Maintenance

If the owner operates and maintains the building the "normal" cost of these items is an expense deductible in the year in which it is made. There never has been, however, a clear-cut understanding or fully applicable rule as to what constitutes "normal" operating expense item and what is a capital expenditure. This can be of major importance to the owner-lessor because operating expenses are immediately deductible whereas capital expenditures must be depreciated over their anticipated useful life.

If, for instance, an owner installs new electrical cables in an entire building, it is clearly a capital improvement, particularly if it is done at one time, under a single contract. If, on the other hand, he rewires a single room, it is clearly a matter of ordinary maintenance. In between these two extremes there are many possible variations in the extent of work which can be done. It is to the interest of the average owner of a successful building to put as much as he can into operating expense. On the other hand, it is to the interest of the government to see that these payments are deferred over a period of years. Almost every owner of income real estate has at one time or another had his tax return reviewed on this specific point.

Depreciation

It would be impossible for us to cover with any thoroughness the subject of depreciation in this chapter, so that we will confine ourselves to a review of the basic principles as reflected in the lessor-lessee relationship.

The theory of depreciation is basically simple. A physical asset loses value with the passage of time. The owner of the asset is entitled to take this loss of value into consideration when computing his taxable income.

Depreciation of any specific item can be claimed by only one of the parties—lessor or lessee. Under no circumstances can both parties make the same charge-off. On the other hand, there are a few specialized cases in which neither party—lessor or lessee—may claim depreciation.

Only the lessor may claim depreciation on buildings and improvements existing at the time when the lease was made. Depreciation of improvements to an existing building made by the lessor are depreciable by the lessor over their useful life.

Expenses of Lessor

Most of the expenses incurred by the lessor in making a lease cannot be deducted in the year in which the expense was incurred. The expense must be pro-rated or amortized over the lease term. Some of the items are:

BONUS PAYMENTS

Bonuses paid by the lessor for the purpose of renting to a new tenant are treated as part of the cost of the new lease. The lessor amortizes the payment accordingly over the lease term.

COMMISSIONS, ATTORNEY'S FEES

Brokerage commissions and attorney fees similarly must be amortized over the lease term.

OTHER EXPENSES

Alteration costs or other items of expense incurred by the landlord on a lease transaction must be amortized over the lease term.

CONSIDERATIONS OF THE LESSEE

Is the Lessee a Tenant?

Rental of space used for business or professional purposes is deductible when computing taxable income. (Residential rental is not deductible.) But it is of primary importance to establish that the lease transaction will be considered a *lease* by the Internal Revenue Service. If a lease deal isn't clear on the facts, the transaction may be held to be a conditional sale.

Whether or not the tenant is allowed a deduction for rent doesn't depend entirely on what the lease says. Although the lease may describe the tenant's payments as rent, the details of the transaction may indicate they are really installments paid on a deferred purchase of the property.

As an example, a long-term lease (for what was equivalent to the entire useful life of a property) was entered into. Under the lease terms, 90 per cent of the total lease payments were made during the first one-quarter of the lease period. In this case, the Treasury would hold that a purchase was intended, the reason being that for the remaining three-quarters of the lease term, the tenant enjoys what amounts to ownership rights in the property and the interpretation is that equitable ownership had passed to the tenant, although legal title remained in the landlord.

In an actual case, a property had been offered in the open market for $48,000 and an offer for it had been received in that amount. The owner did not accept the offer of sale but leased the property to a business tenant with payments as follows: $10,000 for the first year; $12,000 for the second year. The lease also contained an option for the lessee to buy the property for an additional $24,000 any time within 10 days after the expiration of the second lease term. Lessee paid $2,000 for the option. The tax court held that this was a sale and disallowed the rental deduction for the two years. The facts showed that the total price paid for the so-called lease arrangement was equivalent to the offer which the owner had received for the property previously.

Some of the earlier sale and leaseback transactions contained options for the lessee to repurchase the property at the lessor's depreciated price after the expiration of a given term of years. This was held in some instances to be 100 per cent financing and the total rental paid was deductible only insofar as it reflected a fair and reasonable *interest rate* on the total purchase price.

Operating Expenses—Real Estate Taxes

Under most lease agreements the tenant is required to pay for the operation and maintenance of the building. This is a normal business expense deductible in the year in which the expenses are incurred. The same warning should be sounded to tenants as to owners in regard to maintenance and expense. The Internal Revenue Service in reviewing the tenant's tax return might construe certain items of maintenance as being capital improvements, in which case the tenant would be required to amortize the cost over the anticipated useful life of the improvement or the remaining lease term, whichever is shorter. Real estate taxes paid by the tenant are usually included as part of the rent and are, of course, deductible items.

Improvements to the Property

Improvements made by the lessee to the real estate, or expenditures by the lessee for fixtures (which are not considered part of the real estate) can be amortized or depreciated over their useful life or the lease term, whichever is shorter.

Renewal Options

With respect to amortization of the cost of purchasing a lease or the cost of leasehold improvements made by the tenant in situations wherein the lease has renewal options, the new law contains some restrictive rules. While a fast write-off of cost can be obtained, deals should be cast within the framework of these rules to assure getting maximum benefits.

1. If a leasehold improvement is constructed, and the lease has a renewal option, the option period need not be taken into consideration in computing the depreciation if the remaining terms of the lease (without renewal periods) is at least 60 per cent of the life of the improvement. Thus improvement cost can be depreciated over the life of the lease (in slightly more than half the time than would be done if the useful life of the improvement were used as a depreciation base). The Treasury can, however, still insist on extending the depreciation over the renewal term if there is reasonable certainty that the lease will be renewed.

For example, a building is constructed on leased land. The building has a 35-year life. The lease has 21 years to run with a renewal option of 10 years. Since the 21-year original term is 60 per cent of the 35-year life of the building, the building cost can be written off over 21 years, unless there is a reasonable certainty that the lease will be renewed.

2. If a lease with renewal options is purchased, the cost of the lease can be written off over the original lease term if at least 75 per cent of the cost is attributable to the remaining term of the lease (without the renewal periods).

For example, a 20-year lease with two renewal options of five years each is purchased for $10,000 and it is stipulated that $8,000 is the cost of acquiring the original 20-year term. The $10,000 can be written off over the 20-year period, unless there is reasonable certainty that the lease will be renewed.

If, however, it was stipulated that only $7,000 were paid for the original 20-year term, the $10,000 cost would have to be written off over the full possible 30-year term, unless it could be shown that it is more probable that the lease will not be renewed.

Sale-Leaseback Transactions

As indicated before, the sale-leaseback transaction in order to receive full tax benefits must qualify as a clear and unequivocal transfer of real estate and a simultaneous leasing at a fair rental value. There are two types of transactions which might be challenged by the taxing authorities.

1. Transaction in which the lessee is given the right to repurchase the property at a depreciated value after a given term of years.

There is danger that this transaction would be regarded as 100 per cent financing and that the lessee would not be entitled to his full rental deduction. He would, on the other hand, be then entitled to a deduction for interest paid and also for depreciation.

2. Transaction where the sales price represents a loss to the seller and the seller claims the loss as a tax deduction.

If it could be proven that the rental being paid under the sale-leaseback transaction is less than the fair rental value, the taxing authority might disallow the loss and consider it as a sum which the lessee is paying for the leasehold. (Such loss deductions have been uniformly disallowed in sale-leaseback transactions where the initial lease term is more than 30 years.)

A typical example of how this situation might work is as follows: A owns a piece of property which currently stands him $500,000 on his books. It can be reasonably well established that the property has a net rental value of $40,000 per annum. He sells the property to B for $400,000 and leases it back for a long period of years at $32,000 per annum. He then deducts his $100,000 loss when computing his income tax return. In this situation there is no doubt but that the ruling would be that he had received $400,000 for the property and had also received a leasehold with a value of $100,000.

Drawing the Lease:
The Lawyer and the Broker

In an earlier chapter we indicated that it is more difficult to draw an airtight lease than to draw a deed, because when a basic agreement has been reached on rentals, there oftentimes ensues a series of secondary negotiations involving the lease terms or covenants.

The owner or lessor, in making a lease, is effecting a transfer of a portion of his estate or property. The tenant is assuming a legal obligation to pay rent, to maintain the property, and possibly to pay other charges. This seems a relatively simple thing but a glance at actual lease instruments will reveal that what seems to be a simple arrangement can be extremely complicated when all of the elements have been given full consideration. Beginning on page 416 is a checklist of items to be considered in preparing a lease. Although many of these apply only to long-term leases, the majority of them must be given consideration in any lease document.

STANDARDIZED LEASES

Many types of leases, particularly short-term leases on apartments, offices and stores are fairly standardized as to content. As a result, most real estate boards have forms covering leases on the types of properties which are actively traded in the area.

These forms are generally adequate and there is no necessity to draft a completely new document for each separate lease agreement. In multi-tenanted apartment houses the owner might, with his attorney's approval, adopt the standard form prepared by the local real estate board. The owner should, of course, submit the form to his attorney for approval. This might result in acceptance of the form with the elimination of some covenants and the addition of others. Once the form has been established, it can be used without legal advice by the owner or by his renting agent. The use of such approved forms by laymen is an accepted practice.

In following this practice, the agent is, in effect, merely filling in the form. Deletions from, or additions to the form by an agent should be cleared first with his principal, who in turn, should clear with his attorney.

A lessee, on the other hand, is ill-advised to sign any lease without advice of legal counsel; this applies even to standard form leases which may have clauses that would prove onerous to a particular tenant. Most standard form leases are prepared by attorneys for owners or lessors. It is natural in the preparation of such a form that the lawyer would give every consideration to his client. These leases are sometimes referred to, not without justification, as "landlord leases." In our experience, when the average prospective lessee refers one of these standard form leases to his attorney for consideration, it usually results in a modification in one or more of the covenants.

STANDARD FORMS NOT ALWAYS ADAPTABLE

As property becomes more specialized in character, or as the proposed lease term increases, there is a diminishing utility to the standard form of lease.

When we reach the long-term ground lease where the tenant agrees to improve the property, each individual case has so many variations peculiar to itself that the use of a lease form would be inadvisable. In preparing these leases, however, attorneys oftentimes find the phraseology used to cover specific situations in previous leases helpful. Many lawyers who specialize in leases maintain a regular book of lease forms. This book is divided into different sections dealing with the various features to be covered. Different wordings of clauses are carefully classified and preserved and used as the occasion may arise. As many as a dozen different forms may be found dealing with one subject, such as the disposition of buildings at the end of the lease term.

CHAIN STORE LEASE FORMS

Many large chain store organizations have their own lease forms which are designed to suit the purposes of the tenant. In these cases the landlord, if he is not expert in negotiating with chain store organizations, needs real estate as well as legal counsel before executing the lease. Many large chains have reached a point of eminence in retailing so that landlords will go out of their way to attract them. This results in lease agreements which favor the tenant. In effect, such a tenant says "These are our terms. We know they are more stringent than those you would get from some other tenant, but if you want to do business with us, this is the way it will be done."

In such a situation the owner needs to know what else he can get in the way of terms from another tenant who might not be as acceptable as the particular chain organization. There is one leading chain, for instance, which will not agree to any percentage leases. It pays what it considers a reasonable value for the space. It also has a limit on the length of the lease term which it will make. The landlord should be acquainted with the terms which competitive chain organizations are willing to make. As a matter of business judgment, he can then determine whether or not he wants the top-ranking tenant with the cumbersome lease restrictions as against a desirable, but not so highly rated, tenant willing to make better lease terms.

THE LAWYER

As we have stated before, the standard type of short-term lease prepared by an attorney may be used by owners or agents without legal consultation in each individual case.

In the cases where the lease is drawn to suit the circumstances of a special deal, the legal counsel for lessor and lessee become the major figure in the consummation of the lease transaction.

For instance, a store lease in a new shopping center might require the lessee to make structural additions to the building on a reimbursable basis; to provide interior finish at his own expense, with some structural items reimbursable; to pay his portion of any tax increase; to pay his pro-rata share of certain operating expnses, such as parking lot maintenance, and so on. In such a case, each separate item must be carefully and unequivocally set forth in the lease agreement. This requires the assistance of legal counsel on both sides.

LETTER OF INTENT—AGREEMENT TO MAKE LEASE

The conditions and covenants of the lease are oftentimes agreed to in advance in a letter of intent which is signed by both parties. The letter of the intent has the legal effect of an agreement or a contract to make a lease, and is oftentimes a necessary preliminary where the lease is going to be a complicated and involved document.

RE-NEGOTIATING THE DEAL

On occasion, difficulties arise when lawyers enter into a lease transaction. Brokers sometimes criticize an attorney for "trying to break up a deal" by "re-negotiating" where there has already been a prior understanding between the parties.

In the writer's experience over many years in the real estate business, he has seen many attempts at so-called "re-negotiations." In some cases he believes they were unwarranted, but in the majority of cases he believes that they were a proper exercise of the lawyer's function. There can be no hard and fast rules as to how a lawyer should comport himself in these situations, because there are no exact or definite limits to the lawyer's duties. Clients engage lawyers for varying purposes. For instance, the real estate operator or investor who makes a business of buying, selling, and leasing real estate uses an attorney primarily as a technician—to see that contracts, deeds, leases, etc., are airtight. Attorneys for chain store organizations are in the same position. In situations such as this, attorneys seldom would interpose their own judgment on business decisions which had been arrived at by the client.

On the other hand, attorneys are often employed as general business advisers, as well as purely legal counsel. How often have we heard expressions like "I wouldn't cross the street without consulting my lawyer." The relationship between lawyer and client sometimes becomes intensely personal. In many instances, the lawyer's knowledge of the workings of the real estate market is better than his client's.

In such cases, an attorney cannot be criticized if he participates in the negotiation on a deal. The surest way to avoid re-negotiation in these cases is to make certain that the client has brought all of the additions and covenants of the lease, particularly if there is any deviation from standard procedure, to the attention of his attorney before the parties meet for the execution of the lease agreement.

The experienced broker will see to it that all matters in dispute are ironed out before the parties meet for formal execution of the agreement. Too often, deals fall apart when what seemed to be relatively insignificant matters are left for last-minute discussion.

SPECIMEN LEASES

There are more men enabled by study than by nature.
CICERO.

Percentage Leases

PERCENTAGE STORE LEASES

(This is a typical percentage lease on a store in a central business district. It is complete, but not too lengthy.)

THIS INDENTURE OF LEASE, WITNESSETH, That ....
COMPANY (hereinafter designated as the "Lessor") has demised and leased, and does hereby demise and lease, unto ...., ...,
.... and ...., partners doing business under the firm name of .... (hereinafter designated as the "Lessee"), whose main office is at No. ...., ..., ..., the premises known as

> The store-room at No. ....
> Avenue in the .... Building in
> the City of ...., County of ....
> State of ....;

said premises to be used and occupied by said Lessee as a rental store for selling (state character of business here) and for no other purpose, for the term of eight (8) years and four (4) months, commencing on the 1st day of March, 19...., and ending on the 30th day of June, 19...., for the rental and upon the terms and conditions following:

1. The Lessee covenants and agrees to pay a rent for said premises, the sum of Twenty Thousand Dollars ($20,000) per annum in equal monthly installments of One Thousand Six Hundred and Sixty-six Dollars and Sixty-seven Cents ($1,666.67), and in addition thereto such sums as may accrue by virtue of the percentage payable upon gross sales as hereinafter more particularly provided, all said rent being payable in gold coin of the United States of America of or equal to the present standard of weight and fineness, or its equivalent in value in lawful money of the United States, as the Lessor may elect. All such sums (unless otherwise provided) are due and payable in advance on the first day of each and every calendar month during said term at the office of

said The .... Company in ...., ..., or such
other place in said city as the Lessor may in writing designate.

2. The Lessee further covenants and agrees to pay to the Lessor as
additional rental for the demised premises, over and above the minimum
rental of Twenty Thousand Dollars ($20,000) per annum, a sum equal
to ten per cent (10%) on the amount of the gross sales in excess of Two
Hundred Thousand Dollars ($200,000) made in, upon or from said prem-
ises for each annual period of said lease, the method and manner of
payment by the Lessee to the Lessor of such additional rental based upon
said gross sales being as follows:

For each and every monthly period during the term of this lease, the
Lessee shall pay to the Lessor as such additional rental on or before the
20th day of the next succeeding month, a sum of money determined by
deducting the sum of One Thousand Six Hundred and Sixty-six Dollars
and Sixty-seven Cents ($1,666.67), being the amount of the minimum
monthly rental payable hereunder for said month, from an amount equal
to ten per cent (10%) on all gross sales made in, upon or from said
demised premises during such preceding month. In the event the aggregate payments made as additional rental under the provisions of this
paragraph for and during any yearly or annual term of this lease shall,
together with the regular monthly installments of minimum monthly
rental, total an amount in excess of a sum equal to ten per cent (10%)
on the total gross business done in, upon or from said premises during
such annual or yearly period, then in that event the Lessor shall refund
and pay to the Lessee the amount of such excess when and as the same
shall be ascertained at the expiration of such yearly period. In no event,
however, shall the rental stipulated to be paid by the Lessee to the Lessor
under the provisions hereof be less than Twenty Thousand Dollars
($20,000) for any such yearly or annual period. It being further pro-
vided that a like adjustment of rental shall be made for the four (4)
month period beginning March 1, 19..., and ending June 30, 19..., and
in no event shall the rental stipulated to be paid by the Lessee hereunder
be less than Six Thousand Six Hundred and Sixty-six Dollars and Sixty-
eight Cents ($6,666.68) for such four (4) month period.

3. The term "gross sales" as herein used shall be held to include the
sales price of all merchandise of every sort whatsoever sold, and the
charges for all services performed for which charge is made by the Lessee
or by other person, persons or corporation selling merchandise or performing service of any sort in, upon or from any part of the said demised
premises, and shall include merchandise sold or services performed either
for cash or for credit, regardless of collections in the case of the latter,
but shall exclude merchandise so purchased which is returned by the
purchaser and accepted by the Lessee, and all allowances made by the
Lessee to its customers.

4. The Lessee further covenants that it will keep separate and accurate records of the gross sales covering all business done or transacted
in, upon or from said demised premises, and that it will give to the Lessor

the right at any and all reasonable times to inspect said records. Said Lessor shall be given access at any and all reasonable times to any other books or records that may be necessary to enable it to make a full and proper audit of the gross income of all business done in, upon or from said demised premises.

On or before the twentieth day of each month during the term of this lease, commencing with the second month thereof, the Lessee shall deliver to the Lessor a correct statement of the gross sales of all business done in, upon or from said demised premises during the next preceding month as shown by the Lessee's records. In addition to such monthly statements, the Lessee shall on the 1st day of February in each year during the term of this lease, and upon the expiration of the lease, render to the Lessor a certified public accountant's statement showing the total gross sales of all business done in, upon or from said demised premises for the year ending the 31st day of December preceding, or for such fractional part of a yearly period as occurs at the beginning and expiration of this lease. If the Lessor is not satisfied with any monthly, annual or other statement thus submitted, then the Lessor shall give notice to the Lessee of such dissatisfaction within thirty (30) days after receipt of the statement complained of. Unless within ten (10) days after the receipt by the Lessee of such notice of dissatisfaction, the Lessee shall satisfy the Lessor with respect to such statement thus complained of, then the Lessor shall have the privilege of having an audit made of the account books and records pertaining to the aforesaid business of the Lessee. Such audit shall be made by certified public accountants in good standing to be selected by the Lessor, which accountants shall work in conjunction with like accountants selected by the Lessee. The expense of such audit shall be borne jointly by the Lessor and the Lessee, and the Lessee shall render all possible assistance to such accountants and shall give them access to all books of accounts and other records that may be necessary to enable such accountants to make a full and complete audit of all gross income of all business done in, upon or from said demised premises.

5. The Lessee agrees to put in a new store front in said leased premises, such new front, however, and the installation thereof to be in all respects subject to the approval of the Lessor, the Lessee to submit plans and specifications for said new front to the Lessor and secure the Lessor's approval thereto before any work is commenced.

6. It is a condition of this lease that said Lessee shall not assign this lease, nor let or underlet said premises or any part thereof, nor sell or permit to be sold liquors, whether spirituous, vinous or fermented, on said premises, nor use the same or permit the same to be used for any other purpose than as above specified, nor make any alterations therein without written consent of the Lessor first had and obtained, and that all additions, fixtures, except movable trade fixtures not attached to the realty, improvements and repairs shall be made and paid for by said Lessee, and shall thereafter be the property of the Lessor. That any personal property in the demised premises shall be at risk of Lessee only,

and Lessor shall not be liable for any damages to said personal property, or to said premises, or to said Lessee, arising from bursting or leaking of water or steam pipes, or from any acts or neglect of co-tenants or other occupants of the building, or any other persons; and that the rules and regulations in regard to said building, which are attached hereto and hereby made a part of this lease, shall, during the continuance of this agreement, be in all things observed and performed by said Lessee, and Lessee's clerks and servants. Said Lessee agrees to pay for all unnecessary damage done to said rooms or building, and for all unnecessary waste of water.

The Lessee shall be responsible for all breakage or injury to plate glass in the demised premises during the term hereof, and shall carry insurance to cover such breakage or injury.

It shall be the duty of the Lessee to take care of and keep clean the sidewalk in front of said store-room and to remove all ice and snow therefrom, the Lessee agreeing to comply with all laws, ordinances and regulations of the public authorities with respect to the care of said sidewalk, and shall indemnify and hold harmless the Lessor from all loss, damage of claim arising out of Lessee's failure in this regard.

7. Said store-room having been leased for the purpose of the Lessee's conducting therein a retail store for selling (state character of business) and for no other purpose, it is understood to be a condition of this lease that said premises be used for no other purpose and that no other merchandise be sold therein, unless the written consent of the Lessor be first had thereto, and the Lessee covenants and agrees to at all times conduct and operate said store and the business thereof as a high grade establishment and in a first-class manner.

8. The Lessor shall furnish the Lessee with water and heat, but not light, free of charge, and the Lessor agrees to furnish the Lessee with whatever electric current the Lessee may use upon the demised premises, for which the Lessee shall pay the Lessor .... cents per kilowatt hour (1000 watt hours). The payment to be made by the Lessee to the Lessor for electric current shall be in addition to the rental hereinabove provided for, and shall be made immediately upon presentation of bills therefor by the Lessor, and any default on the part of the Lessee in the payment of such bills for electric current shall be deemed and treated in all respects in a similar manner as a default in rent, with all rights and remedies to the Lessor in connection therewith which are herein provided in case of a default in rent.

It is mutually understood and agreed that any default on the part of the Lessor to furnish heat, water, light, elevator service, or electric current, by reason of accidents to machinery or equipment, strikes, fire or other causes beyond the control of the Lessor, shall not entitle the Lessee to claim any damages or rebate of rent on account of such default. It is hereby further agreed that if, during the continuance of this agreement said premises shall be so injured by fire as to be rendered untenantable, the damage in so far as the same pertains to the building itself, other than the tenant's fixtures, shall be repaired by the Lessor at its own expense as speedily as possible, provided, however, that if the damage be so extensive as to be impracticable of repair within sixty (60) days, it shall be optional with either party hereto to cancel this agreement, and in case of any such cancellation the rent shall be paid to the day of such fire.

9. It is mutually covenanted and agreed that if default be made in the punctual payment of said rent or any part thereof, or in the observance or performance of any of said conditions or agreements, the Lessor may, without notice to the Lessee, and without demand for rent due, terminate the lease aforesaid, and re-enter the said premises, and remove all persons and property therefrom, using such force as may be necessary. Lessee hereby waives all demand and any and all service of notice (in writing or otherwise), prescribed by any statute or any other law whatever, of intention to re-enter, and waives all claims for damages that may be caused by the Lessor in re-entering and taking possession of the premises. It is also agreed that Lessee shall pay all costs, expenses, costs of courts and attorney's fees incurred by Lessor in making collection of said rent or in enforcing any of the provisions of this lease. If this lease shall be terminated before its expiration by reason of Lessee's default, or if the Lessee shall abandon or vacate said premises before the termination of this lease, the same may be re-let by the Lessor for such rent and upon such terms as the Lessor may see fit, and if the full rental hereinbefore named shall not thus be realized, the Lessee hereby agrees to pay all deficiency, and any expenses incurred by such re-letting. It is agreed by both parties hereto that if the said Lessee shall make an assignment under any insolvency act, or in event bankruptcy proceedings are brought against the Lessee, or a voluntary petition in bankruptcy filed by them, or in the event of any proceedings in law or equity to subject the interest of the Lessee in this lease, then this lease shall not pass, except by written consent of the Lessor, and in such event the Lessor may, at its option, terminate this lease.

10. It is understood and agreed that the Lessor shall not take advantage of any covenant or condition for the forfeiture or termination of the lease until after ten (10) days from the mailing of notice by registered mail directed to the Lessee at its principal office, No. .... St., ..., or such other place as Lessee may hereafter designate, during which period of ten (10) days, said Lessee shall have the right to pay any arrearage of rent or rectify any breach of covenant.

11. The words "Lessor" and "Lessee", as used herein, include, apply to, bind and benefit the heirs, executors, administrators, successors and assigns of the Lessor and the Lessee.

All rights and remedies of Lessor under this lease or this instrument shall be cumulative, and none shall be exclusive of any rights or remedies allowed by law.

IN WITNESS WHEREOF, the parties hereto have signed these presents in duplicate, this ...... day of ...., A. D. 19.....

(Signatures, acknowledgments, and so forth.)

Rules and Regulations

1. No sign, advertisement or notice shall be inscribed, painted or affixed on any part of the outside or inside or said building, except on the glass of the doors and windows of the room leased, and on the directory board, and then only of such color, size, style and material as shall be first specified by the lessor, in writing, endorsed on this lease. No show case shall be placed in front of said building by lessee, without the written consent of lessor endorsed on this lease. The lessor reserves the right to remove all other signs and show cases, without notice to the lessee, at the expense of the lessee. At the expiration of the term, lessee is to remove all his signs from such windows and doors.

2. Lessee shall not put up or operate any steam engine, boiler, machinery, or stove upon the premises or carry on any mechanical business on said premises, or use oil, burning fluids, camphene or kerosene for heating, warming or lighting, or anything, except gas or incandescent electric lights, without the written consent of the lessor first had and endorsed on this lease, and all stoves which may be allowed in said premises shall be placed and set up according to the city ordinances. No articles deemed extra hazardous on account of fire and no explosives shall be brought into said premises.

3. Upon the termination of this lease lessee will surrender all keys of premises and building, and give to lessor or its officer or agent, the explanation of the combination of all locks on the doors of the vaults.

4. All safes shall be carried up or into the premises at such times and in such manner as shall be specified by the lessor; the lessor shall in all cases retain the power to prescribe the proper position of such safes, and any damage done to the building by taking in or putting out a safe, or from overloading the floor with any safe, shall be paid by the tenant causing it. Furniture, boxes or other bulky articles belonging to tenants, shall be carried upon the freight elevator of the said building at hours prescribed by lessor.

5. The lessor, or its officers or agent, shall have the right to enter the premises to examine the same, or to make such repairs, alterations and additions as he or they shall deem necessary for the safety, preservation and improvement of the said premises or building; and the lessor or its officers or agent may place on the windows and bulletin boards of said premises a notice "to rent," for one month prior to the termination of this lease.

6. The premises leased shall not be used for the purpose of lodging or sleeping rooms, or for any immoral or illegal purpose.

7. The rent of an office will include occupancy of office, water in standing bowls, steam heat and elevator service; but lessor shall not be liable for any damages from the stoppage of the elevators for necessary or desirable repairs or improvements.

8. If lessee desires telegraphic or telephonic connections, the lessor will direct the electricians as to where and how the wires are to be introduced, and without such written direction endorsed on this lease, no boring or cutting for wires will be permitted.

9. If lessee desires awnings or shades over and outside of the windows, they must be of such shape, color, material and make as prescribed by the lessor in writing on this lease. Awnings must not be placed without first obtaining permission from lessor in writing.

10. The lessor reserves the right to make such other and further reasonable rules and regulations as in its judgment may from time to time be needful for the safety, care and cleanliness of the building and for the preservation of good order therein.

11. It is understood and agreed between the lessee and the lessor, that no assent or consent to changes in or waiver of any part of this indenture, in spirit or letter, shall be deemed or taken as made except the same be done in writing and endorsed thereon by the lessor.

12. The lessee shall not allow anything to be placed against or near the glass in the partitions between the premises leased and the halls or corridors of the building which shall diminish the light in the halls or corridors.

13. The lessor reserves the right to enter upon any premises vacated by the lessee before the termination of lease to make repairs and alterations.

PERCENTAGE LEASE EVOLVED IN CHICAGO

(The following percentage lease was drafted by a Chicago broker for the Institute of Real Estate Brokers.)

THIS INDENTURE, made in triplicate this ...... day of ...., 19...., by and between BLANK CORPORATION, an Illinois Corporation, with offices in the City of Chicago, Illinois, party of the first part, sometimes hereinafter called the Lessor, and LESSEE, INC., an Illinois Corporation, party of the second part, sometimes hereinafter called the Tenant;

WITNESSETH:

2. Description of property. The Lessor is the owner of the following described property, situated in the City of Middleton, County of Center, Illinois:

(Legal description.)

3. Demise. The Lessor has agreed to let and hereby does let, and said Tenant has agreed to take and hereby does take, for a term of (10) years, commencing on the (First) day of (May), 19.., and terminating on the (Thirtieth) day of (April), 19.., at twelve o'clock midnight, the first floor and part of the basement thereunder in a building to be erected by the Lessor upon the westerly portion of the above described premises known as No. XX First Street, immediately south of the First Street building line of said premises, and upon so much more of said premises as Lessor may elect, in said City of Middleton, Illinois, which first floor (hereinafter referred to as the "store") and basement shall conform to the following specifications:

4. Description of premises. Said store shall front on First Street, with an inside width, east and west, of approximately twenty-one feet four inches (21' 4") and an inside depth, north and south, of approximately one hundred ninety feet (190'), together with an area contiguous thereto on the east and fronting on Back Street described as follows: Beginning at a point approximately twenty-one feet four inches (21' 4") east of the premises hereinabove described on the Back Street front thereof and running north approximately forty-one feet nine inches (41' 9"); thence east approximately eleven feet five inches (11' 5"); thence south approximately thirteen feet (13'); thence west approximately two feet seven inches (2' 7"); thence south approximately twenty-eight feet nine inches (28' 9"); thence west approximately eight feet nine inches (8' 9") to the place of beginning, as shown more particularly in the accompanying plan, marked "Exhibit A" and made a part hereof; together, also, with basement space wholly or partly under said store, commencing approximately sixty-eight feet (68') south of the First Street lot line and measuring approximately eighteen feet (18') wide, east and west, and approximately eighty-three feet nine inches (83' 9") deep, north and south, inclusive of a utility room in the basement for heating and ventilating equipment, (as shown on the accompanying diagram, marked "Exhibit B" and made a part hereof).

5. Erection of building. The Lessor hereby covenants to erect upon the westerly portion of the premises first hereinabove described, immediately south of the First Street building line of said premises, known as No. XX First Street, and upon so much more of said premises as Lessor may elect, a concrete fireproof building, consisting of at least one story and basement, conforming to the specifications hereinabove set out and to the terms of a memorandum signed by the parties hereto, bearing even date herewith and made a part hereof.

6. Lessor's right to alter premises. It is understood and agreed that the Lessor may desire during the term of this Lease to install elevators or stairways, or both, on that portion of the demised premises described as follows:

Beginning at the southwest corner of that part of the premises fronting on Back Street and running east approximately thirty feet one inch (30' 1"); thence north approximately twenty-three feet five inches (23' 5"); thence west approximately thirty feet one inch (30' 1"); thence south approximately twenty-three feet five inches (23' 5"), containing approximately seven hundred five (705) square feet, as shown more particularly by the dotted lines on the accompanying plan, marked "Exhibit A", and made a part hereof.

In the event that the Lessor shall desire to erect such elevators and/or stairways and gives notice to the Tenant of its intention so to do, this Lessee shall, at the expiration of sixty (60) days from the giving of such notice, terminate as to the portion of the premises described in this paragraph, and the Lessor may repossess itself thereof, with or without process of law, and the Tenant agrees to surrender possession of and to vacate and relinquish that part of the premises herein referred to. In the event of the construction of said elevators and/or stairways, as aforesaid, the Lessor, at its expense, shall construct walls so as to enclose the remaining area leased by the Tenant, which walls shall conform to the specifications for first floor walls as set out in memorandum hereinabove referred to, signed by the parties hereto and bearing even date herewith. The vacation and relinquishment of the premises hereinabove described by the Tenant by reason of the right hereinabove reserved by the Lessor to cancel the Lease in respect thereto shall not in any manner affect the amount of rent agreed to be paid by Tenant to the Lessor under the terms of this indenture, nor shall any of the other terms of this indenture be affected thereby.

7. **Maintenance of equipment by tenant.** Tenant covenants and agrees that all operation, upkeep, and repairs of the heating plant and air-conditioning equipment, and fuel and cost of operation thereof, will be at its own cost and expense and under its complete control.

8. **No change of name.** Tenant agrees, upon becoming entitled to possession of the demised premises, as herein provided, to promptly install and thereafter operate and maintain through the term of this Lease a women's retail ready-to-wear store which is comparable to that conducted or maintained by Tenant at other locations throughout the United States in its "Lessee" stores, so far as the demised premises are adaptable therefor, and at which store Tenant will offer for sale a complete line of all grades of women's ready-to-wear garments sold by Tenant and known as "Lessee." Tenant agrees to operate its store in the demised premises under the trade name "Lessee," provided that if at any time Tenant shall be prohibited or prevented from using said trade name by causes beyond its control, then the Tenant may operate such store under such other trade name as a majority of the other stores of Tenant in the metropolitan district are operated at which what are now known as "Lessee" are being sold. It is further agreed that if in two successive years falling within the term of this Lease, commencing on (May 1st) and ending on the next succeeding (30th) of (April), the gross sales and business transacted by Tenant and Tenant's licensees, if any, shall be less than $154,300 in each of such two successive years, then Tenant may, upon the expiration of such two successive years, change its trade name "Lessee" to the trade name "Second" or to any other name which Tenant may select, provided said name is satisfactory to Lessor.

9.   Rental.   The said Tenant covenants and agrees to pay to the Lessor as rent for said premises a sum equal to seven per cent on all sales and business transacted (as hereinafter defined) on the premises, it being understood and agreed, however, that Tenant shall pay a minimum annual rental during the term of this Lease of the sum of ($10,800.00) payable ($900.00) Dollars monthly in advance, on the first of each and every month during said term. Said percentage rental over and above the minimum rental is to be paid on or before the (20th) day of (January) in each year for the preceding calendar year or fraction thereof. The percentage rental on sales for a fractional part of a calendar year, over and above said minimum rental, shall be computed on a pro rata basis by treating the minimum rental for such fractional part of said year at the rate of ($900.00) Dollars per month, and any percentage rental as to such fractional part of a year, over said minimum rental, shall be payable on or before the (20th) day following the end of such fractional period.

10.   Definition of "sales."   The term "sales and business transacted" means the selling price of all goods, wares and merchandise sold in, upon or from any part of the demised premises by the Tenant or any other person, firm or corporation, and the charges for all services performed, for which charge is made by the Tenant or by any other person or corporation selling merchandise or performing services of any sort in, upon or from any part of the demised premises, and shall include sales and charges for cash or credit, regardless of collections in the case of the latter, but shall exclude returns and refunds and the amount of any sales tax or occupational tax or similar tax or imposition whatsoever and howsoever imposed for such sales and charges, where such sales tax, occupational tax or similar tax or imposition is billed to the purchaser as a separate item. Where garments are sold by Tenant which require alterations, the cost of such alterations shall not be included in "sales and business transacted" if such alterations are made by a person not in the regular employ of the Tenant where the charge to the customer is paid over in full to such person, without deduction of any amount directly or indirectly.

11.   Accounting.   Tenant covenants and agrees to keep at its principal office in the City of Middleton, Illinois, proper books of account and to furnish a true and accurate statement monthly of the total daily sales and business transacted on said premises (returns and refunds excluded) and to give the Lessor access to the books and records of the business transacted in the store, during reasonable hours. The Lessor covenants and agrees that said information shall be strictly confidential.

12.   Additional charges.   The Tenant covenants and agrees to pay for all water, gas, electricity consumed on the premises. In the event that the Lessor at any time during the term of this Lease shall sell electric current controlled by a Master Meter, or through an individual electric plant, for the purpose of serving tenants of the Lessor, the Tenant agrees to buy current from the Lessor, provided that at no time shall the Lessor charge the Tenant more for said current than the price at which the Tenant can buy the same from the public utility company.

13. Discontinuance of electric current. It is further understood and agreed that in case Lessor is furnishing electric current to Tenant no charge for current shall be for less than fifty cents (50¢) per month per meter, irrespective of the number of lights connected. The charge for electric current shall be due and payable on or before the tenth day of the month following the period for which the charge is made, and in case the Tenant shall fail to make payment for electric current, as in this clause provided, and such failure to make payment shall continue for five (5) days after giving of written notice by Lessor to Tenant in the manner hereinafter provided for the giving of notices, the Lessor may, without notice to the Tenant, shut off and discontinue the supply of electric current for lighting and power in said premises, and such act of shutting off the electric current shall not be held to be or pleaded as an eviction or as a disturbance in any manner whatever of the Tenant's possession or relieve the Tenant from the payment of rent when due, or vary or change any other provision of this Lease, or render the Lessor liable for any damages whatsoever. In case, after Lessor shall have discontinued furnishing of electric current for failure to pay the charges therefor as above provided, Tenant shall cure such default in payment, Lessor agrees promptly to again furnish electric current to Tenant, subject to the provisions of this paragraph. It is mutually agreed that the Lessor, upon giving thirty (30) days' prior notice of its intention so to do, may discontinue supplying electric current to the Tenant, without in any way affecting the other provisions of this Lease, and the Lessor agrees that before it shall discontinue supplying electric current to the Tenant, it will provide for the Tenant another source of supply of electric current and will connect the demised premises with such other source of supply.

14. Subordination of lease. Tenant covenants and agrees to execute any instrument or instruments permitting a mortgage or trust deed to be placed on the premises first hereinabove described, or any part thereof of which the demised premises are a part, as security for any indebtedness of up to 60% of the then value of the premises covered by said trust deed or mortgage, and subordinating this Lease to said trust deed or mortgage.

15. Completion of premises. In the event the said demised premises shall be completed and notice of completion given to Tenant by Lessor prior to (April 1st), 19 , then the Tenant agrees to take possession of the same upon completion thereof and receipt of notice of completion by Tenant from Lessor and start the payment of rent on (May 1st), 19.., at the minimum rate of $900.00) Dollars per month plus percentage of sales in the manner above provided. In the event that said demised premises shall be completed and notice of completion given subsequent to (April 15th), 19.., then the rent stipulated to be paid hereunder by the Tenant shall proportionately abate until eighteen (18) days after the date of completion of said premises and giving of said notice of completion, or the opening of said store, whichever is earlier, provided, however, that in no event shall the Tenant be obliged to pay rent for any period prior to (May 1st), 19... In the event said premises shall not be completed on or before the (1st) day of (July), 19.., then the Tenant shall have the option for a period of fifteen (15) days after (July 1st), 19.., of cancelling this Lease, upon written notice to Lessor. In the event of such cancellation, no further liability shall accrue to either party by reason hereof. For the purpose of this paragraph, the demised premises shall be deemed to be completed when the Lessor shall have (1) notified the Tenant of all leases made by it to any part of the premises first hereinabove described under the terms of which it is contemplated that the tenants shall take possession on or before (May 1st), 19.., and (2) mailed to the Tenant, at the address hereinafter given for the mailing of notices, a certificate by JOHN DOE, the architect in charge of the erection of the demised premises, to the effect that the said demised premises have been substantially completed pursuant to the plans and specifications as set out in memorandum signed by the parties hereto under even date herewith (except as the same may have been modified by agreement of the parties) and a further certificate from the same party to the effect that the First Street fronts of all other stores leased by the tenants referred to in (1) hereof have been substantially completed.

16. Damage by fire, etc. It is further covenanted and agreed between the parties to these presents that in case the demised premises shall be partially destroyed by fire or by the elements, the same shall be repaired as speedily as possible at the expense of the Lessor, and a just and proportionate part of the rent is to be abated until the premises have been put in complete repair. If, however, the said premises are totally destroyed by fire or by the elements at any time prior to twelve months from the end of the term, the rent shall be paid to the time of such destruction, and the Lessor is immediately to construct a building upon the same location and shall give the Tenant, as soon as it reasonably can do so, as much floor space and frontage therein as is contained in said demised premises, and, upon such completing and furnishing Tenant with said space, the rent herein set out shall commence and accrue thereafter until the termination of this Lease; provided, however, that if said demised premises be substantially destroyed by fire, or the elements, during the last twelve months of the term, then and in that event this Lease shall thereupon be terminated, and from that time on be null and void, and rent shall be paid by Tenant up to the date of such termination.

17. Condemnation of premises. It is mutually covenanted, agreed and understood that if at any time during the term of this lease the premises hereby demised shall be condemned or declared unsafe or shall be ordered or directed to be repaired or rebuilt by the Building authorities or inspectors or other duly constituted authorities, the said Lessor will, at its own expense and without delay, make such changes, alterations, and repairs as may be required or directed by the said duly constituted authorities except such repairs to the interior as Tenant has herein undertaken; provided, however, that the Lessor shall be under no obligation to make such changes, alterations or repairs until it shall have had an opportunity, if it so desires, to contest the validity of any such condemnation, order or direction, and in such event the Lessor shall not be required to make any such changes, alterations or repairs until such condemnation, order or direction has been finally sustained. If the Tenant shall be prevented from using the demised premises by reason of any action on the part of the duly constituted authorities, which action is not caused by the acts of the Tenant, in such event the rent herein provided shall abate during such period.

18. Repairs. The Tenant covenants to keep in repair the interior of said premises. The Lessor covenants to keep in repair the exterior parts of the building, including roof, walls, conductor pipes and sidewalks. Tenant further agrees, whenever necessary, to remove snow and ice from the sidewalk in front of the demised premises and to remove snow and ice from that portion of the roof above the store, so long as it is or shall remain a one-story building, unless the said roof is occupied by or rented out to other tenants.

19. Lessor's right to examine premises. The Tenant agrees to allow the Lessor and its agents free access to the demised premises during reasonable hours for the purpose of examining the same to ascertain if the same are in good repair, to make reasonable repairs or alterations which the Lessor is obligated to make, and to exhibit the same to prospective purchasers and to prospective tenants, provided that the use of demised premises by Tenant is not unreasonably interfered with. In the event that the Lessor at any time while this Lease is in force shall increase the height of the building of which the demised premises are a part and by reason thereof erects scaffolding or any other obstructions upon the sidewalk in front of that portion of Lessor's building occupied by the Tenant in such manner as to interfere with full and complete access to the First Street entrance of the demised premises, the Tenant shall receive a credit upon the rent herein reserved equal to the excess, if any, of the prorated minimum monthly rental for the period during which such obstruction continues over seven per cent (7%) of the sales (as herein defined) for such period.

20. Warranty to tenant. Lessor hereby covenants that it has full authority to execute this Lease, and that it is the sole owner of the premises, and further agrees that Tenant, upon paying said rent and performing the covenants of this Lease, shall and may quietly have, hold and enjoy the demised premises during the term hereof.

21. Removal of trade fixtures. Any and all trade fixtures of whatsoever name and nature that Tenant may have put in the premises at its own expense, shall be removable by it at the termination of this Lease, or any renewal thereof, provided the same can be removed without injury to the premises.

22. Assigning and subletting. The Tenant shall not have the right to assign the within Lease, nor sublet the demised premises, in whole or in part, without first obtaining the written consent of the Lessor. The Lessor covenants and agrees that it will not unreasonably or arbitrarily withhold such consent. Nothing in this paragraph contained, however, shall prevent the sale on the demised premises of any merchandise which Tenant has the right to sell thereon under the terms of this Lease (with the exception of ladies' dresses, suits and coats which shall be sold by Tenant only) through licensees or concessionaires who conduct their business under Tenant's trade name (and the sales and business of such licensees and concessionaires shall be part of the sales above referred to).

23. Default, bankruptcy, etc. If the Tenant shall make any assignment for the benefit of creditors or shall be adjudged a bankrupt, or if a receiver is appointed for the Tenant or its assets or of Tenant's interest under this Lease, and if the appointment of such Receiver is not vacated within five (5) days, or if a voluntary petition is filed under Section 77B of the Bankruptcy Act by the Tenant, or if an involuntary petition is filed under Section 77B of the Bankruptcy Act against the Tenant and if said petition is approved by the Court in which filed, then and in any such event, the Lessor may, upon giving the Tenant ten (10) days' notice of such election, either terminate Tenant's right to possession of the demised premises or terminate this Lease as in the case of a violation by the Tenant of any of the terms, covenants or conditions of this Lease, as hereinafter provided.

24. No partnership created. Notwithstanding the agreement herein contained for the payment by the Tenant of additional rent based upon a percentage of sales, as above provided, it is expressly understood that the Lessor shall not be construed or held to be a partner or associate of the Tenant in the conduct of its business, it being expressly understood and agreed that the relationship between the parties hereto is and shall at all times remain that of Landlord and Tenant.

25. Liability insurance. The Tenant covenants and agrees to protect and save harmless the Lessor of and from any and all claims for injuries to person or property by reason of any accident or happening upon the demised premises. The Tenant agrees to carry public liability insurance, protecting both the Lessor and/or its Agent and Tenant, and will at the request of Lessor, furnish certificate showing such insurance in force.

26. Plate glass—tenant's risk. The Tenant covenants and agrees at its own expense to replace all plate glass and other glass in the demised premises which may become damaged or broken.

27. Restriction of use. The demised premises are to be used only for the purpose of displaying and selling at retail women's outer and intimate wearing apparel, skirts, sweaters, blouses, purses and costume jewelry, except shoes and hosiery. Without in any wise limiting the effect of the foregoing, the Tenant specifically agrees that throughout the term of this Lease and until the possession of the demised premises shall have been surrendered to the Lessor, the demised premises shall not be used or operated, in whole or in part, as or for a variety store of the type which at the present time is commonly known as a (Dollar) store, or the like, nor shall said premises be used during the terms of the Lease as a (Women's Shoes) retail store.

28. Restriction of conduct. The Tenant agrees not to permit any unlawful or immoral practice to be committed or carried on on the demised premises and not to make or permit any use of the premises other than hereinbefore specified and not to allow said premises to be used for any purpose which will increase the rate of insurance thereon and not to keep or use or permit to be kept or used on said premises or on any place contiguous thereto any inflammable fluid or explosive without the written permission of Lessor first had and obtained and not to use or permit the use of the premises for any purpose whatsoever that will injure the reputation of the premises or of the building of which they form a part, or which will disturb the tenants of said building or the inhabitants of the neighborhood. Tenant shall have the right to keep in a suitable place on said premises in a closed container not to exceed one-half gallon of cleaning fluid.

29. Compliance with laws. The Tenant covenants and agrees to comply with all laws, ordinances, rules and regulations of any governmental authority, provided, however, that the Tenant shall be under no obligation to make any structural changes in said building.

30. Alterations by tenant. The Tenant shall have the right to make such alterations and changes in such parts of the premises occupied by it and which are not of a structural nature as it finds necessary for its purpose at its own expense, provided that such alterations will not injure the premises and are made in a first-class workmanlike manner and will comply with all laws, rules and regulations of any governmental authority or the Board of Fire Insurance Underwriters.

31. Lessor not liable for defects. Lessor shall not be liable to Tenant for any damage or injury to it or its property occasioned by wind or by any defect of plumbing, electric wiring or of insulation thereof, gas pipes or steam pipes, or from broken stairs or from the backing up of any sewer pipe or from the bursting, leaking or running of any tank, tub, washstand, water closet or waste pipe, drain or any other pipe or tank in, upon or about said demised premises, nor from the escape of steam or hot water from any boiler, or radiator, nor for any such damage or injury occasioned by water, snow or ice being upon or coming through the roof, stairs, walks or any other place upon or near said demised premises, nor for any such damage or injury done or occasioned by the falling of any fixture, plaster or stucco, nor for any such damage or injury caused by the act, omission or negligence of co-tenants or of other persons, occupants of the same building or of adjacent buildings or contiguous buildings or owners of adjacent or contiguous property, all claims as against the Lessor for any such damage or injury being hereby expressly waived by Tenant.

32. Violations of lease. In the event the Tenant violates any of

the terms, covenants or conditions in this Lease on its part to be performed and such violation continues for fifteen (15) days after written
notice to Tenant in the case of non-payment of rent, or thirty (30) days
in the case of any other violation, after written notice to the Tenant, then
and in any such case the Tenant's right to possession of the demised
premises shall thereupon terminate if the Lessor so elects, but not otherwise, upon Lessor giving Tenant ten (10) days' notice of such election,
and the mere retention of possession thereafter by Tenant, shall constitute a forcible detainer of said premises, or, in any such event, if the
Lessor so elects, but not otherwise, this Lease shall terminate upon
Lessor giving Tenant ten (10) days' notice of such election, and in the
event of such termination of this Lease, the above-mentioned term shall
cease at the expiration of said ten (10) days' notice, in the same manner
and to the same effect as if that were the expiration of the original term
of this Lease, and the Tenant hereby expressly waives any provision of
law now in force or which may hereafter be enacted giving the Tenant
the right under any condition after default to the redemption and
repossession of the leased premises or any part thereof. In the event
of the termination of Tenant's right of possession, as aforesaid, other
than if this Lease is terminated, Tenant agrees to immediately surrender possession of the demised premises at the expiration of said ten
(10) days' notice of Lessor's election to terminate Tenant's right to
possession without any notice to quit or demand for possession of the
demised premises whatsoever, and hereby grants Lessor full and free
entrance to, into or upon said premises or any part thereof to take possession thereof with or without process of law and to expel and remove
Tenant or any other person occupying said premises or any part thereof,
and Lessor may repossess itself of said premises as of its former estate,
but said entry of said premises shall not constitute a trespass or forcible
entry or detainer, nor shall it cause a forfeiture of rents due by virtue
hereof nor a waiver of any covenant, agreement or promise in this
Lease contained to be performed by Tenant. If Tenant's right to possession of said premises shall be terminated as aforesaid, said premises
or any part thereof may be re-let by Lessor for the account and benefit
of Tenant for such rent, and upon such terms and to such person or
persons and for such period or periods as may seem fit to Lessor, but
Lessor shall not be required to accept nor receive any tenant offered
by Tenant, nor do any act whatsoever nor exercise any diligence whatsoever in or about the procuring of any occupant or tenant to mitigate
the damage of Tenant or otherwise, Tenant hereby waiving the use of
any care or diligence by Lessor in the re-letting; and if a sufficient sum
shall not be received from such re-letting to satisfy the rent reserved in
this Lease, after paying the expenses of re-letting and collection, including commissions to agents, Tenant agrees to pay and satisfy all
such deficiency; but the acceptance of a tenant by Lessor, in place of
Tenant, shall not operate as a cancellation of this Lease, nor to release
Tenant from the performance of any covenant, promise or agreement
herein contained, and the performance of any substitute tenant by the

payment of rent, or otherwise, shall constitute only satisfaction pro tanto of the obligations of Tenant arising hereunder.

33. Exclusives. Lessor covenants and agrees that so long as this Lease shall be in force the Lessor will not operate or use or permit the operation or use of the premises first hereinabove described, or of any building thereon, except the demised premises, as or for a retail women's ready-to-wear store, and will not operate or use or permit the operation or use of such premises first hereinabove described, with the exception of the demised premises and the easterly portion of the premises first hereinabove described now under lease to A. Store, for the sale of women's dresses, coats, suits and skirts, sweaters, blouses, and costume jewelry and intimate wearing apparel (which shall not include shoes and hosiery); provided, however, that no such prohibited operation or use of the premises first hereinabove described, or any building thereon, shall constitute a breach of the foregoing covenant until written notice of such prohibited operation or use is given by Tenant to Lessor, and until the Lessor has had a reasonable time thereafter within which to bring about a termination of such prohibited operation or use, Lessor agreeing that upon such notice, it will promptly take proper steps to remedy said prohibited operation; and provided further that the Tenant hereby acknowledges that it is fully informed that the Lessor is negotiating for a lease of part of the premises first hereinabove described to Second Store, Inc., under a lease which permits said Second Store, Inc., to conduct upon said premises a women's shoe store for the sale of women's shoes and such accessories as are commonly included in other stores now operated by Second Store, Inc., and Tenant further acknowledges that it is fully informed that the Lessor has entered into a lease with A. Store, of the premises immediately east and adjoining the store proposed to be leased to Second Store, Inc., which lease permits said A. Store to conduct upon said premises a variety store of the type which is at the present time commonly known as (A Dollar Store), and Tenant agrees that the Lessor may at any time operate or use or permit the operation or use of the premises first hereinabove described, or any building thereon, except the demised premises, as or for such a variety store of the type which is at present time commonly known as (A Dollar Store), or for a store for the sale of ladies' shoes and accessories.

34. Proper notices. All notices required under this Lease shall be deemed to be properly served if sent by Registered Mail to the last address previously furnished by the parties hereto. Until hereafter changed by the parties by notice in writing, notices shall be sent to the Lessor at (.............), (.............), (.............), and to the Tenant at (.............), (.............), (...........). Date of service of such notice shall be the date such notice is deposited in a post office of the United States Post Office Department.

35. Installation of fixtures. The Tenant may commence to install its fixtures and merchandise in the premises before the completion of the building, provided such installation will not unreasonably interfere with the progress of the work.

36. Surrender of premises. The Tenant agrees to surrender the premises at the end of the term, or at any other time, as herein provided, in good condition and repair, ordinary wear and tear excepted.

IN WITNESS WHEREOF, the Lessor has executed this instrument by its President and Secretary thereunto duly authorized, and has affixed hereto its corporate seal, and the Tenant has executed this instrument by its President and Secretary thereunto duly authorized, and has affixed hereto its corporate seal, the day and year first above written.

(Signatures, acknowledgments, and so forth.)

PERCENTAGE LEASE USED IN KNOXVILLE

(This percentage lease was devised by the Brownlow Realty Organization of Knoxville, Tenn. realtors more than 20 years ago. It is included here to show that the substantiative matters in lease agreements have changed little since that date.)

THIS INDENTURE, made this . . . ., 19. . . ., between . . . ., agent for (Name of Lessor here), of first part, hereinafter referred to as "Lessor", and (Name of Lessee here), of the second part, hereinafter referred to as "Lessee",

WITNESSETH, That Lessor, for and in consideration of the rents, covenants and agreements of Lessee hereinafter contained, hath let, demised and leased and doth hereby let, demise and lease unto Lessee those certain premises described as follows:
(Description of premises here)
to be used for the purposes of (Nature of occupancy here) and no other.

TO HAVE AND TO HOLD the said demised premises to Lessee for and during the term of (Term of years here) from and after 12:01 a.m., (Date beginning) . . . ., 19. . . ., yielding and paying therefor to Lessor,
(Annual rental here)
to be paid in equal monthly installments on the first day of each month in advance during the term of this lease.

PROVIDED ALWAYS, and these presents are upon the following express conditions:

1. If the rent hereby reserved, or any part thereof, shall be and remain unpaid and in arrears for the space of ten days after any of the times when the same becomes due and payable, as herein provided, then at the option of Lessor this lease shall terminate forthwith.

2. Lessee or any court or officer thereof or any receiver in bankruptcy shall not assign or transfer this lease or any part thereof or interest therein, or sublet said premises or any part thereof, without the consent in writing of Lessor, and will always remain liable for any default of any such assignee, transferee or sub-tenant, and will at the end of said term quietly surrender said premises to Lessor in as good physical condition as said premises are now in, ordinary wear and tear and damage by fire and the elements excluded, except as may be elsewhere herein otherwise provided.

3. Lessee shall immediately make good any injury or breakage done by him or his agents, employees or visitors, or any damage caused by the overflow of water, steam or gas resulting from the negligence of him or his agents, employees or visitors. He agrees that prior to the date of commencement of this lease and prior to his taking possession of said leased premises he will thoroughly inspect the glass therein and report immediately any that may be broken or cracked, to be replaced by Lessor with sound glass. Thereafter Lessee shall immediately replace any glass that may be broken or cracked by any cause whatsoever, other than fire, and Lessee shall pay for the unstopping of any sewer line or plumbing fixture unless the stoppage be reported to Lessor within two days of Lessee taking possession of the within leased premises. If Lessee is already a tenant of the leased premises, then the liability of replacing glass and unstopping sewer lines and plumbing fixtures devolves solely upon Lessee.

4. If at any time the leased premises, or the building of which the leased premises are a component part, should be damaged by fire, or other major casualty not the fault of the Lessee, and if the cost of repairing the damage should not exceed 20% of the value of the improvements of the premises herein leased, or the building of which the within leased premises are a component part, then Lessor shall as soon as practicable repair the damage caused by said fire or other casualty. If, however, the damage should exceed 20% of the value of the improvements of the premises herein leased, or the building of which the within leased premises are a component part, then Lessor shall have the option of either restoring said premises as set out above or terminating this lease as of the date of said fire or other casualty. If the damage should render the leased premises uninhabitable the rental from the date of said fire, or other major casualty not the fault of Lessee, to the date of the completion of the restoration of the premises shall be abated, such abatement being figured on a pro rata basis of the rentals herein provided for.

5. Unless hereinafter provided to the contrary, Lessor shall repair as promptly as possible any defects in the roof, foundations and outer walls not caused by the negligence of Lessee, his employees or visitors, but in no event shall Lessor be liable for any damage to property or person from any water, gas, smoke or electricity which may leak into or flow from any part of said premises, or from the pipes or plumbing works of same.

6. If said leased premises are now warmed from a central heating plant at the expense of Lessor, then Lessor shall furnish heat in the said leased premises in such a degree as it is furnished other tenants in the same building, but in as much as no additional rent is charged for such heat, Lessor shall not be liable for any failure to supply the same not due to gross negligence on his part.

7. Lessor reserves the right to require Lessee to remove any exterior sign from said leased premises, which in the judgment of Lessor may be objectionable, and Lessee hereby assumes full responsibility for any damage to person or property that may be caused by the displacement of any sign used by or affixed to the said leased premises by him.

8. Lessee shall not do, nor permit to be done, on the said premises anything which will increase the rate of fire insurance on said premises or its contents, or conflict with any municipal ordinance or state or Federal law or with any rules of the government of the City of Knoxville.

9. Lessor shall have the right to enter said leased premises to examine same or to make such alterations or repairs as may be necessary, and may, during the last sixty day period of this lease, display in a prominent position (in the front of the show window if the premises contain a show window) a "For Rent" card not to exceed 30x24 inches in size. Lessor reserves the right to place on the exterior of the leased premises above the first floor ceiling level, a blue and white enamel agency sign, not to exceed 8x30 inches, reading "J. B. & W. G. Brownlow, Agents for This Building".

10. Should Lessee occupy said premises after the termination of this lease, such tenancy shall in no event be from year to year, but shall be at the will of Lessor.

11. Lessee shall pay for all water, gas, heat and electricity used on said leased premises unless otherwise expressly stated herein.

12. In case the said premises be deserted or if default be made in the payment of the rent (and Lessor by receiving partial payment of rent in arrears, does not thereby waive the right of forfeiture for non-payment of rent or any part thereof) at the time or times specified herein, or if default be made in the performance of any of the covenants and agreements or conditions herein contained, then Lessor shall have the right as agent of Lessee to enter said premises, either by force or otherwise, without being liable for any prosecution or claim therefor, and to re-let said premises as the agent of Lessee and to receive the rent therefor, and to apply the same to the payment of the rent due by these presents, holding Lessee liable for any deficiency; or, at the option of Lessor upon default as aforesaid, this lease shall become terminated in the same manner and with the same effect as if that were the expiration of the original term of said lease, and Lessor is hereby authorized to re-enter said premises, either by force or otherwise, and dispossess and remove therefrom Lessee or other occupants and their effects, without being liable to any prosecution or claim therefor, and to hold the same as if this lease had not been made, Lessee hereby expressly waiving the service of legal notice of intention to re-enter or of instituting legal proceedings to that end.

13. It is agreed by the landlord, Lessee and agent that the rents herein mentioned shall be paid through the real estate agency of J. B. & W. G. Brownlow which shall retain a 5% commission as its agency fee on all rentals accruing under this lease. It is understood that, with the exception of this paragraph, J. B. & W. G. Brownlow is acting solely in the capacity as agent for the landlord to whom Lessee must look as regards all covenants, agreements and warranties herein contained, and that J. B. & W. G. Brownlow shall never be liable to Lessee as regards any matter which may arise by virtue of this lease. It is also agreed by all parties hereto, that if Lessee, his successors in interest, or any one from whom Lessee may subsequently secure possession of said leased premises, or any part thereof, should continue in said leased premises beyond the expiration of this lease by virtue of any agreement hereinafter made with the landlord, or his successor in interest, then this paragraph shall be embodied in said agreement. Nothing in this paragraph entails any obligation upon Lessee relative to those matters pertaining solely to the relationship between the landlord and J. B. & W. G. Brownlow.

14. It is agreed and made a part consideration for this lease that all electrical wiring, outlets, light fixtures and reflectors and all linoleum cemented to (or over felt cemented to) the floors of the premises herein leased, shall, upon their, or its, installation become a part of the real estate and the property of the landlord.

15. Wherever Lessor and Lessee are herein referred to such reference shall be construed as applying to their respective successors in interest and in the singular or plural number and in the masculine, feminine or neuter gender, whichever is properly applicable.

16. Failure of either party to exercise any right or privilege herein conveyed or retained at the time or times that such right or privilege may be exercised shall not be construed as a waiver of the exercise of such right or privilege at some subsequent date or of any other right or privilege herein contained.

17. Lessee agrees to keep the leased premises opened for business on such days and during such hours as may prevail in Knoxville for the conduct of Lessee's type of business.

18. Lessee agrees to keep up all repairs at his own expense except those which elsewhere herein are specifically mentioned to be made by Lessor.

19. Whenever either party desires to give any notice to the other party hereto, it shall be considered as legally given if sent by U. S. registered mail to the last known address of the recipient.

20. Notice is hereby given to the public that Lessor shall never be liable for any claims of mechanics, journeymen, supplymen or of any one whomsoever, which may arise because of Lessee's tenancy of the property herein leased and Lessee binds himself to save Lessor harmless from any claims which may arise because of said tenancy. Lessee also agrees that if any suit should be threatened or filed against Lessor because of Lessee's said tenancy, Lessee will pay the reasonable attorney's fees which may be thus incurred by Lessor.

21. Lessor covenants to keep Lessee, as tenant, in quiet possession of the leased premises during the term of this lease, provided Lessee shall pay the rent and keep and perform the covenants and agreements herein provided.

22. In addition to the rentals mentioned on the first page hereof, lessee shall on or before the 10th day of each month, beginning with the 10th day of April, 19.., and ending with the 10th day of July, 19.., certify to lessor over the signature of a responsible officer of lessee, the amount of gross sales of both merchandise and services made during the preceding calendar month by lessee, its sub-tenants and concessionaires in and from the said leased premises. The term "gross sales" shall not include any transfers, exchanges or sales taxes paid by lessee's customers. In addition to the other considerations mentioned herein, lessee shall pay to lessor, when the aforesaid certificate of monthly sales is made to lessor, a sum of money equivalent to 12% of all gross sales made by lessee as described above, in excess of $5,000 during the preceding calendar month. It is understood that if lessor is unable to deliver to lessee the leased premises on the date of the beginning of this lease, any fractional part of a month shall be paid for by lessee on a pro rata basis of the basic rent set out on page one hereof and the percentage payment herein mentioned for said fractional part of a month shall be equivalent to 12% of the excess of sales over and above the amount of the prorated basic rent herein mentioned.

Lessor, or any agent of lessor, shall have the right of inspecting lessee's books of account for the purpose of checking lessee's gross sales, as herein defined, and lessee shall keep in the within leased premises such books of account and such other records as will enable lessor, or lessor's agent, to make such inspections.

23. It is understood that the premises herein leased have been partially destroyed by fire and it is the duty of lessor to restore the premises to substantially their original condition. It is understood that lessor may install a new front above the first floor, giving lessee the same amount of floor space on the second floor which it formerly occupied but changing the window to a different type.

24. Lessee agrees that during the life of this lease, neither lessee nor any affiliate or associate of lessee will operate another retail men's hat store in Knoxville, Tennessee.

IN WITNESS WHEREOF, the said parties of the first and second parts have hereunto set their hands and seals the day and year first above written.

(Signatures, acknowledgments, and so forth.)

CHAIN STORE PERCENTAGE LEASE

(The following percentage lease was drafted and used by a midwestern chain store organization.)

THIS INDENTURE made this .... day of ...., 19.., by and between .... hereinafter designated as the "Landlord," and ...., a New York corporation, having its principal office at ...., hereinafter designated as the "Tenant," as follows:

WITNESSETH: That for the consideration to be paid by the Tenant to the Landlord as hereinafter provided, the Landlord does hereby demise, let, rent and lease unto the Tenant and the Tenant hereby hires and rents from the Landlord the following described premises with all the appurtenances, rights of way and easements thereunto belonging, situate, lying and being in the City of ...., County of .... and State of ...., known as No. .... and described as follows:

TO HAVE AND TO HOLD the same unto the Tenant for the term of .... beginning on the .... day of ...., and ending on the .... day of .... upon the following terms, covenants and conditions:

First. The Tenant hereby covenants and agrees to pay to the Landlord, the following rentals:

A minimum annual "fixed" rental of $.......... payable in equal "fixed" monthly installments of $.......... each in advance on the first day of each and every month during said period. Notwithstanding that the commencement date of the term of this lease is as above specified, it is agreed that the Tenant shall not be obligated to pay any rent until the Tenant shall open its store in the demised premises to the public. The Tenant agrees, however, to use reasonable diligence and in no event shall the rent be suspended beyond .... months from the date above stated for the commencement of the demised term.

Said rent shall be paid to the Landlord at the office of the said Landlord, No. ...., or at such other place as the said Landlord may from time to time designate in writing.

In addition to the minimum annual "fixed" rental of $.............., the Tenant agrees to pay to the Landlord as "additional" rental, an amount equal to ...... per cent of the gross sales made by the Tenant upon the demised premises in excess of $.......... in any fiscal year during the demised term.

Such "additional" rental, if any, shall be computed and paid as follows: The Tenant shall on or before the fifteenth day of each and every month during the demised term, and on or before the fifteenth day of the month following the end of the term, deliver to the Landlord a "statement of sales" setting forth the amount of the "gross sales" made by the Tenant for the month immediately preceding the delivery of such "statement of sales."

The Tenant shall also on or before thirty (30) days after the expiration of each fiscal year during the term hereof deliver to the Landlord an annual "statement of sales" setting forth the amount of the "gross sales" of each and every month made by the Tenant for the fiscal year immediately preceding the delivery of such "statement of sales."

If such "gross sales" during any fiscal year of the term hereof shall exceed the sum of $.........., then simultaneously with the delivery of such annual "statement of sales," the Tenant shall pay to the Landlord at the Landlord's office, an amount equal to .... per cent of such excess.

The term "gross sales" as herein provided, shall not include returns, refunds or allowances made by said Tenant to its customers upon the demised premises or any inter-company transfers of merchandise.

Where the term "fiscal year" is used herein it means the year commencing on the .... day of ...., and ending on the .... day of ....

The said Tenant hereby agrees at all times during the term hereof, to keep true, full and accurate books of account wherein there shall at all times be promptly entered a complete statement of all "gross sales" of merchandise made by said Tenant in and upon the demised premises. The Landlord, its agents and accountants shall at reasonable intervals and during the business hours of the Tenant, have the right to examine said books of account either at the demised premises or at the office of the Tenant for the purpose of verifying the "statements of sales" submitted by the Tenant to the Landlord as aforesaid.

The landlord agrees that any "statements of sales" delivered by the Tenant hereunder are to be regarded as confidential and that the information therein contained shall not be divulged or published by the Landlord but the same may be introduced in evidence in any proper action or proceedings between the parties.

Second. The Tenant agrees during the term hereof, at its own expense, to keep the interior of the demised premises in good repair (excepting, however, that the Tenant shall not be obligated to make any structural repairs) and upon the expiration of the term hereof, to deliver the demised premises to the Landlord in substantially as good a condition as upon the commencement of the term hereof, reasonable wear and tear and damage by fire of the elements or from other causes beyond its control, excepted. The Landlord hereby covenants and agrees to make all other repairs to said premises and the building of which the same are a part at the Landlord's expense. All trade fixtures, furniture and equipment installed, attached to or built upon the demised premises, whether installed during the term of this lease or prior to the commencement thereof under any previous tenancy or occupancy owned by the Tenant shall remain the sole property of the Tenant and may be removed upon vacating the said premises and such right of removal shall extend during the period of any renewal of this lease or any other lease hereafter made between the parties or their successors in interest, and any renewal thereof. All other property attached to or built upon the demised premises shall become the property of the Landlord and shall remain the property of the said Landlord at the termination or forfeiture or surrender of this lease.

The Tenant agrees to replace all the glass in the premises which may be injured or broken during the demised term with glass of the same kind and quality unless the same shall be broken by fire.

Third. The Landlord agrees that the Tenant may make any alterations, repairs, rebuilding or additions to the demised premises, provided that all work shall be done in a good and workmanlike manner and the structural integrity of the building shall not be impaired and that no liens shall attach to the premises by reason thereof.

Fourth. The Tenant agrees promptly to observe, comply with and execute at the Tenant's own cost during the term hereof all laws, and valid and lawful rules, requirements and regulations of the city, county and state in which the demised premises are located and of any and all governmental authorities or agencies and of any board of fire underwriters respecting the demised premises and the manner in which said premises are used by the Tenant provided, however, that in no event shall the Tenant be required to make any structural and/or exterior alterations or changes in complying with said laws, rules, requirements and regulations. The Landlord covenants that it will at its own expense make any and all exterior and/or structural alterations or changes which may be required by any of the authorities having jurisdiction over the demised premises.

Fifth. The Tenant shall at all times have the right to assign this lease and/or sublet the demised premises or any part or parts thereof providing, however, that the Tenant shall remain and continue liable hereunder for the due performance of all the terms, covenants and conditions of this lease and that any assignment or subletting shall be subject to all the terms, covenants and conditions of this lease.

Sixth. In the event of the damage or destruction of the demised premises by fire or other cause, the premises shall be promptly and fully repaired or restored, as the case may be, by the Landlord at the expense of said Landlord. If the building on the demised premises shall be rebuilt or reconstructed, the same shall be reconstructed or rebuilt in such manner that the demised premises shall be in character and appearance equal to the premises damaged or destroyed and the frontage and area thereof shall be the same as immediately prior to such damage or destruction. It is agreed that in the event of such damage or destruction this lease shall continue in full force and effect but if such damage or destruction shall be of such extent that the Tenant cannot conduct its business in regular course therein, then the rent and other payments, if any, which the Tenant is obligated to make hereunder shall abate until the premises have been fully and completely restored by the Landlord and possession thereof shall have been delivered to the Tenant. Any rent paid in advance shall be proportionately rebated. If the Tenant can continue to conduct its business in the demised premises but is deprived of the use of a part or parts thereof by reason of such damage or destruction, then the rent and other payments, if any, which the Tenant is obligated to make hereunder shall equitably abate in proportion to the rental value of the space which the Tenant is unable to use until the demised premises shall have been fully and completely restored by the Landlord.

All of the foregoing shall be subject to the proviso that if the demised premises are damaged or destroyed during the last year of the term hereof, to the extent of fifty (50%) per cent or more of the retail selling space thereof, and the Tenant is deprived of the use of fifty (50%) per cent or more of said retail selling space, then it shall be optional with the Tenant to call upon the Landlord to repair and restore the said building or to cancel this lease. Such option shall be exercised by written notice given by the Tenant to the Landlord within fifteen days after such damage or destruction. If the Tenant shall exercise its option to cancel this lease, then this lease shall terminate as of the date of such damage or destruction with the same full force and effect as if the same had terminated by limitation of time and the Landlord shall repay to the Tenant a proportionate part of any rent paid in advance. If the Tenant shall fail to give any notice to the Landlord within the aforesaid period of fifteen days, the Tenant shall be deemed to have exercised the option to continue the lease for the balance of its term in which case the Landlord shall promptly repair and restore the building.

Seventh. In case the Tenant shall fail to pay to the Landlord the rent or other sums of money payable to the Landlord as and when due and payable hereunder, and such default shall continue for a period of fifteen (15) days after written notice thereof shall be given to the Tenant by the Landlord, or in case the Tenant shall fail to comply with any other provision or condition of this lease on its part to be kept and performed, and such default shall continue for a period of thirty (30) days after written notice thereof shall be given to the Tenant by the Landlord, then upon the happening of any such event, the term hereof, at the option of the Landlord, shall cease and determine and from thenceforth it shall and may be lawful for the Landlord to re-enter into or upon the demised premises or any part thereof and the same to have again, repossess and enjoy as of its former state. The Landlord shall not be entitled to recover possession, sue for any rent or to maintain any other action (including but not limited to any summary proceedings) against the Tenant based on any alleged default by the Tenant hereunder unless the Tenant shall be notified in writing of such alleged default and shall fail to rectify or cure the same within the periods above mentioned.

Notwithstanding the foregoing, in case the default complained of shall be of such a nature that the same cannot be rectified within such thirty (30) day period aforesaid, then such default shall have been deemed rectified if the Tenant shall have commenced the compliance of the provisions hereof breached by it within said thirty (30) day period and shall with all diligence prosecute the work until there shall have been full compliance.

Eighth. Landlord agrees to deliver physical possession of the entire demised premises to the Tenant upon commencement of the term hereof free and clear of all tenants and claims of tenants and free and clear of all violations filed or unfiled, or any statutes, ordinances, rules, orders, regulations and requirements of the Federal, State, County and City Governments and of any and all of their Departments and Bureaus applicable to the demised premises whether or not involving structural, extraordinary or ordinary alterations, additions or repairs; and in accordance and compliance with all rules, orders and regulations of any and all boards of fire underwriters having jurisdiction over the demised premises and free and clear of any conditional bills of sale or chattel mortgages or similar instruments.

Ninth. Landlord warrants and represents that Landlord is indefeasibly seized in fee simple of the demised premises; that Landlord has full right, power and authority to make this lease and that Landlord will defend all and singular the title of the Tenant in and right of possession by the Tenant to said property against all parties whomsoever for the entire term hereof.

Tenth. The Landlord covenants that the Tenant, upon paying the rent herein reserved and performing the conditions and agreements herein contained on its part to be kept and performed, shall at all times during the term hereof peaceably and quietly have, hold and enjoy the said demised premises.

Eleventh. For all purposes hereunder the addresses of the parties hereto are as follows:

LANDLORD:

(Fill in addresses here)

TENANT:

(Fill in addresses here)

The parties hereto shall have the right from time to time to designate different addresses than those above given by giving written notice to the other party designating such new address.

Any notice or demand which may under the terms of this lease be given by either party to the other shall be in writing and shall be served upon the party to which such notice or demand shall be directed by sending the same postpaid through the United States Post Office, by registered mail, addressed to such party at the address above given or such other address as such party may from time to time designate in accordance with the provisions hereof.

Twelfth. The .... covenants and agrees that .... will, at .... own expense, furnish heat to the demised premises sufficient comfortably to heat the same during the business hours of the Tenant during the usual heating seasons.

Thirteenth. The Tenant agrees to pay all charges for gas, power and electricity used or consumed by the Tenant in the demised premises.

Fourteenth. The Landlord may at any reasonable time or times during the business hours of the Tenant enter upon the demised premises for the purpose of inspecting the same or to make any necessary repairs. The Tenant agrees to permit the Landlord three (3) months prior to the expiration of the term hereby granted to place in one or more conspicuous places upon the exterior of the premises, signs advertising the premises "For Sale" and "To Let" provided that said signs shall not obstruct the windows or entrances to the demised premises or otherwise interfere with the operation of the Tenant's business.

Fifteenth. In consideration of the making of this lease and to induce the Tenant to execute the same, the Landlord hereby grants to the Tenant, its successors and assigns, the option and privilege to a renewal of this lease for a period of .... years from the expiration of the term hereby demised, at the same rent and upon all of the terms, covenants and conditions contained in this lease, excepting that from and after the expiration of said renewal term there shall be no further right of renewal. The said option for such renewal of this lease shall be exercised by the service of a written notice (in the manner in this lease prescribed for the service of notices) by the Tenant upon the Landlord not later than four (4) months prior to the expiration of the term of this lease, setting forth the Tenant's intention to exercise such option of renewal, and if the Tenant shall give such notice in the manner aforesaid this lease and the estate hereby demised shall be extended and renewed for such period of .... years from the date of the expiration hereof at the rent and upon all of the terms, covenants and conditions herein contained.

Sixteenth. This lease shall enure to the benefit of and be binding upon the parties hereto and their respective heirs, executors, administrators, successors and assigns.

Seventeenth. It is agreed that the headings and phrases as to the contents of particular paragraphs are inserted only as a matter of convenience and for reference and in no way are or are intended to be a part of this lease or in any way to define, limit or describe the scope or intent of the particular paragraphs to which they refer.

IN WITNESS WHEREOF this Indenture has been duly executed by the parties hereto as of the day and year first above written.

(Signatures, acknowledgments, and so forth.)

LOS ANGELES PERCENTAGE LEASE

(The following is a form of percentage lease compiled and used by a Los Angeles firm.)

THIS LEASE, made as of the .... day of ...., 19....,
by and between .... and ....
.... hereinafter called respectively the "Landlord" and "Tenant," without regard to number or gender, WITNESSETH:

1. Premises. That the Landlord hereby leases to the Tenant and the Tenant hires from the Landlord, those certain premises with all appurtenances thereto situated in the City of ...., County of .... and State of California, and described as follows:

· ·

2. Term. The term shall be for .... years and ....
months commencing on the .... day of ...., 19...., and terminating on the .... day of ...., 19.....

3. Rent. Said tenant shall pay as a fixed rent for said premises for said term the sum of .... in lawful money of the United States of America which Tenant agrees to pay Landlord without deduction or offset at such place or places as may be designated from time to time by Landlord, in installments as follows:

· ·

Dollars ($..........) at the time of the execution of this lease and as a consideration for the execution thereof by the Landlord, it being understood that said payment is not paid as security and does not apply upon any particular period of the term of this lease; the balance of said rent so reserved to be paid in monthly installments in advance on the .... day of each month as follows:

· ·

The fixed rent above specified for the period from ....
through .... shall be free provided the Tenant is not then in default of any of the terms, covenants, or conditions of this lease to be performed by him.

It is further mutually agreed between the parties hereto as follows:

4. Delivery of possession. The Landlord agrees to deliver possession of the premises of the Tenant on or before the first day of the term hereof but if the Landlord for any reason whatsoever should be unable to deliver possession of the said premises to the Tenant at or prior to the commencement of the term hereinbefore specified then he shall deliver such possession as soon as reasonably possible thereafter and this lease shall not be subject to cancellation on account thereof nor shall the Landlord be liable for any damages or compensation of any nature on account thereof nor shall the termination date or other dates specified herein be affected thereby but in such event there shall be a pro-rata per diem abatement of rent covering the period between the specified commencement of the said term and the time of delivery of possession.

5. Use of premises. The Tenant agrees to take actual possession of and occupy and use the premises as soon as reasonably possible after the delivery of said premises to the Tenant for ....
and agrees not to use or permit said premises or any part thereof to be used for any other purpose or purposes and the Tenant further agrees to conform to and comply with at his own expense all requirements of law or duly constituted authority pertaining to said premises, and/or the carriers of any insurance on the premises or on the building or buildings of which the premises are a part, and all such requirements of any Board of Underwriters, rating bureau or similar organization having jurisdiction of said premises or building or buildings and agrees that should any act or omission of or by or permitted by the Tenant in or about said premises result in an increase in any insurance premium rate or rates then applicable to said premises or to any building or buildings of which said premises are a part, the Tenant shall pay to the Landlord, when such increase in rate becomes effective and payable by the Landlord, the amount of any increase in the Landlord's insurance costs occasioned thereby. It is further agreed that the Tenant shall pay all lawful fees for the inspection or examination of said premises or any part thereof or anything appurtenant thereto, that any public authority having jurisdiction over said premises may require to be paid. The Tenant shall not commit or suffer to be committed any waste upon the said premises, or any public or private nuisance, or other act or thing which may disturb the quiet enjoyment of any occupant of nearby premises or of the building in which the demised premises are located. **Alterations.** The Tenant shall not make or suffer to be made, any additions to or alterations of the said premises or any part thereof, without the written consent of the Landlord first had and obtained, and any additions to or alterations of the said premises, except movable furniture and trade fixtures, shall become at once a part of the realty and belong to the Landlord, subject to the option of the Landlord, hereby reserved, to require the Tenant to restore the premises to their prior condition without cost to the Landlord upon any termination of this lease.

6. Repairs. The Tenant shall, at his own expense, keep and maintain the said premises and appurtenances and every part thereof, excepting exterior walls and roof, but including (without limitation of the foregoing) all glazing, sidewalks adjacent to said premises, and store front and the entire interior of the premises, in good sanitary order, condition and repair, hereby waiving all right to make repairs at the expense of the Landlord as provided in Section 1942 of the Civil Code of the State of California, and all rights provided for by Section 1941 of said Civil Code. In the event any repairs become necessary to the exterior walls or roof of the said premises during the term of this lease, then upon written notice from the Tenant to the Landlord stating the necessity therefor and the nature thereof the Landlord shall with reasonable promptness and at his own cost and expense, after receipt of such written notice, make any such necessary repairs specified in such notice. The phrase "exterior walls or roof," as above used shall not be so construed as to require the Landlord to make repairs to the interior surfaces thereof. Should the Tenant fail to make with reasonable promptness after notice from the Landlord any repairs which are the obligation of the Tenant hereunder the Landlord may at his option make the same and all costs and expenses incurred by the Landlord in connection therewith shall become immediately due and payable by the Tenant to the Landlord as so much additional rental hereunder and the respective obligations of the Landlord and Tenant hereinabove set forth to make any other or additional or future repairs shall not be affected thereby. **Surrender.** By entry hereunder, the Tenant accepts the premises as being in good, sanitary order, condition and repair and agrees on the last day of said term, or other termination of this lease, to surrender unto the Landlord the said premises with the said appurtenances in the same condition as when received, reasonable use and wear thereof and damage by fire, earthquake, or other of the elements excepted.

7. **Entry for repairs, etc.** The Tenant shall permit the Landlord and his agents to enter into and upon said premises with any needed equipment at all reasonable times for the purpose of inspecting or repairing the same, or for the purpose of making repairs, alterations or additions to any other portion of the building in which the premises are situated, or for the purpose of placing upon the property in which the said premises are located, any usual or ordinary "For Sale" signs, and shall permit the Landlord at any time within thirty days prior to the expiration of this lease, to place upon said premises any usual or ordinary "To Let" or "To Lease" signs, without any compensation or abatement of rent in any of said events on account thereof. Any such work done or notices or signs posted or placed by the Landlord shall be performed in such manner as to cause as little inconvenience to the Tenant as reasonably possible.

8. **Abandonment.** The Tenant shall not vacate or abandon the premises at any time during the term; and if the Tenant should abandon, vacate or surrender said premises, or be dispossessed by process of law or otherwise, any personal property left on the premises shall be deemed to be abandoned, at the option of the Landlord, except any such property as may be mortgaged to the Landlord. The Tenant shall not conduct or permit to be conducted any sale by auction on the said premises, nor shall the Tenant place or permit to be placed any decoration, sign, marquee or awning on or about the exterior of said premises without the prior written consent of the Landlord. The Tenant upon the request of the Landlord shall immediately remove any decoration, sign, marquee or awning which the Tenant has placed or permitted to be placed on or about the exterior of the premises without the consent of the Landlord, and which in the opinion of the Landlord, is objection-

able or offensive, and if the Tenant fails to do so, the Landlord may enter upon said premises and remove the same.

9.   Taxes and charges.   The Tenant shall pay during the term hereof, all water rates, rents or charges, all electric, gas or other lighting, power or heating charges, and any and every charge for utility or other services furnished said premises or any part thereof and shall also pay all taxes and assessments levied or assessed on or against or in connection with any and all fixtures, equipment and improvements installed or made by the Tenant in or to or about the leased premises and shall bear and pay all taxes and public charges levied or assessed in connection with the operation of the Tenant's business.

10.   Damages and claims.   The Tenant, as a material part of the consideration to be rendered the Landlord under this lease, hereby waives and releases any and all claims against the Landlord for injury or damage of any kind or nature to person or property, in, upon or about said premises, from any cause whatsoever, arising at any time after the execution of this lease and agrees to indemnify and hold the Landlord exempt and harmless from and on account of any such injury or damage or claim therefor to any person or property.

11.   Casualty; restoration.   If at any time after the execution hereof, the improvements herein leased are damaged by fire or earthquake or other of the elements to the extent of less than 50% of their then insurable value the Landlord shall forthwith repair the same and this lease shall not be affected thereby except that the Tenant shall be entitled to an equitable abatement of rent during the period of such damage and repair based on the extent to which such damage and repair interferes with the usefulness of the premises for the business carried on by the Tenant therein, provided however, that should any such damage occur to the extent of 10% or more of the then insurable value of the improvements at any time when the then remaining term of this lease is less than three years the Landlord may at his option cancel this lease by giving notice to the Tenant within 20 days after the occurrence of such damage of his intention so to do, but if the Landlord does not exercise said option to cancel then he shall promptly repair such damage. Should the improvements herein leased be so damaged or destroyed at any time after the execution hereof to the extent of 50% or more of their then insurable value the Landlord may at his option within said 20 day period thereafter, cancel this lease but otherwise shall repair the premises all as above provided, but in any of said events the Tenant shall be entitled to said equitable abatement of rent. It is further agreed that if any building or buildings of which the leased premises are a part are damaged or destroyed to the extent of 50% or more of their then insurable value at any time after the execution hereof or to the extent of 10% or more of such value at any time when the then remaining term of this lease is less than three years then in either of said events the Landlord may cancel this lease whether or not the leased premises are damaged. In respect to any damage or destruction which the Landlord is obligated or elects to repair under the provisions of this paragraph the Tenant waives the provisions of Section 1932, subdivision 2, and of Section 1933, subdivision 4, of the Civil Code of the State of California.

12. Condemnation. In the event that the demised premises or any part thereof shall at any time after the execution of this lease be taken for public or quasi public use or condemned under eminent domain, the Tenant shall not be entitled to claim, or have paid to the Tenant any compensation or damages whatsoever for or on account of any loss, injury, damage or taking of any right, interest or estate of the Tenant but the Landlord shall be entitled to claim, and have paid to him for the use and benefit of the Landlord all compensation and/or damages for and/or on account of and/or arising out of such taking and/or condemnation without deduction from the amount thereof for or on account of any right, title, interest or estate of the Tenant in or to said property. In case of any such taking and/or condemnation referred to in this paragraph then, if and when there is an actual taking of physical possession of the demised premises or of any part thereof in excess of 10% of the ground floor area thereof then either the Landlord or the Tenant may cancel and terminate this lease as to the whole of the demised premises by giving notice to the other party within five (5) days after such actual taking of physical possession of such intention to terminate and should such an actual taking of physical possession of any part of the demised premises (whether more or less than 10% of the ground floor area thereof) occur at any time when the then remaining term of this lease is less than three (3) years, then either party hereto may likewise cancel and terminate this lease by giving notice to the other party within said five (5) day period of such intention to terminate. If this lease is not terminated as above provided for following any of said actual takings then the Landlord shall repair the premises at his own expense.

Percentage rent. Commencing with the date on which the Tenant opens its said store to the public for business the Tenant covenants and agrees to pay to the Landlord as a percentage rent in addition to the fixed rent provided for in section three (3) of this lease, a sum equal to the amount if any by which .... per cent (....%) on all sales and business transacted (as hereinafter defined) on the premises during each calendar month exceeds the fixed rental paid for such month said percentage rental for each calendar month or fraction thereof is to be paid on or before the fifth (5) day of the following calendar month.

The term "sales and business transacted" means the selling price of all goods, wares and merchandise sold in, upon or from any part of the demised premises by the Tenant or any other person, firm or corporation, and the charges for all services performed, for which charge is made by the Tenant or by any other person, firm, or corporation selling merchandise or performing services of any sort in, upon or from any part of the demised premises, and shall include sales and charges for cash or credit, regardless of collections in the case of the latter, but shall exclude returns and refunds, and the amount of any sales tax or similar tax or imposition whatsoever and howsoever imposed for such sales and charges, where such sales tax, or similar tax or imposition is billed to the purchaser as a separate item.

The Tenant covenants and agrees to keep on the demised premises true and complete records and accounts of the sales and business transacted and to furnish a true and accurate statement monthly at the times when rents are paid of the total daily sales and business transacted on said premises (showing but not including the amount of returns and refunds) which said statement shall be certified by the Tenant to be correct and agrees to give the Landlord access during reasonable hours to the books and records of the business transacted in the store. The Tenant also agrees to furnish to the Landlord true and complete copies of all reports of sales taxes or any similar tax or imposition on sales and business transacted on the premises at the times such reports are made to any taxing authority.

The Tenant covenants to, and it is of the essence of this lease that the Tenant shall, continuously during the term of this lease, during all usual business hours, not including Sundays and holidays, occupy and use the premises for the purpose set forth in section five (5) of this lease (except during any times when the premises may be untenantable by reason of fire or other casualty). The Tenant further agrees that in the operation of its said store in the premises it will at all times carry a full and complete stock of seasonable merchandise offered for sale at competitive prices and will maintain an adequate personnel for the efficient service of its customers and in general employ its best judgment, efforts and abilities to operate said store in the manner calculated to produce the maximum volume of profitable sales obtainable. Should the Tenant at any time during the term hereof vacate the leased premises or cease operating said store therein (except during any times when the premises may be untenantable by reason of fire or other casualty) the Tenant shall pay to the Landlord, in addition to the fixed rent provided for in section three (3) of this lease, monthly in advance for each month or fraction thereof during said term during which said store is not continuously conducted in the premises a sum per month in cash equal to the average monthly percentage rental earned hereunder prior thereto which said payment shall in no wise abridge or affect any other right or remedy which the Landlord may have on account of or in connection with such breach of covenant by the Tenant, nor limit or affect the recovery by the Landlord of any damages the Landlord may have sustained by reason of such default of Tenant. Should the Tenant fail to open its store in said premises to the public for business within a period of seven (7) days after the premises are delivered to the Tenant then the Tenant shall pay to the Landlord an additional rental for said premises at the rate of .... Dollars ($..........) per day from and after said seven (7) day period to but not including the date on which the Tenant actually opens its said store to the public for business, such additional rental to be paid at the close of each calendar month or fractional part thereof during which any such rental accrues.

Mechanics' liens.   The Tenant shall at all times pay any and all

liens and claims that may be asserted against said premises by reason
of anything done or ordered to be done by or under the Tenant in, on
or about said demised premises, and should any such liens or claims
remain due and unpaid for thirty days, the Landlord may at his option,
and without any liability to inquire into the correctness or validity of
the same, assume and pay the same, together with any penalties added
thereto, and upon such assumption or payment by the Landlord the
amount assumed or paid shall immediately thereafter be due and payable by the Tenant to the Landlord as additional rent. The Landlord
shall have the right to enter the demised premises and keep posted any
and all notices of non-responsibility or other matters provided or permitted by law for the Landlord's protection in connection with any
such construction or work.

Subordination.   The lien of this lease shall be subject and subordinate to the lien of any bona fide mortgage or trust deed hereafter executed covering all or any part of the leased premises and the tenant agrees
to execute and deliver to the Landlord any instrument or instruments requested by the Landlord consenting to any such mortgage or trust deed
placed or to be placed upon the premises and subordinating this lease
thereto.

Insolvency, remedies, etc.   If the Tenant shall become insolvent or
make an assignment for the benefit of creditors, or file a petition in
bankruptcy or seek the benefit of any bankruptcy, composition or insolvency law or act or if the Tenant shall be adjudged bankrupt or if a
receiver or trustee of the property of the Tenant shall be appointed, or
this lease shall by operation of law devolve upon or pass to any person
or persons other than the Tenant then in each such case the Landlord
shall have the right and option to terminate this lease at any time, and
with or without demand or notice and with or without legal process
enter into the demised premises and take possession thereof and may
use all force necessary to effect such entry and/or to hold such possession and/or to remove the Tenant and/or any person and/or any property from the demised premises.

In case of any default by the Tenant in the making of any of the payments herein reserved or in the event of a breach of any of the other
terms, conditions, covenants or provisions herein contained on the part
of the Tenant to be kept and performed, the Landlord, beside other rights
and remedies he may have, shall have the same immediate right of re-
entry and removal of all persons and property from the premises provided for in the foregoing paragraph hereof and any property removed
by the Landlord may be stored in any public warehouse or elsewhere
at the cost of, and for the account of the Tenant and the Landlord shall
not be responsible for the care or safe keeping thereof and the Tenant
hereby waives any and all loss, destruction and/or damage or injury
which may be occasioned by any of the aforesaid acts. It is further
agreed that in the event of any such default or breach the Landlord
may either terminate this lease and recover from the Tenant all damage he may incur by reason of said breach, including the recovery of

possession, or, he may from time to time, without terminating this lease, relet said premises or any part thereof, for all or any portion of the remainder of said term to a tenant or tenants satisfactory to him, and at such rental or rentals as he may deem advisable, with the right to make alterations and repairs and should such rental or rentals actually received during any month be less than that agreed to be paid during that month by the Tenant hereunder, the Tenant agrees to pay such deficiency to the Landlord, and to pay to the Landlord as soon as ascertained, the cost and expenses incurred by him in such reletting, such deficiency to be calculated and paid monthly, or the lessor may declare all rental and other payments which would accrue to the lessor to the end of the term hereof and which then are unpaid, immediately due and payable and may commence action immediately thereon and recover judgment therefor. No such re-entry or taking possession of the said premises by the said Landlord shall be construed as an election on his part to terminate this lease unless a written notice of such intention is given to the Tenant, or unless the termination thereof be decreed by a court of competent jurisdiction. Notwithstanding any such reletting without termination the Landlord may at all times thereafter elect to terminate this lease for such previous breach. The waiver by the Landlord of any breach of any term, covenant or condition herein contained shall not be deemed to be a waiver of any subsequent breach of the same or any other term, covenant or condition and any and all rights, remedies and options given in this lease to the Landlord shall be cumulative and in addition to and without waiver of or in derogation of any right or remedy given to him under any law now or hereafter in effect. Should either of the parties to this lease obtain a judgment against the other by reason of a breach of this lease a reasonable attorney's fee to be fixed by the court shall be added to such judgment.

Notices.   All notices under this lease shall be given in writing delivered personally or by registered mail or telegram addressed to the Landlord at .... or to the Tenant at .... or to such other person or place as either party may hereafter designate in writing to the other for the service of notices to the party making such designation and any such notices served by registered mail shall be deemed to have been served and valid and sufficient for all purposes within 24 hours after being deposited in the United States Post Office registered postage prepaid and addressed as above required.

Holding over.   Any holding over after the expiration of the said term, or any extension or renewal thereof, with the consent of the Landlord, shall be construed to be a tenancy at will upon the terms, covenants and conditions in effect prior to such holding over and terminable by either party hereto giving to the other party thirty (30) or more days' notice of such intention to terminate said tenancy.

Construction of lease.   The covenants and conditions herein contained shall subject to the provisions as to assignment, apply to and bind the heirs, executors, administrators, successors and assigns of all of the parties hereto; and all of the parties hereto shall be jointly and severally liable hereunder. No captions or titles on this lease shall be considered in the interpretation of any of the provisions hereof. Time is of the essence of this lease.

IN WITNESS WHEREOF, the Landlord and the Tenant have executed these presents in duplicate, the day and year first above written.

(Signatures, acknowledgments, and so forth.)

SHOPPING CENTER LEASE

(This is a lease form used in a regional shopping center in Michigan.)

THIS LEASE, made and entered into this .... day of .... 19...., by and between ...., a Michigan corporation, party of the first part, hereinafter called "Landlord," and party of the second part, hereinafter called "Tenant,"

WITNESSETH: That

Landlord does hereby lease, demise and let unto Tenant the following described premises: ....
....

Said Shopping Center is located in the City of ...., ...
County, Michigan, being bounded and described as follows:

TO HAVE AND TO HOLD, together with appurtenances, with a quiet and undisturbed possession to Tenant, for a term of .... years commencing on the ... day of .... 19...., and ending on the ... day of .... 19...., on the following terms and conditions:

Article I. Acceptance of Premises and Notice of Readiness for Occupancy

Section 1: Landlord agrees prior to the commencement of the term of this lease, at Landlord's sole cost and expense, to construct on the site of the Shopping Center, a new building in which the demised premises are to be located, in accordance with the outline specification entitled "Description of Landlord's Work" annexed hereto and made a part hereof and it is understood and agreed by Tenant that no minor changes from the plans that have been agreed upon by and between the parties hereto which may be necessary during the preparation of the demised premises for Tenant or during construction will affect or change this lease or invalidate same.

Section 2: Except as hereinafter provided, Landlord covenants that actual possession of the demised premises shall be delivered to Tenant on or before the date specified for the commencement of the term hereof.

It is understood that delivery of possession prior to such commencement date shall not affect the expiration date of the term of this lease. Landlord shall, from time to time during the course of construction, provide to Tenant information concerning the progress of construction of said building and shall, when construction progress so permits, notify Tenant in advance of the exact or approximate date by which the demised premises will be ready for occupancy, and will notify Tenant when said premises are in fact ready for occupancy. It is agreed that by occupying said premises as a tenant, Tenant formally accepts the same and acknowledges that the demised premises are in the condition called for hereunder. The rentals herein reserved shall commence on the date when the premises are ready for occupancy, provided, that for the first two (2) weeks after acceptance of possession, Tenant shall be permitted to occupy the said premises without the payment of rent for the purpose of installing fixtures in the said building. Tenant, prior to delivery of possession, shall be permitted to install fixtures and other equipment so long as such activities do not interfere with construction work and it is agreed by Tenant that Landlord shall have no responsibility or liability whatsoever for any loss of, or damage to, any fixtures or other equipment so installed or left on the premises.

Section 3: Failure of Landlord to deliver actual possession of said premises at the time and in the condition herein provided, shall postpone the date of commencement of the term of this lease and extend the date of the expiration thereof for a period of time equal to that which shall have elapsed between the first day of said term as stated herein and the date on which the demised premises are delivered to and accepted by Tenant. Solely for the purpose of computing the term of this lease, the commencement date shall be deemed to be the first day of the month next following the expiration of the two-week free rent period hereinbefore provided.

Section 4: If for any reason the demised premises are not ready for occupancy on the first day of April, 19.., then for a period of thirty (30) days thereafter Tenant shall have the option and for a period of forty-five (45) days thereafter Landlord shall have the option of cancelling and terminating this lease by written notice, one to the other, and in the event that either party shall exercise such option, this lease shall be null and void, all obligations one to the other shall cease with neither party being liable in damages, or otherwise, and any money deposited hereunder shall be returned to Tenant. In the event that neither Tenant or Landlord gives such written notice of cancellation prior to May 1, 19.. in the case of Tenant, and prior to June 16, 19.. in the case of Landlord, then this lease shall be considered as continuing in full force and effect until such time as the demised premises are ready for occupancy and the commencement of the term of this lease shall be extended accordingly for a period of time equal to that which shall have elapsed between the commencement date hereinabove specified and the date on which the demised premises are delivered to and accepted by Tenant.

Section 5: The demised premises shall be deemed as ready for occupancy when

(a) Landlord shall have substantially completed construction of the said premises in accordance with the Description of Landlord's Work as referred to in Section 1 of this Article, in accordance with all lawful statutes or ordinances and regulations affecting said premises, and when

(b) Building "A" as identified on the attached Map of Shopping Center has been occupied and opened for business as a department store by ...., and when

(c) a minimum of one-half of the parking facilities provided for in Section 2 of Article VII of this lease have been completed and are available for use.

Article II. Lease Consideration

Section 1: As partial consideration for the execution of this lease, Tenant has this day paid Landlord the sum of .... dollars ($........) in the form of .... the receipt of which is hereby acknowledged. If Tenant shall have fully and faithfully complied with all of the covenants, agreements, terms, and conditions of this lease upon termination of this lease or any modification or extension thereof, but not otherwise, said consideration or such part and any accrued increment thereof, as shall not have been applied to correction or payment of damages for any violation of the terms hereof, shall promptly be refunded to Tenant, its heirs, administrators, its successors or assigns, or to such other person as Tenant or any court of competent jurisdiction shall direct.

Article III. Rent

Section 1: Tenant shall and hereby agrees to pay to Landlord, at such place or places as Landlord shall designate from time to time in writing, rent for said premises as follows:

Section 2: Said annual percentage rental shall be paid in semi-annual installments as follows: Within thirty (30) days after the end of the first six-month period in each lease year and again within thirty (30) days after the end of each lease year, Tenant shall pay to Landlord, after deducting therefrom the minimum rental paid for said six-month period, a sum of money equal to the percentage of its gross sales for said six-month period computed on the above formula, except that the dollar amounts of gross sales in said formula to which said percentages shall apply shall be reduced by one-half. In the event that the total of the semi-annual payments of percentage rentals for any lease year does not equal the annual percentage rental computed on the amount of gross sales for such twelve-month period in accordance with the formula in Section 1 above set forth, then Tenant shall pay to Landlord any deficiency or Landlord shall refund to Tenant any overpayment, as the case may be, within thirty (30) days after the end of each lease year. In no event, however, shall the rent to be paid by Tenant and retained by Landlord for any lease year be less than the annual minimum rental herein specified. For the purpose of computing the annual percentage rental hereunder, the first lease year shall be deemed to end twelve (12) months after the first of the month next following the expiration of the two (2) week free rent period, provided for in Article I above, and each succeeding twelve-month period shall be deemed a lease year. For any fractional part of a lease year prior to the commencement of the first full lease year as defined herein, gross sales in, upon, and from the demised premises shall be included with gross sales for such first full lease year for all purposes.

Article IV. Gross Sales

Section I: The term "Gross Sales" as used herein shall be construed to include the entire amount of the actual sales price, whether for cash or otherwise, of all sales of merchandise, service and other receipts whatsoever of all business conducted in or from the demised premises, including mail or telephone orders received or filled at the demised premises, and including all deposits not refunded to purchasers, orders taken, although said orders may be filled elsewhere, and sales by any sublessee, concessionaire or licensee or otherwise in said premises; provided that nothing herein shall prevent Landlord from requiring an additional or different percentage rental as a condition to approval of any sublessee, concessionaire or licensee of Tenant hereunder. No deduction shall be allowed for uncollected or uncollectible credit accounts. Said term shall not include, however, any sums collected and paid out for any sales or excise tax imposed by any duly constituted governmental authority nor shall it include the exchange of merchandise between the stores of Tenant, if any, where such exchanges of goods or merchandise are made solely for the convenient operation of the business of Tenant and not for the purpose of consummating a sale which has theretofore been made at, in, from or upon the demised premises and/or for the purpose of depriving Landlord of the benefit of a sale which otherwise would be made at, in, from or upon the demised premises, nor the amount of returns to shippers or manufacturers, nor the amount of any cash or credit refund made upon any sale where the merchandise sold, or some part thereof, is thereafter returned by the purchaser and accepted by Tenant, nor sales of fixtures.

Article V. Sales Reports

Section 1: Tenant shall and hereby agrees that it will submit to Landlord within thirty (30) days after the expiration of each six-month period of each lease year and within thirty (30) days after the expiration of each full lease year period, at the place where the rent herein reserved is then payable, a complete certified statement showing in all reasonable detail the amount of gross sales as defined in Article IV of this lease made from the demised premises during said periods. Tenant shall require of its sub-tenants, if any, to furnish similar statements.

Section 2: In the event Landlord is not satisfied with the semi-annual and annual statements as submitted by Tenant and its sub-tenants, then and in that event Landlord shall have the right to have its auditors make a special audit of Tenant's and its sub-tenants' books and records pertaining to sales on, or in connection with, the premises leased herein. If any such statement is found to be incorrect to an extent of more than three percent (3%) in amount over the figures submitted by Tenant, and its sub-tenant, Tenant shall promptly pay for such special audit as an addition to the next minimum rental payment, and if such audit proves Tenant's and sub-tenants' statements to be correct or together to vary not more than three per cent (3%) from the results of the special audit, then the expense of such audit shall be borne by Landlord. Landlord's right to examine Tenant's and its sub-tenants' books and records, as hereinbefore set forth, or to make an audit thereof in respect to any lease year period, shall be available to Landlord only for a six-month period after the annual statement for such lease year period shall have been furnished to Landlord.

Article VI. Books and Records

Section 1: Tenant shall and hereby agrees that it and its sub-tenants will keep in the demised premises, or some other location in metropolitan Detroit, ...
....
a permanent, accurate set of books and records of all sales of merchandise and all revenue derived from other departments of the business conducted in said premises, during each day of the term hereof, and all supporting records, including state sales tax and business and occupation tax reports. Tenant further agrees that it and its sub-tenants will so keep, retain and preserve for at least seven (7) months after the expiration of each lease year, all sales slips and other pertinent records.

Article VII. Operation and Maintenance of Common Areas

Section 1: For the purpose of this Article and wherever else used in this lease, the "Mall Area" shall be defined as that portion of the Shopping Center which is enclosed within the line identified on the attached Map of Shopping Center as "Building Perimeter Curb," the latter being the line of the exterior face of the curb at the edge of the sidewalk surrounding the building group. It is expressly understood and agreed that if a lesser or greater number of buildings than shown on the Map of Shopping Center shall be in existence at any time, then the line of the "Building Perimeter Curb" shall be constricted or enlarged accordingly, as the case may be, so as to enclose only the area actually occupied by buildings.

Section 2: Landlord agrees at Landlord's sole cost and expense to hard-surface, properly drain, adequately light and landscape a parking area, or areas, together with the necessary access roads, within the limits of the Shopping Center having a minimum capacity for five thousand (5,000) passenger automobiles of standard American make, and Landlord hereby grants to Tenant and Tenant's employees, agents, customers and invitees the right, during the term hereof, to use, in common with others entitled to the use thereof, the parking area, or areas, and access roads within the limits of the Shopping Center. Landlord further agrees to operate, manage and maintain, during the term of this lease, all parking areas, roads, sidewalks, landscaping and drainage and lighting facilities within the Shopping Center. The manner in which such areas and facilities shall be maintained, and the expenditures therefor, shall be at the sole discretion of Landlord and the use of such areas and facilities shall be subject to such reasonable regulations as Landlord shall make from time to time.

Section 3: Tenant agrees to pay upon demand, in addition to the rental set forth in Article III of this lease, a proportionate share of the cost of operation, lighting, cleaning, snow removal, line painting, policing and maintenance including such replacement of paving, curbs, walkways, landscaping and drainage and lighting facilities as may be from time to time necessary, of all of that portion of the Shopping Center which is exclusive of the Mall Area and exclusive of any other areas which may be rented or occupied by tenants other than those occupying the buildings located in the Mall Area. Tenant further agrees to pay a proportionate share of the cost of operation, lighting, cleaning, snow removal, line painting, policing and landscaping of the Mall Area and the underlying public spaces consisting of the truck road and loading platforms, but not including the cost of any repair or replacement of paving, curbs, platforms and walkways therein. Cost of operation and maintenance shall not include taxes, assessments or depreciation of the original investment except as hereinafter provided in Section 4 of this Article. The proportionate share to be paid by Tenant shall be computed on the basis that the total floor area of the herein demised premises bears to the total floor area rented or occupied by all of the occupants, whether as tenants or owners, of the buildings in the Mall Area. With each demand for payment as herein provided of Tenant's proportionate share Landlord shall submit a statement showing in reasonable detail for the period in question all income, if any, and disbursements made in connection with the operation and maintenance herein described.

Section 4: In the event that Landlord shall require the payment of any fee or charge by the general public for the use of the parking area, or areas, which may be by meter or otherwise, then and in that event only, all taxes and assessments levied upon the land contained within the Shopping Center, exclusive of that in the Mall Area and in any other areas rented or occupied by tenants other than those occupying the buildings within the Mall Area, shall become part of the cost of operation and maintenance as provided in Section 3 of this Article and the total revenue derived from all such fees and charges shall be applied on the said cost of operation and maintenance before apportionment among the occupants as further provided in Section 3 of this Article.

Article VIII. Use of Premises

Section 1: It is understood and agreed between the parties hereto that said premises during the continuance of this lease may be used and occupied only for .... and for no other purpose or purposes without the written consent of Landlord. Tenant agrees to operate 100% of the leased premises during the entire term of this lease, unless prevented from doing so by causes beyond Tenant's control, and to conduct its business at all times in a high class and reputable manner. Tenant shall promptly comply with all laws, ordinances and lawful orders and regulations affecting the premises hereby leased, and the cleanliness, safety, occupation and use of same. No auction, fire, or bankruptcy sales may be conducted in the herein demised premises without the previous written consent of Landlord. Tenant agrees that it will conduct its business in the leased premises during the regular and customary hours for such type business and on all business days and will conduct such business in a lawful manner and in good faith and in such manner that Landlord will at all times receive the maximum amount of rental for the operation of such business in and upon the leased premises. Tenant shall not use the sidewalks adjacent to the demised premises for business purposes without the written consent of Landlord. Notwithstanding anything in this Article contained, there shall be no obligation on the part of Tenant to comply with any of the laws, directions, rules and regulations referred to which may require structural alterations, structural changes, structural repairs or structural additions, unless made necessary by act or work performed by Tenant, in which event Tenant shall comply at its expense.

Article IX. Care of Premises

Section 1: Tenant shall not perform any acts or carry on any practices which may injure the building or be a nuisance or menace to other tenants in the Shopping Center, and shall keep the premises under its control, including the sidewalks adjacent to the premises and the basement loading platform areas allocated for the use of Tenant, clean and free from rubbish and dirt at all times, and shall store all trash and garbage within the leased premises and arrange for the regular pick-up of such trash and garbage at Tenant's expense. Tenant shall not burn any trash or garbage of any kind in or about the building.

Section 2: Tenant shall not keep or display any merchandise or signs on or otherwise obstruct the sidewalks or areaways adjacent to the premises without the written consent of Landlord. Tenant shall not use or permit the use of any portion of said premises as sleeping apartments, lodging rooms, or for any unlawful purpose or purposes. Tenant shall maintain the show windows and signs in a neat and clean condition.

Tenant shall not make any structural changes in the demised premises without the written consent of Landlord.

Article X. Utility Services

Section 1: Landlord agrees to provide and maintain the necessary mains and conduits in order that water, gas and electricity may be furnished to the demised premises. If Tenant shall use water, gas and/or electricity for any purpose in the leased premises and Landlord shall elect to supply the water, gas and/or electricity Tenant shall accept and use the same as tendered by Landlord and pay therefor at the applicable rates filed with the proper regulating authority and in effect from time to time covering such services.

Section 2: Landlord agrees at its own cost and expense to construct, operate and maintain a central plant together with the necessary distribution mains for the production of steam in adequate volume to heat the entire Shopping Center. Tenant agrees to accept and use for heating purposes steam as tendered by Landlord and to pay for the same monthly at rates to be fixed from time to time by Landlord, which schedule of rates shall be on a sliding scale in accordance with the volume of steam consumed monthly by Tenant and calculated on the same ratio as that used by the Detroit Edison Company in downtown Detroit. Each twelve-month period ending July 31 shall be deemed a heating year and within thirty (30) days after the end of each heating year Landlord shall compute the total cost of furnishing steam to the Shopping Center for the preceding heating year and shall allocate the same on the basis that the amount billed to Tenant during said period bears to the total amount of billing to all tenants. To the extent Tenant's pro rata share of such cost for any heating year is greater or less than the sum actually billed to Tenant for steam consumed during said heating year the difference shall be billed or refunded to Tenant as the case may be and at the same time Landlord shall furnish to Tenant a statement showing in reasonable detail the basis for determining such cost. Operating cost of the central steam plant shall be considered as all of those items of expense which in usual accounting practice are treated as operating costs and including, but not limited to, such items as fuel, water, electricity, supplies, wages, including wages of supervisory personnel, compensation insurance, payroll taxes, boiler insurance and ordinary maintenance and repairs, including that to the air handling equipment within the demised premises, to the total sum of which there shall be added fifteen (15%) per cent; but operating cost shall not include depreciation, real and personal property taxes, maintenance of the four outer walls and roof of heating plant or any major replacements and repairs of the type ordinarily charged as capital expense in usual accounting practice. For any fractional part of a heating year during which Tenant is in possession during the term of this lease there shall be an equitable adjustment of any refund or billing by Landlord.

Section 3: Landlord agrees at its own cost and expense to construct, operate and maintain a central plant together with the necessary distribution mains for the production of chilled water in adequate volume to air condition the entire Shopping Center. Tenant agrees to accept and use for air conditioning purposes such chilled water as tendered by Landlord and to pay for the same monthly at rates to be fixed from time to time by Landlord. Each twelve-month period ending January 31st shall be deemed an air conditioning year and within thirty (30) days after the end of each air conditioning year Landlord shall compute the total cost of furnishing chilled water to the Shopping Center for the preceding air conditioning year and shall allocate the same on the basis that the amount billed to Tenant during said period bears to the total amount of billing to all tenants. To the extent Tenant's pro rata share of such cost for any air conditioning year is greater or less than the sum actually billed to Tenant for chilled water consumed during said air conditioning year the difference shall be billed or refunded to Tenant as the case may be and at the same time Landlord shall furnish to Tenant a statement showing in reasonable detail the basis for determining such cost. Operating cost of the central chilled water plant shall be considered as all of those items of expense which in usual accounting practice are treated as operating costs and including, but not limited to, such items as fuel, water, electricity, supplies, wages, including wages of supervisory personnel, compensation insurance, payroll taxes, real and personal property taxes, compressor insurance and ordinary maintenance and repairs, including that to the air handling equipment within the demised premises, to the total sum of which there shall be added fifteen (15%) percent; but operating cost shall not include depreciation, maintenance of the four outer walls and roof of central plant or any major replacements and repairs of the type ordinarily charged as capital expense in usual accounting practice. For any partial air conditioning year during which Tenant is in possession during the term of this lease there shall be an equitable adjustment of any refund or billing by Landlord. Tenant further agrees in addition to pay in equal monthly installments a fixed charge computed at the rate of .... per year per square foot of floor area served by the air conditioning installation within the herein demised premises which shall be not less than the total area of the first floor of said premises. Subsequent to the installation of the air conditioning duct system in the demised premises and prior to the commencement of the term of this lease Landlord shall notify Tenant in writing of the number of square feet of floor area served by the air conditioning installation. The amount of such annual fixed charge shall be payable by Tenant at the same time and in the same manner as provided for the payment of the minimum guaranteed rent as provided in Article III of this lease.

Section 4: Payment for any and all water, gas, electricity, steam and chilled water used by Tenant and furnished by Landlord shall be made monthly and within ten (10) days of the presentation by Landlord to Tenant of bills therefor, the Landlord reserving, and it is hereby covenanted and agreed by the parties hereto, that Landlord is to have the right to cut off and discontinue, without notice to the Tenant, said water, gas, electricity, steam and chilled water or any other service whenever and during any period for which bills for the same or for rent are not promptly paid by Tenant. The obligation of Tenant to pay for water, gas, electricity, steam and chilled water as herein provided shall commence as of the date on which possession of the premises is delivered to Tenant as provided for in Article I, Section 2 of this lease, without regard to any free rental period or formal commencement date of this lease.

Section 5: Landlord shall not be liable in damages or otherwise should the furnishing of any services by it to the demised premises be interrupted by fire, accident, riot, strike, act of God, or the making of necessary repairs or improvements or other causes beyond the control of Landlord.

Section 6: Meters for the measurement of consumption of steam and consumption of chilled water by Tenant are designed to be used in common with occupants of the other stores identified as .... and Tenant agrees that all charges for the consumption of steam and chilled water as computed from the reading of the said meters shall be shared by Tenant together with all other tenants herein above designated in the following manner:

(a) Tenant shall pay for consumption of steam proportionately to the amount that the total floor area in the herein demised premises bears to the total floor area of all occupied stores in the above designation.

(b) Tenant shall pay for consumption of chilled water proportionately to the amount that the floor area served by the air conditioning system within the herein demised premises bears to the total amount of floor area served by the air conditioning system within all of the occupied stores included in the above designation.

Article XI. Maintenance of Building

Section 1: Landlord shall keep the foundation, the four outer walls and roof of demised premises in good repair, except that Landlord shall not be called on to make any such repairs occasioned by the act or negligence of Tenant, its agents, or employees, except to the extent that Landlord is reimbursed therefor under any policy of insurance permitting waiver of subrogation in advance of loss. Landlord shall not be called upon to make any other improvements or repairs of any kind upon said premises, and said premises shall at all times be kept in good order, condition and repair by Tenant, and shall also be kept in a clean, sanitary, and safe condition in accordance with the laws of the State of Michigan, and in accordance with all directions, rules and regulations of the health officer, fire marshal, building inspector or other proper officers of the governmental agencies having jurisdiction, at the sole cost and expense of Tenant, and Tenant shall comply with all requirements of law, ordinance and otherwise, touching said premises. Tenant shall permit no waste, damage or injury to said premises, and Tenant shall at its own cost and expense replace any glass windows and doors in the premises which may be broken. At the expiration of the tenancy created hereunder, Tenant shall surrender the premises in good condition, reasonable wear and tear, loss by fire or other unavoidable casualty excepted. Notwithstanding anything in this Article contained, there shall be no obligation on the part of Tenant to comply with any of the laws, directions, rules and regulations referred to which may require structural alterations, structural changes, structural repairs, or structural additions, unless made necessary by act or work performed by Tenant, in which event Tenant shall comply at its expense.

Article XII. Signs and Alterations

Section 1: Tenant shall not erect or install any exterior or interior window or door signs or advertising media or window or door lettering, or placards without the previous written consent of Landlord. Tenant agrees not to use any advertising media that shall be deemed objectionable to Landlord or other tenants, such as loud speakers, phonographs or radio broadcasts in a manner to be heard outside the leased premises. Tenant shall not install any exterior lighting or plumbing fixtures, shades or awnings, or any exterior decorations or painting, or build any fences or make any changes to the store front without the previous consent of Landlord.

Section 2: All alterations, additions, improvements and fixtures, other than trade fixtures, which may be made or installed by either of the parties hereto upon the premises and which in any manner are attached to the floors, walls or ceilings shall be the property of Landlord and at the termination of this lease shall remain upon and be surrendered with the premises as a part thereof, without disturbance, molestation or injury. Any linoleum or other floor covering of similar character which may be cemented or otherwise adhesively affixed to the floor of the herein leased premises shall be and become the property of Landlord absolutely.

Article XIII. Covenant to Hold Harmless

Section 1: Landlord shall be defended and held harmless by Tenant from any liability for damages to any person or any property in or upon said premises and the sidewalks adjoining same and the loading platform area allocated to the use of Tenant, including the person and property of Tenant, and its employees and all persons in the building at its or their invitation or with their consent. It is understood and agreed that all property kept, stored or maintained in the demised premises shall be so kept, stored or maintained at the risk of Tenant only. Tenant shall not suffer or give cause for the filing of any lien against the herein demised premises.

Article XIV. Insurance

Section 1: Tenant shall not carry any stock of goods or do anything in or about said premises which will in any way tend to increase the insurance rates on said premises and/or the building of which they are a part. Tenant agrees to pay as additional rental any increase in premiums for insurance against loss by fire that may be charged during the term of this lease on the amount of insurance to be carried by Landlord on said premises and/or the building of which they are a part, resulting from the business carried on in the leased premises by Tenant, whether or not Landlord has consented to the same. If Tenant installs any electrical equipment that overloads the lines in the herein leased premises, Tenant shall at its own expense make whatever changes are necessary to comply with the requirements of the Insurance Underwriters and governmental authorities having jurisdiction.

Section 2: Tenant shall, during the entire term hereof, keep in full force and effect a policy of public liability insurance with respect to the demised premises and the business operated by Tenant, and/or any subtenants of Tenant in the demised premises, in which both Landlord and Tenant shall be named as parties covered thereby, or which provides equivalent protection to and is approved by Landlord, and in which the limits of liability shall be not less than one hundred thousand dollars ($100,000) per person and two hundred thousand dollars ($200,000) for each accident or occurrence for bodily injury and ten thousand dollars ($10,000) for property damages. Tenants shall furnish Landlord with a certificate or certificates of insurance, or other acceptable evidence that such insurance is in force at all times during the term hereof.

Article XV. Abuse of Plumbing, Walls, Etc.

Section 1: The plumbing facilities shall not be used for any other purpose than that for which they are constructed, and no foreign substance of any kind shall be thrown therein, and the expense of any breakage, stoppage, or damage resulting from a violation of this provision shall be borne by Tenant, who shall, or whose employees, agents, invitees, or licensees shall, have caused it. Tenant, its employees, or agents, shall not mark, paint, drill or in any way deface any walls, ceilings, partitions, floors, wood, stone or iron work without the written consent of Landlord.

Article XVI. Exterior and Window Lighting

Section 1: If requested by Landlord, Tenant shall keep the display windows in the leased premises well lighted from dusk until 11:00 o'clock P.M., or such other reasonable time as determined by Landlord, during each and every weekday except Sundays and holidays of the term of this lease, unless prevented by cause beyond the control of Tenant. Landlord agrees to provide time clocks for control of such lights.

Section 2: Landlord agrees to provide facilities for the lighting of the parking area located adjacent to the demised premises during such hours of darkness as Tenant is open for business.

Article XVII. Receiving, Delivery and Tenant Parking

Section 1: Tenant agrees that all receiving and delivery of goods and merchandise and all removal of merchandise, supplies, equipment, garbage and refuse shall be made only by way of the underground truck road and the loading platform adjacent thereto. Landlord hereby grants to Tenant and Tenant's employees, agents and invitees the right, during the term hereof, to use, in common with others entitled to the use thereof, such underground truck road and loading platform subject to reasonable regulations as Landlord shall make from time to time.

Section 2: Notwithstanding any other provision of this lease Tenant and its employees shall park their cars only in areas specifically designated for that purpose by Landlord from time to time. Tenant further agrees that upon written notice from Landlord it will within five (5) days furnish to Landlord the automobile license numbers assigned to its car and the cars of all its employees.

Article XVIII. Assignment

Section 1: Tenant agrees not to assign or in any manner transfer this lease or any estate or interest therein without the previous written consent of Landlord, and not to sublet said premises or any part or parts thereof or allow anyone to come in with, through or under it without like consent. Consent by Landlord to one or more assignment of this lease or to one or more subletting of said premises shall not operate to exhaust Landlord's rights under this Article.

Section 2: Tenant agrees not to change the advertised name of the place of business operated in the herein described premises without the written permission of Landlord.

Article XIX. Access to Premises

Section 1: Landlord shall have the right to enter upon the leased premises at all reasonable hours for the purpose of inspecting the same, or of making repairs, additions or alterations to the demised premises or any property owned or controlled by Landlord. If Landlord deems any repairs required to be made by Tenant necessary, it may demand that Tenant make the same forthwith, and if Tenant refuses or neglects to commence such repairs and complete the same with reasonable dispatch, Landlord may make or cause such repairs to be made and shall not be responsible to Tenant for any loss or damage that may accrue to its stock or business by reason thereof, and if Landlord makes or causes such repairs to be made, Tenant agrees that it will forthwith, on demand, pay to Landlord the cost thereof with interest at seven per cent (7%) per annum, and if it shall default in such payment, Landlord shall have the remedies provided in Article XXIII hereof.

Section 2: For a period commencing ninety (90) days prior to the termination of this lease, Landlord may have reasonable access to the premises herein demised for the purpose of exhibiting the same to prospective tenants.

Article XX. Eminent Domain

Section 1: If the whole of the premises hereby leased shall be taken by any public authority under the power of eminent domain then the term of this lease shall cease as of the day possession shall be taken by such public authority and the rent shall be paid up to that day with a proportionate refund by Landlord of such rent as may have been paid in advance.

Section 2: If a part only of the leased premises shall be taken under eminent domain Tenant shall have the right either to terminate this lease and declare same null and void or, subject to Landlord's right of termination as set forth in Section 4 of this Article, to continue in the possession of the remainder of the leased premises and shall notify Landlord in writing within ten (10) days after such taking of Tenant's intention. In the event Tenant elects to remain in possession, all of the terms herein provided shall continue in effect, except that the minimum rent shall be reduced in proportion to the amount of the premises taken and Landlord shall at its own cost and expense make all the necessary repairs or alterations to the basic building, store front and interior work as covered by Description of Landlord's Work attached hereto so as to constitute the remaining premises a complete architectural unit.

Section 3: All damages awarded for such taking under the power of eminent domain whether for the whole or a part of the leased premises shall belong to and be the property of Landlord whether such damages shall be awarded as compensation for diminution in value to the leasehold or to the fee of the premises; provided, however, that Landlord shall not be entitled to the award made to Tenant for loss of business, depreciation to, and cost of removal of stock and fixtures.

Section 4: If more than fifty per cent (50%) of the first floor area of the building in which the demised premises are located shall be taken under power of eminent domain Landlord may, by written notice to Tenant delivered on or before the date of surrendering possession to the public authority, terminate this lease. In the event Landlord elects to so terminate, Landlord shall indemnify Tenant for the unamortized cost of Tenant's fixtures and leasehold improvements by paying to Tenant a sum of money which shall be determined by either

(a) the depreciated amount at which such fixtures and leasehold improvements are carried on Tenant's books or

(b) the depreciated amount as determined by multiplying the original capital cost by a fraction the numerator of which shall be the number of years of the term of this lease that shall not have expired at the time of such damage and the denominator of which shall be the number of years of the term of this lease which shall not have expired at the time of the making of such expenditures,

whichever sum is the lesser, and further providing that from such sum of indemnity shall be deducted an amount equal to that which Tenant shall have received or is receivable by Tenant from the public authority as an award for damages to such fixtures and leasehold improvements as a result of the taking.

Article XXI. Damage

Section 1: In case the demised premises shall be partially or totally destroyed by fire or other casualty insurable under full standard extended coverage insurance, as to become partially or totally untenantable, the same shall be repaired as speedily as possible at the expense of Landlord, unless Landlord shall elect not to rebuild as hereinafter provided, and a just and proportionate part of the rent shall be abated until so repaired. The obligation of Landlord hereunder shall be limited to the basic building, store front and interior work as covered by Description of Landlord's Work attached hereto.

Section 2: If more than fifty per cent (50%) of the first floor area of the building in which the demised premises are located shall be destroyed by fire, or other casualty, as to become wholly untenantable, then Landlord may, if it so elects, rebuild or put said building in good condition and fit for occupancy within a reasonable time after such destruction or damage, or may give notice in writing terminating this lease. If Landlord elects to repair or rebuild said building, it shall, within thirty (30) days after such injury, give Tenants thereof notice of its intention to repair and then to proceed with reasonable speed to repair. In case Landlord elects to rebuild or repair, as herein provided, then the obligation of Landlord hereunder shall be limited to the basic building, store front and interior work as covered by Description of Landlord's Work attached hereto.

Section 3: In the event that Landlord elects not to rebuild under the conditions of Section 2 of this Article, then Landlord shall indemnify Tenant for the unamortized cost of Tenant's fixtures and leasehold improvements by paying to Tenant a sum of money which shall be determined by either

    (a) the depreciated amount at which such fixtures and leasehold improvements are carried on Tenant's books or

    (b) the depreciated amount as determined by multiplying the original capital cost by a fraction the numerator of which shall be the number of years of the term of this lease that shall not have expired at the time of such damage and the denominator of which shall be the number of years of the term of this lease which shall not have expired at the time of the making of such expenditures,

whichever sum is the lesser, and further providing that from such sum of indemnity shall be deducted an amount equal to that which Tenant shall have received or is receivable by Tenant from insurance carried by it on the said fixtures and leasehold improvements.

Article XXII. Bankruptcy

Section 1: Neither this lease, nor any interest therein nor any estate thereby created shall pass to any trustee or receiver or assignee for the benefit of creditors or otherwise by operation of law.

Section 2: In the event the estate created hereby shall be taken in execution or by other process of law, or if Tenant shall be adjudicated insolvent or bankrupt pursuant to the provisions of any state or Federal insolvency or bankruptcy act, or if a receiver or trustee of the property of Tenant shall be appointed by reason of Tenant's insolvency or inability to pay its debts, or if any assignment shall be made of Tenant's property for the benefit of creditors, then and in any of such events, Landlord may at its option terminate this lease and all rights of Tenant hereunder, by giving to Tenant notice in writing of the election of Landlord to so terminate.

Section 3: Tenant shall not cause or give cause for the institution of legal proceedings seeking to have Tenant adjudicated bankrupt, reorganized or rearranged under the bankruptcy laws of the United States, and shall not cause or give cause for the appointment of a trustee or receiver for Tenant's assets, and shall not make any assignment for the benefit of creditors, or become or be adjudicated insolvent. The allowance of any petition under the bankruptcy law, or the appointment of a trustee or receiver of Tenant or its assets, shall be conclusive evidence that Tenant caused, or gave cause therefor, unless such allowance of the petition, or the appointment of a trustee or receiver, is vacated within thirty (30) days after such allowance or appointment. Any act described in this Section 3 shall be deemed a material breach of Tenant's obligations hereunder, and upon such breach by Tenant, Landlord may at its option and in addition to any other remedy available to Landlord terminate this lease and all rights of Tenant hereunder, by giving to Tenant notice in writing of the election of Landlord so to terminate.

Article XXIII. Non-Payment of Rent

Section 1: If any rental payable by Tenants to Landlord shall be and remain unpaid for more than fifteen (15) days after same is due and payable, or if Tenant shall violate or default any of the other covenants, agreements, stipulations or conditions herein, and such violation or default shall continue for a period of thirty (30) days after written notice of such violation or default, then it shall be optional for Landlord to declare this lease forfeited and the said term ended, and to re-enter said premises, with or without process of law, using such force as may be necessary to remove all persons or chattels therefrom, and Landlord shall not be liable for damages by reason of such re-entry or forfeiture; but notwithstanding such re-entry by Landlord, the liability of Tenant for the rent provided for herein shall not be relinquished or extinguished for the balance of the term of this lease. And it is further understood that Tenant will pay, in addition to the rentals and other sums agreed to be paid hereunder, such additional sums as the court may adjudge reasonable as attorney's fees in any suit or action instituted by Landlord to enforce the provisions of this lease, or the collection of the rentals due Landlord hereunder.

Article XXIV. Holding Over

Section 1: In the event Tenant remains in possession of the herein leased premises after the expiration of this lease and without the execution of a new lease, it shall be deemed to be occupying said premises as a tenant from month to month, subject to all the conditions, provisions and obligations of this lease insofar as the same are applicable to a month to month tenancy.

Article XXV. Waiver

Section 1: One or more waivers of any covenant or condition by Landlord shall not be construed as a waiver of a subsequent breach of the same covenant or condition, and the consent or approval by Landlord to or of any act by Tenant requiring Landlord's consent or approval shall not be deemed to waive or render unnecessary Landlord's consent or approval to or of any subsequent similar act by Tenant.

Article XXVI. Subordination

Section 1: Tenant agrees that this lease shall be subordinate to any mortgages or trust deeds that may hereafter be placed upon said premises and to any and all advances to be made thereunder, and to the interest thereon, and all renewals, replacements, and extensions thereof, provided the mortgagee or trustee, named in said mortgages or trust deeds shall agree to recognize the lease of Tenant in the event of foreclosure if Tenant is not in default. In the event of any mortgagee or trustee electing to have the lease a prior lien to its mortgage or deed of trust, then and in such event, upon such mortgagee or trustee notifying Tenant to that effect, this lease shall be deemed prior in lien to the said mortgage or trust deed, whether or not this lease is dated prior to or subsequent to the date of said mortgage or trust deed.

Article XXVII. Notices

Section 1: Whenever under this lease a provision is made for notice of any kind, it shall be deemed sufficient notice and service thereof if such notice to Tenant is in writing addressed to Tenant at the last known post office address of Tenant or at the leased premises and sent by registered mail with postage prepaid, and if such notice to Landlord is in writing, addressed to the last known post office address of Landlord and sent by registered mail with postage prepaid. Notice need be sent to but one tenant or landlord where tenant or landlord is more than one person.

Article XXVIII. Construction

Section 1: Nothing contained herein shall be deemed or construed by the parties hereto, nor by any third party, as creating the relationship of principal and agent or of partnership or of joint venture between the parties hereto, it being understood and agreed that neither the method of computation of rent, nor any other provision contained herein, nor any acts of the parties herein, shall be deemed to create any relationship between the parties hereto other than the relationship of landlord and tenant. Whenever herein the singular number is used, the same shall include the plural, and the masculine gender shall include the feminine and neuter genders.

Article XXIX. Non-Liability

Section 1: Landlord shall not be responsible or liable to Tenant for any loss or damage that may be occasioned by or through the acts or omissions of persons occupying adjoining premises or any part of the premises adjacent to or connected with the premises hereby leased or any part of the building of which the leased premises are a part or for any loss or damage resulting to Tenant or his property from burst, stopped or leaking water, gas, sewer, or steam pipes or for any damage or loss of property within the demised premises from any cause whatsoever to the extent that payment therefor is made to or on behalf of Tenant pursuant to any insurance contract which at the time of such loss permits waiver of subrogation rights prior to a loss thereunder.

Article XXX. Common Toilets and Washrooms

Section 1: Toilet and washroom facilities for the use of Tenant and its employees are designed to be used in common with occupants of the other stores identified as ....
and Tenant agrees to cooperate with the occupants of the herein designated stores to the end that the said common facilities, including the halls, stairways and areaways connecting them with the demised premises, shall at all times be kept and maintained in a clean, orderly and sanitary manner. Tenant further agrees to share in an equitable manner with occupants of the other designated stores the expenses of thus maintaining the common facilities including the expense of furnishing the usual toilet and washroom supplies of paper, soap and towels.

Section 2: In the event that the common facilities as set forth in Section 1 above shall not be kept and maintained in a clean, orderly and sanitary manner, Landlord shall have the right in its sole discretion to assume such obligation and charge the expense thereof to Tenant in an amount proportionate to the ratio that the total floor area of the herein demised premises bears to the total floor area of all of the stores identified in Section 1 above as sharing in the use of said common facilities.

Article XXXI. Consent not Unreasonably Withheld

Section 1: Landlord agrees that whenever under this lease provision is made for Tenant securing the written consent of Landlord such written consent shall not be unreasonably withheld.

IN WITNESS WHEREOF, Landlord and Tenant have signed their names and affixed their seals the day and year first above written.

**Description of Landlord's Work
for Annexation to Lease**

A. Structure

1. The structural frame, columns, beams and joists shall be of steel and concrete construction. The roof shall be concrete type construction. The floor slabs shall be reinforced concrete, designed to carry the following live loads:

Basement	250 lbs.
First Floor	125 lbs.
Mezzanine	100 lbs.

    The clear height of floors between the floor slab and finished ceiling shall be not less than 10' 0" in the basement; 14' 0" on the first floor; 8' 0" under the mezzanine; and 7' 6" over mezzanine.
2. The reinforced concrete exterior walls of the basement shall be waterproofed, and the roof shall be a bonded, built-up, 20-year roof, and will provide the equivalent of 1 in. rigid insulation.
3. Fire-resistant partitions shall be provided between the leased area and other leased areas, as well as between public or common spaces in the basement and the leased area.
4. Where the leased space occupies more than one level, a stairway as required by the Building Code of the City of Detroit shall be provided.

B. Public Spaces and Services

1. A 4' 0" wide labeled metal door shall be provided between the leased space and loading dock in the basement and a 3' 6" wide metal door at other openings between the leased space and public or common corridors. Electrically operated dumbwaiter service with a maximum platform size of 9 sq. ft. and a car capacity of 300 lbs. at 50 ft. per minute, shall be available to serve the basement and first floor.

    (a) The following public or common spaces shall be provided in each building: On the first floor, a covered walkway surrounding the building; in the basement a truck road and loading platform; and in the basement and/or on the first floor, corridors connecting the leased premises with access to loading platform.

(b) Employees' toilets and washrooms shall be provided in size and number, and contain the number of plumbing fixtures with hot water, cold water, sewer connections and ventilation as required by the Detroit Code. These toilet rooms shall be enclosed by a wall of structural glazed tile and equipped with the necessary number of doors. Landlord has, at his discretion, the right to arrange common toilet facilities for a number of tenants where such an arrangement would be more advantageous from a planning point of view.

C. Store Fronts

1. Store fronts shall be designed by Landlord's architect and installed by Landlord, subject to the approval of tenant for design, and approval of Landlord for both design and cost. The term, *Store Front*, shall refer to the enclosing wall separating the heated area of the leased space from the covered sidewalk or other public area and specifically shall not include any portion of the construction which shall extend within the said enclosing wall.

2. Entrance and exit doors shall be provided in number and size as required to conform with Building Code. These doors may be single doors or pairs of doors and shall consist of metal frames with plate glass inserts or tempered glass panels. They shall be equipped with the necessary standard hardware such as door pulls, and handles, door closers and hinges.

D. Utilities

Steam

1. Steam from the central plant shall be brought to the leased space or fan room where it will be made accessible and metered for the tenant's use.

Electricity

2. Electrical work shall be provided as follows:
   (a) Service shall be brought to individual panel boards containing circuit breakers for branch circuits.
   (b) After consultation with tenant, and in consideration of tenant's needs and wishes, a distribution system, to suit the normal operating requirements of tenant, will be provided.

Water

3. (a) Water shall be brought to the leased space or fan room where it will be made accessible to the individual tenants and its consumption metered.
   (b) Cold water supply lines shall be supplied for all toilets and washrooms and roughed in for all tenant supplied equipment.
   (c) Hot water supply lines shall be supplied for all toilets and washrooms and roughed in for all tenant supplied equipment.
   (d) A water heating system capable of supplying 150° F. water shall be provided for all toilets and washrooms required to be installed by Landlord in accordance with B. 1(b) above.

Gas

4. Gas mains shall be brought to the leased space or fan room where gas will be made available to the individual tenants and its consumption metered.

Sewer

5. Waste lines shall be supplied to all toilets and washrooms and roughed in for all tenant supplied equipment.

E. Heating and Air Conditioning

Heating

1. Adequate heating coils will be provided for the space heating of the air conditioned area to 70° when outside air is at minus 10° F. Supplementary radiation by convectors, exposed pipe, or radiators will be provided at store fronts and in basement or service areas, and connected to the steam main. This supplementary radiation will be limited to that necessary to prevent steaming or frosting of the show windows, and to provide a minimum of 60° F. in the storage and service areas.

Air Conditioning

2. (a) Chilled water will be produced in a central plant and piped to a fan room where it will be metered for tenant's consumption.
   (b) After consultation with tenant, and in consideration of tenant's needs and wishes, a duct system, to suit the normal operating requirements of tenant, will be provided.
   (c) Air handling equipment, including fans, chilled water coils, filters, connections and controls, will be provided and attached to the duct system.

(d) The system will be designed to maintain in the conditioned space a maximum temperature of 80° F. and to maintain a relative humidity not exceeding 50% within the limits of plus or minus 1° F. at the controlling instrument, and a rise of not more than 3° from 80° F. at peak periods. These design standards are subject to the following conditions:

(1) An outside dry bulb temperature of 95° F., coincident with a wet bulb temperature of 75° F.

(2) An installed lighting load of 6 watts per square foot of conditioned space.

(3) An occupancy load of 1 person per 40 square feet of conditioned space.

(4) Ventilation to the conditioned space of 10 c.f.m. per person.

(5) A maximum of 1.73 c.f.m. per square foot and .0046 tons per square foot.

F. Interior Finishes

1. Floors for leased space will be smooth cement finish.
2. Where tenant desires to install other floor materials at his expense, provision to accommodate such floors will be made, however, information concerning such floors must be in the possession of Landlord in sufficient time not to delay construction.
3. Ceilings will be finished as follows:
   (a) In all storage and service areas the exposed structure shall receive two coats of oil base paint.
   (b) In sales areas a smooth plaster or dry-built hung ceiling with standard acoustic fiber tile construction will be installed on a metal suspension system.
4. Interior side of all walls enclosing the leased space in sales areas only shall receive smooth plaster finish ready for painting by tenant.

G. Limitations and Exceptions

1. The Landlord's work shall be limited to that covered in the foregoing paragraphs. The tenant shall be responsible for but not limited to,
   (a) All electric fixtures within the leased space and their installation.
   (b) All interior curtain walls.
   (c) All light coves or other special hung ceilings.
   (d) All interior painting and decor other than in storage and service areas in the basement.
   (e) All furnishings and fixtures.
   (f) All show window backgrounds, show window floors, show window ceilings and show window lighting fixtures within the leased space.
   (g) All mechanical equipment, elevators, escalators, freight ele-

vators, conveyors, and their shafts, pent houses, doors, etc., within the leased premises. All such work shall be done in a manner to conform with governing codes and ordinances, and only with the approval of Landlord.

(h) All floor coverings.

(i) Interior vestibules and storm doors.

(j) All store signs.

2. All work which tenant wishes to undertake at his own expense during the general construction period shall be awarded to the contractors approved by Landlord.

3. All work undertaken by tenant at his own expense and which is connected to the structure must be installed in such a way as not to damage the structure or any part thereof.

4. Mezzanines: Mezzanines will be limited to not more than one-third of the first floor area and not closer than 10′ 0″ to the store front line.

Architectural and Construction Standards

A. All entrance doors must be recessed in such manner that doors opening to the outside will not cross the general store front line.

B. The depth of the arcade in an arcade front shall be limited to its width.

C. To secure a clear separation of one tenant store from the other, and to avoid possible clashing in materials and treatments, there shall be a neutral strip between each store of a minimum of 12 inches in width. The centerline of this neutral strip shall coincide with the lines defining the leased spaces.

D. To avoid areas which will not provide points of interest to pedestrian customers, continuous blind wall sections of more than 10 percent of the total exposed perimeter shall not be permitted. The break separating each blind wall area must be of a major character, such as a glass wall view into the store or a large scale show window, except in stores of less than 100 lineal feet of perimeter where the limit shall be 20 percent.

E. It is the desire of Landlord to give the tenants the greatest possible freedom in the choice of store front materials but such materials must be fireproof and lend themselves to easy upkeep and maintenance, and must offer a pleasant, orderly appearance.

F. It is the desire of Landlord to give the tenants the greatest possible freedom in the choice of store front colors, but—

(1) Colors must harmonize with the color scheme of the Center itself and, especially, with the columns of the colonnade.

(2) Colors must harmonize with the color scheme of the surrounding stores. To assist the tenants, a general color range will be developed, with a sufficiently large selection to permit a wide latitude of individual expression.

G. No store front or any part thereof shall project beyond the lines describing the leased premises, with the exception that signs may project beyond the general store front line not more than 12 inches.

H. The Center provides general sun and weather protection by covered colonnades sufficient to cut off the sun's rays down to a 45 degree angle. In certain cases additional protection will be provided by awnings, to be furnished by Landlord and operated by the tenant. In such cases the awnings will carry a standard, uniform sign panel with the name of the store in front of which the awning is hung.

I. Signs on all multi-occupancy buildings shall be restricted in location to the store front proper below the colonnade ceiling, shall have no part more than 4' 0" high and shall have no flashing or moving lights.

CONCESSION LEASE

(This is a complete lease agreement for the operation of a concession or "leased department" within a general merchandise or department store.)

AGREEMENT, made this   day of   , 19 , between   , a   Corporation, with its principal office and place of business at   Street, City of   , State of   , herein referred to as the "Licensor" and   with offices at   , herein referred to as "Licensee."

WITNESSETH:

The Licensor conducts a large department store in the City of   , State of   , and the Licensee desires to operate and conduct a department in said store for the sale at retail of the articles, merchandise, and/or services set forth in Article I hereof,

NOW, THEREFORE, in consideration of the promises and of the agreements herein contained, the parties agree with each other as follows:

1st. The Licensor hereby grants unto the Licensee the right and privilege of conducting, subject to the approval of Licensor, a department to be known as No.   , for

**Location of
Department**

only at such location in the Licensor's store at   Street in the City of   , and State of   , as the Licensor may from time to time designate. Licensee agrees not to engage in the business hereinabove provided to be operated by Licensee, within the city (or other specified geographical area) mentioned other than in the store of Licensor, unless this provision is modified by the written consent of the Licensor.

Charges

2nd. The Licensee hereby covenants and agrees that it will pay to the licensor as compensation for said rights and privileges granted to the Licensee,   percent (%) of the net sales arising and to arise from the business conducted by it and upon said space and premises. Net sales shall be defined as gross sales less returns, (some thought should also be given to defining the types of sales to be included, i.e., cash sales, charge sales, installment sales and lay-a-way sales). In addition to the percentage to be paid to the Licensor, it should also be provided that the Licensee shall pay to the Licensor a minimum of   dollars. This minimum, however, shall not be in addition to the percentage of net sales paid to the Licensor, but shall only be in effect where such percentage does not equal the minimum amount stated.

Term

3rd. Operations under this agreement shall commence on   , or such earlier date as may be mutually agreed upon by the parties hereto

Cancellation

in writing and this agreement shall continue in effect for a period of 52 weeks from the effective date of such commencement of operations—and shall continue thereafter at will, subject to the right of either party to cancel this agreement by giving at least sixty (60) days prior written notice to the other, sent as provided in Paragraph 16, at the address hereinabove recited, or at such address as may be subsequently designated in writing.

**Substituted
Location**

4th. The expense of moving fixtures of the Licensee from one location to another shall be borne by the Licensor, except that if the cause of such moving shall have been beyond the control of the Licensor, as in the case of fire, or an act of God, demand of any governmental authority, insurance companies, insurance exchange or departments, Building Department or Fire Department, or any other Governmental agency or officer or officers of any of them, the expense shall be borne by the Licensee.

Settlements

5th. Settlements between the Licensor and Licensee of the business of each accounting month shall be made on or about the tenth (10th) day of each succeeding month. In addition to the percentage of net sales payable to the Licensor, which Licensor is hereby authorized to deduct and retain from gross receipts, it may also reimburse itself for all obligations due to it from the Licensee, including supplies purchased by the Licensee from the Licensor, and any employees' salaries which may have been incurred or paid by the Licensor for the Licensee, advertising costs, and service charges, and any and all other expenses authorized by and chargeable to the Licensee, and all matters of obligations due to the Licensor from the Licensee. All settlements shall be made according to the books of the Licensor, subject to correction for errors. Upon any monthly statement each party agrees to pay to the other any amount disclosed by such statement to be due from such party to the other.

Sales Receipts and Records

6th. The Licensee agrees that the receipts (including checks accepted by the Licensor) from the operation of said department to be conducted by the Licensee, shall go through the regular channels of the business of the Licensor, according to its usual and ordinary methods of doing business in the same manner as sales made by the Licensor for its own account in its general business, and shall be retained by the Licensor in trust for the Licensee, subject to payment as herein provided. By this provision the parties intend and agree that the receipts shall be transmitted from said department to the cashiering department of the Licensor and shall not be retained in the said department or handled by the employees thereof except for the purpose of transmitting the receipts from the customer to said cashiering department. Sales books shall be used by the employees of said department similar to the sales books used by employees in other departments of the Licensor's store, and with each sale shall be transmitted the record thereof in such form as the Licensor may require. The Licensor shall have the right at any and all times to inspect any and all such books, and may require the installation by the Licensee in said department of such measures for preventing losses, thefts and shortages, and for detecting inaccuracies, as it may desire. The Licensee agrees to make such installations at its expense. The Licensee agrees that the Licensor may rely upon all such sales records and other records and representations made by the employees in said department, and the Licensee agrees that such records shall be conclusive as against it.

Advertising

7th. The Licensee agrees that it will not advertise its business carried on in said store in said department without the approval of the Licensor as to the advertising medium and text; it being understood that the business name of the Licensor is its exclusive property and under no circumstances is to be used by the Licensee without the consent of the Licensor. The Licensee, during the term of this agreement and any renewal or extension thereof, agrees to spend a sum equal to   (%) percent of the gross receipts from the business done in said department, to advertise in newspapers the materials and merchandise of the Licensee. The Licensee shall prepare its own advertising subject to the approval of the Licensor. Where, however, the Licensee desires the Licensor to prepare the advertisements the Licensee agrees to pay   (%) percent of the cost of advertising as a service charge for the preparation of the advertising matter, to include drawings, lay-outs and copy. The Licensor agrees to give the Licensee the benefit of all advertising rates and discounts enjoyed by the Licensor.

**Window
Display
and
Exhibitions**

8th. The Licensor agrees that the Licensee shall have the use, from time to time, of a window display and bargain booths together with the sales counters and fixtures as shall be installed in the location from time to time designated to the Licensee, and suitable room for storage of stock. The Licensor shall have the right to control the displays and public exhibitions and any other demonstrations within the store or adjacent thereto, and in connection with the said business conducted by the Licensee from and in the store of the Licensor. The Licensee shall supply material and fixtures for window display, and such display shall be subject to the approval and control of the Licensor.

Services

9th. The Licensor shall furnish free of cost to the Licensee the usual and customary heat, light, water service, porter service, and elevator service and make same available to the Licensee for the proper conduct of said department. Delivery service will be made by the   Parcel Service, or by such other method, as may be employed by the Licensor, and the Licensee agrees to pay the cost of delivery and that the Licensee hereby assumes the liability of damage

in delivery except insofar as the Licensor may recover for such damaged delivery from the

Parcel Service or similar carrier. The Licensee shall
not make any charge to customers for delivery and
shall prepare all packages wrapped and addressed
ready for delivery in the general style of packages
of other departments of the Licensor, and shall bear
the name of the Licensor as "   ."

**First
Class
Department**

10*th*. The Licensee agrees to maintain and conduct
a modern first class department in keeping with the
standards of the Licensor and to employ in said department all necessary sales persons and employees to
properly conduct said department.

**Employees:
Rules
Regulations
Hours and
Wages**

11*th*. All persons employed in and about or in connection with the said business to be conducted by the
Licensee in said department shall be and hereby are
recognized to be the employees of the Licensee. They
shall conform to all rules, regulations and requirements now in force in the business of the Licensor,
as well as all rules and regulations as hereafter may be
promulgated or put into operation by it. The Licensee
agrees to be responsible for all acts of omission or
commission of its employees. All persons employed in
said department shall be selected and recommended
by the Licensee and upon Licensor's approval engaged by the Licensor for and on behalf of the Licensee. All employees shall be first subject to the
approval of the Licensor who shall have the right
to require the Licensee to immediately dismiss from
its employment any employee deemed unsuitable, or
who shall violate any of the rules or regulations of
the Licensor, or shall in any way conduct themselves
to the dissatisfaction of the Licensor, and the Licensee
shall immediately comply with such request in such
cases. The Licensee shall have the right to regulate
and fix the salaries, commissions and bonuses of its
employees but such salaries, commissions and bonuses
shall conform to the general standard of the Licensor
and may be advanced in the first instance by the Licensor in the usual and regular way in which the
Licensor pays or hereafter may pay wages to its own
employees and the wages so advanced shall be
charged against the Licensee, who hereby agrees to
repay the same to said Licensor. The Licensee shall
furnish to the Licensor all information desired by the
Licensor with respect to the Licensee's payroll.

The parties agree that the employees will at all
times work for the mutual interest of the parties

hereto. It is further agreed that the Licensor will not make any loans or personal advances to the Licensee's employees out of the money in its hands due to the Licensee unless authorized by the general office of the Licensee. The Licensee agrees to follow the Licensor's policy on paid vacations and legal holidays. Licensee agrees that before dismissing from its employ any of its employees, it will first obtain the consent of the Licensor.

Merchandise Price

Customers' Adjustments

12*th*. Licensee further agrees that the merchandise in said department shall be sold at prices first named to customers and said prices shall compare favorably with prices put upon similar goods by competitors of the Licensee. The Licensee also agrees that it will adhere faithfully to the doctrine of selling "strictly at one price" and all merchandise shall be marked in plain figures. Settlements of disputes with customers in regard to merchandise shall in the first instance be under the control of the Licensee and shall be settled by it in accordance with the policy prevailing in the Licensor's business. In the event that the Licensee is unable to settle such disputes to the entire satisfaction of the customer, the matter shall be referred to the Bureau of Adjustments of the Licensor, and the Licensor shall have the right to make such adjustments as it may deem proper and may charge all such allowances or refunds to the account of the Licensee, who will abide by the Licensor's decision in the premises. The Licensor agrees that it will adjust any controversy in a reasonable manner.

Licensee's Purchases

13*th*. With the prior approval of the Licensor the Licensee shall have charge of the purchasing of all merchandise for said department, all of which shall be purchased in the name of and on the credit of the Licensee and shall be paid for directly by the Licensee, and the Licensee agrees not to pledge the credit of the Licensor.

Taxes

14*th*. The Licensee agrees to take care of and pay all license fees and taxes, including but not limited to Social Security and Unemployment taxes, which are now imposed or may hereafter be imposed on the business carried on in said department or on Licensee's merchandise.

Property Damage

15*th*. It is further agreed that the Licensee shall have free access to entrances or any elevators or stairways in the said store for its own use and the use of its employees and customers at such time as the store is open but the hours of opening and closing the store shall be under the control of the Licensor. The Licensor shall not be liable to the Licensee for any damage to the Licensee's property occasioned by failure to keep the said store or any portion thereof, or any elevator therein in repair or running condition or caused by plumbing, heating apparatus, water, electric light, gas or steam pipes of any kind or nature, or the bursting, leaking or running of any waste pipe in said store. The Licensee hereby assumes complete responsibility for all its stock of merchandise and other property which may at any time be in said store, and for all thefts thereof, losses, stock and shrinkages or injury to or loss of said stock from any cause whatsoever, whether herein specifically mentioned or not.

Notices

16*th*. All notices and demands shall be sent to either party at the address herein above recited or to such place as the parties hereto may designate in writing. Notices and demands may be given by registered mail or in person.

Waiver

17*th*. No waiver or any right, agreement or condition hereof, shall be binding upon the Licensor or Licensee unless in writing, and waiver of any covenant or condition shall be a waiver only to such default and not as to subsequent provisions or defaults.

Bankruptcy, Insolvency, etc.

18*th*. It is understood and agreed that if the Licensor or the Licensee shall become insolvent or be adjudged bankrupt, or request an extension of credit or if any execution or attachment issue against it, and be levied against the merchandise or assets, or if it give a chattel mortgage or deed of trust or deed of assignment or bill of sale conveying its merchandise or assets in bulk, or if a receiver or receivers be appointed for the business of it, then and in such event the other party unfavorably affected shall thereby have the right and option immediately to terminate the within agreement and shall have a prior lien on the goods, chattels and effects of the other party to secure any sums due.

Fire

19*th*. It is further agreed that in the event the Licensor's store shall be destroyed by fire or other cause so as to make it impossible to carry on business therein the license and provisions herein provided shall terminate and be of no further force and effect. In the event said store is partially destroyed by fire or other cause and is repaired by the Licensor within a reasonable length of time, the Licensee will be excused from performance during the time said store is not open for business as usual, and the license contained herein shall continue to the end of the term.

Telephone

20*th*. The Licensor agrees to supply the Licensee with telephone service connecting the said department with all other departments of the store and enabling calls to be made from the outside to the said department. The Licensee shall pay for all outside telephone calls made from said department at the rate of ( ) cents per call and all toll charges. If an outside telephone instrument is provided for the Licensee's separate use it shall pay ( ) cents per month for the use of such instrument.

Fixtures and Signs

21*st*. That attached hereto and marked Exhibit "A" is an inventory of all equipment and fixtures located in said department and owned by the Licensor. Such fixtures as shall be supplied by the Licensor shall remain the property of the Licensor and the Licensee agrees to maintain in good repair, at its own cost and expense, the fixtures, equipment and machinery supplied by the Licensor for the use in said department, ordinary wear and tear excepted. The Licensee agrees to install such fixtures, counters, show cases, machinery or equipment as it shall find necessary in the operation of said department, at its own cost and expense. All such improvements shall blend with harmonious effect with the present fixtures of the Licensor's adjoining department. All such fixtures and improvements must first be approved in writing by the Licensor. No signs shall be installed or displayed without the written approval of the Licensor. At the expiration of this agreement the entire department, including all the equipment, fixtures and machinery, except such fixtures that have been installed or brought into the department by the Licensee, and are the property of the Licensee and which may be removed without any injury or damage whatsoever to the Licensor or its property, shall be delivered to the Licensor in good working order and condition, reasonable wear and tear excepted.

Employees' Discount

22*nd*. The Licensee agrees to give all employees of the Licensor a discount of (%) percent of the sale price upon all merchandise purchased in the said department.

Insurance

23*rd*. The Licensee agrees to fully insure all its merchandise, fixtures and equipment in the said department, or in any warehouse or any other building of the Licensor, against loss by fire or water, and the Licensee also agrees to secure and pay for workmen's compensation insurance, and such other insurance as may be required by law. The Licensee agrees to reimburse the Licensor for the cost of public liability and products liability insurance covering the said department which insurance shall include the interest of both Licensor and Licensee.

Statute and Ordinances

24th. The Licensee shall take good care of and shall not do or permit to be done any acts or omissions which may be detrimental or cause damage to the Licensor's store or anything contrary to laws, rules or regulations of any governmental authority. Licensee shall promptly execute and comply with all statutes, rules, orders, ordinances and regulations of any governmental authority or legislature or of the State Board of Fire Underwriters, or of the State Fire Insurance Exchange, or with the recommendations of any insurance company, or of any duly constituted authority, all at the cost and expense of the Licensee arising out of or resulting from Licensee's business.

Assignment

25th. This agreement and the right and privilege granted to the Licensee hereunder are personal and shall not be assigned or underlet by the Licensee by agreement of any type or by operation of law. This agreement shall terminate in the event of death, incapacity of the Licensee or if the Licensee permits any other person or persons, firm or corporation to transact the Licensee's business in said department other than employees as same are herein defined without first obtaining the written consent of the Licensor. The Licensor may, whenever in its opinion the operation of the department by the Licensee interferes with the business of the Licensor, terminate this agreement and the right and privilege hereto upon 10 days notice in writing to the Licensee.

Injuries to Person or Property

26th. The Licensor shall not be liable for any damage or loss in any respect or particular, on account of any matter or thing whatsoever to Licensee, and Licensee hereby assumes all responsibility for injuries to persons or property of customers, employees, and other arising in the department conducted by it or out of transactions, acts or omissions therein or connected therewith and agrees and hereby covenants to hold the Licensor absolutely free and harmless from any claim of customers, employees or others for damages arising out of injuries to anyone, or transactions with anyone, whether employee or otherwise, in said department, or arising through or from the business of said department or for violation of agreements made with customers, employees or others by said Licensee, or from any claim of any sort whatsoever, made by third parties, and arising out of dealings with said departments, and Licensee agrees to indemnify the Licensor for any loss sustained or expenses incurred on account of any actions or claims mentioned herein. Nothing in this paragraph shall be construed, however, as relieving the Licensor from liability for its own acts of negligence, omission or commission or from its liability to the Licensee for default or violation of any of the terms of this agreement.

Negligence

Employees' Acts

27*th*. The Licensee hereby expressly assumes all responsibility for any act done by any employee in its said business, providing such act is done within the scope of the Licensee's business, and it expressly agrees that it will indemnify the Licensor against any claim or claims, action or actions for damages arising in the conduct of said business, and against any liability therefor.

Repairs

28*th*. The Licensor shall have complete control of its store and its representatives shall have the right to inspect all departments therein and make such repairs and alterations as may be deemed necessary by the Licensor.

Copyrights and Patents

29*th*. The Licensee agrees to hold the Licensor free and harmless, and indemnify the Licensor for any loss sustained or expense incurred on account of any suit or claim whatsoever arising out of the infringement of any patent or copyright in any manner affected or claimed to be affected on account of sales, advertisements, or operations by Licensee during the term of this agreement, or any renewals, thereof, as well as to defend any actions brought against the Licensor for such infringement.

Lost Property

30*th*. The Licensee, its representatives, and employees, shall deliver to the Licensor, all articles and money which may be found in or about the department, or any part of the store.

Chattel Mortgages Assignments etc.

31*st*. No chattel mortgage, conditional sales, hypothecation, or assignment of stock or equipment, located in this department, shall be executed by Licensee without the consent, in writing, of the Licensor.

Defaults

32*nd*. If Licensee vacates or abandons the department or fails to exercise and carry out its right and privilege, or if the said Licensee shall discontinue the conduct of the business therein, or shall violate or fail to observe and perform any one or more of the terms and conditions thereof, on its part to be performed, it being understood and agreed that the breach of any one or more of the terms and conditions imposed upon the said Licensee shall be deemed a material breach of the terms of this agreement, or if the said Licensee shall become insolvent, or if a petition in bankruptcy shall be filed by or against it, or if it shall make general assignment for the benefit of creditors, or if an execution shall issue against the Licensee, then, upon the happening of any of the said events, the said Licensor shall have the right to terminate this agreement at once, and upon such election, this agreement and the term hereby granted and all rights of the said Licensee hereunder shall absolutely cease and come to an end, as though the term hereof had originally been made to expire at that time; and upon such termination or on termination for any reason hereinbefore or hereinafter provided the said Licensor shall have the right to lock out or prohibit the Licensee from entering the store and to remove the fixtures and merchandise of the said Licensee from the said store, at the expense of the said Licensee.

33*rd*. It is definitely understood and agreed that nothing in this agreement shall in any way be construed to constitute a co-partnership between the parties hereto, or the relationship of Landlord and Tenant.

Wrapping Paper Boxes and Other Supplies

34*th*. The Licensee agrees to requisition and purchase from the Licensor all necessary supplies, including wrapping paper, boxes, twine, etc., as shall be necessary for the use in said department and the Licensee agrees to pay for such supplies as shall be requisitioned or used in said department at the Licensor's cost price. The Licensee will not use or permit to be used any wrapping paper, boxes, twine, shopping bags, or other supplies that bear any other insignia, trade mark, slogan or name other than the name of the Licensor.

Cash Receipts and Funds

35*th*. All sales shall be made in the name of the Licensor and shall be recorded by the Licensee at its expense. All moneys received by the Licensee or its employees, representing the proceeds of the sale of goods sold in said department, shall immediately be turned over to the Licensor. All moneys and accounts so received by the Licensor on account of sales in said department, shall be held by the Licensor in trust for the Licensee and if mingled with the Licensor's funds, either in the cash drawer, or deposit in the bank, or wherever such co-mingling may be effected, such funds shall, nevertheless, be and remain trust funds, and are to be so held by the Licensor in trust for the Licensee until the Licensor has paid to the Licensee the total amount of such sales and receipts in accordance with the provision hereof.

In the event title to said funds shall at any time be called into question, the parties hereto desire to clearly specify that these funds are trust funds irrespective of whether they are co-mingled or not, and said funds will be so held for the benefit of the Licensee and not otherwise.

Licensor's Books and Records

36th. The Licensor agrees to keep a true and correct account of all moneys received, growing out of the Licensee's sales (including an account with respect to the Licensee's credit or charge sales) also an account of all moneys disbursed on the Licensee's authorization and exhibit said records to the Licensee or its representatives upon reasonable request to do so. The Licensee agrees to keep a true and correct account of all sales made by it, and the Licensor shall at all reasonable times have access to said accounts. Both the Licensor and Licensee hereto shall have the right to examine not only the books of account, but all sales slips and records pertaining to Licensee's sales.

Personal Contract

37th. It is understood and agreed that this contract is personal between the parties hereto and the Licensor agrees that it will continuously conduct a mercantile business of its own, in said store during the period of this agreement, consisting of the sale, at retail, of wearing apparel, home furnishings, and furniture and other merchandise, and rendering service to customers, and in the event that the Licensor shall in any manner dispose of its lease to the store or its interest in said business, the Licensee may, at its option, immediately terminate this agreement.

Labor Unions

38th. That in the event the Licensor shall make any contract or agreement with any Unions or Labor organizations respecting the conditions of employment, hours, or wages of its employees, the Licensee agrees to abide by and adhere to the provisions of each contract or agreement, as the same affect its employees.

Advertising Penalty

39th. Notwithstanding the provisions contained in Paragraph "7th" hereof, if the Licensee neglects or fails to expend the amount stipulated to be spent for advertising contained in said paragraph, then the Licensee agrees to pay to the Licensor an additional sum equal to one-half of the difference between the actual amount spent for advertising and the amount specified in Paragraph *"7th"* hereof.

NEWS STAND PERCENTAGE LEASE

(This is a typical percentage lease where a large hotel leased the rights for a news, cigar, and confectionery stand in its lobby for $12,000 and a percentage of the receipts.)

THIS AGREEMENT made this .... day of ...., Nineteen Hundred and ...., by and between .... of ...., incorporated under the general laws of ...., hereinafter called the lessor, and .... of the City of ...., State of ...., hereinafter called the lessee.

WITNESSETH: That the said lessor has, in consideration of the rents, covenants and agreements hereinafter agreed to be paid, kept and performed by the said lessee, demised and leased, and by these presents does demise and lease unto the said lessee, for a term beginning ...., and ending ...., the space now occupied by the cigar and news stand in the lobby of the .... Hotel, ..., and also the privilege for sale of Cigars, Cigarettes, Periodicals, Confectionery, Theatre Tickets and Novelties, which are sold throughout the Hotel ...., during the term hereby demised.

The lessee hereby agrees to pay as rent to the lessor:

15% on the gross receipts from the sale of cigars, cigarettes, tobacco, etc.

15% on the gross receipts from the sale of confectionery, novelties, etc.

15% on the gross profits from the sale of theatre tickets.

10% on the gross receipts from the sale of newspapers, periodicals, etc.

it being understood and agreed, however, that the minimum rental which shall be paid by the lessee, shall be Twelve Thousand Dollars ($12,000) per annum and this amount shall be payable in equal installments of One Thousand Dollars ($1,000) each on the first day of each and every month during the term of this agreement as rent in advance for the month next ensuing, and the lessee shall, at the end of each month, render to the lessor, a statement showing the gross sales as itemized above and on the .... day of ...., and on the .... day of .... of each succeeding year during the term of this agreement, the lessee shall render an annual statement to the lessor showing gross sales of all merchandise and gross profit on all theatre tickets for the twelve (12) preceding months and pay as additional rent, any excess earned over and above the Twelve Thousand Dollars ($12,000) in accordance with the percentage as set forth above which excess, if any, shall be payable on the first day of .... of each year.

1. The lessor agrees during the term of this agreement, to furnish the lessee with necessary heat and light.

2. The lessee hereby agrees to pay to the lessor in cash on ...., the sum of Eleven Hundred and Twenty-Eight Dollars ($1,128), for the present fixtures, which fixtures shall be maintained during the term of this agreement at the cost of the lessee, which fixtures, however, shall remain the property of the lessor and shall be turned back to it in good order and condition at the termination of this lease, natural wear and tear excepted.

3. The lessee further agrees to pay to the lessor on .... the sum of Two Hundred and Fifty Dollars ($250), as purchase price for a cash register in use on the premises.

4. The lessee further covenants and agrees that he will well and truly pay or cause to be paid to the lessor, the rent herein reserved at the time or times the same shall become due or payable and whether demand therefor shall be made or not.

5. Provided always, that in case the building of which demised premises form a part shall be so damaged by fire or other casualty or happening as to substantially destroy the same, then this lease shall cease and come to an end, and any unearned rent paid in advance by the lessee shall be refunded to it, but in case of such damage or destruction of the demised premises as shall not substantially destroy the building, then the demised premises shall be restored to their condition immediately prior to such damage or destruction with due diligence by the lessor, and a just proportion of the rent hereinbefore reserved, according to the extent of the injury or damage sustained by the demised premises shall be suspended and abated until the demised premises shall have been so restored and put in proper condition for use and occupation. In the event that the building including the demised premises shall be condemned or declared by any authority having jurisdiction of the premises, as unsafe, the demised premises shall be repaired and so restored forthwith by the lessor, and a just proportion of the rent hereinbefore reserved shall be suspended and abated until the demised premises shall have been put in safe and proper condition for use and occupation. In the event that by reason of such condemnation or other action on the part of any authority, it shall become necessary to demolish and remove the said building including the demised premises, then and upon the happening of any such event this lease shall cease and come to an end and any unearned rent paid in advance by the lessee shall be refunded to him.

6. It is further covenanted and agreed, that if the said rent or any part thereof shall be ten (10) days in arrears, the lessor may distrain therefor; and provided further that if the said rent or any part thereof shall remain unpaid and be at any time, thirty (30) days in arrears, or if the lessee shall default in any of the covenants or provisions hereof obligatory on him and such default shall continue for fifteen (15) days after written notice thereof given to him or left on said premises, then this lease shall, at the option of the lessor, be null and void, and the lessor may proceed to recover possession of the said premises under and by virtue of a seven (7) days' summons, under the provisions of an Act of Congress to establish a Code of Law for the District of Columbia, approved March 3rd, 1901, or by such legal action or proceedings as may at the time be in operation in like cases.

7. It is further understood and agreed that the lessor reserves the right to audit the books of the lessee in the conduct of his business and if found to be incorrect expense for same to be paid by said lessee.

8. It is further covenanted and agreed, that no waiver of breach of any covenant herein contained shall be construed to operate as a waiver of any subsequent breach of the same covenant or of the covenant itself.

9. The character of goods to be sold by said lessee on the premises hereby demised and the General Management of the places leased under these presents shall be to the satisfaction of said lessor.

10. It is further covenanted and agreed that all provisions of this agreement shall be binding upon the lessor or its assigns and the lessee, his heirs, executors, administrators and assigns.

11. The lessor hereby reserves the right to change any space that may be assigned from time to time to the said lessee to be used for the purpose of this lease, excepting space now allotted in the main lobby of the hotel building.

IN TESTIMONY WHEREOF, the lessor has caused this agreement to be signed by ...., its ...., and duly attested by ...., its ...., and its Corporate Seal attached hereto, and the lessee has hereunto affixed his name and seal, on the day and year first hereinbefore written.

(Signatures, acknowledgments, and so forth.)

Short-Term Leases

OFFICE LEASE

(This is the standard office lease formerly used by the Institute of Real Estate Management of the National Association of Real Estate Boards. They have discontinued publication of this lease form. Used by permission.)

THIS INDENTURE, Witnesseth, That the Lessor, ...
does hereby lease unto the Lessee, ...
.........................., the premises known and described as
Rooms ...., ..., and .... at Nos. ....
.... as shown on plats hereto attached, marked "A," in the
City of .... State of .... for the term of
.... Years and .... Months beginning on the ......
day of .... and ending on the .... day of ....
IN CONSIDERATION of said demise the lessee covenants:

1. To pay to the Lessor as rent for said premises the sum of ....
.... Dollars in United States Gold Coin of the present
standard of fineness, in .... installments of ....
.... for the period beginning ...., and ending
.............., payable one each on the .... day of every calendar
month of the term of this lease. All of said payments shall be made at
the office of ...., ...,
or at such other place in .... as the lessor
shall from time to time, by written notice left at said demised premises,
appoint; that each and every installment of rent accruing under the
provisions of this lease, and all other sums of money payable hereunder
by the lessee to the lessor shall bear interest at the maximum legal rate
per annum from the date when the same shall respectively become payable under the terms of this lease until the same shall be paid.

2. That the lessee will use and occupy said premises for ....
....
and for no other use or purpose, and that the lessee will at his own expense keep said demised premises in good repair and tenantable condition

225

during said term and that the lessee will replace at his own expense any and all broken glass in and about said premises with glass of the same size and quality, including all signs thereon.

3. That no representations, except such as are contained herein or endorsed hereon, have been made to the lessee respecting the condition of said premises. The taking possession of said premises by the lessee shall be conclusive evidence as against the lessee that said premises were in good and satisfactory condition when possession of the same was so taken; and the lessee will, at the termination of this lease, by lapse of time or otherwise, return said premises to the lessor in as good condition as when received, loss by fire and ordinary wear excepted.

4. That the lessee will not assign this lease or any interest hereunder; and will not permit any assignment hereof by operation of law; and will not sublet said premises or any part thereof; and will not permit the use of said premises by any parties other than the lessee, and the agents and servants of the lessee.

5. That the lessee will make no alterations in, or additions to, said premises without first obtaining the lessor's written consent and that all the erections, additions, fixtures and improvements, whether temporary or permanent in character (except only the movable office furniture of the lessee), made in or upon said premises, either by the lessee or the lessor, shall be the lessor's property, and shall remain upon said premises at the termination of said term by lapse of time or otherwise, without compensation to the lessee.

6. That the lessee will not use or permit upon said premises anything that will invalidate any policies of insurance now or hereafter carried on said building or that will increase the rate of insurance on said demised premises, or on the building of which said demised premises are a part; that the lessee will pay all extra insurance premiums on the said building which may be caused by the use which said lessee shall make of said demised premises; that the lessee will not use or permit upon said premises anything that may be dangerous to life or limb; the lessee will not in any manner deface or injure said building or any part thereof, or overload the floors of said demised premises, it being mutually agreed that in no event shall any weight placed upon the said floors exceed seventy-five (75) pounds per square foot of floor space covered; that the lessee will not permit any objectionable noise or odor to escape or be emitted from said premises, or do anything or permit anything to be done upon said premises in any way tending to create a nuisance, or tend-ing to disturb any other tenant in said building, or the occupants of neighboring property, or tending to injure the reputation of the said building; the lessee will comply with all governmental, health, and police requirements and regulations respecting said premises and will not use said premises for lodging or sleeping purposes.

7. That the lessor shall not be liable for any damage either to person or property, sustained by the lessee or by other persons due to the building or any part thereof, or any appurtenances thereof becoming out of repair, or due to the happening of any accident in or about said building, or due to any act or neglect of any tenant or occupant of said building, or of any other person. This provision shall apply especially (but not exclusively) to damage caused by water, snow, frost, steam, sewerage, illuminating gas, sewer gas or odors, or by the bursting or leaking of pipes or plumbing works, and shall apply equally whether such damage be caused by the act or neglect of other tenants, occupants, or janitors of said building, or of any other persons, and whether such damage be caused or occasioned by any thing or circumstances above mentioned or referred to, or by any other thing or circumstances, whether of a like nature or of a wholly different nature. If any such damage shall be caused by any act or neglect of the lessee, the lessor may, at his option, repair such damage, whether caused to the building, or to tenants thereof, and the lessee shall thereupon reimburse the lessor for the total cost of such damage both to the building and to the tenants thereof. The lessee further agrees that all personal property upon the demised premises shall be at the risk of the lessee only and that the lessor shall not be liable for any damage thereto or theft thereof.

8. It is mutually agreed that all the rules and regulations printed upon the back of this instrument shall be and are hereby made a part of this lease, and the lessee covenants and agrees that he and his servants and agents will at all times observe, perform and abide by said rules and regulations.

9. If the term of any other lease for premises in said building, held by the lessee, shall be terminated at any time after the date hereof and prior to the first day of the term of this lease on account of default by the lessee, such termination shall of itself terminate and cancel this lease and render it of no further force or effect.

10. That if default shall at any time be made by said lessee in the payment of the rent hereby reserved, or any installment thereof, or if default shall be made in any of the other covenants herein contained, to be kept, observed and performed by the lessee, or if the leasehold interest shall be levied on under execution, or if the lessee shall be declared bankrupt or insolvent according to law, or if any assignment of his property shall be made for the benefit of creditors, or if a receiver shall be appointed for the lessee, then, and in any of said cases, the lessor may, at his option, at once, without notice to the lessee or to any other person, terminate this lease; and upon the termination of said lease at the option of the lessor as aforesaid, or at the expiration by lapse of time of the term hereby demised, the lessee will at once surrender possession of said premises, to the lessor, and remove all effects therefrom, and if such possession be not immediately surrendered, the lessor may forthwith re-enter said premises and re-possess himself thereof as of his former estate and remove all persons and effects therefrom using such force as may be necessary without being deemed guilty of any manner of trespass or forcible entry or detainer. And the lessee expressly waives the service of any notice of intention to terminate this lease or to re-enter said premises, and waives the service of any demand for payment of rent or for possession, and waives the service of any and every other notice or

demand prescribed by any statutes of the State of ....
No receipt of moneys by the lessor from the lessee, after the termination
in any way of this lease, or after the giving of any notice, shall reinstate,
continue or extend the term of this lease, or affect any notice given to
the lessee prior to the receipt of such money, it being agreed that after
the service of notice or the commencement of a suit, or after final judgment for possession of said premises, the lessor may receive and collect
any rent due, and the payment of said rent shall not waive or affect
said notice, said suit or said judgment. If the lessee shall not remove
all effects from said premises as above agreed, the lessor may, at his
option, remove the same or any of the same in any manner that the
lessor shall choose, and store the same without liability on the part of
the lessor for loss thereof, and the lessee will pay the lessor, on request,
any and all expenses incurred in such removal and also storage on said
effects for any length of time during which the same shall be in the
lessor's possession; or the lessor may at his option, without notice, sell
the said effects or any of the same for such price as the lessor may deem
best and apply the proceeds of such sale upon any amounts due under
this lease from the lessee to the lessor, including the expenses of the removal and sale.

11. That in case the lessee shall vacate said premises or abandon the
same during the life of this lease, or in case the lessee shall make default
in the payment of the rent hereby reserved or any installment thereof,
or shall make default in any of the covenants herein contained to be
kept, observed and performed by the lessee, the lessor may at his option,
without terminating this lease, but the lessor shall not be under any
obligation so to do, enter into said premises, remove the lessee's property
and signs therefrom, and re-let the same, for the account of the lessee,
for such rent and upon such terms as shall be satisfactory to the lessor;
without such re-entry working a forfeiture of the rents to be paid and
the covenants to be performed by the lessee during the full term of this
lease; and for the purpose of such re-letting the lessor is authorized to
make any repairs, changes, alterations or additions in or to said demised
premises that may be necessary or convenient, and if a sufficient sum
shall not be realized monthly from such re-letting, after paying all of
the costs and expenses of such repairs, changes, alterations, or additions
and the expenses of such re-letting and the collection of the rent accruing
therefrom each month to satisfy the monthly rent above provided to be
paid by the lessee, then the lessee will satisfy and pay such deficiency
each month upon demand therefor.

12. That the lessee will pay to the lessor at once upon the termination
of this lease, in accordance with the provisions hereof, or upon the vacation of said premises by the lessee, a sum of money equal to the entire
amount of rent by this lease provided to be paid and at that time remaining unpaid, including double rent as herein provided as the liquidated damages of the lessor, and upon making such payment the lessee
shall be entitled to receive from the lessor all rents received by the lessor

from other tenants on account of said premises during the term originally demised by this lease, provided, however, that the moneys to which the lessee shall so become entitled shall in no event exceed the liquidated damages last aforesaid, with lawful interest thereon.

13. To pay all attorney's fees and expenses of the lessor incurred in enforcing any of the obligations of the lessee under this lease, or in any litigation or negotiation in which the lessor shall, without his fault, become involved through or on account of this lease.

14. That the lessor shall have a first lien upon the interest of the lessee under this lease, to secure the payment of all moneys due under this lease, which lien may be foreclosed in equity at any time when money is overdue under this lease; and the lessor shall be entitled to a receiver of said leasehold interest to be appointed in any such foreclosure proceeding, who shall take possession of said premises and who may re-let the same under the orders of the court appointing him and the lessor is also hereby given a first lien for all moneys due under this lease upon any and all personal property belonging to said lessee.

15. That the lessee will pay to the lessor, as liquidated damages, double rent for all the time the lessee shall retain possession of said premises or any part thereof after the termination of this lease, whether by lapse of time or otherwise; but the provisions of this clause shall not operate as a waiver by the lessor of any right of re-entry hereinbefore provided; nor shall any waiver by the lessor of his right to terminate this lease for breach of covenant affect his right to terminate this lease for any later breach of the same or another covenant.

16. It is understood and agreed that this lease does not grant any rights to light and air over property, except public streets adjoining the land on which said building is situated.

17. That the lessee shall pay all gas and electric bills rendered against or charged upon said premises, and in case the lessee shall not pay the same when due and payable the lessor may pay the same, and the amount so paid is hereby declared to be so much additional rent and shall be due and payable to the lessor from the lessee forthwith.

18. If the lessor shall furnish electric current for lighting or power to other tenants of the building during the term of this lease, then the lessee agrees to purchase electric current for lighting or power from the lessor only, and to pay to the lessor for such electric current consumed and measured by meter, installed by the lessor, at the rate customary in the building. The charge for electric current shall be due and payable on or before the tenth day of the month following the period for which the charge is made; and in case the lessee shall fail to make payment for electric current as in this clause provided, the lessor may, without notice to the lessee, shut off and discontinue the supply of electric current for light and power in said premises, and such act of shutting off the electric current shall not be held or pleaded as an eviction or as a disturbance in any manner whatever of the lessee's possession, or relieve lessee from the payment of rent when due, or vary or change any other provision of this lease, or render the lessor liable for damages of any kind whatsoever.

19. That the lessee shall not conduct, nor permit to be conducted on said premises, any business which is contrary to any of the laws of the United States of America, or the State of ...., or contrary to the ordinances of the City of ...., and it is expressly agreed that a violation of this clause shall, at the option of the lessor, work a forfeiture of this lease.

20. That in consideration of the execution of this lease by the lessor, the lessee shall not use said premises for any purpose except that which is above specified, and in particular will not expose nor offer for sale on said premises, any alcoholic or other liquors, tobacco, drugs, flowers, candies, confections, nor any other thing or things whether of a like or of a wholly different nature, without the written consent of the lessor, the right being hereby reserved to the lessor to grant to any person, firm or corporation, the exclusive right and privilege to conduct any particular business in said building, and such exclusive right and privilege so granted shall be binding upon the lessee hereunder the same as though specifically incorporated in this lease.

21. In case of injury by fire or other casualty to the demised premises or any part thereof, the lessor shall have .... days within which to repair and restore the same, without terminating this lease. Further, the lessor and lessee covenant with each other that if, during the life of this lease said premises shall be so injured by fire or other casualty as to be untenantable, then unless said injury be repaired within .... days thereafter as hereinbefore specified, either party hereto upon written notice to the other party given not later than .... days after said fire may terminate this lease, in which case rent shall be apportioned and paid to the date of such fire.

22. That in the event that the lessor, during the term hereby demised, shall be required by the City of ...., the order or decree of any court, or any other governmental authority, to repair, alter, remove, reconstruct, or improve any part of the demised premises or of the building of which said premises are a part, then such repairing, alteration, removal, reconstruction or improvement may be made by and at the expense of the lessor and shall not in any way affect the obligations or covenants of the lessee herein contained, and the lessee hereby waives all claims for damages or abatement of rent because of such repairing, alteration, removal, reconstruction or improvement.

23. That if the lessee shall move from said premises at any time prior to the termination of this lease, the lessor shall have the right to enter upon said premises for the purpose of decorating the same or making alterations or changes therein, without such entry in any manner affecting the obligations of the lessee hereunder.

24. No waiver of any condition expressed in this lease shall be implied by any neglect of the lessor to declare a forfeiture or take any other action on account of the violation of such condition if such violation be continued or repeated subsequently, and no express waiver shall affect any condition other than the one specified in such waiver, and that one only for the time and in the manner specifically stated; if the lessor shall not take action of any kind upon any failure of the lessee to pay any installments of rent when due, such forbearance or failure or neglect to take prompt action shall not be construed as a waiver by the lessor of any right reserved to the lessor herein, but the lessor shall have the right at any and all times thereafter to enforce a prompt and strict compliance with the terms of this lease, regardless of any and all former acts of forbearance or failure to insist upon a prompt or strict compliance with any of the terms, covenants and conditions of this lease.

25. In every case where under the provisions of this lease it shall be necessary or desirable for the lessor to give to or serve upon the lessee any notice or demand it shall be sufficient either (1) to deliver or cause to be delivered to the lessee a written or printed copy of such notice or demand, or (2) to send a written or printed copy of said notice or demand by mail, postage prepaid, addressed to the lessee at the demised premises, or (3) to leave a written or printed copy of said notice or demand upon the demised premises, or to post the same upon the door leading into said premises.

26. The lessee hereby constitutes and appoints any attorney of any court of record to be his true and lawful attorney, for him and in his name and stead to enter his appearance in any suits that may be brought in any court in the State of .... at any time when any money is due hereunder for rent as aforesaid, to waive the issuing of process and service thereof and trial by jury or otherwise and to confess a judgment or judgments for such money so due and for costs of suit and for a reasonable attorney's fee in favor of the lessor, to be fixed by the court, and to release all errors that may occur or intervene in such proceedings, including the issuance of execution upon any such judgment, and to stipulate that no writ of error or appeal shall be prosecuted from such judgment or judgments, nor any bill in equity filed, nor any proceedings of any kind taken in law or equity to interfere in any way with the operation of such judgment or judgments or of execution issued thereon, and to consent that execution may immediately issue thereon.

Further, the lessor and lessee covenant with each other (A) That all rights and remedies of the lessor under this lease shall be cumulative, and none shall exclude any other rights and remedies allowed by law.

(B) That the words "lessor" and "lessee" wherever used herein shall be construed to mean lessors and lessees in all cases where there is more than one lessor or lessee, and the necessary grammatical changes required to make the provisions hereof apply either to corporations or individuals, men or women, shall in all cases be assumed as though in each case fully expressed.

(C) Each of the provisions of this lease shall extend to, and shall, as the case may require, bind or inure to the benefit not only of the lessor and of the lessee, but also of their respective heirs, legal representatives and assigns in the event that this lease shall be assigned with the written consent of the lessor.

IN WITNESS WHEREOF, the parties hereto have caused this instru-

ment to be executed under their seals this .... day of ....
A.D. 19.....

(Signatures, acknowledgments, and so forth.)

Rules and Regulations

(Applicable only to the premises demised by the within lease and to
the lessee thereof.)

Rule 1. No sign, picture, advertisement, or notice shall be displayed,
inscribed, painted, or affixed on any part of the outside or inside of said
building, or on or about the premises hereby demised, except on the glass
of the doors and windows of said premises and on the Directory Board of
the building, and then only of such color, size, style and material as shall
be first specified by the lessor in writing on this lease. No "For Rent"
signs shall be displayed by the lessee, and no showcases, or obstructions,
signs, flags, barber poles, statuary, or any advertising device of any kind
whatever shall be placed in front of said building or in the passageways,
halls, lobbies or corridors thereof by the lessee; and the lessor reserves the
right to remove all such showcases, obstructions, signs, flags, barber poles,
statuary, or advertising devices and all signs other than those provided
for without notice to the lessee and at his expense. No newspaper, magazine or other advertising is to be done from the said premises, or referring
to the said premises, unless the same is first approved by the lessor, or
his agent, and any breach of this covenant shall be restrainable by injunction.

Rule 2. The tenant shall not (without the lessor's written consent)
put up or operate any steam engine, boiler, machinery or stove upon the
premises, or carry on any mechanical business thereon, or do any cooking
thereon, or use or allow to be used upon the demised premises oil, burning fluids, camphene, or kerosene for heating, warming or lighting, or
anything (except gas or incandescent electric lights, and those only of
such company or companies as may be supplying the building) for
illuminating said premises. No article deemed extra hazardous on account of fire and no explosives shall be brought into said premises.

Rule 3. No additional locks shall be placed upon any doors of the
premises, and the lessee will not permit any duplicate keys to be made
(all necessary keys will be furnished by the lessor), but if more than two
keys for any door-lock shall be desired, the additional number must be
paid for by the lessee. Upon the termination of this lease the lessee shall
surrender to the lessor all keys of the premises and give to the lessor the
explanation of the combinations of all locks in safes, safe cabinets and
vault doors in the premises.

Rule 4. Safes, furniture, boxes or other bulky articles shall be carried
up into the premises only with written consent of the lessor first obtained,
and then only by means of the elevators, by the stairways or through the
windows of said building as the lessor may in writing direct, and at such

times as the lessor may direct. Safes and other heavy articles shall be placed by the lessee in such places only as may be first specified in writing by the lessor, and any damage done to the building or to the tenants or to other persons by taking a safe or other heavy article in or out of the demised premises, from overloading a floor, or in any other manner, shall be paid for by the lessee causing such damage.

Rule 5. Elevator service shall be furnished by the lessor daily from .... to .... (Sundays and Holidays excepted).

Heat will be furnished by the lessor daily from 8:00 A.M. to .... (Sundays and Holidays excepted), whenever, between .... such heat shall, in the lessor's judgment, be required for the comfortable occupation and use of said premises; but the lessor shall not be liable in damages by abatement of rent, or otherwise, for failure to furnish or delay in furnishing elevator service, heat, electric current, janitor service, or water, when such failure to furnish or delay in furnishing is occasioned by needful repairs, renewals, or improvements, or in whole or in part by strike, lock-out, or other labor controversy, or by inability to secure coal at the building after reasonable effort to do so, or by any accident or casualty whatsoever, or by the act or default of the lessee, or other parties, or by any cause or causes beyond the reasonable control of the lessor; nor shall the lessor be liable for any act or default of the janitors, or other employees not authorized by the lessor; and such failure, delay, or default in furnishing elevator service, heat, janitor service, or water, or any unauthorized act or default of the janitors, or employees shall not be considered or construed as an actual or constructive eviction of the lessee, nor shall it in any way operate to release the lessee from the prompt and punctual performance of each and all of the other covenants herein contained by the lessee to be performed.

Rule 6. The lessor shall furnish janitor service in said demised premises, but any and all electric current used in the performance of janitor service, and also in making repairs and alterations in said premises during the term of this lease shall be at the expense of the lessee.

No person shall be employed by the lessee to do janitor work in said demised premises, and no persons, other than the janitors of said building, shall clean said premises, unless the lessor shall endorse on this lease his written consent thereto.

Any person employed by the lessee, with the lessor's consent as aforesaid, to do janitor work, shall, while in said building and outside of said demised premises, be subject to, and under the control and direction of the superintendent of said building (but not as agent or servant of said superintendent or of the lessor).

Rule 7. The lessor and his agents may retain a pass key to the premises and shall have the right to enter the demised premises at all reasonable hours for the purpose of exhibiting the same, and may place and keep on the windows and doors of said premises at any time during the last sixty (60) days of the term of this lease signs advertising the premises for rent.

Rule 8. The lessor, and his agents, shall have the right to enter the demised premises at all reasonable hours for the purpose of making any repairs, alterations, or additions which he or they shall deem necessary for the safety, preservation, or improvement of said premises or said building, and the lessor shall be allowed to take all material into and upon said premises that may be required to make such repairs, improvements, and additions, or any alterations for the benefit of the lessee without in any way being deemed or held guilty of an eviction of the lessee; and the rent reserved shall in no wise abate while said repairs, alterations, or additions are being made; and the lessee shall not be entitled to maintain a setoff or counter-claim for damages against the lessor by reason of loss or interruption to the business of the lessee because of the prosecution of any such work. All such repairs, decorations, alterations, additions and improvements shall be done during ordinary business hours, or, if any such work is at the request of the lessee to be done during any other hours, the lessee shall pay for all overtime.

Rule 9. If the lessee desires awnings or shades, either inside or outside of the windows, they must be furnished, installed and maintained at the expense of the lessee and at his risk, and must be of such shape, color, material, quality, design and make as may be prescribed by the lessor.

Rule 10. If the lessee desires telegraphic or telephonic connections, or the installation of any other electric wiring, the lessor will, upon receiving a written request from the lessee, direct the electricians as to where and how the wires are to be introduced and run, and without such directions no boring, cutting or installation of wires will be permitted. The lessee shall not install any radio antenna connected to said building, either inside or outside the demised premises.

Rule 11. The lessee shall not allow anything to be placed against or near the glass in the partitions, between the premises leased and the halls or corridors of the building, which shall diminish the light in, or prove unsightly from, the halls or corridors.

Rule 12. No electric current, intended for light or power purposes, shall be used by the tenants, excepting that furnished or approved by the lessor; nor shall electric or other wires be brought into the premises, except upon the written consent and approval of the lessor.

Rule 13. The lessee, when closing his office for business, at any time, shall see that all awnings are pulled up and that all windows are closed, thus avoiding possible damage from fire, storms, rain or freezing.

Rule 14. The lessee shall not allow anything to be placed on the outside window ledges of the premises, nor shall anything be thrown by the lessee, or his employees, out of the windows of the building; nor shall they undertake to regulate the thermostats, if any, which control the heat.

Rule 15. Water on the said premises shall not be wasted by the lessee or his employees by tying or wedging back the faucets of the wash bowls or otherwise.

Rule 16. No bicycle or other vehicle, and no animal shall be brought into the offices, halls, corridors, elevators or any other parts of said building by the lessee, his agents or employees.

Rule 17. Ice, mineral water, towels and toilet supplies shall be obtained by the said lessee only from such persons as may be satisfactory to the lessor.

Rule 18. No person shall disturb the occupants of this or any adjoining building or premises by the use of any musical instrument, unseemly noises, whistling, singing or in any other way.

Rule 19. The premises leased shall not be used for lodging or sleeping, or for any immoral or illegal purposes or for any purpose that will damage the premises or the reputation thereof.

Rule 20. The lessor reserves the right to make such other and further reasonable rules and regulations as in his judgment may from time to time be needful for the safety, care and cleanliness of the premises, and for the preservation of good order therein, and any such other or further rules and regulations shall be binding upon the parties hereto with the same force and effect as if they had been inserted herein at the time of the execution hereof.

LEASE IN NEW OFFICE BUILDING

(This is based on standard office lease of the Real Estate Board of New York.

Address _____

Premises _____

TO

STANDARD FORM OF

Office
Lease

The Real Estate Board of New York, Inc.
©Copyright 1970. All Rights Reserved.
Reproduction in whole or in part prohibited.

Dated   19   .

Rent per Year

Rent per Month

Term
From
To

Drawn by..............................Checked by..........................
Entered by............................Approved by........................

Agreement of Lease,

made as of this   day of   19   , between

party of the first part, hereinafter referred to as LANDLORD, and

party of the second part, hereinafter referred to as TENANT,

Witnesseth: Landlord hereby leases to Tenant and Tenant hereby hires from Landlord

in the building known as
in the Borough of   , City of New York, for the term of

(or until such term shall sooner cease and expire as hereinafter provided) to commence on the
    day of   nineteen hundred and   , and to end on the
    day of   nineteen hundred and

both dates inclusive, at an annual rental rate of

which Tenant agrees to pay in lawful money of the United States which shall be legal tender in payment of all debts and dues, public and private, at the time of payment, in equal monthly installments in advance on the first day of each month during said term, at the office of Landlord or such other place as Landlord may designate, without any set off or deduction whatsoever, except that Tenant shall pay the first   monthly installment(s) on the execution hereof (unless this lease be a renewal).

In the event that, at the commencement of the term of this lease, or thereafter, Tenant shall be in default in the payment of rent to Landlord pursuant to the terms of another lease with Landlord or with Landlord's predecessor in interest, Landlord may at Landlord's option and without notice to Tenant add the amount of such arrearages to any monthly installment of rent payable hereunder and the same shall be payable to Landlord as additional rent.

The parties hereto, for themselves, their heirs, distributees, executors, administrators, legal representatives, successors and assigns, hereby covenant as follows:

Rent   1. Tenant shall pay the rent as above and as hereinafter provided.
Occupancy   2. Tenant shall use and occupy demised premises for

and for no other purpose.

Alterations: **3.** Tenant shall make no changes in or to the demised
premises of any nature without Landlord's prior written
consent. Subject to the prior written consent of Landlord,
and to the provisions of this article, Tenant at Tenant's expense, may
make alterations, installations, additions or improvements which are
non-structural and which do not affect utility services or plumbing and
electrical lines, in or to the interior of the demised premises by using
contractors or mechanics first approved by Landlord. All fixtures and
all panelling, partitions, railings and like installations, installed in the
premises at any time, either by Tenant or by Landlord in Tenant's behalf,
shall become the property of Landlord and shall remain upon and
be surrendered with the demised premises unless Landlord, by notice
to Tenant no later than twenty days prior to the date fixed as the termination of this lease, elects to have them removed by Tenant, in which event,
the same shall be removed from the premises by Tenant forthwith, at
Tenant's expense. Nothing in this article shall be construed to prevent
Tenant's removal of trade fixtures, but upon removal of any such trade
fixtures from the premises or upon removal of other installations as may
be required by Landlord, Tenant shall immediately and at its expense,
repair and restore the premises to the condition existing prior to installation and repair any damage to the demised premises or the building due
to such removal. All property permitted or required to be removed by
Tenant at the end of the term remaining in the premises after Tenant's
removal shall be deemed abandoned and may, at the election of Landlord, either be retained as Landlord's property or may be removed from
the premises by Landlord at Tenant's expense. Tenant shall, before making any alterations, additions, installations or improvements, at its expense,
obtain all permits, approvals and certificates required by any governmental or quasi-governmental bodies and (upon completion) certificates
of final approval thereof and shall deliver promptly duplicates of all such
permits, approvals and certificates to Landlord and Tenant agrees to carry
and will cause Tenant's contractors and sub-contractors to carry such
workman's compensation, general liability, personal and property damage
insurance as Landlord may require. Tenant agrees to obtain and deliver to
Landlord, written and unconditional waivers of mechanic's liens upon
the real property in which the demised premises are located, for all work,
labor and services to be performed and materials to be furnished in
connection with such work, signed by all contractors, sub-contractors,
materialmen and laborers to become involved in such work. Notwithstanding the foregoing, if any mechanic's lien is filed against the demised
premises, or the building of which the same forms a part, for work
claimed to have been done for, or materials furnished to, Tenant,
whether or not done pursuant to this article the same shall be discharged
by Tenant within ten days thereafter, at Tenant's expense, by filing the
bond required by law.

Repairs: **4.** Landlord shall maintain and repair the public portions of the building, both exterior and interior. Tenant shall, throughout the term of this lease, take good care of the demised premises and the fixtures and appurtenances therein and at its sole cost and expense, make all non-structural repairs thereto as and when needed to preserve them in good working order and condition, reasonable wear and tear, obsolescence and damage from the elements, fire or other casualty, excepted. Notwithstanding the foregoing, all damage or injury to the demised premises or to any other part of the building, or to its fixtures, equipment and appurtenances, whether requiring structural or non-structural repairs, caused by or resulting from carelessness, omission, neglect or improper conduct of Tenant, its servants, employees, invitees or licensees, shall be repaired promptly by Tenant at its sole cost and expense, to the satisfaction of Landlord reasonably exercised. Tenant shall also re-pair all damage to the building and the demised premises caused by the moving of Tenant's fixtures, furniture or equipment. All the aforesaid repairs shall be of quality or class equal to the original work or construction. If Tenant fails after ten days notice to proceed with due diligence to make repairs required to be made by Tenant, the same may be made by the Landlord at the expense of Tenant and the expenses thereof incurred by Landlord shall be collectible as additional rent after rendition of a bill or statement therefor. Tenant shall give Landlord prompt notice of any defective condition in any plumbing, heating system or electrical lines located in, servicing or passing through the demised premises and following such notice, Landlord shall remedy the condition with due diligence but at the expense of Tenant if repairs are necessitated by damage or injury attributable to Tenant, Tenant's servants, agents, employees, invitees or licensees as aforesaid. Except as specifically provided in Article 9 or elsewhere in this lease, there shall be no allowance to Tenant for a diminution of rental value and no liability on the part of Landlord by reason of inconvenience, annoyance or injury to business arising from Landlord, Tenant or others making or failing to make any repairs, alterations, additions or improvements in or to any portion of the building or the demised premises or in and to the fixtures, appurtenances or equipment thereof. The provisions of this Article 4 with respect to the making of repairs shall not apply in the case of fire or other casualty which are dealt with in Article 9 hereof.

Window Cleaning: **5.** Tenant will not clean, nor require, permit, suffer or allow any window in the demised premises to be cleaned, from the outside in violation of Section 202 of the Labor Law or any other applicable law or of the rules of the Board of Standards and Appeals, or of any other board or body having or asserting jurisdiction.

Requirements **6.** Prior to the commencement of the lease term, if Tenant
of Law,   is then in possession, and at all times thereafter, Tenant,
Fire Insurance, at Tenant's sole cost and expense, shall promptly comply
Floor Loads: with all present and future laws, orders and regulations of
all state, federal, municipal and local governments, departments, commissions and boards and any direction of any public officer pursuant to law, and all orders, rules and regulations of the New York Board of Fire Underwriters or any similar body which shall impose any violation, order or duty upon Landlord or Tenant with respect to the demised premises or the building arising out of Tenant's use or manner of use or occupancy thereof. Nothing herein shall require Tenant to make structural repairs or alterations unless Tenant has by its manner of use of the demised premises or method of operation therein, violated any such laws, ordinances, orders, rules, regulations or requirements with respect thereto. Tenant may, after securing Landlord to Landlord's satisfaction against all damages, interest, penalties and expenses, including, but not limited to, reasonable attorneys' fees, by cash deposit or by surety bond in an amount and in a company satisfactory to Landlord, contest and appeal any such laws, ordinances, orders, rules, regulations or requirements provided same is done with all reasonable promptness and provided such appeal shall not subject Landlord to prosecution for a criminal offense or constitute a default under any lease or mortgage under which Landlord may be obligated, or cause the demised premises or any part thereof to be condemned or vacated. Tenant shall not do or permit any act or thing to be done in or to the demised premises which is contrary to law, or which will invalidate or be in conflict with public liability, fire or other policies of insurance at any time carried by or for the benefit of Landlord with respect to the demised premises or the building of which the demised premises form a part, or which shall or might subject Landlord to any liability or responsibility to any person or for property damage, nor shall Tenant keep anything in the demised premises except as now or hereafter permitted by the Fire Department, Board of Fire Underwriters, Fire Insurance Rating Organization or other authority having jurisdiction, and then only in such manner and such quantity so as not to increase the rate for fire insurance applicable to the building, nor use the premises in a wrongful manner which will increase the insurance rate for the building or any property located therein over that in effect prior to the commencement of Tenant's occupancy. Tenant shall pay all costs, expenses, fines, penalties or damages, which may be imposed upon Landlord by reason of Tenant's failure to comply with the provisions of this article and if by reason of such failure the fire insurance rate shall, at the beginning of this lease or at any time thereafter, be higher than it otherwise would be, then Tenant shall reimburse Landlord, as additional rent hereunder, for that portion of all fire insurance premiums thereafter paid by Landlord which shall have been charged because of

such failure by Tenant, and shall make such reimbursement upon the first day of the month following such outlay by Landlord. In any action or proceeding wherein Landlord and Tenant are parties a schedule or "make-up" of rate for the building or demised premises issued by the New York Fire Insurance Exchange, or other body making fire insurance rates applicable to said premises shall be conclusive evidence of the facts therein stated and of the several items and charges in the fire insurance rate then applicable to said premises. Tenant shall not place a load upon any floor of the demised premises exceeding the floor load per square foot area which it was designed to carry and which is allowed by law. Landlord reserves the right to prescribe the weight and position of all safes, business machines and mechanical equipment. Such installations shall be placed and maintained by Tenant, at Tenant's expense, in settings sufficient, in Landlord's judgment, to absorb and prevent vibration, noise and annoyance.

Subordination: **7.** This lease is subject and subordinate to all ground or underlying leases and to all mortgages which may now or hereafter affect such leases or the real property of which demised premises are a part and to all renewals, modifications, consolidations, replacements and extensions of any such underlying leases and mortgages. This clause shall be self-operative and no further instrument of subordination shall be required by any ground or underlying lessee or by any mortgagee, affecting any lease or the real property of which the demised premises are a part. In confirmation of such subordination, Tenant shall execute promptly any certificate that Landlord may request.

Property— **8.** Landlord or its agents shall not be liable for any dam-
Loss, Damage, age to property of Tenant or of others entrusted to em-
Reimburse- ployees of the building, nor for loss of or damage to any
ment, Indem- property of Tenant by theft or otherwise, nor for any in-
nity: jury or damage to persons or property resulting from any
cause of whatsoever nature, unless caused by or due to the negligence of Landlord, its agents, servants or employees; nor shall Landlord or its agents be liable for any such damage caused by other tenants or persons in, upon or about said building or caused by operations in construction of any private, public or quasi public work. If at any time any windows of the demised premises are temporarily closed, darkened or bricked up (or permanently closed, darkened or bricked up, if required by law) for any reason whatsoever including, but not limited to Landlord's own acts, Landlord shall not be liable for any damage Tenant may sustain thereby and Tenant shall not be entitled to any compensation therefor nor abatement or diminution of rent nor shall the same

release Tenant from its obligations hereunder nor constitute an eviction. Tenant shall not move any safe, heavy machinery, heavy equipment, bulky matter, or fixtures into or out of the building without Landlord's prior written consent. If such safe, machinery, equipment, bulky matter or fixtures requires special handling, all work in connection therewith shall comply with the Administrative Code of the City of New York and all other laws and regulations applicable thereto and shall be done during such hours as Landlord may designate. Tenant shall indemnify and save harmless Landlord against and from all liabilities, obligations, damages, penalties, claims, costs and expenses for which Landlord shall not be reimbursed by insurance, including reasonable attorneys fees, paid, suffered or incurred as a result of any breach by Tenant, Tenant's agents, contractors, employees, invitees, or licensees, of any covenant or condition of this lease, or the carelessness, negligence or improper conduct of the Tenant, Tenant's agents, contractors, employees, invitees or licensees. Tenant's liability under this lease extends to the acts and omissions of any subtenant, and any agent, contractor, employee, invitee or licensee of any sub-tenant. In case any action or proceeding is brought against Landlord by reason of any such claim, Tenant, upon written notice from Landlord, will, at Tenant's expense, resist or defend such action or proceeding by counsel approved by Landlord in writing, such approval not to be unreasonably withheld.

Destruction, **9.** (a) If the demised premises or any part thereof shall **Fire and Other** be damaged by fire or other casualty, Tenant shall give **Casualty:** immediate notice thereof to Landlord and this lease shall continue in full force and effect except as hereinafter set forth. (b) If the demised premises are partially damaged or rendered partially unusable by fire or other casualty, the damages thereto shall be repaired by and at the expense of Landlord and the rent, until such repair shall be substantially completed, shall be apportioned from the day following the casualty according to the part of the premises which is usable. (c) If the demised premises are totally damaged or rendered wholly unusable by fire or other casualty, then the rent shall be proportionately paid up to the time of the casualty and thenceforth shall cease until the date when the premises shall have been repaired and restored by Landlord, subject to Landlord's right to elect not to restore the same as hereinafter provided. (d) If the demised premises are rendered wholly unusable or (whether or not the demised premises are damaged in whole or in part) if the building shall be so damaged that Landlord shall decide to demolish it or to rebuild it, then, in any of such events, Landlord may elect to terminate this lease by written notice to Tenant given within 90 days after such fire or casualty specifying a date for the expiration of the lease, which date shall not be more than 60 days after the giving of such notice, and upon the date specified in such notice the term of this lease shall expire as fully and completely as if such date were the date set forth above for the termination of this lease and Tenant shall forthwith quit, surrender and vacate the premises without prejudice however, to Landlord's rights and remedies against Tenant under the lease provisions in effect prior to such termination, and any rent owing shall be paid up to such date and any payments of rent made by Tenant which were on account of any period subsequent to such date shall be returned to Tenant. Unless Landlord shall serve a termination notice as provided for herein, Landlord shall make the repairs and restorations under the conditions of (b) and (c) hereof, with all reasonable expedition subject to delays due to adjustment of insurance claims, labor troubles and causes beyond Landlord's control. (e) Nothing contained hereinabove shall relieve Tenant from liability that may exist as a result of damage from fire or other casualty. Notwithstanding the foregoing, each party shall look first to any insurance in its favor before making any claim against the other party for recovery for loss or damage resulting from fire or other casualty, and to the extent that such insurance is in force and collectible and to the extent permitted by law, Landlord and Tenant each hereby releases and waives all right of recovery against the other or any one claiming through or under each of them by way of subrogation or otherwise. The foregoing release and waiver shall be in force only if both releasors' insurance policies contain a clause providing that such a release or waiver shall not invalidate the insurance and also, provided that such a policy can be obtained without additional premiums. Tenant acknowledges that Landlord will not carry insurance on Tenant's furniture and/or furnishings or any fixtures or equipment, improvements, or appurtenances removable by Tenant and agrees that Landlord will not be obligated to repair any damage thereto or replace the same. Any differences or disputes between Landlord and Tenant in respect to any matters in this article shall be summarily determined by submitting the same to the American Arbitration Association in New York City. Both parties shall cooperate in expediting the hearing. (f) Tenant hereby waives the provisions of Section 227 of the Real Property Law and agrees that the provisions of this article shall govern and control in lieu thereof.

Eminent Domain: 10. If the whole or any part of the demised premises shall be acquired or condemned by Eminent Domain for any public or quasi public use or purpose, then and in that event, the term of this lease shall cease and terminate from the date of title vesting in such proceeding and Tenant shall have no claim for the value of any unexpired term of said lease.

Assignment, Mortgage, Etc.: 11. Tenant, for itself, its heirs, distributees, executors, administrators, legal representatives, successors and assigns, expressly covenants that it shall not assign, mortgage or encumber this agreement, nor underlet, or suffer or permit the demised premises or any part thereof to be used by others, without the prior written consent of Landlord in each instance. If this lease be assigned, or if the demised premises or any part thereof be underlet or occupied by anybody other than Tenant, Landlord may, after default by Tenant, collect rent from the assignee, under-tenant or occupant, and apply the net amount collected to the rent herein reserved, but no such assignment, underletting, occupancy or collection shall be deemed a waiver of this covenant, or the acceptance of the assignee, under-tenant or occupant as tenant, or a release of Tenant from the further performance by Tenant of covenants on the part of Tenant herein contained. The consent by Landlord to an assignment or underletting shall not in any wise be construed to relieve Tenant from obtaining the express consent in writing of Landlord to any further assignment or underletting.

Electric Current:
☞

12. Rates and conditions in respect to submetering or rent inclusion, as the case may be, to be added in RIDER attached hereto. Tenant covenants and agrees that at all times its use of electric current shall not exceed the capacity of existing feeders to the building or the risers or wiring installation and Tenant may not use any electrical equipment which, in Landlord's opinion, reasonably exercised, will overload such installations or interfere with the use thereof by other tenants of the building. The change at any time of the character of electric service shall in no wise make Landlord liable or responsible to Tenant, for any loss, damages or expenses which Tenant may sustain.

Access to Premises:

13. Landlord or Landlord's agents shall have the right (but shall not be obligated) to enter the demised premises in any emergency at any time, and, at other reasonable times, to examine the same and to make such repairs, replacements and improvements as Landlord may deem necessary and reasonably desirable to the demised premises or to any other portion of the building or which Landlord may elect to perform following Tenant's failure to make repairs or perform any work which Tenant is obligated to perform under this lease, or for the purpose of complying with laws, regulations and other directions of governmental authorities. Tenant shall permit Landlord to use and maintain and replace pipes and conduits in and through the demised premises and to erect new pipes and conduits therein. Landlord may, during the progress of any work in the demised premises, take all necessary materials and equipment into said premises without the same constituting an eviction nor shall the Tenant be entitled to any abatement of rent while such work is in progress nor to any damages by reason of loss or interruption of business or otherwise. Throughout the term hereof Landlord shall have the right to enter the demised premises at reasonable hours for the purpose of showing the same to prospective purchasers or mortgagees of the building, and during the last six months of the term for the purpose of showing the same to prospective tenants

---

☞ Rider to be added if necessary.

and may, during said six months period, place upon the premises the usual notices "To Let" and "For Sale" which notices Tenant shall permit to remain thereon without molestation. If Tenant is not present to open and permit an entry into the premises, Landlord or Landlord's agents may enter the same whenever such entry may be necessary or permissible by master key or forcibly and provided reasonable care is exercised to safeguard Tenant's property and such entry shall not render Landlord or its agents liable therefor, nor in any event shall the obligations of Tenant hereunder be affected. If during the last month of the term Tenant shall have removed all or substantially all of Tenant's property therefrom, Landlord may immediately enter, alter, renovate or redecorate the demised premises without limitation or abatement of rent, or incurring liability to Tenant for any compensation and such act shall have no effect on this lease or Tenant's obligations hereunder. Landlord shall have the right at any time, without the same constituting an eviction and without incurring liability to Tenant therefor to change the arrangement and/or location of public entrances, passageways, doors, doorways, corridors, elevators, stairs, toilets, or other public parts of the building and to change the name, number or designation by which the building may be known.

Vault,
Vault Space,
Area:
14. No Vaults, vault space or area, whether or not enclosed or covered, not within the property line of the building is leased hereunder, anything contained in or indicated on any sketch, blue print or plan or anything contained elsewhere in this lease to the contrary notwithstanding. Landlord makes no representation as to the location of the property line of the building. All vaults and vault space and all such areas not within the property line of the building, which Tenant may be permitted to use and/or occupy, is to be used and/or occupied under a revocable license, and if any such license be revoked, or if the amount of such space or area be diminished or required by any federal, state or municipal authority or public utility, Landlord shall not be subject to any liability nor shall Tenant be entitled to any compensation or diminution or abatement of rent, nor shall such revocation, diminution or requisition be deemed constructive or actual eviction. Any tax, fee or charge of municipal authorities for such vault or area shall be paid by Tenant.

Certificate of
Occupancy:
15. Tenant will not at any time use or occupy the demised premises in violation of the certificate of occupancy issued for the building of which the demised premises are a part.

Bankruptcy:
16. (a) If at the date fixed as the commencement of the term of this lease or if at any time during the term hereby demised there shall be filed by or against Tenant in any court pursuant to any statute either of the United States or of any state,

a petition in bankruptcy or insolvency or for reorganization or for the appointment of a receiver or trustee of all or a portion of Tenant's property, and within 60 days thereof, Tenant fails to secure a dismissal thereof, or if Tenant make an assignment for the benefit of creditors or petition for or enter into an arrangement, this lease, at the option of Landlord, exercised within a reasonable time after notice of the happening of any one or more of such events, may be cancelled and terminated by written notice to the Tenant (but if any of such events occur prior to the commencement date, this lease shall be ipso facto cancelled and terminated) and whether such cancellation and termination occur prior to or during the term, neither Tenant nor any person claiming through or under Tenant by virtue of any statute or of any order of any court, shall be entitled to possession or to remain in possession of the premises demised but shall forthwith quit and surrender the premises, and Landlord, in addition to the other rights and remedies Landlord has by virtue of any other provision herein or elsewhere in this lease contained or by virtue of any statute or rule of law, may retain as liquidated damages, any rent, security deposit or moneys received by him from Tenant or others in behalf of Tenant. If this lease shall be assigned in accordance with its terms, the provisions of this Article 16 shall be applicable only to the party then owning Tenant's interest in this lease.

(b) It is stipulated and agreed that in the event of the termination of this lease pursuant to (a) hereof, Landlord shall forthwith, notwithstanding any other provisions of this lease to the contrary, be entitled to recover from Tenant as and for liquidated damages an amount equal to the difference between the rent reserved hereunder for the unexpired portion of the term demised and the fair and reasonable rental value of the demised premises for the same period. In the computation of such damages the difference between any instalment of rent becoming due hereunder after the date of termination and the fair and reasonable rental value of the demised premises for the period for which such instalment was payable shall be discounted to the date of termination at the rate of four per cent (4%) per annum. If such premises or any part thereof be re-let by the Landlord for the unexpired term of said lease, or any part thereof, before presentation of proof of such liquidated damages to any court, commission or tribunal, the amount of rent reserved upon such re-letting shall be deemed to be the fair and reasonable rental value for the part or the whole of the premises so re-let during the term of the re-letting. Nothing herein contained shall limit or prejudice the right of the Landlord to prove for and obtain as liquidated damages by reason of such termination, an amount equal to the maximum allowed by any statute or rule of law in effect at the time when, and governing the proceedings in which, such damages are to be proved, whether or not such amount be greater, equal to, or less than the amount of the difference referred to above.

Default: **17.** (1) If Tenant defaults in fulfilling any of the covenants of this lease other than the covenants for the payment of rent or additional rent, or if the demised premises become vacant or deserted, or if the demised premises are damaged by reason of negligence or carelessness of Tenant, its agents, employees or invitees, then, in any one or more of such events, upon Landlord serving a written five (5) days notice upon Tenant specifying the nature of said default and upon the expiration of said five (5) days, if Tenant shall have failed to comply with or remedy such default, or if the said default or omission complained of shall be of a nature that the same cannot be completely cured or remedied within said five (5) day period, and if Tenant shall not have diligently commenced curing such default within such five (5) day period, and shall not thereafter with reasonable diligence and in good faith proceed to remedy or cure such default, then Landlord may serve a written three (3) days' notice of cancellation of this lease upon Tenant, and upon the expiration of said three (3) days, this lease and the term thereunder shall end and expire as fully and completely .as if the expiration of such three (3) day period were the day herein definitely fixed for the end and expiration of this lease and the term thereof and Tenant shall then quit and surrender the demised premises to Landlord but Tenant shall remain liable as hereinafter provided.

(2) If the notice provided for in (1) hereof shall have been given, and the term shall expire as aforesaid; or (2a) if Tenant shall make default in the payment of the rent reserved herein or any item of additional rent herein mentioned or any part of either or in making any other payment herein required; or (2b) if any execution or attachment shall be issued against Tenant or any of Tenant's property whereupon the demised premises shall be taken or occupied by someone other than Tenant; or (2c) if Tenant shall make default with respect to any other lease between Landlord and Tenant; or (2d) if Tenant shall fail to move into or take possession of the premises within fifteen (15) days after the commencement of the term of this lease, of which fact Landlord shall be the sole judge; then and in any of such events Landlord may without notice, re-enter the demised premises either by force or otherwise, and dispossess Tenant by summary proceedings or otherwise, and the legal representative of Tenant or other occupant of demised premises and remove their effects and hold the premises as if this lease had not been made, and Tenant hereby waives the service of notice of intention to re-enter or to institute legal proceedings to that end. If Tenant shall make default hereunder prior to the date fixed as the commencement of any renewal or extension of this lease, Landlord may cancel and terminate such renewal or extension agreement by written notice.

Remedies of **18.** In case of any such default, re-entry, expiration and/or
Landlord and dispossess by summary proceedings or otherwise, (a) the
Waiver of rent shall become due thereupon and be paid up to the
Redemption: time of such re-entry, dispossess and/or expiration, together with such expenses as Landlord may incur for legal
expenses, attorneys' fees, brokerage, and/or putting the demised premises
in good order, or for preparing the same for re-rental; (b) Landlord
may re-let the premises or any part or parts thereof, either in the
name of Landlord or otherwise, for a term or terms, which may at Landlord's option be less than or exceed the period which would otherwise have
constituted the balance of the term of this lease and may grant concessions or free rent or charge a higher rental than that in this lease, and/or
(c) Tenant or the legal representatives of Tenant shall also pay Landlord
as liquidated damages for the failure of Tenant to observe and perform
said Tenant's covenants herein contained, any deficiency between the rent
hereby reserved and/or covenanted to be paid and the net amount, if any,
of the rents collected on account of the lease or leases of the demised
premises for each month of the period which would otherwise have constituted the balance of the term of this lease. The failure or refusal of
Landlord to re-let the premises or any part or parts thereof shall not release or affect Tenant's liability for damages. In computing such liquidated
damages there shall be added to the said deficiency such expenses as Landlord may incur in connection with re-letting, such as legal expenses, attorneys' fees, brokerage, advertising and for keeping the demised premises in
good order or for preparing the same for re-letting. Any such liquidated
damages shall be paid in monthly instalments by Tenant on the rent day
specified in this lease and any suit brought to collect the amount of the
deficiency for any month shall not prejudice in any way the rights of
Landlord to collect the deficiency for any subsequent month by a similar
proceeding. Landlord, in putting the demised premises in good order or
preparing the same for re-rental may, at Landlord's option, make such alterations, repairs, replacements, and/or decorations in the demised premises as Landlord, in Landlord's sole judgment, considers advisable and
necessary for the purpose of re-letting the demised premises, and the making of such alterations, repairs, replacements, and/or decorations shall
not operate or be construed to release Tenant from liability hereunder as
aforesaid. Landlord shall in no event be liable in any way whatsoever for
failure to re-let the demised premises, or in the event that the demised
premises are re-let, for failure to collect the rent thereof under such re-
letting, and in no event shall Tenant be entitled to receive any excess,
if any, of such net rents collected over the sums payable by Tenant to
Landlord hereunder. In the event of a breach or threatened breach by
Tenant of any of the covenants or provisions hereof, Landlord shall have
the right of injunction and the right to invoke any remedy allowed at law
or in equity as if re-entry, summary proceedings and other remedies were
not herein provided for. Mention in this lease of any particular remedy,
shall not preclude Landlord from any other remedy, in law or in equity.
Tenant hereby expressly waives any and all rights of redemption granted

by or under any present or future laws in the event of Tenant being evicted or dispossessed for any cause, or in the event of Landlord obtaining possession of demised premises, by reason of the violation by Tenant of any of the covenants and conditions of this lease, or otherwise.

Fees and Expenses: **19.** If Tenant shall default in the observance or performance of any term or covenant on Tenant's part to be observed or performed under or by virtue of any of the terms or provisions in any article of this lease, then, unless otherwise provided elsewhere in this lease, Landlord may immediately or at any time thereafter and without notice perform the same for the account of Tenant, and if Landlord makes any expenditures or incurs any obligations for the payment of money in connection therewith including, but not limited to, attorneys' fees in instituting, prosecuting or defending any action or proceeding such sums paid or obligations incurred with interest and costs shall be deemed to be additional rent hereunder and shall be paid by Tenant to Landlord within five (5) days of rendition of any bill or statement to Tenant therefor.

No Representations by Landlord: **20.** Neither Landlord nor Landlord's agents have made any representations or promises with respect to the physical condition of the building, the land upon which it is erected or the demised premises, the rents, leases, expenses of operation or any other matter or thing affecting or related to the premises except as herein expressly set forth and no rights, easements or licenses are acquired by Tenant by implication or otherwise except as expressly set forth in the provisions of this lease. Tenant has inspected the building and the demised premises and is thoroughly acquainted with their condition, and agrees to take the same "as is" and acknowledges that the taking of possession of the demised premises by Tenant shall be conclusive evidence that the said premises and the building of which the same form a part were in good and satisfactory condition at the time such possession was so taken, except as to latent defects. All understandings and agreements heretofore made between the parties hereto are merged in this contract, which alone fully and completely expresses the agreement between Landlord and Tenant and any executory agreement hereafter made shall be ineffective to change, modify, discharge or effect an abandonment of it in whole or in part, unless such executory agreement is in writing and signed by the party against whom enforcement of the change, modification, discharge or abandonment is sought.

End of Term: **21.** Upon the expiration or other termination of the term of this lease, Tenant shall quit and surrender to Landlord the demised premises, broom clean, in good order and condition, ordinary wear excepted, and Tenant shall remove all its property. Tenant's obligation to observe or perform this covenant shall sur-

vive the expiration or other termination of this lease. If the last day of
the term of this lease or any renewal thereof, falls on Sunday, this lease
shall expire at noon on the preceding Saturday unless it be a legal holi-
day in which case it shall expire at noon on the preceding business day.

Quiet   **22.** Landlord covenants and agrees with Tenant that upon
Enjoyment: Tenant paying the rent and additional rent and observing
                      and performing all the terms, covenants and conditions,
on Tenant's part to be observed and performed, Tenant may peaceably
and quietly enjoy the premises hereby demised, subject, nevertheless, to
the terms and conditions of this lease including, but not limited to, Article
30 hereof and to the ground leases, underlying leases and mortgages
hereinbefore mentioned.

Failure   **23.** If Landlord is unable to give possession of the
to Give   demised premises on the date of the commencement of
Possession: the term hereof, because of the holding-over or retention
                     of possession of any tenant, undertenant or occupants,
or if the premises are located in a building being constructed, because
such building has not been sufficiently completed to make the premises
ready for occupancy or because of the fact that a certificate of occupancy
has not been procured or for any other reason, Landlord shall not be
subject to any liability for failure to give possession on said date and the
validity of the lease shall not be impaired under such circumstances, nor
shall the same be construed in any wise to extend the term of this lease,
but the rent payable hereunder shall be abated (provided Tenant is not
responsible for the inability to obtain possession) until after Landlord
shall have given Tenant written notice that the premises are substantially
ready for Tenant's occupancy. If permission is given to Tenant to enter
into the possession of the demised premises or to occupy premises other
than the demised premises prior to the date specified as the commencement of the term of this lease, Tenant covenants and agrees that such
occupancy shall be deemed to be under all the terms, covenants, conditions and provisions of this lease, except as to the covenant to pay rent.
The provisions of this article are intended to constitute "an express provision to the contrary" within the meaning of Section 223-a of the New
York Real Property Law.

No Waiver: **24.** The failure of Landlord to seek redress for violation
                     of, or to insist upon the strict performance of any cov-
enant or condition of this lease or of any of the Rules or Regulations set
forth or hereafter adopted by Landlord, shall not prevent a subsequent act
which would have originally constituted a violation from having all the
force and effect of an original violation. The receipt by Landlord of rent
with knowledge of the breach of any covenant of this lease shall not be
deemed a waiver of such breach and no provision of this lease shall be

deemed to have been waived by Landlord unless such waiver be in writing signed by Landlord. No payment by Tenant or receipt by Landlord of a lesser amount than the monthly rent herein stipulated shall be deemed to be other than on account of the earliest stipulated rent, nor shall any endorsement or statement of any check or any letter accompanying any check or payment as rent be deemed an accord and satisfaction, and Landlord may accept such check or payment without prejudice to Landlord's right to recover the balance of such rent or pursue any other remedy in this lease provided. No act or thing done by Landlord or Landlord's agents during the term hereby demised shall be deemed an acceptance of a surrender of said premises and no agreement to accept such surrender shall be valid unless in writing signed by Landlord. No employee of Landlord or Landlord's agent shall have any power to accept the keys of said premises prior to the termination of the lease and the delivery of keys to any such agent or employee shall not operate as a termination of the lease or a surrender of the premises.

Waiver of Trial by Jury: 25. It is mutually agreed by and between Landlord and Tenant that the respective parties hereto shall and they hereby do waive trial by jury in any action, proceeding or counterclaim brought by either of the parties hereto against the other (except for personal injury or property damage) on any matters whatsoever arising out of or in any way connected with this lease, the relationship of Landlord and Tenant, Tenant's use of or occupancy of said premises, and any emergency statutory or any other statutory remedy. It is further mutually agreed that in the event Landlord commences any summary proceeding for non-payment of rent, Tenant will not interpose any counterclaim of whatever nature or description in any such proceeding.

Inability to Perform: 26. This lease and the obligation of Tenant to pay rent hereunder and perform all of the other covenants and agreements hereunder on part of Tenant to be performed shall in no wise be affected, impaired or excused because Landlord is unable to fulfill any of its obligations under this lease or to supply or is delayed in supplying any service expressly or impliedly to be supplied or is unable to make, or is delayed in making any repair, additions, alterations or decorations or is unable to supply or is delayed in supplying any equipment or fixtures if Landlord is prevented or delayed from so doing by reason of strike or labor troubles or any cause whatsoever including, but not limited to, government preemption in connection with a National Emergency or by reason of any rule, order or regulation of any department or subdivision thereof of any government agency or by reason of the conditions of supply and demand which have been or are affected by war or other emergency.

Bills and   **27.** Except as otherwise in this lease provided, a bill,
Notices: statement, notice or communication which Landlord may
desire or be required to give to Tenant, shall be deemed
sufficiently given or rendered if, in writing, delivered to Tenant personally
or sent by registered or certified mail addressed to Tenant at the building
of which the demised premises form a part or at the last known residence address or business address of Tenant or left at any of the aforesaid premises addressed to Tenant, and the time of the rendition of
such bill or statement and of the giving of such notice or communication shall be deemed to be the time when the same is delivered to
Tenant, mailed, or left at the premises as herein provided. Any notice
by Tenant to Landlord must be served by registered or certified mail
addressed to Landlord at the address first hereinabove given or at such
other address as Landlord shall designate by written notice.

Services Pro-   **28.** As long as Tenant is not in default under any of the
vided by Land- covenants of this lease, Landlord shall provide: (a) nec-
lord—Water,   essary elevator facilities on business days from 8 a.m.
Elevators,   to 6 p.m. and on Saturdays from 8 a.m. to 1 p.m. and
Heat, Cleaning, have one elevator subject to call at all other times; (b)
Air Condi-   heat to the demised premises when and as required by
tioning: law, on business days from 8 a.m. to 6 p.m. and on
Saturdays from 8 a.m. to 1 p.m.; (c) water for ordinary
lavatory purposes, but if Tenant uses or consumes water for any other
purposes or in unusual quantities (of which fact Landlord shall be the
sole judge), Landlord may install a water meter at Tenant's expense
which Tenant shall thereafter maintain at Tenant's expense in good
working order and repair to register such water consumption and
Tenant shall pay for water consumed as shown on said meter as
additional rent as and when bills are rendered, and on Tenant's
default in making such payment, Landlord may pay such charges and
collect the same from Tenant. Such a meter shall also be installed and
maintained at Tenant's expense if required by Law or Governmental
Order. Tenant, if a water meter is so installed, covenants and agrees
to pay its proportionate share of the sewer rent and all other rents
and charges which are now or hereafter assessed, imposed or may
become a lien on the demised premises or the realty of which they are
a part; (d) cleaning service for the demised premises at Landlord's expense provided that the same are kept in order by Tenant. If, however,
said premises are to be kept clean by Tenant, it shall be done at Tenant's
sole expense, in a manner satisfactory to Landlord and no one other than
persons approved by Landlord shall be permitted to enter said premises or
the building of which they are a part for such purpose. Tenant shall pay
Landlord the cost of removal of any of Tenant's refuse and rubbish from
☞   the building. (e) RIDER to be added in respect to rates
          and conditions for air conditioning/cooling and ventila-

---

☞ Rider to be added if necessary.

tion if the entire building in which the demised premises is located is serviced by a central air conditioning/cooling and ventilating system. If applicable, air conditioning/cooling will be furnished from May 15th through September 30th on business days (Mondays through Fridays, holidays excepted) from 8:00 a.m. to 6:00 p.m., and ventilation will be furnished on business days during the aforesaid hours except when air conditioning/cooling is being furnished as aforesaid. If Tenant requires air conditioning/cooling or ventilation for more extended hours or on Saturdays, Sundays or on holidays, Landlord will furnish the same at Tenant's expense. (f) Landlord shall have no responsibility or liability for failure to supply the services agreed to herein. Landlord reserves the right to stop services of the heating, elevators, plumbing, air-conditioning, power systems or cleaning or other services, if any, when necessary by reason of accident or for repairs, alterations, replacements or improvements necessary or desirable in the judgment of Landlord for as long as may be reasonably required by reason thereof or by reason of strikes, accidents, laws, order or regulations or any other reason beyond the control of Landlord. If the building of which the demised premises are a part supplies manually-operated elevator service, Landlord at any time may substitute automatic-control elevator service and upon ten days' written notice to Tenant, proceed with alterations necessary therefor without in any wise affecting this lease or the obligations of Tenant hereunder. The same shall be done with a minimum of inconvenience to Tenant and Landlord shall pursue the alterations with due diligence.

Captions: 29. The Captions are inserted only as a matter of convenience and for reference and in no way define; limit or describe the scope of this lease nor the intent of any provision thereof.

Definitions: 30. The term "office", or "offices", wherever used in this lease, shall not be construed to mean premises used as a store or stores, for the sale or display, at any time, of goods, wares or merchandise, of any kind, or as a restaurant, shop, booth, bootblack or other stand, barber shop, or for other similar purposes or for manufacturing. The term "Landlord" as used in this lease means only the owner, or the mortgagee in possession, for the time being of the land and building (or the owner of a lease of the building or of the land and building) of which the demised premises form a part, so that in the event of any sale or sales of said land and building or of said lease, or in the event of a lease of said building, or of the land and building, the said Landlord shall be and hereby is entirely freed and relieved of all covenants and obligations of Landlord hereunder, and it shall be deemed and construed without further agreement between the parties or their successors in interest, or between the parties and the purchaser, at any such sale, or the said lessee of the building, or of the land and building, that the purchaser or the lessee of the building has assumed and agreed to carry out any and all covenants and obligations of Landlord, hereunder. The words "re-enter" and "re-entry" as used in this lease are not restricted to their technical legal meaning. The term "business days" as used in this lease shall exclude Saturdays (except such portion thereof as is covered by specific hours in Article 28 hereof), Sundays and all days observed by the State or Federal Government as legal holidays.

Adjacent **31.** If an excavation shall be made upon land adjacent **Excavation—** to the demised premises, or shall be authorized to be **Shoring:** made, Tenant shall afford to the person causing or authorized to cause such excavation, license to enter upon the demised premises for the purpose of doing such work as said person shall deem necessary to preserve the wall or the building of which demised premises form a part from injury or damage and to support the same by proper foundations without any claim for damages or indemnity against Landlord, or diminution or abatement of rent.

Rules and **32.** Tenant and Tenant's servants, employees, agents, **Regulations:** visitors, and licensees shall observe faithfully, and comply strictly with, the Rules and Regulations and such other and further reasonable Rules and Regulations as Landlord or Landlord's agents may from time to time adopt. Notice of any additional rules or regulations shall be given in such manner as Landlord may elect. In case Tenant disputes the reasonableness of any additional Rule or Regulation hereafter made or adopted by Landlord or Landlord's agents, the parties hereto agree to submit the question of the reasonableness of such Rule or Regulation for decision to the Chairman of the Board of Directors of the Management Division of The Real Estate Board of New York, Inc., or to such impartial person or persons as he may designate, whose determination shall be final and conclusive upon the parties hereto. The right to dispute the reasonableness of any additional Rule or Regulation upon Tenant's part shall be deemed waived unless the same shall be asserted by service of a notice, in writing upon Landlord within ten (10) days after the giving of notice thereof. Nothing in this lease contained shall be construed to impose upon Landlord any duty or obligation to enforce the Rules and Regulations or terms, covenants or conditions in any other lease, as against any other tenant and Landlord shall not be liable to Tenant for violation of the same by any other tenant, its servants, employees, agents, visitors or licensees.

Successors **33.** The covenants, conditions and agreements contained **and Assigns:** in this lease shall bind and inure to the benefit of Landlord and Tenant and their respective heirs, distributees, executors, administrators, successors, and except as otherwise provided in this lease, their assigns.

In Witness Whereof, Landlord and Tenant have respectively signed and sealed this lease as of the day and year first above written.

Witness for Landlord:

....

CORP. SEAL

....   [L. S.]

Witness for Tenant:

....

CORP. SEAL

....   [L. S.]

ACKNOWLEDGMENTS

CORPORATE LANDLORD
STATE OF NEW YORK, } ss.:
County of

On this   day of   , 19   , before me

personally came
to me known, who being by me duly sworn, did depose and say that he resides

in   ;

that he is the   of

the corporation described in and which executed the foregoing instrument, as LANDLORD; that he knows the seal of said corporation; that the seal affixed to said instrument is such corporate seal; that it was so affixed by order of the Board of Directors of said corporation, and that he signed his name thereto by like order.

....

CORPORATE TENANT
STATE OF NEW YORK, } ss.:
County of

On this   day of   , 19   , before me

personally came
to me known, who being by me duly sworn, did depose and say that he resides

in   ;

that he is the   of

the corporation described in and which executed the foregoing instrument, as TENANT; that he knows the seal of said corporation; that the seal affixed to said instrument is such corporate seal; that it was so affixed by order of the Board of Directors of said corporation, and that he signed his name thereto by like order.

....

GUARANTY

FOR VALUE RECEIVED, and in consideration for, and as an inducement to Landlord making the within lease with Tenant, the undersigned guarantees to Landlord, Landlord's successors and assigns, the full performance and observance of all the covenants, conditions and agreements, therein provided to be performed and observed by Tenant, including the "Rules and Regulations" as therein provided, without requiring any notice of non-payment, non-performance, or non-observance, or proof, or notice, or demand, whereby to charge the undersigned therefor, all of which the undersigned hereby expressly waves and expressly agrees that the validity of this agreement and the obligations of the guarantor hereunder shall in no wise be terminated, affected or impaired by reason of the assertion by Landlord against Tenant of any of the rights or remedies reserved to Landlord pursuant to the provisions of the within lease. The undersigned further covenants and agrees that this guaranty shall remain and continue in full force and effect as to any renewal, modification or extension of this lease and during any period when Tenant is occupying the premises as a "statutory tenant." As a further inducement to Landlord to make this lease and in consideration thereof, Landlord and the undersigned covenant and agree that in any action or proceeding brought by either Landlord or the undersigned against the other on any matters whatsoever arising out of, under, or by virtue of the terms of this lease or of this guaranty that Landlord and the undersigned shall and do hereby waive trial by jury.

Dated New York City.. 19............

WITNESS:

....

Residence ....

Business Address ....

Firm Name ....

....[L. S.]

RULES AND REGULATIONS ATTACHED TO AND MADE A PART OF THIS LEASE IN ACCORDANCE WITH ARTICLE 32.

1. The sidewalks, entrances, driveways, passages, courts, elevators, vestibules, stairways, corridors or halls shall not be obstructed or encumbered by any Tenant or used for any purpose other than for ingress to and egress from the demised premises and for delivery of merchandise and equipment in a prompt and efficient manner using elevators and passageways designated for such delivery by Landlord. There shall not be used in any space, or in the public hall of the building, either by any Tenant or by jobbers or others in the delivery or receipt of merchandise, any hand trucks, except those equipped with rubber tires and sideguards. If said premises are situate on the ground floor of the building Tenant thereof shall further, at Tenant's expense, keep the sidewalks and curb in front of said premises clean and free from ice, snow, dirt and rubbish.

2. The water and wash closets and plumbing fixtures shall not be used for any purposes other than those for which they were designed or constructed and no sweepings, rubbish, rags, acids or other substances shall be deposited therein, and the expense of any breakage, stoppage, or damage resulting from the violation of this rule shall be borne by the tenant who, or whose clerks, agents, employees or visitors, shall have caused it.

3. No carpet, rug or other article shall be hung or shaken out of any window of the building; and no Tenant shall sweep or throw or permit to be swept or thrown from the demised premises any dirt or other substances into any of the corridors or halls, elevators, or out of the doors or windows or stairways of the building, and Tenant shall not use, keep or permit to be used or kept any foul or noxious gas or substance in the demised premises, or permit or suffer the demised premises to be occupied or used in a manner offensive or objectionable to Landlord or other occupants of the building by reason of noise, odors and/or vibrations, or interfere in any way with other Tenants or those having business therein, nor shall any animals or birds be kept in or about the building. Smoking or carrying lighted cigars or cigarettes in the elevators of the building is prohibited.

4. No awnings or other projections shall be attached to the outside walls of the building without the prior written consent of Landlord.

5. No sign, advertisement, notice or other lettering shall be exhibited, inscribed, painted or affixed by any Tenant on any part of the outside of the demised premises or the building or on the inside of the demised premises if the same is visible from the outside of the premises without the prior written consent of Landlord, except that the name of Tenant may appear on the entrance door of the premises. In the event of the violation of the foregoing by any Tenant, Landlord may remove same without any liability, and may charge the expense incurred by such removal to Tenant or Tenants violating this rule. Interior signs on doors and directory tablet shall be inscribed, painted or affixed for each Tenant by Landlord at the expense of such Tenant, and shall be of a size, color and style acceptable to Landlord.

6. No Tenant shall mark, paint, drill into, or in any way deface any part of the demised premises or the building of which they form a part. No boring, cutting or stringing of wires shall be permitted, except with the prior written consent of Landlord, and as Landlord may direct. No Tenant shall lay linoleum, or other similar floor covering, so that the same shall come in direct contact with the floor of the demised premises, and, if linoleum or other similar floor covering is desired to be used an interlining of builder's deadening felt shall be first affixed to the floor, by a paste or other material, soluble in water, the use of cement or other similar adhesive material being expressly prohibited.

7. No additional locks or bolts of any kind shall be placed upon any of the doors or windows by any Tenant, nor shall any changes be made in existing locks or mechanism thereof. Each Tenant must, upon the termination of his Tenancy, restore to Landlord all keys of stores, offices and toilet rooms, either furnished to, or otherwise procured by, such Tenant, and in the event of the loss of any keys, so furnished, such Tenant shall pay to Landlord the cost thereof.

8. Freight, furniture, business equipment, merchandise and bulky matter of any description shall be delivered to and removed from the premises only on the freight elevators and through the service entrances and corridors, and only during hours and in a manner approved by Landlord. Landlord reserves the right to inspect all freight to be brought into the building and to exclude from the building all freight which violates any of these Rules and Regulations or the lease of which these Rules and Regulations are a part.

9. No Tenant shall obtain for use upon the demised premises ice, drinking water, towel and other similar services, or accept barbering or bootblacking services in the demised premises, except from persons authorized by Landlord, and at hours and under regulations fixed by Landlord. Canvassing, soliciting and peddling in the building is prohibited and each Tenant shall co-operate to prevent the same.

10. Landlord reserves the right to exclude from the building between the hours of 6 P.M. and 8 A.M. and at all hours on Sundays, and legal holidays all persons who do not present a pass to the building signed by Landlord. Landlord will furnish passes to persons for whom any Tenant requires same in writing. Each Tenant shall be responsible for all persons for whom he requests such pass and shall be liable to Landlord for all acts of such persons.

11. Landlord shall have the right to prohibit any advertising by any Tenant which, in Landlord's opinion, tends to impair the reputation of the building or its desirability as a building for offices, and upon written notice from Landlord, Tenant shall refrain from or discontinue such advertising.

12. Tenant shall not bring or permit to be brought or kept in or on the demised premises, any inflammable, combustible or explosive fluid, material, chemical or substance, or cause or permit any odors of cooking or other processes, or any unusual or other objectionable odors to permeate in or eminate from the demised premises.

13. If the building contains central air conditioning and ventilation Tenant agrees to keep all windows closed at all times and to abide by all rules and regulations issued by the Landlord with respect to such services. If Tenant requires air conditioning or ventilation after the usual hours, Tenant shall give notice in writing to the building superintendent prior to 3:00 P.M. in the case of services required on week days, and prior to 3:00 P.M. on the day prior in the case of after hours service required on weekends or on holidays.

APARTMENT LEASE

(This is the standard apartment lease used by the Institute of Real Estate Management of the National Association of Real Estate Boards. Used by permission.)

TENANT COPY
OWNER COPY
OFFICE COPY

APARTMENT LEASE

TO

Location

Commences

Expires

APARTMENT LEASE

This Lease, made this _____ day of _____

19_____, by and between _____ hereinafter designated

_____

as lessor, and _____

_____ hereinafter designated as lessee,

WITNESSETH .

1. The lessor, in consideration of the rent reserved herein to be paid by said lessee and of the other covenants, agreements and conditions hereinafter contained to be kept, performed and observed by said lessee, does hereby let and lease unto said lessee Apartment _____ in the _____

_____ Apartments located at _____ in the City of

_____ County of _____ State of _____, to be used and occupied by the lessee and his immediate family as a private residence, and for no other purpose,

DESCRIPTION AND TERM

for the term beginning on the _____ day of _____ , 19 ____ and ending on the _____ day of _____ , 19 ____

RENT

2. The lessee, in consideration of the demise and of the covenants and agreements made herein by said lessor, leases said premises for said term and does hereby promise to pay to said lessor, his representatives and assigns as rental for said premises the sum of _____

_____ dollars in lawful money of the United States, payable as follows:

_____

_____

_____

_____

CONDITION OF PREMISES

3. The lessee accepts said premises in their present condition and agrees to keep said premises in a good clean condition; to make no alterations or additions to the same; to commit no waste thereon; to obey all laws and ordinances affecting said premises; to replace all glass broken or cracked; to repay the lessor the cost of all repairs made necessary by the negligent or careless use of said premises; and, to surrender the premises at the termination hereof in like condition as when taken, reasonable wear and damage by the elements excepted.

DELIVERY OF POSSESSION

4. It is understood that if the lessee shall be unable to enter into and occupy the premises leased at the time above provided by reason of said premises not being ready for occupancy, or by reason of the holding over of any previous occupant of said premises, or as a result of any cause or reason beyond the direct control of the lessor, the lessor shall not be liable in damages to the lessee therefor but during the period the lessee shall be unable to occupy said premises as hereinbefore provided the rental therefor shall be abated. If said lessor is not able to deliver possession to said lessee within _____ days of the date named for the commencement of said term, the lessee may cancel and terminate this lease.

UTILITIES

5. The lessor shall furnish heat during the usual heating season, elevator service either manually operated or automatic, electric current for lighting and operation of household equipment, gas for cooking, and hot and cold water for ordinary household use; but lessor shall not be liable for failure to furnish any of the above named services from any cause whatsoever, nor shall failure so to do be grounds for eviction provided lessor exercises reasonable diligence to remedy such failure.

DESTRUCTION OF PREMISES

6. In case of partial destruction or injury to said premises by fire, the elements or other casualty, the lessor shall repair the same with reasonable dispatch after notice to him of such destruction or injury. In the event said premises are rendered totally untenantable by fire, the elements or other casualty, or in the event the building of which the demised premises are a part (though the demised premises may not be effected) be so injured or destroyed that the lessor shall decide within a reasonable time not to rebuild, the term hereby granted shall cease and the rent shall be paid up to the date of such injury or damage.

RIGHT OF RE-ENTRY

7. The lessor, his agent, janitor, watchman and employees may enter said premises at any time with pass key or otherwise to examine same or to make needed repairs to said premises and if the premises consist of only a part of a structure owned or controlled by the lessor, the lessor, his agent, janitor or watchman or employees may enter the demised premises at reasonable times to install or repair pipes, wires and other appliances deemed by the lessor essential to the use and occupation of other parts of the building.

ASSIGNMENT OR SUBLETTING

8. The lessee further covenants that he will not allow anyone to share said premises, keep roomers or boarders, nor assign, sublet or transfer said premises or any part thereof without the lessor's consent endorsed in writing hereon; also, that the written assent hereon to one assignment or transfer of this lease or subletting shall not be considered as a waiver of this covenant by the lessor to any subsequent assignment, transfer or subletting, nor shall such written assent to any assignment or transfer, release said lessee from liability hereunder.

CONDEM-NATION

9. It is agreed by and between the lessor and the lessee that if the whole or any part of said premises hereby leased shall be taken by any competent authority for any public or quasi-public use or purpose, then and in that event, the term of this lease shall cease and terminate from the date when the possession of the part so taken shall be required for such use or purpose. All damages awarded for such taking shall belong to and be the property of the lessor.

**NON-
LIABILITY
OF LESSOR**

10. The lessee covenants that the lessor shall not be liable for any damage or injury of the lessee, the lessee's agents or employees or to any person entering the premises or the building of which the demised premises are a part or to goods or chattels therein resulting from any defect in the structure or its equipment, or in the structure or equipment of the structure of which the demised premises are a part, and, further to indemnify and save the lessor harmless from all claims of every kind and nature.

EVICTION

11. The lessee covenants that in event of a partial eviction occasioned by act or neglect of the lessor that does not materially affect the beneficial use by the lessee, the obligation to pay rent shall not abate but possession shall be restored or the rental reduced proportionately at the option of the lessor.

**PAYMENT
OF RENT**

12. All payments of rents shall be made at the office of _____, agents for the lessor, or at such other place as the lessor may designate in writing.

**RULES
AND
REGULATIONS**

13. The lessee covenants and agrees that all rules and regulations printed upon the back hereof, or hereafter adopted by the lessor and made known to lessee, shall have the same force and effect as covenants of said lease, and the lessee covenants that he, his family and guests will observe all such rules and regulations.

VACATING UPON TERMINATION

14. Lessee further covenants and agrees that upon tne expiration of said term, or upon the termination of the lease for any cause, he will at once peacefully surrender and deliver up the whole of the above described premises together with all improvements thereon to the lessor, his agents and assigns.

HOLDOVER TENANCY

15. The lessee covenants that his occupancy of the said premises beyond the term of this lease shall not be deemed as a renewal of this lease for the whole term or any part thereof, but that the acceptance by the lessor of rent accruing after the expiration of this lease shall be considered as a renewal of this lease for one month only and for successive periods of one month only.

RIGHT TO MORTGAGE

16. The lessor may encumber the premises by mortgage or mortgages, securing such sum or sums and upon such terms and conditions as the lessor may desire, and any such mortgage or mortgages so given shall be a first lien on the land and buildings superior to the rights of the lessee herein.

QUIET ENJOYMENT

17. Said lessor covenants that said lessee on payment of all of the aforesaid installments and performing all the covenants and observing all the rules and regulations shall and may peacefully and quietly have, hold and enjoy the said demised premises for the term aforesaid.

DEFAULT

18. Provided that in case any rent shall be due and unpaid or if default shall be made in any of the covenants herein contained, or if said premises shall be abandoned, deserted or vacated, then it shall be lawful for the said lessor, his agents, attorneys, successors or assigns to re-enter, repossess the said premises and the lessee and each and every occupant to remove and put out, and upon re-entry as aforesaid this lease shall terminate. In the event of re-entry by the lessor as herein provided lessee shall be liable in damages to said lessor for all loss sustained.

19. It is understood and agreed that the terms lessor and lessee shall include the executors, administrators, successors, heirs and assigns of the parties hereto.

IN WITNESS WHEREOF, the lessor and the lessee have executed these presents, the day and year first above written.

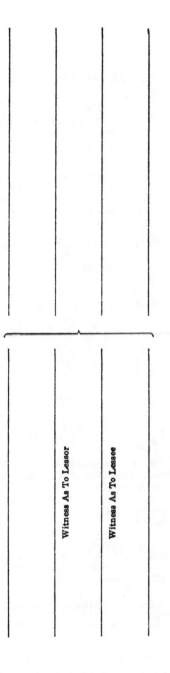

Witness As To Lessor

Witness As To Lessee

RULES AND REGULATIONS

1. Children shall not play in the public halls, stairways or elevator.

2. No baby carriages, velocipedes or bicycles shall be allowed in passenger elevators, if any, or in the halls, passageways, areas or courts of the building.

3. The passenger elevators, unless automatic and if any, shall be operated only by employees of the lessor and must not in any event be interfered with by the lessee, his family, servants or visitors. Elevators, unless automatic, will be operated only during such hours as the lessor may from time to time determine.

4. No animals or pets of any kind shall be kept or harbored in the demised premises without written permission of the lessor.

5. No wires, cables or aerials for radio or television purposes shall be installed upon the roof or other parts of the building without the lessor's written permission.

6. Nothing shall be thrown by the tenants, their servants, employees or visitors from the windows or doors or in the passageways or hallways. If the building is equipped with an incinerator all garbage shall be well wrapped and placed in incinerator. Boxes and debris shall be disposed of as directed.

7. Nothing shall be placed upon the outer windowsills and dust mops, clothing, tablecloths, rugs, etc., shall not be shaken or cleaned in any of the public halls or from any of the windows, doors, or landings.

8. Lessee shall report promptly all leaking faucets or toilets and shall turn off electric lights when not needed.

9. No furniture or bulky articles shall be brought into the building except through service entrance.

10. In order to reduce noise and prevent unnecessary dirt being brought into the building, the lessee shall use only those trades people such as milkmen, drycleaners and paper boys as the lessor shall approve.

11. The lessee's family and guests shall have due regard for the comfort and enjoyment of other tenants in the building. No musical instrument, radio or television shall be played after 11:00 p.m. No musical instrument shall be practised upon at any time.

12. If storage space be provided in the basement or other part of the building it shall not be considered a part of the leased premises or part of the consideration for which rent is paid. All goods or property stored in said space shall be at the sole risk of the lessee.

LEASE FOR FURNISHED HOUSE OR APARTMENT

(This lease may be conveniently adapted to the leasing of either a furnished house or apartment.)

THIS LEASE executed at ...., Pennsylvania, this .... day of ...., 19...., by and between John Jones of ...., Pennsylvania, the Lessor, and Wm. Smith of ...., Pennsylvania, the Lessee, witnesseth: That said Lessor, in consideration of the rents and covenants hereinafter stipulated to be paid and performed by said Lessee, does hereby demise, let and lease unto said Lessee, the following described premises, to-wit:
(Description of premises.)
and the appurtenances thereunto belonging, and also all the furniture, carpets, dishes, crockery, glassware, kitchen utensils and other personal property specified in the schedule hereto annexed marked "Exhibit A" and made a part hereof:

To have and to hold the same, unto the said Lessee, to be used by said Lessee as a dwelling, and for no other purpose, for the term of .... years, beginning on ...., 19...., and ending on ...., 19...., for the yearly rent of .... dollars ($..........) payable in equal monthly installments of .... dollars ($..........) each, in advance, on the first day of each and every month during said term at .... in the city of ...., Pennsylvania, or such other place in said city as the Lessor may direct.

And said Lessee does hereby covenant and agree with said Lessor, his heirs and assigns, as follows: That he will pay said rent at the times and place in the manner aforesaid; that he will pay all bills and charges for water, gas and electric current which may be assessed or charged against the occupant of said premises during said term or any extension thereof; that he will use and occupy said premises, and said furniture, etc., in a careful, safe and proper manner, and will carefully conduct and guard all fires that may be conducted thereon; that he will not commit or suffer any waste therein; that he will not use or occupy said premises for any unlawful purpose; that he will not sell, or permit to be sold, on the said premises, during said term, spiritous, vinous, malt or any intoxicating liquor, without the written consent of said Lessor; that he will not assign this lease nor underlet said premises, nor any part thereof, without the written consent of said Lessor; that he will not use or occupy said premises, or permit the same to be used or occupied, for any purpose deemed extra-hazardous on account of fire or otherwise; that he will make no alterations or additions in or to said premises without the written consent of said Lessor; that he will permit said Lessor, or his agents, to enter upon said premises, at all reasonable times, to examine the condition thereof; that he will surrender and deliver up said premises, and all of said furniture, carpets, dishes, crockery, and glassware, kitchen utensils and other personal property, in as good order and condition as the same now are, reasonable use and ordinary wear and tear thereof, and damage by fire or other unavoidable casualty excepted; and that he will replace all such furniture or other articles of personal property, as shall be broken, damaged, or missing, with other articles of equal value, and of as near the same pattern as possible.

Provided, however, that if said rent, or any part thereof, shall at any time be in arrears and unpaid, and without any demand being made therefor, or if said Lessee, or his assigns, shall fail to keep and perform any of the covenants, agreements or conditions of this lease, on his part to be kept and performed, or if said Lessee shall be adjudged a bankrupt, or shall make an assignment for the benefit of creditors, or if the interest of said Lessee therein shall be sold under execution or other legal process, it shall be lawful for said Lessor, his heirs or assigns, to enter into said premises, and again have, repossess and enjoy the same as if this lease had not been made, and thereupon this lease and everything herein contained on the part of said Lessor to be done and performed shall cease, determine and be utterly void; without prejudice, however, to the right of the Lessor to recover from said Lessee, or assigns, all rent due up to the time of such entry. In case of any such default and entry by said Lessor, said Lessor may relet said premises for the remainder of said term for the highest rent obtainable and may recover from said Lessee any deficiency between the amount so obtained, and the rent hereinbefore reserved.

And provided further, that in case any buildings on said premises, or any part thereof, without any fault or neglect of said Lessee, shall be destroyed or so injured by the elements, or other cause, as to be unfit for occupancy, said Lessee may thereupon surrender possession of said premises to said Lessor, and thereupon this lease shall cease, determine and be utterly void.

And said Lessor, for himself, and for his heirs, executors, administrators and assigns, hereby covenants and agrees with said Lessee, his executors and administrators, that, said Lessee paying the rents, and keeping and performing the covenants of this lease on his part to be kept and performed, said Lessee shall peaceably and quietly hold, occupy and enjoy said premises, during said term, without any let, hindrance or molestation by said Lessor or his heirs or any person or persons lawfully claiming under him or them.

It is mutually covenanted and agreed by and between said Lessor and said Lessee that, as security for the said rents to be paid and the covenants to be performed by said Lessee, or assigns, a lien is hereby reserved upon the premises hereby leased, and the interest of said Lessee and assigns in and to the same, in favor of said Lessor, his heirs and assigns, prior and superior to any and all other liens thereupon whatsoever.

In witness whereof, the said Lessor and Lessee have set their hands to duplicates hereof on the .... day of ...., 19.....

(Signatures, acknowledgments, and so on.)

THEATER LEASE

(This is an excellent form of theater lease. Note the reference to equipment and provisions for its preservation. Also, note provisions regarding special police legislation, and the observation of laws and ordinances, and so forth.)

THIS INDENTURE OF LEASE entered into at ...., ..., this .... day of ...., 19...., by and between ...., party of the first part, hereinafter designated the Lessor, and ...., party of the second part, hereinafter designated the Lessee, WITNESSETH:

1. That the Lessor does hereby let and lease unto the Lessee the following described premises, to-wit:

> The .... Theater, so-called, located at No. .... Street, in the City of ...., together with the entrance lobby leading thereto and all exits and exit-ways therefrom; also all carpets, chairs, stage equipment, scenery and other theatrical fixtures and appurtenances belonging thereto, as at present constituted; a schedule of the foregoing personal property included in the demised premises, identified by the signatures of the parties, is hereto attached, marked "Exhibit A" and made part hereof.

The aforesaid premises shall be used by the Lessee for the purpose of conducting therein a high class (insert herein the kind of theater) theater, and nothing of an improper, illegal or immoral nature shall be permitted therein.

2. TO HAVE AND TO HOLD the demised premises unto the Lessee for the term of .... (......) years, beginning on the .... day of ...., 19...., and ending on the .... day of ...., 19.....

3. The Lessor covenants with the Lessee that, conditioned upon the performance by the Lessee of the covenants and agreements hereof by it to be performed and observed, the Lessee shall have the peaceable possession and enjoyment of the demised premises, without the lawful let, hindrance or disturbance of any person or persons whomsoever.

4. During the term of this lease the Lessee will pay to the Lessor, at such place in the city of ...., ..., as the Lessor may from time to time designate, in equal .... payments in advance, commencing the .... day of ...., 19...., rent as follows:

(Insert schedule of rentals.)

5. The Lessee shall pay all special taxes and assessments or license fees levied, assessed or imposed by law or ordinance, by reason of the use of said premises and property for the aforesaid purposes, and shall keep the Lessor harmless and free from any loss, cost, damage or expense by reason of the same, as well as on account of any penalties or damage resulting from any violation of law or ordinance resulting from the use of said demised premises by the Lessee.

6. The Lessee shall promptly pay all charges for electric current, water and heat furnished to the Lessee and/or the demised premises during the period of this lease.

7. The Lessee agrees to comply with all lawful rules, orders and regulations relating to the demised premises, the use thereof, and in connection with the operation of said theater. However, it is agreed that no failure on the part of the Lessee to comply with any law or ordinance prohibiting the operation of theaters on Sundays or after prescribed hours, shall be treated as a default on the part of the Lessee under this lease, anything in this lease to the contrary notwithstanding.

provided that the Lessor's estate and interest in the demised premises be not in any manner endangered thereby.

8. The Lessee will keep and maintain all of the personal property, equipment, furnishings and furniture included in the demised premises in good condition and in good repair during the period of this lease, and will surrender the same to the Lessor at the expiration of the period of this lease in as good condition as such property shall have been at the time of the commencement of the term hereof, except for the consequences of ordinary use and natural wear. The Lessee will promptly repair any of said property that may become damaged, broken or so worn as to be unfit for use; provided that if as the result of ordinary wear any of said property should become unfit for use for the purposes intended, the Lessee shall replace the same with other property of the same kind and character. The Lessee shall replace all broken glass with glass of the same size and quality as that broken.

9. The Lessee will not assign this lease without the written consent of the Lessor first had; nor will the Lessee sublet said premises or any part thereof without the consent of the Lessor first had; and will not permit any transfer by operation of law of Lessee's interest in said premises acquired through this lease.

10. The Lessor may have free access to the premises at all reasonable times for the purpose of examining the same, or to make any alterations or repairs to the building that the Lessor may deem necessary for its safety or preservation, and also during the last three months of the term of this lease for the purpose of exhibiting said premises and putting up the usual notice "To Rent" or "For Sale," which notice shall not be removed, obliterated or hidden by the Lessee.

11. The Lessor shall not be liable for any damage occasioned by failure to keep said premises in repair and shall not be liable for any damage done or occasioned by or from plumbing, gas, water, steam or other pipes, or sewage, or the bursting, leaking or running of any cistern, tank, washstand, water closet, or waste pipe in, above, upon or about said premises or building, nor any damage occasioned by water, snow or ice being upon or coming through the roof, skylight, trap door or otherwise, nor for any damage arising from acts or negligence of co-tenants or other occupants of the same building, or any owners or occupants of adjoining or contiguous property.

12. If default be made in payment of the rentals reserved hereunder, or any part thereof, or in fulfillment of any of the covenants or agreements herein specified to be fulfilled by the Lessee, or if any waste be committed or unnecessary damage done upon or to said premises, the Lessor may, at the Lessor's election, at any time while such default continues, or before the replacement or repair of such waste or damage, without notice, declare the said term ended, and enter into possession of said premises, and sue for and recover all rents and damages accrued or accruing under this lease or arising out of any violation thereof; or the Lessor may sue and recover without declaring this lease void or entering into possession of said premises.

13. Every demand for rent due, wherever and whenever made, shall have the same effect as if made at the time it falls due and at the place of payment, or on the premises; and after the service of any notice or commencement of any suit, or final judgment therein, the Lessor may receive and collect any rent due, and such collection or receipt shall not operate as a waiver of nor affect such notice, suit or judgment. Any notice or summons to be served by or on behalf of the Lessor upon the Lessee under this lease, or in connection with any proceeding or action growing out of this lease, or the tenancy arising therefrom, may be sufficiently served by leaving such notice or summons addressed to the Lessee upon the demised premises.

IN WITNESS WHEREOF the parties hereto have set their hands to duplicates hereof the day and year first above written.
In presence of:

(Signatures, acknowledgments, and so forth.)

LEASE ON MANUFACTURING SPACE

(The following lease used in Baltimore makes use of the "primary" and "secondary" rentals referred to in Chapter 2. This accomplishes the same objective as the standard "escalation clause.")

THIS AGREEMENT, Made this .... day of ...., 19...., between The Blank Co., Agents, of the City of Baltimore, State of Maryland, hereinafter called the Lessors; and ....
.... hereinafter called the Lessee.

WITNESSETH, That the Lessors, for and in consideration of the payment of the rental and performance of the covenants and agreements hereinafter mentioned, including the rules and regulations hereunto attached and made a part of this lease, do hereby let and lease to the Lessee, the following premises, situated in the City of Baltimore, State of Maryland, known and described as follows: ....
....
....
Said space above described, being in building known as "The Majestic Building."

TO HAVE AND TO HOLD the same for a term of .... years, commencing upon the .... day of ...., 19...., and ending on the .... day of ...., 19.....

THE CONDITIONS OF THIS LEASE are as follows: The Lessee hereby covenants to pay the sum of .... Dollars per annum, as rent for the above described premises, which said sum is to be paid in twelve (12) equal installments by said Lessee, on the

.... day of each and every calendar month in advance during the continuance of this lease; it being agreed between the parties hereto that in determining the rent aforesaid, a "Primary" rate of .... cents per square foot for the area of .... square feet hereby demised is established to produce a net return to the owner of the said "The Majestic Building," free and discharged from all operating expenses thereon, while a "Secondary" rate of .... cents per square foot on the said area of .... square feet is established to cover the operating expenses of the said building, which operating expense shall cover taxes, insurance, water, heat, elevator service, watchman service, general maintenance of the building, together with any other charges or costs of a like and similar character. The Primary rate shall remain fixed for the continuance of the lease, while the Secondary rate shall be subject to adjustment at the close of each calendar year and is determined by dividing the total operating cost for the current calendar year by the rentable area of the building, which rentable area is 590,809 square feet. Should the cost of such operations be in excess of .... cents per square foot, the Lessee agrees to pay as the Secondary rate hereunder such increased rate within thirty (30) days after demand therefor, and should the cost of operating the said building be less than .... cents per square foot, the Lessors hereby agree to refund to the Lessee within thirty (30) days from the close of the calendar year, such amount as to adjust the Secondary rate to operating costs.

(A.) It being agreed between the parties hereto that in the event of the termination or cancellation of this lease prior to the close of any calendar year, that the operating cost to such date of termination or cancellation of the then current year shall be the basis upon which the Secondary rate shall be determined.

In the event of the failure or refusal of the Lessee to pay said rent as above stated, the Lessors may distrain therefor and reserve the right to declare this lease forfeited after ten (10) days' written notice to the Lessee. And thereupon said Lessors shall have the right to enter into possession of the demised premises and to sue for and recover all the rent due at the rate aforesaid, or which may become due as aforesaid.

IT IS FURTHER covenanted and agreed that if said Lessee shall move out or abandon said demised premises or any part thereof, the Lessors may, if they shall so elect, re-let the same or any part thereof, on such terms, conditions and rentals as they may deem proper, and apply the proceeds that may be collected from the same, less the expense of re-letting upon the rent to be paid by the Lessee, and hold the Lessee for any balance that may be due under this lease; and such re-letting shall not operate as a termination of this lease or a waiver or postponement of any rights of the Lessors against the Lessee.

THE ABOVE DESCRIBED demised premises are to be used by the Lessee for the following specific purposes and none other: ....
....
And in the event said Lessee shall use said demised premises for any

other purposes than those above mentioned, or in the event that said Lessee shall cause any unnecessary damage to be done to the same, the Lessors reserve the right at their election to declare this lease forfeited, and to re-enter upon and resume possession of the demised premises in like manner as upon failure or refusal of the Lessee to pay rent.

THE SAID LESSEE FURTHER covenants and agrees that said premises shall be used and occupied for the purposes above mentioned, in a careful, safe and proper manner; that said premises, or any part thereof, shall not be used for any purpose except as heretofore described, nor shall said premises be underlet in whole or in part, nor shall this lease be assigned without the written consent of the Lessors, under pain of forfeiting the residue of the term hereby granted at the election of the Lessors in like manner as for failure or refusal to pay rent. The Lessee further covenants and agrees, that in the event of the waiver at any time by the Lessors of any particular covenant or condition of this lease, that said waiver shall extend to the particular case only and for the particular time and in the particular manner specified, and such waiver shall not be construed or understood as waiving any further or other rights of any character whatever.

SAID LESSEE FURTHER covenants and agrees that said demised premises, with all appurtenances, were in good order and condition when received by him, and that during the continuance of this lease the Lessee will keep said demised premises and appurtenances in like good order and repair and in a clean and wholesome condition, without charge or expense to the Lessors, and will not allow any waste or misuse of the water or electricity, and will pay for all damage to the building, as well as all damage to the tenants or occupants thereof, caused by any waste, misuse or neglect of said premises, its apparatus or appurtenances by said Lessee, his clerks, agents, servants or employes. Said Lessee further covenants that at the expiration of the time mentioned in this lease, or at the sooner termination thereof, by forfeit or otherwise, said Lessee will yield up said demised premises, together with all its appurtenances, to said Lessors, in good order and condition, and will surrender all keys of the several doors, and such other things as pertain to said demised premises.

IT IS FURTHER covenanted that any alterations in the demised premises which may be made during the continuance of this lease, shall be at the expense of the Lessee and by the mechanics of the Lessors, and no alterations of any character shall be made unless a plan of the same be first submitted to the Lessors, and until the Lessors shall have given their written permission for such alterations to be made.

THE LESSEE FURTHER COVENANTS and agrees that he will not drill into any column, girder, beam, floor, ceiling or wall for the purpose of attaching shafts, pulleys, machinery, or for any other purpose without the written consent of the Lessors.

THE LESSORS RESERVE the right at any time during the continuance of this lease to enter upon the said demised premises, either in person or through their designated agents or employes, for the purpose of inspecting said demised premises and ascertaining the condition of the same, or for any other purpose whatsoever.

IT IS FURTHER COVENANTED that the Lessors shall not be liable for any loss or damage to any property caused by the Automatic Sprinkler with which said building is equipped.

IT IS FURTHER COVENANTED that the Lessors shall not be liable for any loss or damage to any property placed in said demi_,d premises, arising from any acts or neglect of co-tenants or other occupants of said building, or by any other person whatsoever, except the Lessors.

THE LESSORS AGREE as a part of the above named consideration, to keep said premises properly heated, to furnish passenger and freight elevator service between the hours of 7:00 A.M. and 6:00 P.M. (Sundays and holidays excepted) and to furnish watchman's service without extra charge to the Lessee; and they further agree to furnish to said Lessee between the hours of 7:00 A.M. and 6:00 P.M. electrical power and electric light and live steam (Sundays and holidays excepted) at the rate as per attached schedule which is hereby made a part hereof.

The covenants herein to furnish heat, elevator service, light, power and live steam shall be subject, however, to the condition that the Lessors are not prevented by reasons beyond their control, from securing necessary fuel to operate their machinery and to the condition that in the event of any breakdown in the machinery of the Lessors, by which said machinery the said Lessors expect to furnish such heat, elevator service, power, light and live steam to the Lessee, so that because of said breakdown in said machinery said Lessors are temporarily unable to furnish said heat, elevator service, power, light and live steam; or, are unable to secure the necessary fuel, then no liability shall attach to the Lessors for such failure. Said Lessors, however, agree to use reasonable care in securing the necessary fuel and in the preservation and maintenance of said machinery, and covenant that in the event of any breakdown or stoppage of said machinery, they will use due diligence in making a prompt repair of same.

IN THE EVENT the said demised premises shall be so damaged or destroyed as to be rendered untenantable by fire, act of God or otherwise, or in the event of the destruction of the machinery of the Lessors by which said machinery said Lessors furnish heat, elevator service, power, light and live steam to the Lessee, so that said machinery cannot be repaired within a period of sixty (60) days, or the Lessors are unable to furnish other electric current to the said Lessee within a period of sixty (60) days, then, and in that event, this lease shall become wholly null and void as to all parties hereto, and all rights of such parties shall cease and become of no further force or effect. And in such event, it is specifically agreed that the Lessee shall be under no further liability to pay rent to the Lessors, and that the Lessors shall be under no liability for damages to the Lessee for failure to comply with the covenants herein contained and the Lessee shall forthwith vacate the premises.

ON FAILURE to pay rent at maturity, or to give possession at the expiration of this lease, and as liquidated damages for such failure, it is agreed that double the rent above specified shall be paid for the time the rent remains due and unpaid, or said tenant holds possession after expiration of lease.

IT IS FURTHER covenanted and agreed that all of the covenants, conditions, agreements and obligations of this lease shall extend to and be binding upon the respective heirs, executors, administrators, successors and assigns of the respective parties hereto.

AND THE LESSORS, upon the performance of the terms and conditions of this lease by the Lessee, will warrant and defend the Lessee in the enjoyment and peaceable possession of the above demised premises during the term aforesaid.

IT IS FINALLY covenanted and agreed that this agreement with all its provisions and covenants shall continue in force from year to year after the expiration of the term above mentioned, provided, however, that the parties hereto, or either of them, can terminate the same at the end of the term above mentioned, or of any year thereafter, by giving at least three (3) months' previous notice thereof in writing.

IN WITNESS WHEREOF, The parties hereunto affixed their hands and seals in triplicate, the day and year first above written.

(Signatures, acknowledgments, and so forth.)

Rules and Regulations

Halls, etc. The halls, entries, passages, corridors, vestibules, elevators and stairways shall not be obstructed, or any rags, paper, dust or ashes, rubbish or other substance placed therein by either the tenants, their employes or the occupants of their demised premises, or be used by them for any other purpose than for ingress and egress to and from their respective rooms or offices.

Elevators. The passenger elevators shall not be used for carrying heavy or bulky articles, and all such articles must be carried up or down on the freight elevators. All carrying of furniture and packages in the freight elevators must be done under the supervision of the janitor, engineer or operator.

Signs. No sign, advertisement, or notice shall be inscribed, placed or exhibited, painted or affixed on, upon or against any part of the outside or inside of the building by any tenant or occupant thereof, save and except upon the glass of the doors and windows of the demised premises, and then only of such form, size and color as the Lessors shall prescribe in writing.

Wires. No electric wires for any purpose shall be brought into the building except with the written permission of the Lessors. If tenants desire telegraphic or telephonic connections, the Lessors reserve the right to direct the electricians as to where and how the wires are to be introduced, insulated and protected, and without such direction no boring or cutting or use of the building will be permitted for each purpose.

Electric lights; safes. Tenants shall furnish and pay for all lamps used by them.

No safe, or other heavy article, shall be put in by any tenant without the written permission of the Lessors, and then only in such manner and place as may be specified by the Lessors.

Keys. Tenants will be furnished three keys to each door for space covered by this lease. Extra keys will be furnished at the rate of twenty-five cents each, which will be refunded to the Lessee at same rate upon being returned. A charge of twenty-five cents will be made for any keys of the original three not returned, upon moving from the building.

Water closets. The water closets and other water fixtures shall not be used for any purpose other than those for which they were constructed, and any damage resulting from misuse thereof shall be borne by the tenant, whether caused by himself, his employes or any occupants of the demised premises.

Window shades; miscellaneous. Tenants will furnish their own shades and awnings under the direction of the Lessors.

Tenants shall keep and maintain the hereby demised premises in a cleanly and sanitary condition and nothing shall be thrown by the tenants, their clerks, servants or agents out of the windows or doors or down the corridors of the building.

No animals or birds, bicycles or other vehicles shall be allowed in the offices, corridors, halls, elevators or elsewhere in the building.

Tenants and occupants must not leave windows open when it rains or snows, and for any default or carelessness in these respects, shall make good any injury sustained by other tenants and to the Lessors for damage to paint, plastering, or other parts of the building, resulting from such default or carelessness.

All glass, locks and trimmings in or upon the doors, and windows, respectively, belonging to the building, shall be kept whole, and when any part thereof shall be broken the same shall be immediately replaced or repaired and put in order by the Lessee, under the direction and to the satisfaction of the Lessors, and shall be left in good repair.

The Lessors will furnish water for the toilets and wash basins, but all water used by the tenant for manufacturing or purposes other than provided in the toilet rooms, shall be paid for by the Lessee.

Tenants shall make necessary provision to prevent water, oil or other liquid materials from leaking or wasting on the floor of said demised premises, and to so keep and use said premises in such manner as to avoid damage to or interference with the Sprinkler System, or the water, steam and plumbing pipes and any other equipment in or that may be put in or on said premises or building, and in the event of damage therefrom, said Lessee shall pay the damage thereby sustained.

Lessee shall pay the Lessors on the first day of each calendar month for the electric current consumed for the preceding month, both for power and light.

The Lessors will provide ample switchboards in the basement for light and power required for all rentable space, but Lessee shall pay for and, under the supervision of the Chief Engineer, carry all feeds for power from said switchboards to and distribute same through that portion or portions of the building covered by this lease.

Tenants shall not do or permit anything to be done in or upon the demised premises which will in any way conflict with the conditions in any insurance policy upon the building or any part thereof, or in any way increase the rate of fire insurance upon the building or on property kept therein, or in any way conflict with the laws or ordinances of the City of Baltimore, or with the rules and regulations of its various departments, or in any way obstruct or interfere with the rights or comforts of other tenants of the building or injure or annoy them, or to allow said demised premises to be used for any improper, immoral, unlawful or objectional purposes, or for the keeping, storing or selling intoxicating liquors, or for any kind of eating house, or for sleeping purposes, or for washing or cooking therein.

Tenants, their clerks, employes or occupants of their demised premises shall not overload any part of the building, or put in or operate any power engine, boiler or stove, or keep or use oils, burning fluid, kerosene, naphtha, gasoline or other combustible material for heating, warming, lighting or any other purpose on the demised premises, or use anything but gas or electricity for illuminating the demised premises without the written consent of the Lessors.

The Lessors, their agent or representative, shall have the right to enter the premises to examine the same in order to make such repairs as shall be deemed necessary for the safety, care or preservation thereof, or of the building, or for the comfort or enjoyment of other tenants, or to cover any emergency that may arise, or at reasonable times to show persons wishing to lease the same; and to place and keep in place upon the doors or windows two months previous to the termination of the lease, a "For Rent" notice.

Tenants, their clerks, employes or the occupants of their demised premises shall not make or permit any improper noises in the building, or do anything that will annoy or disturb or interfere in any way with other tenants or those having business with them.

The water shall not be left running, or the electricity left burning, unless in actual use in the demised premises.

No spikes, screws, hooks or nails shall be put into the walls or woodwork of the building, nor shall the walls be marred in any manner.

The Lessors reserve the right to change or rescind any of these Rules and Regulations, or to make such other and further reasonable changes as in their judgment may, from time to time, be necessary for the safety, care and convenience or cleanliness of the premises or for the comfort of the tenants.

It is understood between the Lessors and the tenants that no assent or consent to any waiver of any part hereof by the Lessors, in spirit or letter, shall be deemed or taken as made, except the same be done in writing and attached to or endorsed hereon by the Lessors.

LOFT LEASE

(This is the standard loft lease of the Property Management Division of the National Association of Real Estate Boards. Used by permission.)

Par. 1. THIS INDENTURE OF LEASE WITNESSETH: That ....
.... of ...., the Lessor, does hereby demise and lease unto ....
....
of ...., the Lessee, the premises known and described as ....
....
in the .... Building at ....
for the term of .... beginning on the first day of ...., 19...., and ending on the last day of ...., 19...., unless the term hereby demised shall be sooner terminated as hereinafter provided.

Rent

Par. 2. In consideration of said demise, the Lessee covenants (Section one) to pay to the Lessor as rent for said premises the sum of ....
.... ($.........) Dollars in equal monthly installments of ....
....
and, in addition thereto, such sums as may accrue by virtue of the provisions of Section .... hereafter, payable in gold coin of the United States of America of or equal to the present standard of weight and fineness, or in its equivalent in value as the Lessor may elect. All such sums are due and payable in advance on the first day of each and every calendar month during said term at the office of the said .... in ...., or such other place in said city as the Lessor may in writing designate. (Section two) ....
....

Services

Par. 3. The Lessor shall supply said premises with electric, water, heat, and gas service during ordinary business hours, and during the time and in the manner customary in said building. The Lessee hereby agrees and binds .... to light said premises with electricity only and to heat said premises with steam only and to buy the electric current and steam for same, during the period of this lease, from said Lessor at the usual rate charged to tenants of its building generally therefor, and to pay for such electric current and steam immediately upon the presentation of bills therefor by the Lessor. Said Lessee further covenants and agrees with said Lessor to pay for any water or gas used by the Lessee in said demised premises at the rates fixed by the Public Service Departments or Public Service Corporations for firms furnishing such service.

It is hereby agreed by the Lessee that the Lessor is to have the right, without notice to the Lessee, to cut off and discontinue said electric current, heat, water, gas, or any other service, whenever and at any time when Lessor's bills for rent or electric current or other service are not promptly paid by the Lessee. The Lessor shall not be liable for damages nor shall the rental hereinbefore stipulated be abated for failure to furnish water, heat, electric, gas, or other service, when such failure to furnish or delay in furnishing is occasioned by needful repairs, renewals or improvements or in whole or in part by any strike, lock-out or other labor controversy or by inability to secure coal after reasonable effort to do so, or by any accident or casualty whatsoever or by any act or default of the Lessee or other parties or by any cause or causes beyond the reasonable control of the Lessor, nor shall the Lessor be liable for any act or default of the janitors or other employees not authorized by the Lessor, and such failure, delay or default in furnishing water, heat, electric, gas, or other service or unauthorized act or default of the janitors or employees shall not be considered or construed as an actual or constructive eviction of the Lessee by the Lessor, nor shall it in any way operate to release the Lessee from the prompt and punctual performance of each and all of the covenants and agreements of this lease.

Additions and Alterations

Par. 4. That the Lessee will make no alterations in or additions or improvements to said premises without in each case the written consent of the Lessor first had and obtained; further that in the event any alterations, additions, or improvements in or to said premises are made necessary by reason of the special use, and (or) occupancy of said premises by said Lessee, then said Lessee covenants and agrees that .... will make such alterations, additions, or improvements in or to said premises at .... own expense. It being further covenanted and agreed that any such alterations, additions, or improvements shall be made under the direction of Lessor and to the satisfaction of the Lessor. The Lessee shall in making any such alterations, additions, or improvements and (or) in using and (or) occupying the premises, comply with the Building Code and ordinances of the City of .... and all the laws of the State of .... pertaining to such work and (or) such use or occupancy; it being further covenanted and agreed that any additions, alterations, or improvements made by the Lessee (except only movable store and office furniture and fixtures) shall become and remain a part of the building and be and remain the property of the Lessor upon the termination of this lease or the Lessee's occupancy of the premises, provided further that the Lessor may by giving written notice to the Lessee prior to the expiration of this lease require the Lessee to restore said premises to the same condition they were in at the commencement of this lease and (or) before any alterations, additions, or improvements had been made in said premises by said Lessee. The Lessee will indemnify and save harmless the Lessor from and against all expenses, liens, claims, or damages to either property or person which may or might arise by reason of any such repairs, alterations, improvements, or additions.

Character of Occupancy

Par. 5. The Lessee agrees that said premises shall be used ....
....
and for no other purpose, and shall be used and occupied in a careful, safe, and proper manner; that no nuisance, trade, or occupation which is known in insurance as extra or especially hazardous shall be permitted therein, that no waste shall be committed or permitted upon or any damage be done to said premises.

Unlawful Use

Par. 6. The Lessee shall not conduct or permit to be conducted on said premises any business or permit any act which is contrary to or in violation of the laws of the United States of America or of the State of .... or of the ordinances of the City of........ ...., nor shall the Lessee store or sell or permit to be sold or stored therein any malt, spirituous, or vinous liquors or any narcotic drugs, and the Lessee agrees that in the use and (or) occupancy of the premises the Lessee will comply with all the provisions of the Building Code and (or) the ordinances of the City of .... and (or) of the laws of the State of .... pertaining to such use and (or) occupancy.

Alterations To Be Made By Lessor

Par. 7. It is covenanted and agreed by and between the Lessee and the Lessor, that any changes and (or) alterations in the demised premises to be made by the Lessor at the expense of the Lessor, are evidenced and shown on the plan of the demised premises, which is attached hreto and made a part of this lease, such plan being identified by the signature of the Lessor and of the Lessee.

Sub-Letting and Assignments—Lessor's Right
to Terminate on Breach

Par. 8. The Lessee agrees that neither said premises nor any part thereof shall be underlet nor shall this lease be assigned without the consent in writing of the Lessor first having been obtained. No assign-

ment for the benefit of creditors or by operation of law shall be effective
to transfer any rights to the said assignee without the written consent of
the Lessor first having been obtained; in case Lessee shall make such
assignment, the Lessor shall have the right to terminate this lease. It
is further agreed between the parties hereto that if the Lessee shall be
declared insolvent or bankrupt, or if any assignment of the Lessee's property shall be made for the benefit of creditors or otherwise, or if the
Lessee's leasehold interest herein shall be levied upon under execution,
or seized by virtue of any writ of any court of law, or if a petition be
filed to declare the Lessee bankrupt or a Trustee in bankruptcy or a
receiver be appointed for the Lessee, whether under the opration of the
State or of the Federal Statutes, then and in any of said cases the Lessor
may at .... option immediately and without notice
to the Lessee or any assignee, transferee, receiver, trustee, or any other
person or persons, terminate this lease and immediately retake possession
of said premises, using such force as may be necessary without being
deemed guilty of any manner of trespass or forcible entry or detainer.
The Lessee expressly waives the service of any notice of intention to
terminate this lease or to retake said premises, and waives service of any
demand for payment of rent or for possession, or of any and every other
notice or demand prescribed by any law of the State of ....
and agrees that the simple breach of any of the covenants herein shall
of itself constitute a wrongful detainer of said premises by the Lessee
within the meaning of the law of the State of ....
governing forcible entry and detainer.

Claim Bankruptcy

It is agreed between the parties hereto that if the rent stipulated herein
at any time shall not be paid when due, or within thirty (30) days thereafter, then the next subsequent twelve (12) installments or such number
of installments of rent up to twelve (12) remaining unpaid, shall forthwith become due and payable at the option of the Lessor without notice
to the Lessee, and in case the said Lessee is declared bankrupt or volun-
tarily offers to creditors terms of composition or in case a receiver is
appointed to take charge of and conduct the affairs of the Lessee, such
claim for further unpaid installments of rent due under this lease shall
be considered liquidated damages and shall constitute a debt provable
in bankruptcy or receivership.

Vacation of Premises

Par. 9. If the said Lessee shall abandon or vacate said premises before the end of the term of this lease or shall suffer the rent to be in
arrear, the Lessor may at its option and without notice enter said premises, remove any signs of said Lessee therefrom and re-let same as it may
see fit without such retaking, avoiding, or terminating this lease, and that
for the purpose of such re-letting, the said Lessor is authorized to make
any repairs, changes, alterations, or additions in or to said demised prem-

ises as may be necessary, in the opinion of the Lessor, for the purpose of such re-letting and if a sufficient sum shall not be realized from such re-letting after paying all the costs and expenses of such repairs, changes, alterations, or additions and the expense of such re-letting, and the collection of the rent accruing therefrom each month to equal the monthly rental above stipulated to be paid by the said Lessee under the provisions of Paragraph Two, Sections .... of this lease, then the Lessee will pay such deficiency each month upon demand therefor.

Loss or Damage to Tenant's Property

Par. 10. All personal property of any kind or description whatsoever in the demised premises shall be at the Lessee's sole risk, and the Lessor shall not be liable for any damage done to or loss of such personal property or damage or loss suffered by the business or occupation of the Lessee arising from any act or neglect of co-tenants or other occupants of the building or of other employees or the employees of the Lessor or of other persons, from bursting, overflowing, or leaking of water, sewer, or steam pipes or from the heating or plumbing fixtures or from electric wires, or from gas, or odors, or caused in any other manner whatsoever except in the case of willful neglect on the part of the Lessor.

Payments After Termination—Removal of Lessee's Property

Par. 11. No payment of money by the Lessee to the Lessor after the termination of this lease, in any manner, or after the giving of any notice by the Lessor to the Lessee, shall reinstate, continue or extend the terms of this lease or affect any notice given to the Lessee prior to the payment of such money, it being agreed that after the service of notice or the commencement of a suit or after final judgment granting the Lessor possession of said premises, the Lessor may receive and collect any sums of rent due or any other sums of money due under the terms of this lease, and the payment of such sums of money, whether as rent or otherwise, shall not waive said notice or in any manner affect any pending suit or any judgment theretofore obtained. If the Lessee shall fail to remove all effects from said premises upon termination of this lease for any cause whatsoever, the Lessor may, at its option, remove the same in any manner that the Lessor shall choose, and store said effects without liability to the Lessee for loss thereof, and the Lessee agrees to pay the Lessor on demand any and all expenses incurred in such removal, including court costs and attorney's fees and storage charges on such effects for any length of time the same shall be in the Lessor's possession, or the Lessor may, at its option, without notice, sell said effects, or any of the same, at private sale and without legal process, for such price as the Lessor may obtain and apply the proceeds of such sale upon any amounts due under this lease from the Lessee to the Lessor and upon the expense incident to the removal and sale of said effects.

Premises Untenantable Because of Fire

Par. 12. The Lessee shall in case of fire give immediate notice thereof to the Lessor, and in case said premises hereby leased, or the building of which the same is a part, shall be partially damaged by fire or other element, the same shall be repaired as speedily as possible at the expense of the Lessor but the rent shall not be abated; but in case the damage should be so extensive as to render the said premises hereby leased untenantable, then the rent shall cease until such time as the premises hereby leased and the means of access to them shall be put in repair, or the Lessor may at its option elect to terminate this lease. In case of the total destruction of the said building containing said premises hereby leased, by fire or otherwise, or so much thereof that the Lessor shall desire to rebuild (whether or not the demised premises be affected), the rent shall be paid up to the time of such destruction, and then and from thenceforth this lease shall cease and come to an end. No compensation or claim will be allowed by the Lessor by reason of inconvenience or annoyance arising from the necessity of repairing, altering, or improving any portion of the building, however the necessity may occur.

Should 25% or more of the rentable area in the building of which the demised premises form a part, be rendered untenantable by fire or other casualty or condemnation, then the Lessor may cancel this lease, although the within premises be not themselves damaged, written notice of cancellation to be given Lessee within thirty days after such damage and Lessee to immediately surrender possession.

Alterations Required by Law

Par. 13. The Lessee agrees that if the Lessor during the term hereby demised shall be required by the City of .... or by any order or decree of any court or by any other governmental authority to repair, alter, remove, reconstruct, or improve any part of the demised premises or of the said building, then such repair, alteration, removal, reconstruction, or improvement may be made by and at the expense of the Lessor and shall not in any way affect the obligations or covenants of the Lessee herein contained, and the Lessee hereby waives all claims for damages or abatement of rent because of such work.

Withholding of Premises

Par. 14. Should the Lessee withhold from the Lessor, possession of the premises after the termination of this lease, whether by lapse of time or by election of either party, and after written notice to vacate the premises has been given by the Lessor, the damages for which the Lessee shall be liable to the Lessor for such detention shall be and are hereby liquidated at a sum equal to double the rate of rental stipultated herein for the period of such detention; or, should the Lessee remain in the demised premises after the termination of this lease, then in that event the Lessor may elect, without notice to the Lessee, to constitute such withholding of the premises as a holdover under this lease, and treat said tenant as a tenant for another year on the same terms and conditions as are contracted in this lease.

Rules and Regulations

Par. 15. No sign, picture, advertisement, or notice may be displayed on any part of the outside or inside of said building or on or about the premises hereby demised, except on the glass of the doors or windows of said premises or other space provided by the Lessor for signs, and then only of such color, size, style, and material as shall be first specified by the Lessor in writing. No "For Rent" signs shall be displayed by the Lessee, and no showcases, merchandise, obstructions, signs, or any advertising device of any kind whatever shall be placed in or on said building or on the sidewalks, areaways, etc., on which it abuts, by the Lessee, and the Lessor may remove any and all such matter, materials or appliances, and all signs other than those herein expressly excepted, placed in violation hereof, without notice to the Lessee and at the Lessee's expense.

The Lessor shall have the right to enter the demised premises at all reasonable hours for the purpose of exhibiting the same, and may place and keep on the windows and doors of said premises at any time within sixty days before the expiration of this lease, usual "For Rent" signs advertising the premises for rent.

The Lessor shall further have the right to enter the demised premises at all reasonable hours for the purpose of making any repairs, decorations, alterations, or additions which the Lessor shall deem necessary for the safety, preservation, or improvement of said premises or of said building, and the Lessor shall be allowed to take all material into and upon said premises that may be required to make such repairs, decorations, improvements, and additions or any alterations for the benefit of the Lessee without in any way being deemed or held guilty of an eviction of the Lessee; and the rent stipulated to be paid shall in no wise abate while said repairs, decorations, alterations or additions are being made, nor shall the Lessee be entitled to maintain a setoff or counter-claim for damages against the Lessor by reason of loss or interruption to the business of the Lessee because of the prosecution of any such work. All such repairs, decorations, alterations, additions, and improvements shall be made during ordinary working hours, or if any such work is, at the request of the Lessee, to be done during any other hours, the Lessee shall pay for any extra cost occurring because of such request.

Condition of Premises

Par. 16. The Lessee has examined the premises herein demised and said premises are known to the Lessee to be in good condition and repair.

Waivers

Par. 17. No waiver of any condition or covenant of this lease by the Lessor shall be deemed to imply or constitute a further waiver of any other like condition or covenant of said lease.

Maintenance of Premises

Par. 18. The Lessee is to keep the premises in a proper state of repair and in the same condition of repair they were in at the commencement of this lease, natural wear, decay, or damage by the elements of electricity (occurring without fault of the Lessee or other persons permitted by the Lessee to occupy or enter the demised premises or any part thereof) or by act of God, insurrection, riot, invasion, or commotion, or of military or usurped power only excepted. All glass both exterior and interior of said premises is at the sole risk of the Lessee and any glass broken during the term of this lease is to be promptly replaced by and at the expense of the Lessee with glass of the same size, kind, and quality.

Quiet Possession

Par. 19. The Lessor shall wararnt and defend the Lessee in the enjoyment and peaceful possession of the premises during the term aforesaid and all terms, conditions, and covenants to be observed and performed by the parties hereto shall be applicable to and binding upon their heirs, administrators, successors, executors, or assigns.

Provision for Use of Elevators by Lessee and Loading Platform

Par. 20. ....

Insurance Clause

Par. 21. ....

Obstructing Halls or Passageways

Par. 22. ....

Cumulative Rights and Remedies

Par. 23. The rights and remedies hereby created are cumulative and the use of one remedy shall not be taken to exclude or waive the right to the use of another.

Deposit as Security

Par. 24. ....
....

Idemnifying the Lessor

Par. 25. The Lessee agrees that .... will, at all times, indemnify and save, protect and keep harmless the Lessor and the said demised premises from every and all costs, loss, damage, liability, expense, penalty and fine whatsoever which may arise from or be claimed against said Lessor or the demised premises, by any person or persons for any injuries to person or property, or damage of whatever kind or character consequent upon or arising from the use or occupancy of said premises by the said Lessee or consequent upon or arising from any neglect or fault of the Lessee or his agents and employees in the use and occupancy of the premises, or consequent upon or arising from the sale or giving away of intoxicating liquors, or consequent upon or arising from any failure by said Lessee to so comply and conform with all laws, statutes, ordinances, and regulations of the United States, the State and Municipality in which said premises are situate, now and hereafter in force; and if any suits or proceedings shall be brought against the Lessor or the said demised premises, on account of any alleged violation thereof, or failure to comply and conform therewith, or on account of any damage, omission, neglect (or use of said premises), by the Lessee or his agents and employees, or any other person on said premises, that he, the Lessee, will defend the same, and will pay whatever judgment or judgments which may be recovered against the Lessor or against the said demised premises on account thereof.

New Construction or Remodeling, etc.

Par. 26. If the premises herein demised are a part of a building to be constructed or now in course of construction or being remodeled by the Lessor, and if the same is not ready for occupancy on the first day of the term herein demised, then the Lessee shall be entitled to an abatement of the monthly installment to be paid for the month or months, or proportionate part of the monthly installment of rent for part of the month, in which said premises are not ready for occupancy; beyond such loss or abatement of rent as aforesaid, the said Lessor shall not be liable for any damages of any kind and nature by reason of any delay, no matter how caused, in rendering said premises ready for occupancy, or for failing to erect said building, nor shall the term hereof be, by reason thereof, in any way extended thereby.

IN WITNESS WHEREOF the parties of this lease have set their hands to duplicates hereof this .... day of ...., A. D., 19.....

(Signatures, acknowledgments, and so forth.)

FARM LEASE

(This a typical form used in leasing a farm. If the farm is leased on a so-called "cropping" basis, and stock is included, a different form should be used to cover those features.)

THIS LEASE, made this .... day of ...., 19...., by and between John Doe, of ...., Lessor, and Richard Roe, of ...., Lessee, witnesseth: That said Lessor does hereby demise, let and lease unto said Lessee, his executors, administrators, and assigns, the following described farm property, situated in the township of ...., county of ...., and state of Iowa, and known as:

(Description of premises.)

....

To have and to hold the same, with the appurtenances thereunto belonging, unto said Lessee, his executors, administrators and assigns, for and during the term of .... years, commencing on the .... day of ...., 19...., and ending on the .... day of ...., 19...., on the following terms and conditions, to-wit:

Said Lessee, for himself, his executors, administrators and assigns, does hereby covenant and agree with said Lessor, his heirs and assigns, as follows:

(*a*) That he will pay to said Lessor, his heirs or assigns at .... in the .... of ...., Iowa, the yearly rent of .... dollars ($.........) payable in equal semi-annual instalments of .... dollars ($.........) each, on the first days of January and July of each year, beginning ...., 19..;

(*b*) That he will cultivate, manure and manage said farm and premises in a husbandlike manner according to the most approved course of husbandry; and that he will not plow up any land now in meadow or pasture without the written consent of the said Lessor;

(*c*) That he will sow all clover and timothy seed that may be necessary and proper to keep said land from deteriorating and becoming less productive;

(*d*) That he will consume on said premises all the hay, straw and fodder produced thereon, and that he will properly distribute and spread on said premises all manure and compost produced thereon;

(*e*) That he will not cut any timber on said premises, except for use in repairing fences thereon;

(*f*) That he will not injure the roots of any trees growing in any fields, or near any fence, on said premises, but in plowing will leave a space around said trees sufficient for their protection;

(*g*) That he will use and occupy said premises in a careful, safe and proper manner, and will carefully conduct and guard all fires that may be conducted thereon;

(*h*) That he will not commit or suffer any waste thereon;

(*i*) That he will not use or occupy said premises for any unlawful purpose;

(*j*) That he will not sell, or permit to be sold, on said premises during said term, spiritous, vinous, malt or any intoxicating liquor, without the written consent of said Lessor;

(*k*) That he will not assign this lease, nor underlet said premises nor any part thereof, without the written consent of said Lessor;

(*l*) That he will make no alterations or additions in or to said premises without the written consent of said Lessor;

(*m*) That he will permit said Lessor, or his agents, to enter upon said premises at all reasonable times to examine the condition thereof;

(*n*) That he will surrender and deliver up said premises at the end of said term, in as good order and condition as the same now are, or may be put by said Lessor, reasonable use and ordinary wear and tear thereof, and damage by fire, or other unavoidable casualty, only, excepted; and that he will leave on said premises all unspent hay, straw and fodder, and all manure and compost, produced thereon.

Provided, however, that if said rent, or any part thereof, shall at any time be in arrears and unpaid, and without any demand being made therefor, or if said Lessee, or his assigns, shall fail to keep and perform any of the covenants, agreements or conditions of this lease on his part to be kept and performed, said Lessor, his heirs or assigns, may enter into said premises and have, repossess and enjoy the same as if this lease had not been made, and thereupon this lease and everything herein contained on the part of said Lessor to be done and performed shall cease, determine and be utterly void; without prejudice, however, to the right of the Lessor to recover from said Lessee, or assigns, all rent due up to the time of such entry. In case of any such default and entry by said Lessor, said Lessor may relet said premises for the remainder of said term for the highest rent obtainable, and may recover any deficiency from said Lessee.

In case of such default and entry by the Lessor, all improvements made and placed upon said premises shall be left upon said premises and become the property of said Lessor.

And said Lessor, for himself and his heirs and assigns, hereby covenants and agrees with said Lessee, his executors and administrators, that, said Lessee paying the rents, and keeping and performing the covenants of this lease on his part to be kept and performed, said Lessee shall peaceably and quietly hold, occupy and enjoy said premises during said term.

It is mutually covenanted and agreed by and between said Lessor and said Lessee, that said Lessee shall do all the work in making the ordinary repairs to the fences on said premises, and that said Lessor shall furnish the nails and wire therefor; provided, however, all accommodation fences shall be constructed at the sole expense of said Lessee, and that all other repairs shall be made by the said Lessee.

It is further agreed that if said Lessee shall pay the rent and perform all the covenants and agreements of this lease on his part to be performed, said Lessee may, at the end of said term, remove the improvements which have been made and placed on said premises by said Lessee.

In witness whereof, the said Lessor and Lessee have hereunto set their hands to duplicates hereof the day and year first above written.

(Signatures, acknowledgments, and so forth.)

ONE FAMILY HOUSE LEASE

(This is a short form of lease for one family dwelling used in Virginia.)

THIS DEED OF LEASE

Made this .... day of .... in the year 19...., between .... of the one part, and .... of the other part, WITNESSETH, That the said part ... of the first part do ... demise unto the said part of the second part .... personal representatives and assigns ....
....
....
from the .... day of ...., 19...., for the term of ..... from thence next ensuing; and to expire on the .... day of ...., 19...., yielding therefor during the said term the rent of .... Dollars, ... payable as follows, to wit: ....
....
the first installment to become due on the .... day of ....
.... next.

The said Lessor .. covenant .. for the Lessee .. quiet enjoyment of ...... term, and that if the said building shall be destroyed or so injured by fire as to render .... untenable, this lease shall be determined ....
....

The said Lessee .. covenant .. to pay the rent in the manner above stated; that ...... will not assign without leave; that ...... will leave the premises in good repair; that the premises shall not be used during the said term for any other purpose or purposes than those above specified; that all gas and electric bills which shall be unpaid at the termination of the tenancy shall be regarded as so much rent due to the lessor .. and be recoverable by all the remedies to which ...... may be entitled for the recovery of the rent hereinbefore reserved; that at the expiration of the said term, to wit, on the .... day of ...., 19...., without any notice requiring ...... so to do, ... will deliver to the Lessor .., ... agents or assigns, quiet and peaceful possession of the said premises. The Lessee .. acknowledge .. the receipt of .... keys and agree .. to return the same, and to replace all glass broken out during ...... tenancy at the expiration of this lease. Any damages caused by the bursting of water pipes, from failure to turn off the water in cold weather, or from the stoppage of water closets, shall be repaired at the expense of the Lessee .... and the Lessee .. covenant .. that the Lessor .. may re-enter for default of .... days in the payment of any installment of rent, or for the breach of any covenant herein contained.

Witness the following signatures and seals:

.... [SEAL]
.... [SEAL]
.... [SEAL]

.... bind .... as security for the fulfillment on part of the Lessee .. of all the obligations and covenants entered into by .... as above, and hereby waive .... homestead exemption as to this obligation.

WITNESS .... hand and seal, this .... day of ...., 19 .....

.... [SEAL]

GAS STATION LEASE

(Gas station leases may be either on a month-to-month basis or of a permanent character. The following form is one used by one of the largest eastern oil companies for establishing gasoline stations. This is a fixed dollar rental. The lease does not provide for any compensation to the owner on the basis of sales volume.)

THIS LEASE, dated this .... day of ...., 19.....

WITNESSETH:

That ...., of ...., State of ...., the Lessor, does hereby let and lease unto The Blank Oil Company, a corpartion organized and existing under the laws of the State of Ohio, Lessee, all that real property situated in ...., County of .... and State of Ohio, described as follows, to-wit:

. . . .
. . . .

TO HAVE AND TO HOLD for the term of . . . . years, commencing on the . . . . day of . . . . and ending on the . . . . day of . . . .

The Lessee, as part of the consideration hereof, is hereby granted the privilege and option of renewing this lease for an additional term of . . . . years at a rental of . . . . Dollars ($. . . . .) . . . . per month, at the expiration of the term herein provided.

The Lessee agrees to pay as rent for said premises the sum of . . . . Dollars ($. . . . .) per month, ...
. . . .
commencing on the . . . . day of . . . ., 19. . . ., and on the . . . . day of each and every month thereafter during said term, subject to terms and conditions as hereinafter provided, and to quit and deliver up the premises to the Lessor peaceably and quietly at the end of said term.

The Lessee as part of the consideration hereof is hereby given the exclusive privilege and option at any time during . . . . the term of this lease, or any renewal thereof, to purchase the demised premises, for the sum of . . . . Dollars, ($. . . . .). This option shall be exercised by delivering, or mailing by registered mail, to the Lessor, addressed to his last known address, at any time within said option period, a written notice of Lessee's election to exercise this option, which exercise shall take effect from the date of delivery or of mailing, as the case may be. Thereupon the Lessor promptly shall cause to be prepared a survey showing boundaries and dimensions of said premises and an abstract showing good title in fee simple in the Lessor, free of liens and incumbrances, which shall be delivered to the Lessee, who shall have a reasonable time for examination and approval thereof and for the correction of any defects shown therein. Promptly upon such examination and approval of such abstract by the Lessee, the Lessor shall deliver to the Lessee a good and valid warranty deed conveying said premises free from all liens, incumbrances and dower interests in exchange for the payment of the purchase price.

The said Lessee shall have the right to cut curbs, use sidewalks, and to construct, maintain and use a driveway over, across and upon said premises for the ingress and egress of vehicles and persons.

The Lessee shall have the right to construct and maintain its standardized metal type of building upon said premises for the purpose of carrying on its business of selling gasoline and other petroleum products, and appliances and containers for same, as well as to install such underground tanks, pipe lines and other equipment as may be desirable in connection therewith and conform with the requirements of the legal authorities having jurisdiction over the same. Said buildings, tanks and other equipment are to be deemed no part of the real estate, and shall be the property of the Lessee; and the said Lessee shall have the right within a reasonable time after the termination of this lease, or any renewal thereof, to remove all of said buildings, tanks and other equipment from said premises.

It is agreed that the permanent improvements to be made by the Lessee on said premises, such as grading, filling in, construction of driveways, and cutting of curbs, will make said premises more valuable in the future for service station site purposes, to the extent of the cost of such improvements not removed or restored by the Lessee at the termination of the lease; and in consideration of said increase in value for said purposes, said Lessor agrees that in case said premises shall be leased or used by any other person, firm or corporation for Gasoline Service Station purposes, within one year after the vacation of said premises by the Lessee, said Lessor, or his assigns, shall pay to the Lessee the actual cost of such improvements, not removed or restored.

The Lessor agrees not to erect or permit to be erected upon any property belonging to the Lessor adjoining said premises, any sign board or advertising device, nor to use or permit to be used any such adjoining premises for purposes similar to those herein contemplated.

It is further agreed that the Lessee, its successors or assigns, may cancel this lease upon giving sixty days' written notice of such cancellation, and thereafter be released from any further obligation hereunder.

The Lessee may cancel this lease on thirty days' notice in the event that it is unable, by reason of injunction or other interference, to use said premises for the purposes above specified.

The said Lessor shall pay all taxes levied upon the above land, but if any taxes are levied upon any improvements placed thereon by said Lessee, then said Lessee shall pay the same.

The Lessor shall warrant and defend the Lessee in the enjoyment and peaceable possession of the above demised premises, during the term aforesaid if the Lessee shall perform all and singular the covenants agreed to be performed on the part of said Lessee.

This lease, subject to the terms hereof, shall be binding upon and inure to the benefit of the parties hereto, their heirs, personal representatives, successors and assigns.

IN WITNESS WHEREOF, these presents are hereby signed in duplicate, the day and year first above written.

(Signatures, acknowledgments, and so forth.)

BILLBOARD AND SIGN LEASE

(This lease is one used by a billboard and electrical sign concern that does a nation-wide business.)

In consideration of .... Dollars ($........) per year, payable at the office of The Blank Co. in .... installments; receipt of the first installment being hereby acknowledged the undersigned Lessor hereby leases exclusively to The Blank Co. the premises described as follows ....

....

with the right of ingress to and egress from the same, for the purpose of erecting and maintaining advertising signs, sign boards, bulletin boards thereon, and for storage purposes, from the .... day of .... 19...., to the .... day of .... 19...., and grants to the Lessee the privilege and option to renew and continue this lease for a like period upon like terms and conditions, provided it shall give written notice to the Lessor at any time within sixty days prior to the expiration of the term herein provided of its election to exercise such option, such notice to be delivered to the Lessor personally or sent by mail to the address given below or such other address as the Lessor may hereafter in writing designate.

It is expressly agreed that the Lessor may terminate this lease by giving the Lessee thirty days' notice in writing and refunding to the Lessee pro rata the rent paid in advance, in case the Lessor improves the said premises by erecting a permanent building thereon, requiring the removal of the Lessee's signs, sign boards or bulletin boards, provided that in case such proposed improvement shall not be made within a reasonable time after the giving of such notice to the Lessee this lease shall at the option of the Lessee be reinstated and continue in full force for the term above provided. Provided, however, that after the improvements are made by the Lessor pursuant to said notice, The Blank Co. shall be given the option to lease said premises for advertising purposes for the remainder of the term herein granted, and upon the terms and conditions herein specified. The rent payable hereunder shall be abated during the time that the Lessee is deprived of the possession and use of said demised premises.

In case any restriction on the construction or maintenance of advertising signs, sign boards or bulletin boards are imposed by statute or by ordinance of the city, town or village in which said premises are located, or, in case any such restriction, statute, ordinance or other rules or regulations, already existing, be enforced, or in case the Federal, State, Municipal or other public authorities shall hereafter establish any rules or regulations, or taxation, which shall have the effect of so restricting the location, construction, maintenance or operation of signs, sign boards or bulletin boards as to diminish the value of said premises for advertising purposes in the judgment of the Lessee, or increasing the cost of using said leased premises for advertising purposes as above provided, or in case the view of the premises shall become obstructed the Lessee may terminate this lease upon giving the Lessor ten days' notice in writing, and the Lessor shall refund, pro rata, any rent paid in advance.

All structures or material placed upon the premises by the Lessee shall remain its property and may be removed by it at any time.

(Signatures, acknowledgments, and so forth.)

OIL WELL LEASE
(Short Form)

AGREEMENT, Made and entered into the .... day of
.... A. D., 19...., by and between ....
State of ...., part .... of the first part, and
........................, party of the second part.

WITNESSETH, That the said part .... of the first part, for
and in consideration of the sum of .... Dollars
in hand well and truly paid by the said party of the second part, the
receipt of which is hereby acknowledged, and of the covenants and
agreements hereinafter contained on the part of the party of the second
part, to be paid, kept and performed ha..... granted, demised, leased
and let and by these presents do..... grant, demise, lease and let unto
the said second party, its successors or assigns, for the sole and only
purpose of mining and operating for oil and gas, and of laying pipe
lines, constructing tanks, buildings, including pumpers' houses, and other
structures thereon to take care of said products, all that certain tract
of land situate in the Township of ...., County of
.... and State of ...., bounded and described as follows, to-wit: ....
....
containing .... acres, more or less.

It is agreed that this lease shall remain in force for the term of ten
years from this date and as long thereafter as oil or gas or either of them
is produced therefrom by the party of the second part, its successors or
assigns.

In consideration of the premises the said party of the second part
covenants and agrees:

First. To deliver to the credit of the first part .... heirs or
assigns, free of cost in the pipe line to which it may connect its wells,
the equal .... part of all oil produced and
saved from the leased premises.

Second. To pay the first part .... Dollars
each year in advance, for the gas from each well where gas only is found,
while the same is being used off the premises, and the first part ....
to have gas free of cost to heat .... stoves in dwelling house on
said premises during the same time.

Third. To pay to first part .... for gas produced from any oil
well and used off the premises at the rate of ....
Dollars per year, for the time during which such gas shall be so used.

The party of the second part agrees to complete a well on said premises within .... from the date hereof, or
pay at the rate of .... Dollars in advance
for each additional .... months such completion is delayed
from the time above mentioned for the completion of such well until

a well is completed: and it is agreed that the completion of such well shall be and operate as a full liquidation of all rent under this provision during the remainder of the term of this lease.

The party of the second part shall have the right to use gas, oil and water produced on said lands for its operation thereon, except water from wells of first part...., and shall have the right to pump wells on adjoining farms from powers located on said premises.

When requested by first part...., second party shall bury its pipe lines below plow depth.

No well shall be drilled nearer than .... feet to house or barn on said premises.

Second party shall pay for damages caused by it to growing crops on said lands.

The party of the second part shall have the right at any time to remove all machinery and fixtures placed on said premises including the right to draw and remove casing.

....

The party of the second part, its successors or assigns shall have the right at any time on payment of .... Dollars to the part .... of the first part .... heirs or assigns, to surrender this lease for cancellation, after which all payments and liabilities thereafter to accrue under and by virtue of its terms shall cease and determine.

All covenants and agreements herein set forth between the parties hereto shall extend to their successors, heirs, executors, administrators and assigns.

(Signatures, acknowledgments, and so forth.)

OIL WELL LEASE

(This lease, used by an oil company operating in Texas, is quite complete and longer than forms used in many territories.)

AGREEMENT, Made and entered into the .... day of .... A. D., 19...., by and between .... of .... County of .... and State of Texas, part .... of the first part, hereinafter called "Lessor"; and the Blank Oil Company, duly authorized to do business in State of Texas, party of the second part, hereinafter called "Lessee":

WITNESSETH: That the said lessor for and in consideration of the sum of .... Dollars in hand well and truly paid by the lessee, the receipt of which is hereby acknowledged, and of the covenants and agreements hereinafter contained on the part of the lessee, to be paid, kept and performed ha.... granted, demised, leased and let and by these presents do... grant, demise, lease and let unto the lessee, its successors or assigns, the lands hereinafter described, for the sole purpose of mining and operating for oil and gas, and of laying pipe lines, constructing tanks, erecting buildings for housing and boarding employees, and other structures, and all other rights and privileges necessary, incident to or convenient for the economical operation of said land, alone or cojointly with neighboring lands, for oil and gas; said land being situate in the County of ...., State of Texas, and more particularly described as follows: ....

....
....
....
....
....
.... containing .... acres more or less.

TO HAVE AND TO HOLD said lands and all rights and privileges granted hereunder to and unto the lessee, its successors and assigns, for the term of five (5) years from the date hereof, and as much longer as oil, gas or either of them shall be produced from said lands by lessee in paying quantities.

In consideration of the premises, the lessee further covenants and agrees:

First. To deliver to the credit of the lessor, free of cost, in the pipe line to which it may connect its wells, the equal one-eighth (⅛) part of all oil produced and saved from the leased premises as royalty, or at lessee's election, to pay the lessor for such royalty the market price prevailing the day the oil is run into the pipe line or run into storage tanks, in which last event, settlement and payment shall be made by the lessee on the 15th day of each month for the royalty so purchased by the lessee during the preceding month.

Second. To pay to the lessor .... Dollars ($..........) each year in advance, for the gas from each well where gas only shall be found, when the same is used off the premises, the lessor to have gas free of cost from any such well for all stoves and inside lights in the principal dwelling house on said land, by making his own connections with the well, the use of such free gas to be at lessor's sole risk and expense at all times; to pay lessor for gas produced from oil wells when such gas is used or sold off the premises, at the rate of five dollars per annum for each well while the gas is being used or sold and when such gas is used for the manufacture of gasoline or any other product there shall be an additional payment at the rate of fifteen dollars per annum for each well while such gas is being so used for the manufacture of gasoline or any other product, said payments to be made each three months in advance.

Third. If operations for the drilling of a well are not commenced on said land on or before the .... day of ...., 19...., this lease shall terminate as to both parties, unless the lessee, on or before that date shall pay or tender the lessor the sum of ....

($..........) Dollars, in the manner hereinafter provided, which payment or tender shall operate as a rental for .... months from and after the date last above stated, and the same shall also cover the rights and privileges of the lessee to defer the commencing of said well during said period of months. In like manner and upon like payments or tenders the commencement of a well may be further deferred for like periods of the same number of months successively during the entire five-year term of this lease. Lessor expressly declares that the down payment or bonus received by him for this lease at the time of execution thereof is a good, valid and substantial consideration and sufficient in all respects to support each and every covenant contained herein, including specifically the option granted the lessee to extend this lease from time to time during the five-year term thereof upon the payment or tender of the rentals hereinbefore provided for. Lessee agrees to immediately offset all paying oil or gas wells drilled on lands adjoining this tract, and it is expressly agreed that no implied covenants regarding the measure of diligence to be exercised by the lessee in the drilling of said land during the original five-year term hereof shall be read into this lease, it being the express agreement of the parties that the provisions of this paragraph set forth the exclusive conditions under which the lessee shall hold this lease for said original term of five years.

Fourth. Lessor shall pay and discharge all liens, taxes and assessments, charges and incumbrances that are now against, or may hereafter accrue, be levied or assessed against said premises before the same have become delinquent and failing so to do, lessee is hereby authorized to advance, but is under no obligation so to do, funds necessary to pay and pay off and discharge the same, and in such event lessee shall have a lien upon said premises together with the rights of enforcement thereof existing in the former holder and all rentals and royalties accruing hereunder to secure such advancement or advancements and may retain such royalties and rentals and apply the same on such advancement or advancements until the same is or are discharged or satisfied in full.

Fifth. All rentals due hereunder shall be paid by lessee's check mailed, postage prepaid, to lessor at .... or to .... Bank of .... for lessor's credit on or before the date any such rental shall become payable; said bank, by power irrevocable, is hereby made the agent of lessor to accept all rentals paid hereunder, and the same shall continue as the depository of such rentals during the life of this lease regardless of changes in the ownership of said land or said rentals. No change in the ownership of said land, or the rentals or royalties due hereunder shall affect or bind the lessee until such purchaser shall have furnished the lessee an abstract of title to such lands, certified to date, showing as a part thereof the title claimed by such purchaser.

Sixth. Should the lessee drill a dry hole on said land, then at the next succeeding rental paying date the lessee shall resume payment of rentals due hereunder, otherwise this lease shall terminate as to both parties.

Seventh. If said lessor owns a less interest in the above described land than the entire and undivided fee simple estate therein, then the royalties and rentals herein provided for shall be paid to the lessor only in the proportion which his interest bears to the whole and undivided fee.

Eighth. The lessee shall have the right to assign this lease, or any portion of the acreage covered thereby, in which last event the lessee shall be liable only for royalties accruing from operations on the acreage retained, and be liable only for such proportions of the rentals due under said lease as the acreage retained by the lessee bears to the entire acreage covered by said lease and the assigns of the lessee shall have corresponding rights and privileges with respect to said royalties and rentals as to the acreage so assigned.

Ninth. The lessee shall have the right to use gas, oil and water produced on said lands for its operation thereon, except water from wells of lessor, and shall have the right to pump wells on adjoining farms from powers located on said premises.

Tenth. The lessee shall have the right at any time to remove all machinery and fixtures placed on said premises including the right to draw and remove casing.

Eleventh. When requested by lessor, lessee shall bury pipe lines below plow depth.

Twelfth. No well shall be drilled nearer than 200 feet to the house or barn on said premises, without the consent of lessor.

Thirteenth. Lessee shall pay for damage caused by operations to growing crops on said land.

WITNESS the hands and seals of the parties hereto the day and year first above written.
WITNESSES:

(Signatures, acknowledgments, and so forth.)

LEASE FOR DRILLING FOR OIL AND GAS

(The following standard lease for the drilling of oil and gas has been prepared by a large southern oil and gas association, and seems to meet fully the requirements of such a situation.)

THIS AGREEMENT, entered into this the .... day of ...., 19...., between ...., hereinafter called the Lessor, and ...., hereinafter called Lessee, does witness:

1. That Lessor, for and in consideration of the sum of .... Dollars ($............), in hand paid and of the covenants and agreements hereinafter contained to be performed by the Lessee, has this day granted and leased and hereby grants, leases and lets unto the Lessee

for the purpose of mining and operating for and producing oil and gas, casinghead gas and casinghead gasoline, laying pipe lines, building tanks, storing oil, building powers, stations, telephone lines and other structures thereon to produce, save, take care of and manufacture all of such substances, and for housing and boarding employes, the following described tract of land in .... County, Oklahoma, to-wit: In Section ...., Township ...., Range .... and containing .... acres more or less.

2. This lease shall remain in force for a term of ten (10) years and as long thereafter as oil, gas, casinghead gas, casinghead gasoline, or any of them is produced.

3. The Lessee shall deliver to the credit of the Lessor, free of cost, in the pipe line to which Lessee may connect its wells the equal one-eighth part of all oil produced and saved from the leased premises as royalty, or at the Lessee's option, to pay to the Lessor for such one-eighth royalty the market price prevailing on the day such oil is run into the pipe line, or into storage tanks.

4. To pay Lessor .... Dollars ($.........) each year for gas from each well where gas only is found while the same is being sold or used off the premises, and to pay to the Lessor the sum of Fifty Dollars ($50.00) each year as royalty on each gas well where gas only is found and same is not used or sold, the Lessor to have gas free of rent from any gas well on the leased premises for all stoves and inside lights in the principal dwelling house on said land by making his own connections with the well, the use of said gas to be at the Lessor's sole risk and expense at all times.

5. To pay to Lessor for gas produced from any oil well and used by the Lessee for the manufacture of gasoline one-eighth of the market value of such gas. If said gas is sold by the Lessee, then one-eighth of the proceeds of the sale thereof.

6. If operations for the drilling of a well for oil or gas are not commenced on said land on or before one year from this date, this lease shall terminate as to both parties unless the Lessee shall, on or before one year from this date, pay or tender to the Lessor, or for the Lessor's credit in the .... Bank at ...., or its successors, which bank and its successors are the Lessor's agent and shall continue as the depository regardless of changes in ownership of said land, or the oil and gas, or assignments of rental hereunder, the sum of .... Dollars ($.........) which shall operate as rental and cover the privilege of deferring the commencement of drilling operations for a period of one year. In like manner and upon like payments or tenders, the commencement of drilling operations may be further deferred for like periods successively. All such payments or tenders may be made by check or draft of the Lessee mailed or delivered on or before the rental paying date.

7. Notwithstanding the death of the Lessor, or his successor in interest, until written notice to the Lessee or its successor in interest of the death of any person to whom such rental should be paid, the payment or tender thereof to his credit to the depository and in the manner provided above, shall be binding on the heirs, devisees, executors, administrators of such person, and after such notice, the rentals which may become due hereunder may be paid or tendered to or deposited to the credit of the executor or administrator of the estate of such person, or at the option of the Lessee, or its successor in interest, tendered to above depository in the manner above provided.

8. If at any time prior to the discovery of oil or gas on this land and during the term of this lease, the Lessee shall drill a dry hole, or holes, on this land, this lease shall not terminate if operations for the drilling of a well shall be commenced by the next ensuing rental paying date, or if the Lessee begins or resumes the payment of rentals in the manner and amount hereinabove provided; in which event preceding paragraph hereof governing the payment of rentals and the manner and effect thereof shall continue in force.

9. If said Lessor owns a less interest in the above described land than the entire and undivided fee simple estate therein, then the royalties and rentals herein provided for shall be paid the said Lessor only in the proportion which his interest bears to the whole and undivided fee.

10. The Lessee shall have the right to use free of cost gas, oil and water produced on said land for its operations thereon, except water from the wells of the Lessor. When required by Lessor, the Lessee shall bury pipe lines below plow depth and shall pay for damage caused by its operations to growing crops on said land. No well shall be drilled nearer than 200 feet to the house or barn now on said premises without written consent of the Lessor. Lessee shall have the right at any time during or after the expiration of this lease to remove all machinery, fixtures, houses, buildings and other structures placed on said premises, including the right to draw and remove all casing.

11. If the estate of either party hereto is assigned (and the privilege of assigning in whole or in part is expressly allowed), the covenants hereof shall extend to their heirs, executors, administrators, successors or assigns; but no change in the ownership of the land or assignment of rentals or royalties or notice thereof shall be binding on the Lessee until after the Lessee has been furnished with the written transfer or assignment or a certified copy thereof; but notwithstanding such changes in ownership, in whole or in part, the Lessee may develop and operate the land covered by this lease as an entirety and there shall be no obligation on his part to offset wells on separate tracts into which the land covered by this lease may be hereafter divided by either sale, devise or inheritance. And it is hereby agreed that in the event this lease shall be assigned as to a part or as to parts of the above described lands and the other holder or owner of any such part or parts shall fail or make default in the payment of the proportionate part of the rents due from him or them, such default shall not operate to defeat or affect this lease insofar as it covers a part or parts of said land upon which the said Lessee or any assignee thereof shall make due payment of said rental.

12. Lessor hereby warrants and agrees to defend the title to the lands herein described, and agrees that the Lessee shall have the right at any time to redeem for Lessor, by payment of any mortgages, taxes or other liens on the above described lands, in the event of the default of payment by Lessor, and be subrogated to the rights of the holder thereof.

13. Notwithstanding anything in this lease contained to the contrary, it is expressly agreed that if Lessee shall commence drilling operations at any time while this lease is in force, this lease shall remain in force and its term shall continue so long as such operations continue, and if production should result therefrom, then as long as production continues.

14. If production on the land shall cease from any cause, then Lessee may resume drilling operations within sixty days from such cessation, and this lease shall remain in force while such operation continues, and if production results therefrom, then as long as production continues.

15. Lessee may, at any time, surrender this lease by placing a release thereof of record in the proper county.

16. It is agreed that this lease shall never be forfeited or cancelled for failure to perform, in whole or in part, any of its implied covenants, conditions or stipulations until it shall have been finally judicially determined that such failure exists, and after such final determination, Lessee is given a reasonable time therefrom to comply with such covenant, condition or stipulation.

17. This lease and all its terms, conditions and stipulations shall extend to and be binding on all successors of said Lessor or Lessee.

(Signatures, acknowledgments, and so forth.)

A SHORT, SHORT FORM OF A HOUSE LEASE

(The acme of simplicity seems reached in this lease form which has been used by realtors in suburban Philadelphia. It can be accurately described as a lease memorandum since most of the tenants have occupied their premises for many years. In effect, it is a renewal without stating the fact that the tenant had previously been in occupancy of the premises.)

Date.......................

No. ....(Street and number here) ....

We will rent you said premises from date to April 30th next upon the following terms:

1. You agree to pay us annually $.............

2. You agree to pay the city for all water used, and real estate tax increase, if any.

3. You agree to pay in equal monthly installments on the first day of each month, in advance, at our office.

4. You agree to take the property as it now is; to make all repairs and renewals (except roof and outside painting), including all drainage to city sewer and all water pipes to city main; to keep your grass cut and your driveway in repair. We agree only to repair the roof and paint the outside of the house.

5. As a guarantee that you will comply with paragraph 4 in a manner satisfactory to us, you agree to deposit with us annually, the sum of $............ This deposit may be used by you at any time for the good of the house but there must be always one year's deposit in our hands. Such balance as may be in our hands when you vacate will be returned to you, after deducting amount for necessary repairs. Our opinion as to condition shall be final.

6. You are not to sublet the premises without our written consent, and not for more than six months.

7. You may continue as tenant upon the above terms, from year to year, or may vacate at any time upon giving us 90 days' notice, in writing. We may terminate this contract (a) at the end of any yearly term by giving you 60 days' notice, in writing, and (b) at the expiration of 30 days after failure to pay rent as herein agreed, by giving you 15 days' written notice to vacate at the expiration of said 15 days.

ACCEPTED: GEORGE WOODWARD, Incorporated,
   (Tenant signs here.)   By.....................
....   President.

To paint the house and repair the roof takes 1% of our rent. Cost of new roof, when put on, will be added to capital investment.

Needed outside repairs will be made always before painting and charged against your deposit.

Long-Term Leases

(OVER 25 YEARS)

COMMITMENT TO PURCHASE IN SALE-LEASEBACK TRANSACTION

(This is a simplified form of a commitment to purchase land and building under a sale-leaseback transaction.)

Dated: ....

John Doe Company, Inc.
New York City,
New York

Gentlemen:

This letter will confirm our agreement to purchase the land and building or buildings to be erected thereon by your company, located at ...., consisting of approximately ...... square feet of land and approximately ...... square feet of building under roof, at a total purchase price to the undersigned equivalent to your cost of land and construction of said building or buildings on said property not to exceed the amount of .... ($.............) Dollars.

Simultaneously with the transfer of title and consummation of said sale, your company will enter into a lease as tenant with the purchaser as landlord on the terms and conditions hereinafter set forth.

The lease shall be for the term of .... years. Annual net rent for the first .... years of said term shall be at a rate equal to .... per cent of our total purchase price, and for the last .... years of said term shall be equal to ..... per cent of our total purchase price. Said rent shall be paid in equal monthly installments in advance. It is further understood that you are to have options to renew lease after the expiration of said .... year term for .... additional .... year terms, upon the same terms and conditions, except that the annual net rental to be paid by

309

you shall be at a rate equal to ..... per cent of our total purchase price. The aforesaid annual net rental shall be strictly net to us.

Said lease shall be in the form annexed hereto and designated as Exhibit "A".

You further agree that you shall cause your parent company, ..., to execute and deliver simultaneously with the execution and delivery of said lease, an agreement of guaranty, guaranteeing the performance of the tenant of the said lease. Said guaranty shall be in the form annexed hereto and marked Exhibit "B".

Satisfactory title evidence and a title policy in the amount of the purchase price provided for herein will be obtained by you from .... all at your own cost and expense.

It is further understood and agreed that title will close and the sale and leaseback shall be consummated on substantial completion of the building or buildings referred to herein.

If the above is in accordance with your understanding please acknowledge to that effect in the place indicated below.

Very truly yours,

X Y Z CORPORATION

By: ....

The above is in accordance with our understanding and is hereby accepted and agreed to:

JOHN DOE COMPANY, INC.

By: ....

LEASE USED IN SALE-LEASEBACK TRANSACTION

(This is an excellent example of a lease used in a sale-leaseback transaction.)

AGREEMENT OF LEASE

THIS AGREEMENT OF LEASE, made as of the day of ...., ..., between .... WITNESSETH, that Landlord, in consideration of the rents and covenants hereinafter specified to be paid and performed by Tenant, hereby leases to Tenant, and Tenant hereby rents from Landlord, the premises hereinafter described, upon the terms and conditions herein set forth.

Article 1

THE LEASED PREMISES—FIXTURES AND EQUIPMENT

Sec. 101. *The Leased Premises.* The leased premises are described in Exhibit A, attached hereto and made a part hereof, and include all easements, improvements, tenements, appurtenances, hereditaments, fixtures, rights and privileges thereto belonging or in any way appertaining, and subject to any restrictions, easements and encroachments, and to any zoning and governmental regulations now or hereafter in effect, relating to or affecting the leased premises.

Sec. 102. *Fixtures, Machinery and Equipment.* All fixtures, machinery and equipment, which are necessary to the general operation and maintenance of the leased premises, shall be the property of Landlord whether owned by Landlord at the commencement of the term, subsequently purchased by Landlord, or purchased by Tenant in accordance with the provisions of this lease. All lighting fixtures and heating and air-conditioning equipment shall be considered necessary to the general operation and maintenance of the premises. Trade fixtures, machinery, partitions, facilities and other equipment, which are supplied and used by Tenant in the conduct of its business, including process machinery and equipment, process boilers, process piping and process electric switch gear (other than building equipment) now installed in the leased premises or which may hereafter be installed therein, shall be the property of Tenant and may be removed by Tenant at any time prior to or upon termination of the lease. If required by Landlord, Tenant shall at its expense remove such trade fixtures at the expiration of the term and repair any damage caused by such removal.

Sec. 103. *"Leased Premises" and "Improvements" Defined.* "Leased premises" shall mean the premises described in Section 101 hereof, and shall include any and all improvements now or hereafter located or constructed thereon, including the fixtures and equipment therein which are the property of Landlord as above described. "Improvements" shall mean all buildings and other improvements now or hereafter located or constructed on the leased premises.

Article 2

TERM OF LEASE—POSSESSION

Sec. 201. *Term-Possession.* The term of this lease shall be the period commencing with the date possession of the leased premises is delivered to Tenant as evidenced by the written stipulation of Landlord and Tenant attached hereto and marked Exhibit B, and ending twenty-five (25) years from such date, or from the last day of the month in which possession of the leased premises is delivered to Tenant if the date of delivery of possession is not the first day of a calendar month.

Sec. 202. *"Lease Year" Defined.* "Lease Year" shall mean the 12 month period beginning on the first day of the term or if such day is not the first day of a calendar month, on the first day of the next succeeding month, or on any anniversary thereof.

Sec. 203. *Hold-Over Tenancy.* If Tenant remains in possession of the leased premises after the expiration of the term of this lease or any extension hereof, without written consent of Landlord, such holding over shall, if rent is accepted by Landlord for any period after the expiration of the term, create a tenancy from year to year at the last annual rental payable hereunder and otherwise upon the terms and conditions of this lease, and either Landlord or Tenant may terminate such tenancy at the end of any such year by giving to the other not less than 90 days' advance notice of termination; provided that Landlord upon notice to Tenant within 60 days after such holding over may elect to consider the tenancy as running from month to month and terminable by Landlord or Tenant at the end of any month on 30 days' notice.

Article 3

RENT—TAXES—INSURANCE

Sec. 301. *Rent.* Tenant shall pay to Landlord as rent during the term of this lease an annual amount equal to   of Landlord's investment, as hereinafter defined, totalling to the sum of
                                                                      per annum
and payable in monthly installments of
                                                                      , in
advance, commencing on the first day of the first calendar month of the term and continuing throughout the balance of the term, which Tenant agrees to pay in lawful money of the United States which shall be legal tender in payment of all debts and dues, public and private, at the time of payment, provided, however, that if the first day of the term is not the first day of a calendar month, Tenant shall, as an addition to the first rent payment, pay to Landlord as rent for the portion of the month prior thereto a pro rata part of the monthly installment of rent. The exact amount of the rent resulting from the application of the provisions of this paragraph shall be agreed upon by Landlord and Tenant and shown in Exhibit B to be attached hereto. Any installments of rent overdue for a period of more than 10 days shall bear interest at the rate of 6% per annum until paid.

Sec. 302. *Taxes and Assessments.* Tenant shall pay as additional rent, as they become due and payable and before they become delinquent, all taxes, assessments and other public charges levied upon or assessed against the leased premises, or arising by reason of the occupancy, use or possession of the leased premises, or the business carried on therein, which are or may become a lien during the term of this lease, all of which are hereinafter collectively referred to as "taxes". Landlord shall promptly forward to Tenant all bills received by Landlord for taxes which Tenant is required by the provisions of this lease to pay and which shall be assessed or levied against Landlord. Tenant shall deliver promptly to Landlord receipts evidencing payment of all such taxes. All taxes for the year in which this lease is terminated shall be pro rated between Landlord and Tenant. Tenant shall not be in default hereunder in respect to the payment of any tax which Tenant is required by any provision hereof to pay so long as Tenant shall in good faith contest such tax, and Tenant may file in the name of Landlord all such protests or other instruments and institute and prosecute proceedings for the purpose of such contest, but shall, at the request of Landlord, furnish reasonable assurance satisfactory to Landlord, indemnifying it against any loss or liability by reason of such contest.

Sec. 303. *Fire Insurance.* Tenant, at its expense, shall keep all buildings erected in and upon the leased premises, insured for the benefit of Landlord and Tenant, as their respective interests may appear, against loss or damage by fire and against such other risks as are covered by endorsement commonly known as supplemental or extended coverage, in responsible insurance companies authorized and licensed to issue such policies in New York and Tenant shall maintain and keep in force such insurance, at all times during the term of this lease, in an amount not less than the full insurable value of said buildings. All such policies of insurance shall provide that the proceeds thereof shall be payable to Landlord and Tenant, as their respective interests may appear, and certificates of such insurance shall be delivered to the Landlord, and shall contain a standard mortgage clause. Tenant shall also carry war damage insurance covering the leased premises providing that such insurance is made available to it by any Governmental authority.

Sec. 304. *Liability Insurance.* Tenant, at its expense, shall provide and keep in force for the benefit of Landlord comprehensive general liability insurance in which Landlord shall be named as an additional assured with minimum limits of liability in respect of bodily injury of $100,000.00 for each person and $300,000.00 for each occurrence and in respect of property damage of $50,000.00 for each occurrence. Such policies shall cover the entire leased premises, including any elevators thereof, and any sidewalks, streets and ways adjoining the leased premises, shall be issued by insurance companies and in form satisfactory to Landlord, shall provide for at least ten days notice to Landlord before cancellation, and such policies or certificates thereof shall be delivered to Landlord.

Sec. 305. *Utility Charges.* Tenant shall pay all charges for water, electricity, gas, telephone and other utility services furnished to the leased premises, and shall also pay sewer charges and taxes.

Sec. 306. *Rent on Net Return Basis.* It is intended that the rent provided for in this lease shall be an absolutely net return to Landlord for the term of this lease, free of any expenses or charges with respect to the leased premises, including taxes and assessments now imposed upon or related to the leased premises commonly known as real estate taxes, and any taxes and assessments whether by way of an income tax or otherwise which may be levied, assessed or imposed by the state in which the leased premises are located or by any political or taxing subdivision thereof upon the income arising from the rents provided herein in lieu of or as a substitute for taxes and assessments imposed upon or related to the leased premises and commonly known as real estate taxes, and that Tenant, and not Landlord, shall be required to, and shall, pay such taxes and assessments, but not to pay any other income tax which may be levied against Landlord.

Article 4

LANDLORD'S INVESTMENT

Sec. 401. *"Landlord's Investment" Defined.* "Landlord's investment" shall mean the amount of Landlord's investment in the leased premises and shall be the total of the cost of acquisition of the leased premises, including, but not limited to, all sums advanced by Landlord for the purchase price of the land and any buildings comprising the leased premises at the time of purchase; title searches and insurance of title to the leased premises; surveys; taxes and assessments required to be paid at settlement or paid by Landlord prior to settlement and allocable to any portion of the term of this lease; and any other reasonable expenses incident to the acquisition of title to the leased premises; provided, however, that Landlord shall not be required to advance more than $ as its investment in the leased premises. Any sum in excess of such maximum amount shall be borne by Tenant.

Article 5

TITLE, CONDITION AND USE OF PREMISES

Sec. 501. *Use—Compliance with Laws and Restrictions.* Tenant shall have the peaceful and quiet use of the leased premises for any lawful purpose without hindrance on the part of Landlord, and Landlord shall warrant and defend Tenant in such peaceful and quiet use against the lawful claims of all persons claiming by, through or under Landlord. Tenant shall not breach or suffer the breach of any of the conditions, agreements and restrictions of record affecting the leased premises and shall hold Landlord harmless from all consequences of any such breach. Tenant shall comply with all present and future laws, ordinances and regulations of duly constituted public authorities now or hereafter in any manner affecting the leased premises, the adjacent sidewalks or any buildings thereon or the use thereof. Tenant shall have the right to contest the validity of any laws, ordinances or regulations adversely affecting its use of the leased premises and shall hold Landlord harmless from the consequences of violation of any such law, ordinance or regulation. Tenant shall not violate or permit to be violated any of the conditions of the policies of insurance described in Sections 303 and 304 hereof and shall perform and satisfy all requirements of the insurers.

Sec. 502. *Continuance of Lease.* If the use of the leased premises for any purpose shall be prohibited or prevented by any public authority for any reason, this lease shall not be thereby terminated, nor shall Tenant be entitled by reason thereof to surrender the leased premises, or to any abatement or reduction in rent, nor shall the respective obligations of Landlord and Tenant be affected.

Sec. 503. *Repairs and Alterations.* Tenant agrees to accept the leased premises in the condition existing on the date of the commencement of the term of this lease, to take good care of the leased premises, and, at its expense, to make all repairs, structural and ordinary as well as extraordinary, in and about the premises necessary to preserve and maintain them in good order and condition. Tenant may make such alterations in and to the leased premises and the buildings thereon as it may deem desirable for its use thereof, provided that if such alterations shall substantially change the basic structure of the building or adversely affect the soundness or value thereof, the prior approval of Landlord shall be obtained before such work is commenced. All repairs and alterations shall be in quality at least equal to the original construction. Subject to the provisions of Sec. 102 hereof, any and all alterations, additions and improvements, made to or placed upon the leased premises by the Tenant as well as all fixtures and articles of personal property attached to, or made part of the demised premises shall immediately become the property of the Landlord and at the termination of this lease shall be surrendered to the Landlord. At the termination of this lease, Tenant shall deliver the premises to Landlord in good condition and repair, allowance being made for ordinary wear and tear and obsolescence. Landlord shall be under no obligation to rebuild, replace, maintain or make repairs to the leased premises or to the buildings situated thereon during the term of this lease, provided, however, that Landlord shall make available to Tenant to the extent of Tenant's actual expenditures therefor any monies received by Landlord in reimbursement or in compensation for damage or loss to the leased premises in connection with any bonds, damage recovery or litigation affecting the leased premises.

Sec. 504. *Changes Requiring Landlord's Prior Approval.* Tenant shall not demolish any building on the leased premises without the written consent of Landlord. Tenant may construct an addition or additions to any building on the leased premises or erect new buildings or other improvements on any unimproved portions of the leased premises, provided (i) the prior written consent of Landlord is obtained if such additions or new construction will cost more than $25,000.00, (ii) such additions or new construction will be of a type which would not detract from existing building, (iii) notice of any proposed construction work costing more than $25,000.00 is given to Landlord, and (iv) when required by Landlord, a copy of the plans and specifications therefor shall be furnished to Landlord. It is also contemplated by both parties hereto that Landlord will be given the opportunity to make an additional investment in the leased premises if it so desires, to cover the cost of such addition, additions, new buildings or other improvements, with a resultant increase in the rent to be paid by Tenant hereunder, and upon such other terms and conditions as may be mutually agreed upon.

Sec. 505. *Landlord's Right to Inspect and Repair.* Landlord shall have the right at any reasonable time to inspect the leased premises. Landlord may make any repairs which are essential for the protection and maintenance of the leased premises or any part thereof, if Tenant fails to commence such repairs within 30 days unless emergency conditions require immediate commencement after notice from Landlord, and any expenditures for such work shall be considered as rent payable in accordance with the provisions set forth in Section 803 hereof.

Sec. 506. *Mechanics' Liens.* Tenant shall not permit any mechanics' or similar liens to remain upon the leased premises for labor or material furnished to Tenant or claimed to have been furnished to Tenant in connection with work of any character performed or claimed to have been performed on the leased premises or at the direction or with the consent of Tenant, whether such work was performed or materials furnished before or after the commencement of the term of this lease. Tenant may, however, contest the validity of any such lien or claim, provided Tenant shall give to Landlord reasonable security to insure payment and to prevent any sale, foreclosure or forfeiture of the leased premises by reason of such nonpayment, if required by Landlord. Upon a final determination of the validity of any such lien or claim, Tenant shall immediately pay any judgment or decree rendered against Tenant or Landlord with all proper costs and charges and shall cause such lien to be released of record without cost to Landlord.

Sec. 507. *Seniority of Lease.* Any liens, mortgages or encumbrances affecting the leased premises which may be created by Landlord, or any subsequent owner, prior to termination of this lease shall be subordinate to this lease and to the rights granted to Tenant hereunder.

Sec. 508. *Tenant to Indemnify Landlord.* The Tenant shall indemnify and hold harmless the Landlord from and against any and all liability, fines, suits, claims, demands and actions, and costs and expenses of any kind or nature of any one whomsoever, due to or arising out of (i) any breach, violation or non-performance of any covenant, condition or agreement in this lease set forth and contained on the part of the Tenant to be fulfilled, kept, observed and performed; and/or (ii) any damage to property occasioned by Tenant's use and occupancy of the demised premises; and/or (iii) any injury to person or persons, including death resulting at any time therefrom, occurring in or about the demised premises and/or on the sidewalks in front of the same. If the Tenant be required to defend any action or proceeding pursuant to this paragraph to which action or proceeding the Landlord is made a party, the Landlord shall be entitled to appear, defend or otherwise take part in the matter involved, at its election, by counsel of its own choosing, provided such action by the Landlord does not limit or make void any liability of any insurer of the Landlord or Tenant hereunder in respect to the claim or matter in question. The Tenant's liability under this paragraph shall be reduced by the net proceeds actually collected of any insurance effected by the Tenant on the risks in question for the Landlord's benefit.

Article 6

DESTRUCTION OR CONDEMNATION OF PREMISES

Sec. 601. *Fire Damage.* Damage to or destruction of any portion of the improvements on the leased premises by fire or any other cause shall not terminate this lease or entitle Tenant to surrender the leased premises or to any abatement of or reduction in rent payable by Tenant or otherwise affect the respective obligations of Landlord and Tenant. In the event of such damage or destruction, Landlord shall proceed with due diligence to collect the proceeds of any available insurance, and Tenant shall promptly restore the improvements to at least as good a condition as existed immediately prior to the casualty. If the insurance proceeds exceed $25,000.00, an architect approved by Landlord shall be selected by Tenant to supervise the restoration, and Landlord shall make advances to Tenant from such proceeds to cover reconstruction costs; otherwise, Tenant shall be reimbursed from such proceeds for its cost of restoring the improvements upon completion of the work. Landlord shall not be required to advance any sums in excess of the insurance proceeds paid to it, nor any amount in excess of Tenant's actual expenditures made to restore the building. No settlement of any claim for loss and damage covered by said insurance policies shall be made by Landlord or Tenant with any insurance company without the written consent of both parties hereto.

Sec. 602. *Condemnation.* In the event the leased premises or any part thereof shall be condemned and taken for a public or quasi-public use, any award made to compensate either Landlord or Tenant for its damages or loss shall be paid to Landlord.

Upon any total taking, Tenant's obligation to pay rent or to discharge any other obligation hereunder, other than the payment of money then due and damages arising out of any breach on the part of Tenant, shall cease, provided that if the total award (less any collection expensses) is not sufficient to permit payment to the Landlord of a sum equal to the then unamortized principal amount shown on Schedule A, as of such date of termination of this lease, Tenant shall pay to Landlord an amount of money equal to such deficiency.

In the event that only a part of the leased premises is condemned and taken, Tenant, in accordance with plans and specifications approved by Landlord, shall promptly restore the remaining portion of the leased premises so that it will constitute a complete architectural unit, and upon completion of such work, and upon payment of the award of compensation, Landlord shall reimburse Tenant to the extent of the total award (less any collection expenses) for costs so expended, and there shall be such abatement in rent and such other adjustments as Landlord and Tenant may agree upon as being just and equitable. If they are unable to agree upon such adjustments, resort shall be had to arbitration as hereinafter provided.

Sec. 603. *Arbitration on Condemnation Award.* If Landlord and Tenant within 30 days after the determination of the condemnation award are unable to agree upon the adjustments to be made in the lease, the adjustments shall be determined by three disinterested arbitrators, one chosen by Landlord, one by Tenant and the third by the two so chosen. The decision of any two of the arbitrators shall be final and conclusive. The decision shall be in writing, and signed copies shall be delivered to Landlord and Tenant. The party desiring arbitration shall give written notice to the other naming therein the arbitrator selected by it. In the event that, within a 15-day period after the giving of such notice, the other party shall fail to give to the party requesting arbitration written notice of the arbitrator selected by it, or in the event that the two arbitrators chosen shall fail within 15 days after their selection to agree upon the third, then on request of the party not in default, or upon the request of either party if neither is in default, any court of general equity jurisdiction in the county in which the leased premises are situated may within 15 days after such request appoint an arbitrator or arbitrators to fill any places remaining vacant.

Article 7

ASSIGNMENT—SUBLEASES—SALE

Sec. 701. *Assignment or Sublease by Tenant.* Tenant may assign or transfer this lease or sub-lease the whole or any part of the leased premises without the written consent of Landlord provided that Tenant shall nevertheless remain primarily liable to Landlord for the payment of all rent and for the full performance of all of the covenants and conditions of this lease. In the event that this lease is so assigned the Tenant shall within a reasonable time thereafter deliver to the Landlord a duplicate original of an instrument of assignments and assumption in and by which the assignee of the lease accepts such assignment and assumes all of the obligations of the Tenant under said lease.

Sec. 702. *Sale by Landlord.* Landlord shall have the right to sell or transfer the leased premises, subject to all of the provisions of this lease. The term "Landlord" as used in this lease means only the owner for the time being of the leased premises, so that in the event of any sale or sales of the leased premises, the said Landlord shall be and hereby is entirely freed and relieved of all covenants and obligations of Landlord hereunder arising after the date of such sale or sales.

Article 8

DEFAULT—BANKRUPTCY

Sec. 801. *Remedies of Landlord.* In the event that during the term of this lease (regardless of the pendency of any bankruptcy, reorganization, receivership, insolvency or other proceeding, in law, in equity, or before any administrative tribunal, which has prevented or might prevent compliance by Tenant with the term of this lease)

    (a) Tenant shall default in the payment of any installment of rent or other sum herein specified to be paid by Tenant and such default shall continue for 30 days;

    (b) Tenant shall default in the observance or performance of any of Tenant's covenants, agreements or obligations hereunder, and such default shall not be cured within 30 days after Landlord

shall have given to Tenant written notice specifying such default
or defaults, or

(c) without further possibility of appeal or review,

(i) Tenant is adjudicated a bankrupt or insolvent, or

(ii) a receiver is appointed for all or substantially all of Tenant's
business or assets on the ground of Tenant's insolvency, or

(iii) a trustee is appointed for Tenant after a petition has been
filed for Tenant's reorganization under the Bankruptcy Act of the
United States, known as the Chandler Act, or any future law of
the United States having the same general purpose, or

(iv) Tenant shall make an assignment for the benefit of its
creditors,

then in any such event Landlord shall have the right, at its election, at
any time thereafter while such default or defaults continue, to re-enter
and take complete and peaceable possession of the leased premises and
any and all improvements then forming part of the leased premises, and
to declare the term of this lease ended, whereupon this lease and all the
right, title and interest of Tenant hereunder shall terminate and be of
no further force or effect. In the event of such declaration, Landlord shall
have the right to sue for and recover all rents and other sums accrued up
to the time of such termination including damages arising out of any
breach on the part of Tenant. Landlord shall also have the right, without re-entering the leased premises or terminating this lease, to sue for
and recover all rents and other sums, including damages, at any time
and from time to time accruing hereunder.

Sec. 802. *Cumulative Rights.* No right or remedy herein conferred
upon or reserved to Landlord is intended to be exclusive of any other
right or remedy herein or by law provided, but each shall be cumulative
and in addition to every other right or remedy given herein or now or
hereafter existing at law or in equity or by statute.

Sec. 803. *Other Remedies of Landlord.* If Tenant shall default in
the performance of any covenant required to be performed by it under
this lease, Landlord may perform the same for the account and at the
expense of Tenant, after first giving notice to Tenant of such default
and a reasonable time to cure such default. If Landlord at any time is
compelled to pay any sum of money, or do any act which will require
the payment of any sum of money, by reason of the failure of Tenant to
comply with any provision hereof, after reasonable notice, or, if Landlord is compelled to incur any expense, including reasonable counsel fees
in instituting, prosecuting or defending any action or proceeding instituted by reason of any default of Tenant hereunder, the sum or sums so
paid by Landlord shall be due from Tenant to Landlord as additional
rent on the next date following the incurring of such expenses upon
which a regular monthly rental payment is due.

Sec. 804. *Effect of Waiver or Forbearance.* No waiver by Landlord
of any breach by Tenant of any of its obligations, agreements or covenants hereunder shall be a waiver of any subsequent breach or of any

other obligation, agreement or covenant, nor shall any forbearance by Landlord to seek a remedy for any breach by Tenant be a waiver by Landlord of its rights and remedies with respect to such or any subsequent breach.

Sec. 805. *Waiver of Redemption.* The Tenant hereby waives, surrenders and gives up all right or privilege which Tenant may or might have under or by reason of any applicable law, regulation or ruling now in effect, or any future law, regulation or ruling, to redeem, occupy or re-occupy the leased premises or have a continuance of this lease for the term hereby demised after having been dispossessed or ejected therefrom by process of law.

Article 9

OPTIONS TO RENEW

Sec. 901. *First Renewal Option.* At the expiration of the term specified in Sec. 201 of Article 2 hereof, said term shall be extended, at the option of Tenant, for an additional period of   years then next ensuing, on the same terms, covenants and conditions as herein set forth, except as to renewals and except that the net yearly rental for said first renewal term, shall be an annual amount equal to   % of Landlord's investment as hereinabove defined, payable in monthly installments of one-twelfth of such amount in advance, commencing on the first day of the first calendar month of said first renewal term and continuing monthly throughout the balance of said first renewal term. Tenant shall give Landlord six months notice prior to the expiration of the term hereof of its desire so to extend such term.

Sec. 902. *Second Renewal Option.* At the expiration of the first renewal term specified in Sec. 901 hereof, said term shall be extended, at the option of Tenant, for an additional   years then next ensuing, on the same terms, covenants and conditions as herein set forth, except as to renewals and except that the net yearly rental for said second renewal term, shall be an annual amount equal to   % of Landlord's investment as hereinabove defined, payable in monthly installments of one-twelfth of such amount in advance, commencing on the first day of the first calendar month of said second renewal term and continuing monthly throughout the balance of said second renewal term. Tenant shall give Landlord six months notice prior to the expiration of said first renewal term of its desire so to extend such term.

Sec. 903. *Third Renewal Option.* At the expiration of the second renewal term specified in Sec. 902 hereof, said term shall be extended, at the option of Tenant, for an additional   years then next ensuing, on the same terms, covenants and conditions as herein set forth, except as to renewals and except that the net yearly rental for said third renewal term, shall be an annual amount equal to   % of Landlord's investment as hereinabove defined, payable in monthly installments of one-twelfth of such amount in advance, commencing on the first day of the first calendar month of said third renewal term and continuing monthly throughout the balance of said third renewal term. Tenant shall give Landlord six months notice prior to the expiration of said second renewal term of its desire so to extend such term.

Sec. 904. *Fourth Renewal Option.* At the expiration of the third renewal term specified in Sec. 903 hereof, said term shall be extended, at the option of Tenant, for an additional   years then next ensuing, on the same terms, covenants and conditions as herein set forth, except as to renewals and except that the net yearly rental for said fourth renewal term, shall be an annual amount equal to   % of Landlord's investment as hereinabove defined, payable in monthly installments of one-twelfth of such amount in advance, commencing on the first day of the first calendar month of said fourth renewal term and continuing monthly throughout the balance of said fourth renewal term. Tenant shall give landlord six months notice prior to the expiration of said third renewal term of its desire so to extend such term.

Article 10

OPTIONS TO BUY

Sec. 1001. *Option to Buy.* At any time subsequent to five (5) years from the commencement of the term hereof as defined in Sec. 201, the Tenant or its successors or assigns shall have the privilege and option of purchasing the leased premises for a purchase price equal to the then appraised value of the leased premises, but in no event less than the then unamortized principal amount shown on Schedule A, provided that Tenant shall not be in default under any provision of this lease, and subject to the following conditions:

(a) That Tenant will acquire or construct a plant, larger in capacity, in the same general locality, and

(b) That Landlord will have the first right of refusal to finance the new plant at a percentage rate equal to or greater than the present rate of   of certified cost.

(c) Tenant shall give Landlord at least three (3) months' notice in writing of the intention of Tenant to purchase said premises.

Sec. 1002. *Appraisal of Premises.* If Landlord and Tenant within 30 days after notice of intention to purchase cannot agree on an appraiser to be appointed, then the appraised value is to be determined by three disinterested appraisers, one chosen by Landlord, one by Tenant and the third by the two so chosen. The decision of any two of the appraisers so chosen shall be final and conclusive. If for any reason the two appraisers chosen by the parties cannot agree upon a third appraiser, then any court of general equity jurisdiction in the county in which leased premises are situated may, upon request of either party, appoint an appraiser to fill the place remaining vacant.

Sec. 1003. *Exercise of Option to Buy.* In the event that said option to buy is exercised, the Landlord hereby covenants and agrees to convey title to Tenant, which title shall be as good and marketable as when title was conveyed to Landlord, free and clear of all liens and encumbrances other than the following: i) liens and encumbrances created or suffered by Tenant, ii) liens of taxes then unpaid, iii) existing leases and iv) liens and encumbrances which are in existence on the date of this lease.

Sec. 1004. *Settlement Procedure.* Landlord shall give Tenant at least thirty (30) days' prior notice of the time and place for the delivery of the deed, which place shall be within the county where the leased premises are located or at such other place as the parties may agree upon. Concurrently with the delivery of the deed, Tenant shall pay to Landlord the stipulated purchase price, together with any unpaid rent. All expenses and taxes incident to the transfer shall be paid by Tenant, except that Landlord shall pay the cost of preparation of the deed.

Article 11

MISCELLANEOUS

Sec. 1101. *Notices.* Any notice provided for herein shall be given by registered mail addressed, if to Landlord, as follows ....
....
and if to Tenant, as follows: ....
....

Sec. 1102. *Change of Address.* The persons and places to which notices are to be mailed may be changed from time to time by Landlord or Tenant upon written notice to the other.

Sec. 1103. *Modification.* This lease may be modified only by written agreement signed by Landlord and Tenant.

Sec. 1104. *Descriptive Headings.* The descriptive headings of this agreement are inserted for convenience in reference only and do not constitute a part of this agreement.

Sec. 1105. *Heirs, Executors, Administrators, Successors and Assigns.* This lease and the covenants, terms and conditions thereof shall be binding upon and inure to the benefit of the heirs, executors, administrators, successors and assigns of the parties hereto.

IN WITNESS WHEREOF, Landlord and Tenant have executed this agreement through their respective authorized officers.

By ....
Landlord

ATTEST:

....
Assistant Secretary

By ....
Tenant

ATTEST:

....
Assistant Secretary

FORTY-YEAR LEASE TO THE WOOLWORTH COMPANY

(Here is an exact copy of a forty-year lease given by the Massachusetts Institute of Technology to the Woolworth Company on a property in a large Massachusetts city, whereby the Institute purchased land, advanced money for the construction of a typical Woolworth store building, and received as rental an amount equal to 5 per cent on the land and building investment plus 1½ per cent of the cost of the building, the latter to care for amortization of the structure. This returns to the lessor 5 per cent on land cost and 6½ per cent on building cost. The Woolworth Company has the right to purchase the premises at cost if the lessor at any time desires to dispose of them. Note that the lease was executed after both parties had entered into an agreement—which follows the lease—which set forth in specific form the terms to be observed. While this lease was drafted more than a quarter of a century ago, its form and its language are still valid.)

THIS INDENTURE made in quadruplicate this eighth day of February, in the year of our Lord one thousand nine hundred and ....
by and between the MASSACHUSETTS INSTITUTE OF TECHNOLOGY, a Massachusetts corporation having its principal place of business in Cambridge, Massachusetts, as Landlord and F. W. WOOLWORTH CO., a corporation existing and doing business under the laws of the State of Pennsylvania, as Tenant:—

WITNESSETH, that the said Landlord has agreed to demise and let, and hereby does demise and let to the Tenant; and the said Tenant has agreed to lease and take, and hereby does lease and take from the Landlord those certain premises situated in the City of ....,
County of ...., and described as follows:

(Legal descriptions here.)

The premises herein leased are more particularly shown on a blue print (or photostat) annexed hereto marked "Exhibit A" and considered a part hereof to the same extent as if fully inserted herein.

Together with any and all of the landord's easements and appurtenances to or used in connection with the demised premises.

Term. To have and to hold the demised premises for a term of forty (40) years to commence on the first day of April, ... and to end on the first day of April, ... at eight o'clock in the forenoon.

Rent.   The said Tenant agrees to pay the said landlord the yearly rent in an amount and payable at the times and in the manner specified in an agreement of even date herewith between the parties hereto. All the terms of said agreement relating to such rental are incorporated herein by reference and made a part hereof as completely as though fully set forth herein. (*Note:* Agreement follows lease.)

Taxes and assessments.   The tenant covenants during the term of this lease to pay when due all taxes, assessments and water rates which shall be charged, assessed or imposed upon the premises herein leased (including the land and any building erected thereon) during the demised term, excepting, however, betterment assessments (meaning thereby assessments for local benefits of a kind tending to increase the value of the property assessed, but not assessments for side-walk improvement) and taxes in the nature of Income Taxes, Excess Profit Taxes, Inheritance, Estate or Transfer Taxes or taxes upon rental by whatever authority imposed or however designated. It is agreed that for the first and last years of the term of this lease all taxes shall be apportioned between the landlord and the tenant according to that part of such years during which the tenant shall have possession of the demised premises.

The tenant covenants that it will indemnify and save harmless the landlord from all liability, loss, cost, damage, expense, and judgments arising from injury of any nature occurring or alleged to have occurred during the term hereof to persons or property on or about the premises herein leased.

Alterations; additions.   The tenant is to erect a new building for its use upon the premises herein leased as provided in said agreement of even date between the parties hereto. After the completion thereof the tenant may, at its own expense, make such alterations, repairs or additions thereto as it finds desirable for its purposes but none such which substantially affect the structure of said new building shall be made without first obtaining on each occasion the consent of the landlord, which consent shall not be unreasonably withheld. The tenant agrees to keep the demised premises, said new building and all additions to or upon same in good condition and repair, both inside and outside, and to bear all expense of and make all repairs, alterations and additions, whether structural or otherwise, which may at any time become necessary or which may be ordered by any governmental authority during the continuance of this lease. All work undertaken by the tenant shall be done in a workmanlike manner, using materials of good quality; and the tenant shall obtain all permits, comply with all governmental requirements and pay the entire cost of such work promptly, leaving the premises herein leased free of all liens for both labor and materials.

Fixtures.   It is agreed between the parties hereto that prior to the expiration of this lease, tenant may remove any or all store fixtures, counters, shelving, show cases and similar trade fixtures which have been installed at the tenant's expense in the demised premises.

At the expiration or other termination of this lease, the tenant agrees to peaceably vacate the demised premises and remove all goods and effects not of the landlord and deliver up to the landlord said premises and all improvements, erections and additions made upon the same, and all plumbing and heating apparatus and landlord's fixtures free and clear and in good repair and condition in all respects, reasonable use, wear and tear and unavoidable casualty alone excepted.

Assignment; subletting. The tenant may sublet the demised premises in whole or in part or may assign this lease, but no assignment or subletting shall in any manner operate to release the tenant from the full performance of all the terms and conditions upon its part to be kept and performed and the tenant shall continue fully liable for the full performance thereof.

Fire clause. It is further agreed between the parties hereto (*a*) that if the said building is destroyed or damaged to any extent by fire or by any other cause at any time prior to May 1, 19...., or damaged by fire or by any other cause on or after May 1, 19.... to the extent of twenty (20) per cent or less of its fair insurable value, the tenant is immediately and at its own expense to repair the damage or to construct a new building, as the case may require, with as much floor space and frontage therein as was contained in the building prior to its damage or destruction, any new building to be constructed in accordance with plans and specifications to be approved by the landlord, which approval will not be unreasonably withheld; (*b*) that if the said building is completely destroyed by fire or by any other cause at any time on or after May 1, 19...., this lease shall be thereby terminated and thenceforth be null and void, and if any rent has been paid in advance the landlord will refund all rent prepaid for any period extending beyond such termination; and (*c*) that if the said building is damaged on or after May 1, 19.... by fire or by any other cause to an extent in excess of twenty (20) per cent of its fair insurable value the tenant will either repair the damage at its own expense or pay to the landlord within sixty (60) days after the damage occurs a sum equal to the damage sustained and in the event of such payment this lease shall be thereby terminated and thenceforth be null and void, and if any rent has been paid in advance the landlord will refund all rent prepaid for any period extending beyond such termination.

Condemnation. The landlord reserves all rights to damages to the premises herein leased and the leasehold hereby created by reason of any taking of all or any portion thereof by governmental or public authority and the tenant hereby grants to the landlord all the tenant's rights to such damages, except for damage to tenant's fixtures and damage to the tenant's business by reason of interference with access during alterations or otherwise. In case any such taking reduces the remaining area of the lot to less than six thousand (6,000) square feet, this lease shall, at the election of the tenant, to be exercised within sixty (60) days of the taking, be thereby terminated and thenceforth be null and void; otherwise, the landlord agrees that it will at its own expense do such work to the building as shall be necessary to repair all damage occasioned by the taking, such work to be done in accordance with plans

and specifications to be approved by the tenant, which approval shall
not be unreasonably withheld, and that the annual rent to be paid hereunder from and after the date upon which the tenant's use of the building is interfered with by any work occasioned by the taking shall be
reduced by a sum equal to five (5) per cent of the amount awarded to
the landlord as damages for such taking, less the cost of the work to
be done by the landlord under the provisions of this paragraph. The
landlord shall not accept any award for such damages unless the tenant
consents thereto until the expiration of thirty (30) days after notice to
the tenant thereof; and if the tenant elects to do so it shall be permitted,
at its own expense, to contest such award by appropriate legal proceedings in the name of the landlord.

Default.   The landlord agrees that it will exercise its right hereinafter established to terminate this lease for default by the tenant until
the expiration of sixty (60) days after notice to the tenant of the alleged default, nor until the expiration of such additional period, if any,
as may be reasonably necessary to make good the default if it is of
such a character as to require more than sixty (60) days to remedy.

Notices.   Any notice or communication from one party to the other
shall be mailed by registered mail, postage prepaid, addressed if to the
landlord at Cambridge, Massachusetts, or at such other address as the
landlord shall from time to time establish by notice to the tenant; and
if to the tenant at 120 Tremont Street, Boston, Massachusetts, and
Executive Office, Woolworth Building, New York City, or at such other
addresses, not exceeding two, as the tenant shall from time to time
establish by notice to the landlord. Any notice so mailed shall be
deemed to have been received unless returned to the sender by the
post office.

Landlord hereby covenants that it has full authority to execute this
lease, and further agrees that tenant upon paying said rent, and performing the covenants of this lease, shall quietly have, hold and enjoy
the demised premises during the term hereof.

PROVIDED ALWAYS, and these presents are upon this condition,
that if the tenant shall fail to perform any of its covenants and agreements herein contained the landlord may, subject to the default provision hereof, enter into and upon the premises herein leased and
repossess the same as of the landlord's former estate and expel the tenant
and those claiming under it and remove their effects without being
deemed guilty of any manner of trespass and without prejudice to any
other remedies, and upon entry as aforesaid this lease shall terminate;
the tenant covenants that in case of such termination, or in case of
termination under the provisions of statute by reason of default by the
tenant, the tenant will indemnify the landlord against all loss of rent
and other payments to be paid by the tenant and other payments which
the landlord may incur by reason of such termination during the residue
of the term hereof; or at the election of the landlord, the tenant will,
upon such termination, pay to the landlord as damages such a sum, if
any, as at the time of such termination represents the excess of the

rent and other payments to be paid hereunder by the tenant above the rental value of the premises for the remainder of said term.

This lease shall bind and enure to the benefit of the parties hereto and their respective heirs, executors, administrators, successors and assigns.

IN WITNESS WHEREOF, the landlord and tenant have signed and sealed these presents in quadruplicate on the day and year first above written.

(Signatures, acknowledgments, and so forth.)

Agreement

THIS AGREEMENT made in quadruplicate this eighth day of February, ..., by and between the MASSACHUSETTS INSTITUTE OF TECHNOLOGY, a Massachusetts corporation having its principal place of business in Cambridge, Massachusetts, hereinafter called the landlord, and F. W. WOOLWORTH CO., a corporation organized under the laws of Pennsylvania, hereinafter called the tenant. WITNESSETH:

WHEREAS said Massachusetts Institute of Technology agrees and proposes to execute simultaneously with this agreement a lease of even date herewith to said F. W. Woolworth Co., of certain real estate situated:

(Premises described here.)

WHEREAS said lease for the rent and terms of payment thereof refer to an agreement of even date therewith and this instrument is the agreement so referred to and is made to supplement and complete said lease and is to be deemed a material part thereof for all purposes to the same extent as if actually set forth therein;

NOW THEREFORE, in consideration of the giving of said lease by the landlord and the acceptance thereof by the tenant, the parties hereto for themselves and their respective successors and assigns agree as follows:

1. The landlord agrees to make an investment not to exceed $........ in the land and in the new building to be built thereon by the tenant. In computing the cost of the land and building, rental paid by tenant before store opening, architectural and designing expenses, reasonable brokerage commission to the negotiating broker for said lease, current taxes so far as not paid by the tenant under said lease, and such expenses of both parties as are properly chargeable to this proposition shall be included.

2. The tenant shall as soon as convenient, but not later than ninety (90) days after landlord obtains possession of said land free of all tenants, commence building a one story and basement mercantile building designed for its occupation according to plans and specifications to be first approved by the landlord, which approval shall not be unreasonably withheld, and the tenant shall make payment therefor and shall within ninety (90) days after its completion give the landlord a full and complete statement of its cost, including the expenses hereinabove referred to. The landlord agrees to pay to the tenant a sum equal to the cost of said building, including said expenses, within thirty (30) days after receiving the statement above referred to; but in no event shall the payment by the landlord to the tenant be greater than the amount by which two hundred thirty thousand dollars ($230,000.00) exceeds the cost to the landlord of the land, including in such cost current taxes so far as not to be paid by the tenant under said lease.

3. Although said lease is for a term beginning April 1, ..., it is agreed:—that the tenant shall pay rent, as hereinafter provided, from and after the date upon which the landlord takes title to the land, whether such date be before or after April 1, ...; and that the tenant's obligations hereunder shall not be affected by any delay in gaining possession which may occur by reason of the failure of any other tenants to vacate. The landlord shall use reasonable efforts to obtain possession of said premises free of all tenants, and agrees that it will abate the rent to be paid by the tenant under Paragraph 4 hereof for such period in excess of sixty (60) days as the landlord shall be unable to obtain possession of said premises free of all tenants.

4. Beginning with the date when the landlord takes title to the land area leased to the tenant up to the date the tenant's store opens for business upon the demised premises, the tenant shall pay to the landlord in one payment on or about the date of the store opening, rental for such period at an annual rate equal to five (5) per cent on the landlord's invested land cost.

5. During the period beginning with the date the tenant's store opens for business upon the demised premises and ending with the date the landlord pays to the tenant the amount expended for building plus expenses, the tenant shall continue to pay to the landlord in equal monthly payments on the fifteenth day of each month for the current month, with appropriate adjustments at the beginning and end of this period, rental for this period at an annual rate equal to five (5) per cent of the landlord's then invested land cost.

6. Beginning with the date the landlord pays to the tenant the amount expended for building, including expenses, the annual rental thereafter shall be five (5) per cent of the landlord's total invested cost, including expenses, of land and building, plus one and 5/100 per cent of the amount paid by the landlord to the tenant toward the cost of the building, including expenses, payable in equal monthly payments on the fifteenth day of each month for the current month during this lease without interruption. It is the intention that these rentals will produce for the landlord five (5) per cent net annual rental on its entire invested cost during the entire lease term and in addition thereto annual amortization of one and 5/100 per cent of the cost to the landlord of the building, including expenses.

7. The landlord agrees that the tenant shall have the right to purchase the demised premises on and after April 1, ... for the landlord's original invested cost of land and building; except that if the landlord at any time desires to sell said premises the foregoing right shall be terminated by notice from the landlord to the tenant; and if so terminated the tenant shall have the right within thirty (30) days of the mailing of such notice to purchase said premises for the landlord's original invested cost of land and buildings.

IN WITNESS WHEREOF, the landlord and tenant have signed and sealed these presents in quadruplicate on the day and year first above written.

(Signatures, acknowledgments, and so forth.)

NINETY-NINE-YEAR LEASE

(This is a standard lease with short, concise paragraphs, properly indexed and quite complete.)

Clause 1.   Parties. This indenture of lease, made this . . . .
. . . . between . . . .
. . . .
. . . .
party of the first part, hereinafter called Lessor, and . . . .
. . . .
. . . .
party of the second part, hereinafter called Lessee,
   Witnesseth:

Clause 2.   Consideration.   That each of the aforesaid parties acknowledges the receipt of a valuable consideration from the other and that they and each of them act herein in further consideration of the engagements of the others as herein stated.

Clause 3.   Premises.   That Lessor has and does hereby demise and lease unto the said Lessee the following described premises:
               (Description in full here.)
. . . .

Clause 4.   Term.   To have and to hold the above described premises unto the Lessee for the period of 99 years commencing on the . . . . . .
day of . . . . 19. . ., and ending on the . . . . day of
. . . . 20. . . ., renewable thereafter forever at same rental as for 99th year.

Clause 5.   Rental.   Lessee hereby covenants and agrees to pay to Lessor as rent for the aforesaid premises the following amounts of money:
. . . .

Clause 6.   When rent is payable.   Each year's rental shall be payable in quarterly installments in advance on the first days of January, April, July and October. Any installment of rent not paid when due shall bear interest at the rate of 8% per annum.

Clause 7.   Rent payable in gold.   All rent reserved and agreed to be paid under this lease shall be paid in standard gold coin of the United

States of America of the present standard of weight and fineness or its equivalent in lawful money of the United States.

Clause 8. Sums due lessor a lien. All money and other sums which shall become due to Lessor hereunder by reason of any provision of this lease is and shall always be a valid and first lien upon the buildings and improvements on said property and upon all of the interests of the Lessee in this lease and paramount to any mortgage which Lessee may execute thereon, or any lien caused by Lessee.

Clause 9. Taxes and assessments. In addition to the rental hereinbefore provided to be paid, Lessee further covenants and agrees to bear, pay and discharge all taxes, assessments, rates, charges for revenue, imposts, and all levies general and special, ordinary and extraordinary, of any name, nature and kind whatsoever, which may be fixed, charged, levied, assessed, or otherwise imposed upon said premises or upon any or all buildings or improvements thereon, but said Lessee shall not be required to pay income taxes or any inheritance or succession taxes which may at any time during the term of this lease be required to be paid upon any gift, devise, deed, mortgage, descent, or other alienation of any part of or all of said leased premises and property. Lessor and Lessee shall pay pro rata the taxes and assessments for the current year.

Clause 10. Tax bills exhibited. Lessee shall exhibit or deliver to Lessor as often as requested so to do, the receipts showing the payment of the aforesaid taxes, assessments, rates, charges, imposts and levies.

Clause 11. New building. Within .... years from date Lessee shall construct and fully complete on said premises a .... building suitable to the neighborhood in which they are situated of a cost value of not less than $............. Said building shall be constructed of good material, erected in a good workmanlike manner and be ready for occupancy on or before .... years from this date, free and clear of all liens of contractors, sub-contractors, mechanics, laborers, material men and other items of like character.

Clause 12. Extension of time for building. If for any reason Lessee shall desire the time extended within which the building provided for in Clause 11 may be completed, the same shall be extended, not, however, beyond .... years on the payment, at the periods provided for in Clause 6, of an increased annual rental equal to .... per cent of the rental provided for in Clause 5, for the extended time.

Clause 13. Bond. Securities acceptable to Lessor or a bond in the sum of .... Dollars ($.........) with surety satisfactory to Lessor shall be executed by Lessee to Lessor contemporaneously with this lease, conditioned for the erection of the aforesaid building together with the payment of rent, taxes, assessments and any and all obligations hereunder until the erection and completion of said building whereupon said bond shall be cancelled and said securities returned. The agreement as to said securities and said bond shall further provide that in case of failure of Lessee to erect said buildings as hereinbefore specified a reasonable amount thereof shall be held to be payable to Lessor as damages for such failure to erect said buildings.

Clause 14. Building now on said premises. There is a building now standing on said premises of the value of .... Dollars ($..........) and which Lessee shall keep in as good repair as it now is up to and until the time when it may be necessary to remove said building for the erection of the new or other buildings as herein provided for and which building shall be insured by Lessee in the amount of 80% of its insurable value exclusive of foundation with the loss if any payable to Lessor. The proceeds of any insurance collected for said building shall be repaid to Lessee to apply on the new or other building herein provided for, such application to be made on the last payment falling due for said new or other buildings.

Clause 15. Insurance. Lessee hereby covenants that Lessee will at all times during the term of this lease, have and keep said building or buildings so to be erected and constructed and completed, or any buildings erected hereafter upon said premises, in constant good condition and repair and insured against loss or damage by fire, in insurance companies of general recognized responsibility and credit, in an amount equal to not less than eighty per cent of the fair insurable value thereof exclusive of foundation.

Clause 16. Policies to be held by trustee. Said policies of insurance shall be deposited with .... (or such other Trust Company as may be designated by the Lessor) as trustee, and all sums arising by reason of loss under said insurance policies shall be available to the Lessee for the reconstruction or repair, as the case may be, of any building or buildings injured or destroyed by fire and shall be by such trustee paid out from time to time on the estimates of any responsible architect, having supervision thereof, certifying that the amount of each estimate is being applied to the payment of the reasonable cost thereof, provided, however, that it first be made to appear to the satisfaction of the trustee that the amount of money necessary to provide for the reconstruction of any building or buildings destroyed or injured, according to the plan adopted therefor, which may be in excess of the amount received upon such insurance policies, has been provided by the Lessee for such purpose and its application for such purpose assured.

Clause 17. Excess of insurance money. Any excess of money received from insurance remaining with the trustee, after the restoration or reconstruction of such building or buildings, if there be no default on the part of the Lessee in the performance of the covenants herein, shall be paid by the trustee to said Lessee, and in case of the Lessee not entering upon the reconstruction or repair of said building or buildings within a period of six months after such destruction or injury by fire or otherwise, and prosecuting the same thereafter with such despatch as may be necessary to complete the same within eighteen months after the damage or loss occurring, then the amount so collected or the balance thereof remaining in the hands of the trustee, as the case may be, shall be retained by it as security for the continued performance and observance by the Lessee of the covenants hereof, and no part thereof shall be paid to the Lessee except after a complete restoration or reconstruction of the building or buildings during the continuance of this lease, and it will be at the option of the Lessor in such case to terminate this lease and retain such amount as liquidated damages resulting from the failure upon the part of the Lessee to promptly, within the time specified, complete such work of restoration or reconstruction.

Clause 18.   Policies to be for the benefit of.   Said trustee shall hold all policies of insurance as provided hereunder for the benefit of Lessor, Lessee and any person, corporation or Trust Company holding a mortgage on the interest of Lessee created under this lease as their respective interests may appear. Lessee shall pay all charges by reason of deposit of said insurance policies or in disbursement of funds received by said Trust Company on said policies.

Clause 19.   Strikes.   Whenever under this instrument a time is stated within which or by which repairs, original construction or reconstruction of said buildings shall be made and during such period a general or sympathetic strike or lock-out occurs, war or rebellion ensues or some event beyond Lessee's power to control, causing delay, the period of such delay so caused shall be added to the period limited herein for the completion of such work.

Clause 20.   Assignments.   Lessee further covenants that Lessee will not, except by way of mortgage of the leasehold estate to secure some actual indebtedness, assign or transfer this lease without the written consent of Lessor, unless there be at the time no existing default on the part of Lessee in observance of the conditions herein, nor unless the first building herein covenanted to be erected shall have been completed, nor unless the assignee of this lease shall expressly assume Lessee's engagements hereunder, nor unless Lessee shall have first placed in the hands of the Lessor for inspection a sufficiently executed instrument of assignment and assumption, which instrument shall be recorded at or about the time of its execution, but after any assignment made in conformity with the above conditions there shall be no further liability under this lease against Lessee herein named, and thereafter all liability shall rest upon the assignee. Any assignment not in conformity with the above shall be void.

Clause 21.   Indemnity against cost or charges.   Lessee further agrees that Lessee will pay and indemnify Lessor against all legal costs and charges including counsel fees reasonably incurred in and about the defense of any suit in discharging the said premises or any part thereof from any liens, judgments or encumbrances, caused or suffered by Lessee.

Clause 22.   Lessor may pay delinquent taxes.   Lessee further covenants that Lessor shall have at all times during the term of this lease or renewals thereof, the right to pay any taxes, assessments, water rates, liens or other charges upon said premises, and the improvements thereon, also to redeem said premises from any sale that may be made of the same for taxes or assessments; that the amount so paid including reasonable expenses shall be so much additional rent due at the next rent date, and be a lien on Lessee's interest in said premises, after such payment.

Clause 23. Validity of taxes or other charges. It is further provided that it shall not be obligatory upon the part of the Lessor to enquire into the validity of any taxes, assessments, liens or other charges, or any tax sale, before making payment as herein provided. If Lessee should in good faith desire to contest any of said items the same may be done on giving Lessor a bond in the amount thereof conditioned for the payment of such items in case Lessee be defeated in the litigation.

Clause 24. Care and use of premises. Lessee further covenants that said premises and all buildings and improvements thereon shall during the term of this lease be used only and exclusively for proper, legitimate and moral purposes and that Lessee will not use nor suffer any person to use in any manner whatsoever the said premises or any building thereon for any purposes in violation of the laws of the United States, the State of Ohio, or of the ordinances and laws of the City of Cleveland that are enforced, or will save Lessor harmless from their violation.

Clause 25. Premises to be kept in good and safe condition. Lessee further covenants that Lessee will at all times keep all buildings and improvements on said premises and all appurtenances thereto and all sidewalks, steps and excavations under sidewalks in good, clean, safe, secure and sanitary condition and repaired and will keep any alley adjoining said premises in a clean, sanitary and safe condition and will conform to all enforced municipal ordinances and laws affecting said premises and will save the Lessor free and harmless from any penalty, damage or other charges imposed for any violation of any of said laws, whether occasioned by the neglect of the Lessee or any agent in the employ of said Lessee, or any person contracting with said Lessee and that Lessee will indemnify and keep harmless Lessor against and from any loss caused by damage or expense arising out of the construction and erection of any buildings or improvements on said premises, or out of any accident or other occurrence causing injury of any person whomsoever, or property whatsoever, and due directly or indirectly to the use of aforesaid premises or any part thereof.

Clause 26. Waiver of breach. It is hereby covenanted and agreed that no waiver of a breach of any of the covenants of this lease shall be construed to be a waiver of any succeeding breach of the same or any other covenant.

Clause 27. Lease not terminated by fire. It is further covenanted and agreed that in case any improvements and buildings upon said premises shall be at any time damaged or destroyed by fire, or other casualty, this lease shall not thereby be terminated, the laws of the state of Ohio to the contrary notwithstanding.

Clause 28. Removing or razing of buildings. Lessee shall have the privilege of removing or razing the building or buildings upon said premises at any time for the purpose of erecting in place thereof a new building or buildings, but prior to such removal or razing a bond or satisfactory security shall be executed to, and deposited with Lessor, in the sum equal to the value of the building removed or razed, conditioned that within two years from the removal or razing of said building or buildings there shall be erected in place thereof a commercial building suitable to the location and of the fair value and cost of construction of not less than the value of the building removed or razed, and in case of failure to erect said building or buildings within the time herein specified reasonable damages for such failure to erect said building or buildings shall be paid to Lessor.

Clause 29.   Old material.   Said Lessee may convert material of the building or buildings removed or razed in accordance herewith to Lessee's own use. If only a part of the building or buildings is sought to be removed and such removal or destruction does not diminish the value of the building or buildings remaining to less than the value of the building required by Clause 11, then the Lessee shall have the privilege of removing such portion for the purpose of erecting a new building instead, first giving a bond or furnishing securities in the amount of said diminished value. But such new structure shall be completed within two years after such removal or destruction.

Clause 30.   Excavation.   In excavating for any building to be erected upon said premises Lessee shall conform to and observe all laws, statutes and ordinances relating to such excavation and will protect all buildings on adjacent premises and at all times have and keep the Lessor's premises hereby leased free and discharged of any liability in favor of the owners of adjoining premises.

Clause 31.   Forfeiture on default.   It is further covenanted and agreed by and between the parties hereto, that any demand for rent made after it becomes due, shall have the same force and effect as if made on the day it falls due, that if any default shall be made by the Lessee in any payment of rents or taxes, assessments, insurance premiums, water rates, or any other sum herein stipulated and agreed to be paid or kept, or the said Lessee shall fail to keep and perform any other covenant, condition or agreement, herein provided on the part of Lessee to be performed, and such default shall exist for a period of sixty (60) days, then, and in that case, the Lessor may serve upon said Lessee written notice of such default; and, if such default shall then continue without being wholly remedied for a period of thirty (30) days after the service of such notice, then it shall and may be lawful for the Lessor, without further notice, to declare said demised term ended, and to re-enter and re-possess the said demised premises, and the building and improvements situated thereon, or any part thereof, either with or without process of law, and the said Lessee does in such event, hereby waive any demand for possession of the demised premises, and any and all buildings and improvements then situated thereon, and the Lessee covenants and agrees, upon the termination of said demised term at the election of said Lessor, or in any other way, to surrender and deliver up said above described premises and property peaceably to said Lessor, or the agents or attorneys of Lessor, immediately upon the termination of said demised term.

Clause 32.   Arbitrators.   The parties hereto covenant and agree that a Board of Arbitrators shall be constituted from time to time when needed, to decide all questions of compliance, interpretation or values, also any and all other questions, some of which are specifically provided for herein, arising under this lease, in regard to which the parties hereto may not agree.

Said Board of Arbitrators shall consist of three disinterested persons appointed, (two of whom may be appointed out of two lists of five persons each to be suggested respectively by the parties hereto) by the presiding judge of the Probate Court of Cuyahoga County, Ohio, which board shall begin at once and proceed with all reasonable dispatch to determine all questions which may be referred to them as herein provided, arising under this lease and such determination shall in each and every instance be final and binding, on the parties hereto.

If either party at any time prefers to have the matter in dispute determined by the courts instead of by arbitrators the same may be done by the party having such preference beginning legal proceedings before the arbitrators are appointed, but not afterwards.

Clause 33.   Questions submitted to arbitrators.   Questions to be submitted to said Board of Arbitrators shall be put in writing by the parties hereto and if either party neglect or fail to act when called upon by the other party, or if any disagreement regarding such questions arise between the parties hereto, said judge of the Probate Court on the application of either party shall put such matters in writing and present the same to said board of arbitrators.

Clause 34.   Report of arbitrators.   Said Board of Arbitrators shall report to the parties hereto and to the Probate Court, within thirty (30) days after the questions have been submitted to them their findings in writing signed by not less than two arbitrators.

Clause 35.   Arbitrators substituted when?   If any one or more of said arbitrators resign, die or become incapacitated before a full and final determination of all questions submitted to them be arrived at, the Judge of the Probate Court shall appoint others in place of the arbitrators no longer acting to make or complete said determination.

Clause 36.   Probate judge.   The Judge of Probate Court herein referred to shall be the official or presiding judge longest acting and then most nearly performing the duties of such official as defined by the laws of Ohio in the year of 19. . . . .

Clause 37.   Expense of arbitrators.   The parties hereto shall share equally the cost and expense of said arbitrators, and all expenses connected therewith.

Clause 38.   Purchase clause.   Lessee is hereby granted the option at any time between 19. . . . and 20. . . ., of buying the fee of the aforesaid premises for the sum of . . . . dollars ($. . . . .) and in case said option be exercised conveyance shall be made by warranty deed and this lease shall thereupon be annulled. The certificate or abstract provided for in Clause 45 extended to date of the lease shall, in case of purchase, be accepted by the buyer as showing satisfactory title.

Clause 39.   Buildings extending on to adjacent land.   Any buildings built on said premises which shall be extended on to adjacent land not owned by Lessor shall be so designed and constructed as to be readily and conveniently separately used by Lessor and have convenient ways of access and egress from and to the aforesaid premises over which such building may extend.

Clause 40.   Appropriations.   1. In the event that the aforesaid land or a part thereof be appropriated by some corporation having the power of eminent domain or be conveyed by the parties hereto to avoid proceedings in appropriation, there shall be ascertained and determined by the Board of Arbitrators, provided for herein, unless the same has been otherwise ascertained and determined:

(a) The value of the land so appropriated or conveyed.

(b) The separate value of any buildings of Lessor standing on the land so appropriated or conveyed.

(c) The separate value of any buildings belonging to Lessee standing on the land so appropriated or conveyed.

(d) Any damage to the residue.

The total of the above four items shall be the amount to be distributed as provided below in this clause.

(e) The total future rentals payable to the Lessor under this lease and apportionable to the land so appropriated or conveyed, and also the total future rentals of the buildings standing thereon belonging to Lessor. In determining future rentals in a lease containing a provision for re-appraisal at a future date, the Board of Arbitrators may disregard said provision if the date for re-appraisal be more than ten years hence, but, in case it be less than ten years hence, said Board may make such re-appraisal at once and determine the future rentals including such re-appraisal.

2. The future rentals payable to Lessor for the land appropriated or conveyed, also the future rentals payable to Lessor for buildings standing on said land belonging to Lessor, (except so much of said building rentals as may accrue on money received for said buildings which the arbitrators may determine shall be used for new construction on the residue of the land) shall be abated.

3. Out of the moneys received for said land appropriated or conveyed, also out of the moneys received for said buildings belonging to Lessor, except so much of said building moneys, as may be used for new construction there shall be paid to Lessor an amount on which the annual interest (computed at the rate determinable by the arbitrators from the lease, as nearly as such rate can be so determined, as the rate on which rentals were contracted for in the lease-hold agreement) shall equal the rentals annually abated.

If there be not sufficient moneys thus received, the full amount thereof, except so much as may be used for new construction, shall be paid to Lessor.

If there be an excess in said moneys so received, over the amount above provided to be paid to Lessor, and used for new construction, there shall also be paid to Lessor from such excess, an amount which placed at interest at the rate of 3% per annum compounded annually, will equal, at the end of the current term of this lease, the amount of said excess.

4. Out of any remaining moneys received for said land appropriated or conveyed, also out of any remaining moneys received for said buildings belonging to Lessor, also out of all moneys received as damages to the residue, also out of all moneys received for buildings standing thereon belonging to the Lessee, there shall be deposited with the trustee then acting, provided for in Clause 16, the amount of money which the arbitrators may determine should be invested in the construction on the residue of said land, of a building suitable to its location, and of the same relative value to said residue as the value of the building provided for in Clause 11 bore to the value of the whole land when the lease was executed, which money shall be available to the Lessee for such purpose, and which building must be built within 18 months thereafter.

5. All remaining moneys shall be paid to Lessee.

Clause 41. Conditions not foreseen. In event of there arising a situation or condition not contemplated by any of the provisions of this lease, which situation or condition affects injuriously the rights and interests of either or both parties hereto, then and thereafter the Board of Arbitrators provided for herein shall be constituted and have full power to decide and determine what each of the said parties hereto shall do and accept in the way of delay or postponement of the requirements of this lease as long as such situation or condition continues, and such decision and determination shall be binding on the parties hereto.

Clause 42. Notices. All notices provided for herein may be served by leaving the same with the trustee provided for in Clause 16, addressed to the party to be served with such notice.

Clause 43. Covenants run to heirs, etc. It is hereby covenanted and agreed between the parties hereto that all covenants, conditions, agreements and undertakings in this lease contained shall extend to and be binding on the respective heirs, executors, administrators, successors and assigns of the respective parties hereto the same as if they were in every case named and expressed and the same shall be construed as covenants running with the land. Also that the terms "Lessor" and "Lessee" shall be construed in the singular or plural number according as they respectively represent one or more than one person.

Clause 44. Buildings at end of lease. If there be a renewal provision in Clause 4 this whole clause (44) shall form no part of this lease, otherwise it shall apply and be part of it.

On or before one year before the expiration of this lease, the parties hereto covenant and agree that one year before the end of the term of this lease Lessor may tender to Lessee an extension hereof for another period of 99 years, at the same rental as for the last year of the current term, and Lessee may accept said extension, in which case no disposition of the buildings upon the premises shall at any time be provided for.

In the event Lessor does not tender said extension of the term of this lease or Lessee fails or refuses to accept such an extension on or before one month after it is received then and in either event the Board of Arbitrators, constituted as hereinbefore provided shall proceed, with dispatch and within three months thereafter shall appraise and determine the full and fair value of the buildings and improvements on said premises belonging to said Lessee and shall at the same time separately appraise and determine the full and fair value of said land and any buildings belonging to Lessor.

Thereupon on or before six months or a ratable period if there have been delays before the expiration of the term of this lease the Lessor shall have the option of buying and taking over said buildings and improvements belonging to Lessee at the value determined by said arbitrators and paying for the same on or before the expiration of the term of this lease, first notifying the Lessee of the intention of Lessor so to do at the beginning of said six months.

In the event that Lessor does not notify Lessee on or before six months or a ratable period if there have been delays before the expiration of this lease of an intention to buy and take over said buildings and improvements belonging to Lessee at the value determined by the arbitrators, Lessee shall thereupon have the option of buying and taking over the fee of said land and any buildings belonging to Lessor at the value thereof determined by said arbitrators and paying for same before the expiration of this lease and such payment being made conveyance shall be made by proper warranty deed.

In the event neither of the parties hereto decide to exercise the options above specified then after the expiration of this lease Lessor and Lessee shall become the owners in common of said premises and said buildings and improvements in proportion to their respective values entering into the same as determined by said arbitrators.

Clause 45. Quiet possession. Lessor hereby covenants that said premises are free and clear from all encumbrances as appears from an abstract or certificate of title accompanying this instrument, also free from any restrictions or limitations on their use which will prevent or interfere with such use for commercial buildings and other like uses, and if Lessee shall keep and perform all the covenants of this lease on the part of Lessee to be performed, Lessor will guarantee to Lessee the quiet peaceful and uninterrupted possession of said premises.

Clause 46. (This clause left blank for any provisions of preliminary agreement not herein provided for.)

Clause 47. Husband or wife joining. .... of said Lessor joins in executing this lease for the purpose of giving consent thereto and waiving any right of dower against Lessee.

Clause 48. Officers of corporations authorized to act. The officers of said Lessor and also of said Lessee are duly authorized to execute this lease on behalf of their respective corporations by resolutions duly passed by their respective boards of directors recorded on page .... of the records of Lessor, and on page .... of the records of said Lessee.

In testimony whereof the above named Lessor ....
....
....
and the above named Lessee ....
....
have hereunto and to two other original instruments of identical tenor and date, set their hands on the day and year first above written.

This instrument consists of .... typewritten pages and each page is signed upon its margin also in all sub-clauses left blank with the initials of said Lessor, or of one of its officers.

(Signatures, acknowledgments, and so forth.)

"SHORT FORM" OF NINETY-NINE-YEAR LEASE

(This form, known as the Henderson lease, is a concise instrument, although not abbreviated in any essential detail.)

THIS INDENTURE, made and entered into this .... day of ...., 19...., by and between .... the Lessor (which expression shall include his heirs, executors, administrators and assigns when the context so admits), and .... the Lessee (which expression shall include his heirs, executors, administrators and assigns when the context so admits), evidences the grants, covenants and agreements now made by and between the parties with reference to the following described premises, to wit:

(Property description here.)

1. ON BEHALF OF THE LESSOR:

Grant. That being the owner in fee of said premises, said Lessor does hereby demise and lease the same to the Lessee for a term of ninety-nine (99) years from and after the first day of ...., 19...., and in connection with such demise covenants with the Lessee that conditioned upon his performance and observance of the Lessee's covenants herein, he shall have the quiet and peaceable possession of said premises during said term and also hereby grants to him the privilege of purchasing said premises at a purchase price of ....
Dollars ($..........) at any time during the .... year of the term hereof, on condition, however, of his not being in default at such time in such performance or observance of such covenants, and also on condition of his first giving to the Lessor six (6) months' written notice of his intention to make such purchase. On such election being so made and such purchase price paid therefor, the Lessor agrees to convey said

premises, subject, however, to the leasehold estate hereby created, to the Lessee by deed of general warranty, accompanied by title abstract showing good title in fee simple, except for such leasehold estate passing under this conveyance, and title free from incumbrances other than such as have been created or suffered by the Lessee and for the discharge of which he is liable under the terms hereof.

2. ON BEHALF OF THE LESSEE IN CONSIDERATION OF SUCH DEMISE:

Rents. (*a*) That he will pay to the Lessor at his office at .... or at such place in the city of .... as said Lessor may from time to time designate in writing, in equal quarterly installments in advance from the beginning of said term, by want of rent, the sum of .... Dollars ($..........) per annum, during the term of this lease.

Taxes. (*b*) That he will, as the same become due and payable, pay the last half of the taxes upon said premises for the year 19..., and also all taxes, assessments or other public charges hereafter during said term levied or assessed upon this lease, the rents herein reserved, the said premises or any building erected thereon and will at all times save harmless the Lessor from the payment thereof, or the payment of any claims or demands becoming chargeable against or payable in respect of said premises, or the use and occupancy thereof. No liability for the payment of taxes, assessments or other charges imposed by state or Federal laws, or the laws of any foreign country upon the income of the Lessor or upon the passing of any interest in the leased premises generally known as "income," or "inheritance," "legacy," "succession" or "estate taxes" is assumed by the Lessee under this provision, these being liabilities of the Lessor. Nothing in this lease, however, shall be construed as preventing or interfering with the contesting by the Lessee, at his own expense, of any liens, claims, or charges of any kind in respect of the premises hereby leased which may be thought by the Lessee to be unlawful or excessive, and the Lessee, upon first furnishing to the Lessor, if the Lessor require the same, reasonable security for the payment of all liability, cost and expenses at the end of the litigation, may so contest the same.

Restrictions upon use. (*c*) That during the term hereof, he will conform to and observe all ordinances, rules and regulations of the said city and state and of all public authorities, boards or officers relating to said premises or the improvements upon the same or use thereof, and will not during such term permit the same to be used for any illegal or immoral purposes, business or occupation, or for the purpose of the sale of intoxicating liquors to be drunk upon the premises, except in connection with a hotel, restaurant, club or drug store, or some other principal business to which such sale of liquor shall be incidental merely, and will not in any case permit such liquors to be sold or dispensed at or over a bar on such premises, except in connection with the use of the same for hotel purposes and in such parts of the building or buildings constructed upon the premises as do not front upon any public street.

Construction of building. (d) That he will, within a period of .... years from the beginning of said term and at a fair and reasonable cost of not less than .... Dollars construct upon the leased premises a building adapted to mercantile, commercial, light manufacturing, apartment, office or hotel purposes (one or more of the same) and that he will thereafter during such term have and keep upon the leased premises, except during any period required for reconstruction, a building of the character and cost of construction above provided for, and will at all times have and keep such building in good condition and repair, except as against loss or damage by fire or other casualty and in case of such loss or damage will, with reasonable dispatch, by suitable repairs or reconstruction, restore the same to the condition it had or should have had before such casualty. In case of the construction or reconstruction of any such building provided for herein being begun within a reasonable time, if there be delay in completion resulting from strikes, lockouts, or causes which could not have been reasonably foreseen, there shall be an allowance of additional time for such completion corresponding with the period of delay resulting from such cause. The Lessee may, however, at any time, for the purpose of reconstruction, remove from the leased premises the building so to be constructed or any building hereafter constructed in its stead on executing and delivering to the Lessor a bond in the sum of .... Dollars ($..........), conditioned for the construction upon the premises of a building of the kind and description above specified within a reasonable time and for the payment of all amounts becoming payable under the terms of this lease until such building shall have been so reconstructed.

Insurance. (e) That he will, during the term hereof, at all times have and keep the interest of the Lessor in such building or buildings insured against loss or damage by fire under policies of insurance companies of recognized responsibility and credit and duly authorized to transact business in the State of Ohio in the full amount of .... Dollars ($..........), or such lesser amount as may at any time represent the full insurable value of the same, with loss or damage arising under such policies made payable to The .... Trust Company, of ...., Ohio, as Trustee, or such other responsible trust company in the City of ...., as the Lessor may from time to time designate, and will procure such policies as issued from time to time to be deposited with such Trustee and pay to it its reasonable charges for the custody of the same as well as for all services by it to be rendered under this clause. All amounts received upon such policies, however, shall be available to the Lessee for the reconstruction or repair, as the case may be, of any such building or buildings, and in case of the work of reconstruction or repair being entered upon promptly and prosecuted with reasonable dispatch and there being no default on the part of the Lessee in the performance and observance of the covenants hereof, the Trustee, from the amounts received on such policies, shall from time to time, as far as is necessary, pay out the amount or amounts by it so received on the estimates of any responsible architect having supervision of such construction or repair certifying that the amount of such estimate is being applied to the payment of the reasonable cost of such construction, subject, however, in case of a plan of reconstruction being adopted which will require an expenditure of an amount in excess of the amount held by the Trustee, to the right of the Trustee to withhold such payments until such time as it be made to appear to his satisfaction that any amount necessary to provide for such reconstruction or repair, according to the plan adopted in excess of the amount held by the Trustee has been provided for by the Lessee and its application to such purposes assured. Any amount remaining in the hands of the Trustee from such source after the restoration or reconstruction of any buildings as herein required shall, if there be at that time no default on the part of the Lessee in the performance of the covenants hereof, be paid to the Lessee.

In case of the Lessee not entering upon the reconstruction or repair of any such building within a period of twelve (12) months after such destruction or injury by fire and thereafter prosecuting the same with such dispatch as would be necessary, in case of the entire reconstruction of the building, to effect completion of the same within a period of two (2) years thereafter, subject, however, to delays resulting from unforeseen causes as hereinbefore provided for in clause (d), then the amount so received by the Trustee or any balance remaining in its hands, as the case may be, shall be retained as security for the continued performance and observance by the Lessee of the covenants hereof, and no part thereof shall be paid to the Lessee or for reconstruction except with the consent of the Lessor and after a restoration of the building or buildings, it being the option of the Lessor in the meantime to terminate this lease on account of any such default and have transferred to him by the Trustee such amount as liquidated damages resulting to him from the failure of the Lessee to promptly and within a reasonable time complete such work of reconstruction or repair.

Mortgagees of leasehold estate may have benefit of fund. (f) In case the Lessee or his assigns in interest shall at any time, by trust deed or mortgage of his leasehold estate, for the purpose of securing the payment of any indebtedness by him or them contracted, authorize the mortgagees or trustees therein named on his behalf or in his stead to enter upon the leased premises and undertake or prosecute the reconstruction or repair of any building on the leased premises damaged or destroyed by fire, and to have and receive for his or their use for such purpose such insurance fund, then in that case such fund shall be equally available to such Trustee or mortgagee as to the Lessee as above provided, and it shall in like manner and to like extent at the request of any such Trustee, be applied to the reconstruction or repair of any such building so injured or destroyed.

Assignment of lease. (*g*) That he will not, except by way of mortgage of his leasehold estate to secure some actual indebtedness, assign or transfer this lease without the written consent of the Lessor during any period when there is an existing default on the part of the Lessee in the performance or observance of the conditions of this lease, or at any time after the loss, destruction or removal of any building upon the premises and before the complete repair or reconstruction of the same, nor shall he make such assignment or transfer unless the assignee shall expressly assume the Lessee's engagements hereunder to the Lessor by written instrument filed forthwith for record in the Recorder's office of said county and an original copy thereof delivered to the Lessor. From and after the time, however, of the making of any such assignment in conformity with the foregoing provisions, there shall exist no further liability under this lease against the Lessee herein named, such liability passing under the instrument of assignment or transfer to the assignee, except that the Lessee herein named shall not be relieved from such liability until the building herein agreed to be erected within such period of .... years has been completed.

Indemnity against cost of litigation. (*h*) That he will pay to and indemnify the Lessor from the payment of all legal costs and charges, inclusive of counsel fees by him lawfully and legally incurred or expended in or about the defense of any suit in discharging the premises, or any part thereof, from any liens, judgment or incumbrances created by the Lessee upon or against the same, or against the Lessee's leasehold estate, or any such costs and charges incurred on account of proceedings in obtaining possession of the premises after the termination of the term of the lease by forfeiture or otherwise.

Lessor may cure certain defaults of lessee. (*i*) That in case of any default on the part of the Lessee in the payment of any amount or amounts herein required to be paid by him other than amounts payable as rent, so called, or in case of any default in the procuring of insurance as herein provided, the Lessor may make any payment or payments proper and necessary to procure such insurance or to cure any default which may be relieved against by the payment of money, and the Lessee will thereupon on demand reimburse and pay to the Lessor the amount so paid or expended, with interest thereon at the rate of eight per cent (8%) per annum from the date of any payment made, and a like rate of interest shall be payable upon all arrearages of rent herein provided to be paid. There is reserved to the Lessor the right at all reasonable times to enter upon the premises for the purpose of inspection of the building and such other purposes as may be necessary or proper for the reasonable protection of his interest in the premises.

Lien of lessor upon leasehold estate. (*j*) That for the payment of all rents hereby reserved and all amounts becoming at any time due hereunder by reason of any engagement of the Lessee, the Lessor shall have a valid and first lien upon all buildings and improvements upon the leased premises and upon the leasehold estate hereby created in favor of the Lessee therein. No act done or suffered by the Lessee shall in any manner affect the reversionary estate of the Lessor in the demised premises or his lien hereby created, and nothing herein contained shall authorize the Lessee on his behalf to perform any act which may in any way incumber or change the title of his said interest in the premises.

3. MUTUAL COVENANTS:

Waiver. (*a*) No waiver of any breach of any covenant, condition or stipulation hereunder shall be taken to be a waiver of any succeeding breach of the same covenant, condition or stipulation.

Lease not extinguished by destruction of building. (*b*) That no damage to or destruction of any building or buildings on the premises by fire or other casualties shall be taken to entitle the Lessee to surrender possession of the demised premises or terminate this lease.

Notice. (*c*) That all notices that may be proper or necessary for the parties hereto to serve upon each other, in case either of them shall have no generally known and recognized place of business within the City of .... may be effectually served by delivering the same to such Trust Company or to such person or persons or institution within the City of .... as may be designated by written notice served by either upon the other.

Demand for rent after same payable. (*d*) Any demand for rent or other payment made upon the Lessee after the same has become due and payable shall have the same effect as though made at the time of its becoming due and payable, and any previous demand therefor is hereby waived.

Fixing rights of parties in land and buildings at end of term. (*e*) During the first six (6) months of the last year of the term of this lease the parties hereto shall by agreement between them ascertain and fix the value of the premises hereby leased in connection with all buildings constructed thereon in like manner as if the same were all under single ownership and this lease extinguished, as well as the value of such building and land separately, that is, the amount which should be apportioned to each of them in making up such gross valuation and thereupon the Lessor shall have the first option and privilege of purchasing said buildings at the expiration of said term at the price so fixed as the value of the same, and in case of his failure or refusal so to make such purchase and pay such price for such building before the expiration of the term, the Lessee shall then immediately have the right and privilege of purchasing the land hereby leased exclusive of buildings and improvements, at the price so fixed upon the same, and in case the Lessee shall not exercise such privilege and make such payment within a period of twenty (20) days from and after the termination of such lease, then from such time forward the Lessor and the Lessee shall be taken to the owners of the entire property, land and buildings in the proportion of interest based upon such relative value of land and buildings as above provided for and mutual conveyance shall be made of the interests so acquired.

If the parties shall not before six (6) months prior to the expiration of such term so agree upon and fix such valuation of land, buildings and entire property as above provided, then each of them shall select a resident free holder of said city as an arbitrator and notify the other of his choice within the first twenty (20) days of the last six (6) months of such last year of said term, and the two (2) so chosen shall within ten (10) days thereafter select a third resident free holder of said city and the three (3) so selected shall proceed to fix such valuation in like manner as above provided in case of the parties doing so and make their report in writing to the parties, the report and award of any two (2) of them being equally conclusive with that of all of them. Should either party fail to so select and notify the other within a period of ten (10) days after being so notified of the selection of the other, then the right to select a second free holder with like effect as if selected by the party so notified and in default, as well as the right to select a third free holder in case the arbitrators selected shall fail to select as above provided shall be vested in the person (or in the eldest one if more than one) then for the longest time consecutively occupying the position of Judge in the Court of Common Pleas, or in case there be no Court of Common Pleas, in the other County Court of general jurisdiction of .... County, Ohio, most nearly corresponding thereto. In case such valuation shall not have been fixed by agreement or arbitration as above provided at or before the termination of this lease by limitation, then the same may, on or before the termination of this lease by limitation, on the application of either party be fixed by any court of competent jurisdiction, and the term of this lease shall in such case be extended until the same by final agreement be so fixed. Thereupon the Lessor shall for a period of ten (10) days have the option given to purchase such building, and in case of his failure so to do, the Lessee shall, for the next succeeding ten (10) days have the option to so purchase the land hereby leased, and in case of his failure so to do, the entire premises shall be held and owned in common as above provided.

Rights of parties in case of appropriation to public use. (*f*) If prior to the exercise of the option of purchase herein provided for, any portion of the leased premises be taken by appropriation to public use, under right of eminent domain, such option of purchase shall thereafter apply to the remaining portion of the premises, except that there shall be an abatement of the amount of the purchase price corresponding with the proportion which the value of the land so taken (exclusive of improvements) may bear to the value of the entire premises (exclusive of improvements) at the time of such taking of the same, and in case of any such taking at any time during the continuance of the term of this lease there shall be a like proportionate abatement of the rent thereafter to be paid, and of the amount awarded for such taking of such portion of the leased premises (inclusive of improvements) the Lessor shall receive the then present worth of his reversionary estate in the portion of the land taken and the then present worth of the future rents covered by such abatement as his portion of the entire damages sustained from such appropriation and the remainder of the amount of such award shall be received by the Lessee as his portion of such damages.

If the entire premises be so taken during the term hereof, this lease shall thereupon be taken to be wholly terminated and the award received for the entire taking of the same (inclusive of improvements) shall be divided between the parties in like manner as above provided.

In case the parties shall not be able to agree upon such proportion of value of the premises so taken within a period of ten (10) days after the time of such taking, then such proportion of value shall be fixed in like manner as is herein provided under clause (e) of the mutual covenants of this instrument.

Conditions of grant. (g) This lease is made upon the condition that Lessee shall perform all the covenants and agreements herein set forth to be performed by him and if at any time there be default on the part of the Lessee in the payment of rent, taxes, assessments or other charges and payments by him to be made, or either of them, or any part thereof, and if such default shall continue for a period of ninety (90) days, or if there shall be default on the part of the Lessee in the performance or observance of any of the remaining covenants or agreements hereof by him to be observed and performed, and such default shall continue for a period of sixty (60) days after written notice of such default being given by the Lessor to the Lessee and to any mortgagee or grantee in trust who shall have given to the Lessor written notice of the existence of the interest held by him in the property, the Lessor at any time thereafter shall without demand or notice (which are hereby waived) have full right, at his election upon sixty (60) days' notice to enter upon the demised premises and take immediate possession thereof and bring suit for and collect all rents, taxes, assessments, payments or other charges which shall have accrued up to the time of such entry; and thereupon from the time of such entry, this lease and all rights herein granted shall become void to all intents and purposes whatsoever and all improvements made on said premises shall be forfeited to the said Lessor, without compensation therefor to the Lessee; provided also that for rents due and non-performance of other conditions the Lessor may sue at once but not enter into possession upon forfeiture, except as above provided.

IN WITNESS WHEREOF, The said Lessor and Lessee have hereunto affixed their names as of the day and year first above written, this instrument being executed in duplicate.

(Signatures, acknowledgments, and so forth.)

BUILDING AGREEMENT

(This building agreement was used by the New York Central Rail-road [now Penn Central Railroad] as part of the lease agreement beginning on page 356. This building agreement provides for the use of the shell of an existing structure.)

BUILDING AGREEMENT made this .... day of ...., 1957, between the NEW YORK STATE REALTY AND TERMINAL COMPANY, hereinafter called the Lessor, party of the first part, and ...., hereinafter called the Lessee, party of the second part;

WHEREAS, The New York Central Railroad Company has constructed certain railroad and terminal structures and improvements within the subsurface of that parcel of land in the Borough of Manhattan, City of New York, bounded and described as follows:
....
....

Subject to such slight variations as may appear upon survey by City Surveyor; and

WHEREAS, the Lessee has by agreement of lease bearing even date and to be delivered simultaneously herewith, hereinafter referred to as the Lease, taken and hired from the Lessor the portion of said parcel of land not used for railroad and terminal purposes (the portion of the parcel of land above described upon which the railroad and terminal structures and improvements are constructed or are to be constructed, which is excepted from the Lease, being herein and therein called the "excepted space," is shown on Plot Plan attached to the Lease); and

WHEREAS, the Lessee is desirous of having the right to reconstruct the present building into a new high-grade building (intended for use for store and office purposes and in connection with such use, if permitted by law and City ordinances, for the parking of cars of occupants of spaces in the building, and for such other purposes as may be approved by the Lessor) upon the portion of said parcel of land not used for railroad and terminal purposes, to which the Lessor consents; and

WHEREAS, the parties hereto desire by this agreement to provide for the reconstruction by the Lessee of such building upon said parcel of land as aforesaid, under and in accordance with the terms and conditions hereinafter set forth;

WITNESSETH:

That the parties hereto for and in consideration of the premises, and of the sum of One Dollar ($1.00) each to the other duly paid, the receipt whereof is hereby acknowledged, do covenant and agree to and with each other as follows:

FIRST. That "as soon as the Lessee shall have obtained possession of premises under tenancies expiring on September 30, 1960," the Lessee shall at its own cost and expense:

(a) Commence the demolition of portions of the building at present constructed upon the parcel of land above described, other than the portions thereof within the excepted space, as shown on the plans and specifications referred to in subdivision (b) hereof, in a manner and in accordance with the rules, regulations and requirements of the departments of the City of New York having supervision over such demolition and also in accordance with such rules, regulations and requirements as may be imposed by the Chief Engineer of the Lessor, herein called the Engineer, having regard to the protection of the railroad, station and terminal tracks and structures within the excepted space and the safe and uninterrupted operation of railroad trains and cars therein; provided, however, that portions of said building at present on said parcel of land (such as columns, supports, foundations, steel work and floor arches) need not be demolished in so far as provision for utilization of such portions is made in the plans and specifications referred to in subdivision (b) hereof; and provided further that, with the consent of the Engineer, new footing work and modifications of existing structures, including those within the excepted space, may be commenced prior to the commencement of the work of demolition;

(b) Cause to be prepared by architects approved by the Lessor, herein called the Architects, plans and specifications for a high-grade fully air conditioned building (designed for store and office purposes and in connection with such use, if permitted by law and City ordinances, for the parking of cars of occupants of spaces in the building, and for such other purposes as may be approved by the Lessor) to be reconstructed upon that portion of the parcel of land above described which is not within the excepted space and upon the easement to maintain supports for the building; said plans and specifications shall provide for a high-grade fully air conditioned building designed for store and office purposes and other uses approved by the Lessor as aforesaid, of skeleton steel construction of not less than twenty (20) stories in height and containing not less than four hundred thousand (400,000) square feet of space; the character, design and type of building shall be subject in all respects to the approval of the Lessor, and the plans and specifications therefor shall be subject in all respects to the approval of the Engineer; and the Lessee shall pay or cause to be paid to the Lessor upon demand the reasonable cost of all work, including engineering, architectural, consultant, accounting and other services performed by the Engineer in checking and approving said plans and specifications;

said plans and specifications shall provide for the changes necessary in the existing columns, supports and foundations of the existing building within the excepted space and the additional columns, supports and foundations necessary to be constructed within the excepted space, in order to support the new building provided for in the plans and specifications, it being understood that all such changes in existing columns, supports and foundations shall be made in such manner and all such additional columns, supports and foundations shall be constructed at such locations within the excepted space and in such manner as shall be approved by the Engineer, having regard in each instance to the protection of the railroad and terminal structures and improvements and railroad operations within the excepted space; any new columns to be constructed within the excepted space shall extend in height to the elevation of the plane described in the Lease, and together with their bracings and foundations, shall be separate from the railroad structures and their foundations in the excepted space and the plans and specifications, in so far as they affect the excepted space, shall be prepared subject in all respects to the approval of the Engineer. Where any piping, wiring, ducts or conduits of the building are to be supported below the ground floor a hung ceiling or basement floor shall be constructed by the Lessee which shall be thoroughly waterproofed and drained into the building drainage system, with enclosing walls built on all sides and plastered on the sides towards the tracks; the changes in the existing columns, supports and foundations in the space excepted from the Lease and the new columns, supports and foundations to be constructed therein, the girders which are to carry the steel work of the building over the excepted space, and the steel to be used in the construction of the basement floor or hung ceiling over the excepted space, are to be furnished and erected by the Lessee and the cost thereof, together with the cost of the basement floor or hung ceiling and the fireproofing of said girders and steel of the basement floor or hung ceiling shall be paid by the Lessee.

Copies of the plans and specifications shall be furnished to the Lessor by the Architects, as soon as reasonably may be after the preparation of said plans and specifications, and upon the completion of the work herein provided for, one copy of all original design, contract, detail and shop drawings, together with one copy of the specifications, shall be corrected for work as built and be turned over by the Architects to the Lessor, to become the property of the Lessor.

In case the Lease shall be terminated by reason of default or otherwise as provided in the Lease, before the construction and completion of the new building in accordance with the terms and provisions of this agreement, then and in such event all plans, reports, estimates and models which shall have been prepared or made in connection with such new building shall become the property of the Lessor, and the Lessee in such event shall deliver or cause to be delivered to the Lessor all such plans, reports, estimates and models.

The word "construct" or "construction" or the words "reconstruct or reconstruction", or any similar words, wherever used in this Building Agreement or in the Lease shall be deemed to refer to the reconstruction of the existing building, or to the construction of the new building, whichever the Lessee elects to undertake.

SECOND. (a) That after the plans and specifications for the building to be constructed upon the parcel of land above described shall have been prepared by the Architects as aforesaid, and approved by the Lessor, and the departments of the City of New York having oversight of said construction, the Lessee shall, within a reasonable time, at its own cost and expense, proceed to construct or cause to be constructed in accordance with said plans and specifications the building, including all girders which are to carry the building columns, the steel to be used in the construction of the basement floor or hung ceiling, the fireproofing of said girders and said steel of the basement floor or hung ceiling, the construction of the basement floor or hung ceiling, the changes in the existing columns, supports and foundations within the space excepted from the Lease and the new columns, supports and foundations to be constructed therein, the curbs and sidewalks, the air intake shafts, ventilating shafts, and pent houses for the use of the Lessor all as shown on the plans and specifications, it being agreed that all work within or affecting the excepted space shall be performed by a contractor approved by the Lessor.

(b) The work of construction provided for in this Paragraph Second shall be done in a good and workmanlike manner and shall at all times be subject to inspection by and the approval of the Architects and the Engineer (the mill, shop and field inspection of steel to be done by the Engineer at the expense of the Lessee) and all such work shall be done in accordance with the plans and specifications and in accordance with the requirements of the various departments of the State of New York and City of New York, having or claiming authority in respect of such construction, and the material used shall be proper and appropriate and approved by the Architects and the Engineer, and the various State and Municipal departments as aforesaid, and as provided for in said plans and specifications.

Special precautions as required by the Terminal Manager of Grand Central Terminal, herein called the Terminal Manager, for the safeguarding of the railroad and terminal structures and improvements and the operation of trains and cars in the excepted space shall be taken by and at the expense of the Lessee and in accordance with the requirements of the plans and specifications, and the erection (except riveting) of all steel and the demolition of the existing building shall be done during such times as the tracks within the excepted space and in 48th Street, 49th Street and Park Avenue are not in use for operating revenue trains unless otherwise permitted by the Terminal Manager, and subject to such rules and regulations as may be prescribed by the Terminal Manager; and the Lessee shall pay for any inspectors, flagmen, and watchmen which the Terminal Manager may place on the work during the demolition of the building and the erection of the steel for the building over the space excepted from the Lease.

THIRD. That the Lessee shall make such arrangements with the Engineer for the performance of engineering and other work as may be required in connection with the preparation of plans and the construction of the foundations within the excepted space, as may from time to time be approved by the Architects and the Engineer, and the Lessee shall pay or cause to be paid upon the rendition of bills therefor the cost of all such engineering and other work so approved and performed as aforesaid, including engineering, architectural, consultant and accounting service, insurance, permits, printing, equipment and office rental, inspection, qualified watchmen, construction of side track, train crews engaged in switching cars by reason of utilization of storage tracks at the site of such work, work train and all other miscellaneous service.

FOURTH. That the Lessee shall at all times indemnify and save harmless the Lessor from any and all mechanics' or other liens filed in connection with the work specified in Paragraph Second hereof or any conditional sales of or chattel mortgages upon any materials, fixtures or articles used in the construction of or appurtenant to the building, to be constructed upon the parcel of land above described, and upon request therefor by the Lessor shall satisfy or discharge, or cause to be satisfied or discharged, all such liens, conditional sales and chattel mortgages, if any. The Lessor may, however, at any time prior to the satisfaction or discharge of such liens, conditional sales or chattel mortgages by the Lessee, satisfy and discharge the same, by bonding or payment (in case the Lessee shall refuse or neglect after thirty (30) days' notice in writing from the Lessor to cause the cancellation of said liens as affecting the lands of the Lessor by bonding or otherwise discharging the same) and the amount paid by the Lessor shall be deemed additional Ground Rental payable under the Lease, falling due on the first day of the month next following the date of such payment and shall be payable by the Lessee at such time, and all the provisions of the Lease in respect of the rights of the Lessor in case of default in payment of the Ground Rental shall be applicable to any default in the payment of such additional Ground Rental under this Paragraph Fourth. Nothing herein contained, however, shall be deemed to prevent the Lessee from contesting in good faith any such liens, conditional sales or chattel mortgages provided the Lessee shall satisfactorily indemnify the Lessor against any loss by reason of its failure to satisfy and discharge the same.

That the Lessee shall do the work specified in Paragraph Second hereof in accordance with the regulations of the departments of the City of New York having supervision of such construction as above provided, and in case of the filing of a notice of violation of any of the regulations of any of said departments against said work or in connection therewith, the Lessee shall at its own cost and expense do all necessary work in order to cause the cancellation of any such notice of violation, and cause the same to be cancelled, and upon the completion of the work shall obtain all certificates required from the various municipal departments of the City of New York in respect thereof; the Lessee shall, however, have the right in good faith, at its own expense, to contest the validity or legality of any notice of violation filed in respect of said work, and pending such contest actively conducted by the Lessee, the non-compliance with the requirement of such notice shall not be deemed a default on the part of the Lessee under this Paragraph, provided the Lessee shall have furnished to the Lessor indemnity satisfactory to the Lessor against any loss on the part of the Lessor by reason of the non-compliance with the requirement of said notice.

The Lessee shall, at all times, indemnify and save harmless the Lessor, The New York and Harlem Railroad Company, The New York Central Railroad Company and The New York, New Haven and Hartford Railroad Company, from any and all damages and costs and claims for same growing out of loss of life or damage or injury to person or property occurring during and in connection with the work of demolishing the present building and constructing the new building upon the parcel of land above described, and shall, at its own cost and expense, cause Casualty, Employers' Liability and Workmen's Compensation Insurance in approved companies to be taken out in such amounts as will protect the Lessor, The New York and Harlem Railroad Company, The New York Central Railroad Company, The New York, New Haven and Hartford Railroad Company and the Lessee from any and all such loss, damage or injury, and shall furnish copies of said policies to the Lessor.

The Lessee shall also furnish to the Lessor policies of fire insurance in companies satisfactory to the Lessor in an amount equal to the expenditures from time to time made by the Lessee in such reconstruction, and in case of any loss or damage to the building to be reconstructed upon the parcel of land above described by fire prior to the completion thereof, the sums recoverable under such insurance policies shall be paid and disbursed as provided in Paragraph Seventh of the Lease.

FIFTH. That the Lessee shall cause the building to be reconstructed upon the parcel of land above described with all reasonable expedition and shall have the same completed free from liens of any kind except the mortgage on the leasehold, if any, and the building ready for occupancy within a reasonable time after the demolition of the existing building upon the parcel of land above described, but not later than September 30, 1963, unless prevented by fire, lock-out, strike, act of war or enemy hostilities, or other cause or casualty beyond the control of the Lessee, and in case of failure to complete the building to be constructed upon the parcel of land above described within the time aforesaid by reason of any or all of said causes, then the Lessee shall have the same completed and the building ready for occupancy within such period after September 30, 1963, as shall be equal to the time that the Lessee shall have been so delayed by any or all of said causes.

SIXTH. That the Lessee shall prior to the time of commencement of the reconstruction of the existing building upon the parcel of land above described, execute and deliver to the Lessor a bond in an amount equal to the estimated cost of the building to be constructed upon the parcel of land above described, as estimated by the Engineer and Architects, with such surety or sureties as shall be satisfactory to the Lessor, conditioned upon the construction and completion of the building to be constructed upon the parcel of land above described, in accordance with the plans and specifications, by the Lessee with all reasonable expedition after the demolition of said existing building, unless prevented by the causes mentioned in Paragraph Fifth hereof, and in case of a delay in completion by reason of any or all of said causes, then conditioned upon the completion of said building as soon as reasonably may be having regard to the time that the Lessee shall have been so delayed by any or all of said causes, in accordance with the plans and specifications, free from all mechanics' liens, chattel mortgages, and conditional bills of sale, and conditioned further upon the due and prompt payment by the Lessee of all sums required to construct and complete the building to be reconstructed upon the parcel of land above described in accordance with the plans and specifications, free from mechanics' liens, chattel mortgages, and conditional bills of sale. As an alternative to the above provision of this Paragraph the Lessee may furnish to the Lessor such other security as may be satisfactory to the Lessor, assuring the reconstruction and completion of the new building upon the parcel of land above described within the time set forth above and in accordance with the plans and specifications, free from mechanics' liens, chattel mortgages, and conditional bills of sale.

If the Lessee shall deposit cash or such other security as shall be satisfactory to the Lessor in a manner approved by the Lessor, and under a deposit agreement satisfactory to the Lessor, which deposit agreement shall contain conditions similar to those above provided for with respect to said bond and shall provide for the application of said deposit towards the cost of the work of reconstruction of the building as such work progresses under certificates approved both as to form and the amount of the payment to be made thereunder by the Engineer, the amount of said bond or the security furnished under the preceding alternative provision shall be decreased by the amount of cash and the value of such security so deposited, and if the cash and the value of such other security shall amount to the estimated cost of reconstructing said building as aforesaid, the bond shall be dispensed with.

SEVENTH. In case the Lessee shall fail to prosecute said work of reconstruction with reasonable diligence, or shall abandon said work before the completion thereof, or shall fail to bond or otherwise discharge any mechanics' liens filed against said work, or to pay and discharge any chattel mortgages, or conditional bills of sale (except in each of the foregoing instances in the case of contest, with indemnity as provided in Paragraph Fourth hereof), upon any materials, fixtures or articles used in the construction of, or appurtenant to the building to be constructed upon the parcel of land above described or shall fail (except in the case of contest provided for in Paragraph Fourth hereof) to proceed in good faith and with all expedition to comply with any notices of violations filed against said work by any of the municipal departments of the City of New York, and if after thirty (30) days' notice to the Lessee and to any Leasehold Mortgagee upon the lease-hold rights of the Lessee under the Lease as mentioned in Paragraph Third of said Lease any such default shall not have been remedied, then the Lessor may, if it elects so to do, upon the service upon the Lessee and any such Leasehold Mortgagee of a thirty (30) days' notice in writing to that effect, take over (unless such default shall meanwhile have been remedied), the completion of the construction of the build-ing to be constructed upon the parcel of land above described, and itself complete such work, or cause the same to be completed. In case the Lessor shall take over the completion of the construction of the build-ing as aforesaid, then unless the Lessee shall, within thirty (30) days after the Architects shall have mailed by registered mail to the Lessor and the Lessee a certificate signed by the Architects stating that the said work is completed and the building ready for occupancy, pay over to the Lessor any and all sums paid, or required to be paid by the Lessor in completing the building as aforesaid, free from liens of every kind as aforesaid, together with interest thereon at the rate of five (5%) per centum per annum, and the reasonable charges and expenses of the Lessor for supervision or otherwise in completing said building (a state-ment of the approximate aggregate amount of which sums shall be presented to the Lessee by the Lessor within five (5) days after request made therefor by the Lessee), the Lease shall cease and determine (time being of the essence of this provision) and all rights of the Lessee in and to the parcel of land above described whether under this agreement or under the Lease shall cease and determine; but the Lessee and in case the bond or bonds mentioned in Paragraph Sixth hereof shall be fur-nished, the sureties thereunder shall nevertheless remain liable in dam-ages to the Lessor for any and all loss and damage sustained by the Lessor by reason of the failure of the Lessee to complete the building in accordance with the terms of this agreement, including any and all sums paid by the Lessor as aforesaid in the completion of the building under this Paragraph Seventh, and in case of the deposit by the Lessee of cash or securities as provided in Paragraph Sixth hereof, the deposit agreement shall provide for the application of such deposit towards the payment of the amount of the expenditures and charges of the Lessor in the completion of the building as aforesaid; provided, however, that in the event the Lessor is reimbursed for all sums paid by the Lessor as aforesaid in the completion of the building within thirty (30) days after the delivery and mailing of said certificate of the Architects as aforesaid, then the Lease shall not cease and determine and all rights of the Lessee and of any such Leasehold Mortgagee shall continue in the same manner as if the Lessor had not taken over completion of the construction of the building as provided in this Paragraph. In case the Lessee shall, within thirty (30) days after the delivery and mailing of said certificate as aforesaid, pay over to the Lessor the approximate aggregate amount of the sums paid or required to be paid by the Lessor in the completion of the building as aforesaid in accordance with the statement presented by the Lessor to the Lessee upon request as aforesaid (less such amounts, if any, as shall have been credited thereon) and if at the time of such payment by the Lessee all the sums required to be paid by the Lessor in the completion of the building shall not as yet have been paid, so that the actual amount required to be paid by the Lessor in the completion of the building is undetermined, then, upon the final payment being made by the Lessor on account of the cost of the completion of the building as aforesaid, an accounting shall be had between the Lessor and the Lessee, whereby the Lessor shall pay over to the Lessee, or the Lessee shall pay over to the Lessor, as the case may be, such sum as the amount paid by the Lessee as aforesaid, shall be in excess of or less than the actual amount, with interest as aforesaid, paid by the Lessor as aforesaid in the completion of said building. Any notice provided for in this agreement shall be given as provided in Paragraph Seventeenth of the Lease. All rights and remedies of the Lessor herein set forth shall be in addition to and not in substitution of the rights and remedies of the Lessor contained in the Lease.

EIGHTH. If any disputes shall arise between the parties hereto in respect of the intent of the said plans and specifications for the building, all and every such question in dispute shall be submitted for determination to a reputable Architect of the City of New York, either to be agreed upon by the parties hereto, or (in case of disagreement between the parties as to such Architect) to be appointed by the person who is then the Presiding Justice of the Appellate Division of the Supreme Court of the State of New York for the First Department upon the application of one of the parties hereto upon reasonable notice to the other party, or in case the person who is then the Presiding Justice of said Appellate Division shall decline to make such appointment, then said Architect shall be appointed by such one of the other Justices of said Appellate Division as shall consent to make such appointment, application being made to said Justices as aforesaid in the order of seniority of designation.

The determination of the Architect so agreed upon or appointed as aforesaid shall be binding and conclusive upon the parties hereto. One-half of the cost and expenses (including the fees of said Architect) of any such determination shall be borne and paid by the Lessor, and one-half of said cost and expense shall be borne and paid by the Lessee.

NINTH. The Lessor hereby consents to the demolition of the present building and the reconstruction of the building as hereinbefore provided. Whenever approval by the Lessor shall be required under the terms of this agreement, such approval shall not be unreasonably withheld or delayed.

IN WITNESS WHEREOF, the parties hereto have caused the execution of this building agreement the day and year first above written.

STATE OF NEW YORK ⎫
COUNTY OF NEW YORK ⎬ ss.:

On the .... day of ...., 1957, before me personally came ...., to me known,
who, being by me duly sworn, did depose and say that he resides at
..................................; that he is ....
President of NEW YORK STATE REALTY AND TERMINAL COM-
PANY, the corporation described in and which executed the above
instrument; that he knows the seal of said Corporation; that the seal
affixed to said instrument was such corporate seal; that it was so affixed
by authority of the Board of Directors of said Corporation, and that he
signed his name thereto by like authority.

STATE OF NEW YORK ⎫
COUNTY OF NEW YORK ⎬ ss.:

On the .... day of ...., 1957, before me personally came ...., to me known,
who, being by me duly sworn, did depose and say that he resides at
..................................; that he is ....
President of ...., the corporation described in and
which executed the above instrument; that he knows the seal of said
Corporation; that the seal affixed to said instrument was such corporate
seal; that it was so affixed by authority of the Board of Directors of said
Corporation, and that he signed his name thereto by like authority.

LEASE OF AIR RIGHTS

*(This is a lease of air rights made by the New York State Realty
and Terminal Company—a subsidiary of the New York Central Railroad—of property on Park Avenue in Manhattan. It is applicable to
long-term lease agreements where there is a provision for re-appraisal
at the end of a specified term of years. This is one of the most complete air rights agreements encountered.)*

AGREEMENT OF LEASE made this .... day of ....,
1957, between NEW YORK STATE REALTY AND TERMINAL COMPANY, a corporation of the State of New York, having its principal office at No. 466
Lexington Avenue, Borough of Manhattan, City and State of New York,
hereinafter called the "Lessor", ...
....
hereinafter called the "Lessee";

WHEREAS, the Lessor, under grant from The New York Central
Railroad Company and The New York and Harlem Railroad Company,
is the owner of a term of twenty-eight (28) years and one (1) month,

with the right to two additional terms of twenty-one (21) years each, in the portion not now to be used for railroad or terminal purposes, of that parcel of land hereinafter described ....

....

WHEREAS, the Lessee is desirous that a lease be made to it of said parcel of land, for the term, at the rentals and additional rentals, upon the covenants, conditions, limitations and agreements, and subject to the exceptions and reservations herein contained, and the Lessor and Lessee are entering into a building agreement bearing even date herewith (hereinafter referred to as the "Building Agreement"), providing for the reconstruction by the Lessee of the building upon said parcel of land, above the space excepted as herein provided;

WITNESSETH:

Demised Premises. That the Lessor has agreed to let, and hereby does let unto the Lessee, and the Lessee has agreed to take and hereby does take and hire from the Lessor, for the term, at the rentals and additional rentals, and upon the covenants, conditions, limitations and agreements herein contained, and with the exceptions and reservations herein set forth, all the portion, not hereinafter excepted, of that parcel of land in the Borough of Manhattan, City of New York, together with the buildings and improvements now or hereafter erected thereon, bounded and described as follows: ....

....

....

Excepted Space. Subject to the usual nuisance restrictions, to existing tenancies, and to such slight variations as may appear upon survey by City Surveyor.

Excepting, however, from the above described parcel of land all the following portion thereof (the elevations hereinafter referred to, and shown on the plot plan marked "Plot Plan No. 1" hereto attached, have reference to the datum plane of The New York Central Railroad Company which takes for its elevation 0'0" mean high water mark of the East River at the foot of East 26th Street): ....

....

The said excepted portion of said parcel of land being shown on plot plan hereto attached, entitled "Plot Plan No. 1, Showing Limits & Planes," dated August 27, 1957, and identified by the signature of F. H. Simpson, Chief Engineer of The New York Central Railroad Company.

The Lessor and the occupants of the excepted space shall also have the right to attach, repair, renew and maintain ducts, pipes, conduits and overhead contact rails and their supports to the underside of the building girders, floor beams and hung ceilings of the Building constructed over said excepted portion of the parcel of land above described.

Reserving also to the Lessor, its successors or assigns, and the occupants of the excepted space, the use of two ventilating ducts or shafts each of an inside area of forty (40) square feet extending up through the Building and above the roof of the Building constructed upon the parcel of land above described at the locations referred to in the Building Agreement, together with the right to construct and maintain penthouses and motors and fans upon the roof of the Building at the locations of said ventilating shafts, and to operate said motors and fans.

Reserving also to the Lessor, the right to maintain the structures required for the support of Park Avenue, and for the support of the paved way hereinafter mentioned, as shown on plot plan hereto attached, dated August 27, 1957, entitled "Plot Plan No. 2, Showing Viaduct Column Locations," and identified by the signature of F. H. Simpson, Chief Engineer of The New York Central Railroad Company.

It is understood and agreed between the parties hereto that there is also demised to the Lessee (1) until the existing building shall be reconstructed as provided in the Building Agreement an easement to maintain within the excepted space for the support of the existing building the columns, supports and foundations of the existing building, and (2) during the term of this lease and any renewal thereof, if any there be, an easement to maintain within the excepted space for the support of the building hereafter to be erected, pursuant to the Building Agreement, upon the parcel of land above described (or any building or buildings erected in the place thereof by the Lessee under the provisions of this lease) the columns, supports and foundations of the existing building now constructed and the columns, supports and foundations which may hereafter be constructed pursuant to the Building Agreement within the excepted space, and the Lessee does hereby covenant and agree at all times during the term of this lease, and any renewal thereof, if any there be, at its own cost and expense to maintain, renew and replace said columns, supports and foundations now or at any time constructed within the excepted space as aforesaid (including any columns erected in substitution for or renewal of any of said columns) of unimpaired strength and in good repair and in accordance with such plans and specifications and under such rules and regulations as the Engineer of the Lessor may from time to time approve and prescribe, for the purpose of safeguarding the railroad and terminal structures and improvements within said excepted space and the operation of the railroads within said excepted space.

Excepting from the above described parcel of land all subsurface rights in and to Park Avenue, and also all subsurface rights in and to the strip of land hereinafter mentioned adjoining on the west the above described parcel of land, a right of way over which is hereinafter granted to the Lessee.

Term. For a term of twenty-eight (28) years to commence on the first day of December, 1957, and to end on the 30th day of November, 1985, YIELDING AND PAYING therefor to the Lessor the following annual rentals or sums (hereinafter referred to as Ground Rental) and the additional rentals hereinafter set forth:

Rental. On the first day of each and every month thereafter, until (a) the date of completion of the new building (as hereinafter defined) to

be constructed upon the premises by the Lessee pursuant to the Building
Agreement, or (b) November 30, 1963, whichever date shall first occur;
and an annual ground rental of ....
....
in advance on the date of completion of the new building, or on December 1, 1963, whichever date shall first occur, and on the first day of each
and every month in each and every year thereafter ensuing during the
balance of the initial term of this lease except as provided in Paragraph
Twelfth in the event that such term is extended.

Date of Completion. The "date of completion of the new building"
herein referred to shall be deemed to be the first day of the month during
which (a) a temporary certificate of occupancy shall be issued, or (b)
any part of the new building shall be occupied by any tenant, occupant
or licensee, or (c) an architect selected by the Lessor shall certify in
writing that the new building is complete and ready for occupancy,
whichever of said events shall first occur. Nothing herein, however,
shall be deemed to alter, modify or affect the provisions of the Building
Agreement specifying the time within which the Lessee shall commence
and complete the construction of the new building.

Subject, however, to the exclusive rights of the Lessor, The New
York Central Railroad Company, The New York and Harlem Railroad
Company and The New York, New Haven and Hartford Railroad Company (hereinafter called the "Railroad Companies") and each of them,
their and each of their successors and assigns, grantees and licensees,
to occupy the excepted space (being that portion of the parcel of land
above described below the plane shown on said Plot Plan No. 1) and
the subsurface of 48th Street, 49th Street and Park Avenue as hereinbefore excepted from the above described parcel of land, and the subsurface of the strip of land hereinafter referred to, adjoining the above
described premises on the west, for the construction, maintenance and
operation of railroad and terminal structures and improvements, and
for such other structures and improvements as the Lessor and the Railroad Companies, their or any of their successors or assigns, may from
time to time or at any time or times hereafter deem advisable to construct
or maintain therein, and for the operation therein and thereunder of
the railroads operated by the respective Railroad Companies, their and
each of their successors and assigns, and of such other companies as shall
lawfully secure the right to use or operate the railroads operated by said
Railroad Companies respectively, and for such other uses and purposes
(exclusive of such other uses and purposes as will injuriously affect the
use and enjoyment of the demised premises by the Lessee) as the Railroad Companies or any of them, their or any of their successors or assigns,
may from time to time, or at any time or times hereafter, deem advisable
to occupy or use said excepted space, or to permit, or to grant the right
to others to occupy or use said excepted space, and the Lessee shall
construct, maintain, renew and replace the columns, supports and foundations of the Building in such manner as will not interfere with the
maintenance, operation and use of the railroad, station and terminal

structures and improvements located within the excepted space and the operation of the railroads operated by the respective Railroad Companies therein; provided, however, that the Lessor shall reimburse the Lessee for any expense incurred by the Lessee in repairing, renewing or replacing columns, supports or foundations of the Building and in repairing the Building where such repair, renewal or replacement is made necessary by reason of damage to such columns, supports or foundations or to the Building caused by the respective Railroad Companies or by any other railroad within the excepted space, or their respective agents, servants or employees.

It is further understood and agreed between the parties hereto:

(a) That there is also demised to the Lessee during the term of this lease the right to use in connection with the premises described in this lease, for the purposes recited in this paragraph and subject to the provisions of this lease, the surface of that portion of the paved way adjoining said premises on the west, which is constructed upon the parcel of land in the Borough of Manhattan, City of New York, bounded and described as follows: ....

....

....

Subject to such encroachments, if any, thereon as may appear upon an accurate survey thereof.

And the Lessee, its successors and assigns, if there be such, shall during the term of this lease, and any renewal thereof, if any there be, have the right to use the surface of the paved way upon the parcel of land described in this paragraph, for the purpose of access to and from 48th Street and to and from 49th Street from and to the building erected upon the parcel of land described in this lease. Such use by the Lessee of the surface of the portion of the paved way which is constructed over the parcel of land described in this paragraph shall, however, be subject to the use thereof by the Lessor and the Railroad Companies, their and each of their successors, officers, agents, employees, passengers, licensees and assigns, and by such other parties as shall be granted the right or permitted by the Lessor and the Railroad Companies, their or any of their successors or assigns, to use said portion of the paved way and shall also be subject to such reasonable rules and regulations as the Lessor may from time to time make in regard to the use thereof and to the payment by the Lessee to the Lessor of the cost of repaving, repairing and otherwise maintaining the surface of said portion of the paved way. No building or other structure shall during the term of this lease, or any renewal or extension thereof, be constructed by the Lessee upon the parcel of land described in this paragraph of a height in excess of 18 feet above the existing established grade of 49th Street at its point of intersection with the center line of said paved way, subject to the proviso that the existing structures now thereon may be maintained thereon.

(b) That in respect of the portion of the paved way which is constructed upon that parcel of land in the Borough of Manhattan, City

of New York, bounded and described as follows: ....
....
....
the Lessor does hereby agree that during the term of this lease and
any renewal thereof, if any there be, the surface of that portion of the
paved way constructed upon the parcel of land described in this paragraph shall be used by the Railroad Companies, their and each of their
officers, agents, employees, licensees and passengers and by such other
parties as shall be granted the right or shall be permitted by the Railroad Companies, their or any of their successors or assigns, to use the
same, only for the purpose of access to and from the premises adjoining
said paved way on the west, or for a restaurant, bar or other purpose in
connection with the said westerly adjoining premises, and that no structure shall be erected upon said parcel of land of a height in excess of
18 feet above the established grade of 48th Street adjoining said parcel
on the south, subject to the proviso that the existing structures now
thereon may be maintained thereon.

And the Lessee does hereby covenant and agree to and with the
Lessor, its successors and assigns, as follows:

Water and Sewer Rents. FIRST. That the Lessee shall well and
punctually pay to the Lessor at Grand Central Terminal, Borough of
Manhattan, City of New York, the Ground Rental above provided on
the days the same is payable, and shall also as additional rental hereunder pay to the proper municipal authorities from time to time as such
water rents, rates and charges and sewer rents shall become payable,
all sums that may during the term of this lease be assessed, imposed
or charged upon the demised premises, or any part thereof, for Croton
or other water rents, rates and charges and sewer rents, whether by
meter or otherwise, exclusive, however, of the sums, if any, imposed
thereon for water used by the Lessor or the Railroad Companies in the
excepted space.

Taxes. That the Lessee shall also as an additional rental hereunder,
during each and every year of the term of this lease, pay to the Lessor
within thirty days after such taxes in any such year shall be payable
(in case said taxes shall be payable in installments, each installment
shall be deemed payable hereunder on the day that such installment
becomes a lien upon the parcel of land above described): (a) a sum of
lawful money of the United States equal to eighty (80%) per centum
of the amount of the taxes, ordinary and extraordinary, for such year,
that may be taxed, charged, imposed or assessed upon the parcel of
land above described (including the portion thereof excepted as aforesaid), or upon the Lessor or the Railroad Companies, or either of them,
their or either of their successors or assigns, on account of the value of
the parcel of land above described, if wholly unimproved; and (b) such
additional sum of lawful money of the United States as will equal the
entire taxes, ordinary and extraordinary, for such year, taxed, charged,
imposed or assessed upon the parcel of land above described (including
the portion thereof excepted as aforesaid), on account of the value of

the improvements thereon (exclusive of the value of the railroad and
terminal structures and improvements within the excepted space), the
value of the improvements being ascertained by deducting from the
assessed value of the land with the improvements thereon the assessed
value of the land if wholly unimproved.

In case in any year the assessment for taxes upon the parcel of land
above described, on account of the value of the improvements constructed thereon, shall include, without separation, the value of the
structures constructed both within and without the excepted space, then,
in arriving at the amount of the taxes on account of improvements payable by the Lessee hereunder, in any such year, a proper deduction
shall be made from the amount of the taxes assessed upon the parcel
of land above described on account of the value of the improvements
constructed thereon, based upon the ratio that the construction cost
of the railroad and terminal structures constructed upon the parcel
of land above described within the excepted space bears to the construction cost of all the structures constructed upon said parcel of
land, including rentals, interest and taxes during construction and any
other items properly chargeable to capital account. In arriving at such
deduction, however, the cost of the columns, supports and foundations
and portions of the Building within the excepted space shall be considered as building structures and not as railroad structures.

The taxes for the year 1957 shall be adjusted as of November 30th,
and the taxes for the last year of the term of this lease, or in case of
renewal, of the last year of such renewal term shall be adjusted as of
November 30th of such last year.

In case, however, at any time or times during the term of this lease
or any renewal or renewals thereof, if any there be, the taxes upon the
parcel of land above described considered as unimproved shall, by
reason of the use of a portion thereof for railroad purposes, be assessed
in a different manner or upon a different basis of assessment than real
estate generally in the City of New York, and in case, by reason thereof,
the taxes so assessed shall be greater or less than if assessed in the same
manner and upon the same basis of assessment as real estate generally in
said City, then there shall be added to or deducted from said taxes, as
the case may be, in arriving at the portion of said taxes payable by the
Lessee hereunder, such sum as shall be equal to the decrease or increase
in such taxes due to such different manner or different basis of assessment.

In case also at any time or times during the term of this lease, or any
renewal or renewals thereof, if any there be, the law in respect of the
method of assessing taxes shall be changed so as to exclude from the
assessment the value, or some portion of the value, of the improvements erected upon lands, and by reason of such change in the method
of assessment the amount of the taxes assessed upon said parcel of land
above described on account of the value of said parcel of land, exclusive
of improvements, shall be increased, then an adjustment shall be had
between the parties hereto as to the amount of the taxes payable by the

parties hereto hereunder respectively subsequent to such time, to the end that the relative proportion of the entire taxes upon said parcel of land (both land and improvements) payable by the parties hereto hereunder prior to such time may thereafter be maintained.

It is further understood and agreed between the parties hereto that no portion of the taxes upon the franchises, business, capital levy, income, profits or revenue of the Lessor, or of the Railroad Companies, its or their respective successors or assigns, shall be payable by the Lessee hereunder, and that no portion of the taxes upon the franchises, business, capital levy, income, profits or revenue of the Lessee, its successors or assigns, shall be payable by the Lessor hereunder.

In case any disagreement shall arise between the parties hereto as to the amount of the taxes payable by the Lessee hereunder, the matter so in disagreement shall be submitted for determination to three arbitrators appointed as provided in Paragraph Fourteenth of this lease, whose decision, or that of a majority of them, shall be binding and conclusive upon the parties hereto. The expense of any such arbitration shall be borne as set forth in said paragraph.

In case of any disagreement as aforesaid, the Lessee shall pay to the Lessor, at the time above provided for the payment of said taxes, on account of the taxes so in disagreement, a sum of money equal to the portion of the taxes of the preceding tax year payable by the Lessee hereunder, and the Lessor shall pay to the proper municipal authorities "under protest" the full amount of the taxes for the tax year so in dispute. Upon the determination by the arbitrators appointed as above provided of the amount of taxes to be paid by the Lessee for such tax year, then the Lessor shall at once pay to the Lessee, or the Lessee shall at once pay to the Lessor, as the case may be, a sum equal to the amount that the sum so paid by the Lessee, on account of said taxes as aforesaid, shall be found to be in excess of or less than the true amount thereof to be paid by the Lessee as determined by said arbitrators, together with interest thereon at the rate of five (5%) per centum per annum.

Assessments and Other Charges. That the Lessee shall also, as an additional rental hereunder, pay to the proper municipal authorities, within thirty (30) days after any such charges or assessments shall be payable, the total amount of any and all other charges and governmental impositions of every kind, and assessments for local improvements or otherwise, that may, during the term of this lease, be taxed, charged, imposed or assessed upon the parcel of land above described (including the portion thereof excepted as aforesaid). The Lessee may arrange for the payment of any such assessment in installments provided, however, that the Lessee shall not arrange for the payment in installments of any such assessment imposed, charged, taxed or assessed upon the parcel of land above described during the last ten years of the term hereof or of any renewal term.

That the Lessee shall, however, have the right, at its own expense, to contest in good faith by legal proceedings conducted promptly, by

legal counsel satisfactory to the Lessor, in the name of the Lessee or
Lessor, any water rents, sewer rents, taxes, charges or assessments imposed upon the parcel of land above described, and in case any such
water rents, sewer rents, taxes, charges or assessments shall, as a result
of any such legal proceedings, be reduced, cancelled, set aside or otherwise discharged, the Lessee shall be entitled to receive its proportion
of such water rents, sewer rents, taxes, charges or assessments, with
interest, if any, thereon recovered, which has theretofore been paid to
the Lessor as herein provided. In case, however, such legal proceedings
shall be conducted in the name of the Lessor, the Lessee shall indemnify
and save harmless the Lessor from any costs, charges or expenses in
connection therewith. The Lessor shall have the right to intervene or
otherwise participate, by its own legal counsel at its own expense, in
the conduct and appeal of any such legal proceedings, and no settlement
of such proceedings shall be made without the consent of both Lessor
and Lessee.

That in case the Lessor shall fail to pay any of the taxes or assessments imposed upon the parcel of land above described within ten days
after receipt from the Lessee of the amount of such taxes or assessments
payable by the Lessee hereunder, the Lesse shall have the right to pay
any such taxes or assessments, with penalties, so unpaid and set off
the amount so paid, with interest thereon at the rate of five (5%) per
centum per annum, *pro tanto* against the rental payments falling due
hereunder subsequent to such time.

SECOND. That for the purposes of this lease the word "Building"
means the existing building as long as the parcel of land first above
described shall be occupied by the building at present located thereon,
and, upon the reconstruction of the existing building as provided in the
Building Agreement, means the building constructed upon the parcel
of land first above described pursuant to the Building Agreement or any
building or buildings at any time constructed in place thereof pursuant
to the terms of this lease.

The words "demised premises" mean the parcel of land first above
described and the improvements at any time constructed thereon, including the columns, supports and foundations of the Building within
the excepted space but excluding the railroad structures and improvements within such space.

The parties declare that all buildings and improvements now standing
upon the premises above described belong to the Lessor, and the Lessor
consents to the demolition of the existing building as provided for in
the Building Agreement. It is agreed that all new buildings, when and
as erected and their appurtenances and additions thereto and any and
all other improvements (excepting trade fixtures installed by and belonging to Lessee or its subtenants) at any time upon said premises shall
immediately, upon erection or installation, become the property and
belong to the Lessor and shall, with the demised premises as a whole,
be surrendered to the Lessor at the termination of this lease.

Repairs, Official Requirements, etc.   That the Lessee shall, during the term of this lease, at its own cost and expense, operate said demised premises, and the elevators and other facilities therein, and maintain and keep in good condition and repair the Building and all parts thereof, both inside and outside (including the columns, supports and foundations of the Building within the space excepted from this lease, except that the Lessor shall reimburse the Lessee for any expense incurred by the Lessee in maintaining, keeping in good condition and repairing the Building and such columns, supports and foundations where such expense is incurred by reason of damage to the Building or to such columns, supports or foundations caused by the respective Railroad Companies or any other railroad therein, or their respective agents, servants or employees) and the fixtures and facilities in the Building or forming part thereof, including all water, drainage, electric lighting, heating, gas, elevator, power, sewer, plumbing and other fixtures and facilities therein, and shall also, at its own cost and expense, comply with, conform to and obey all laws, ordinances, rules, orders and notices of the United States, of the State of New York, of the City of New York, and of the various departments and bureaus of the United States and of said State and City having or claiming any right or authority in respect of the demised premises or the use thereof, or the surfacing of, or removal of snow and ice from, the sidewalks and curbs adjacent to the same; the Lessee shall also indemnify and save harmless the Lessor and the Railroad Companies of and from any and all damages and costs and claims for same growing out of loss of life or damage or injury to persons or property occasioned in the maintenance, repair, use and operation of the demised premises and the fixtures and facilities therein contained, or occasioned by the failure of the Lessee properly to maintain the same in good condition and repair, or properly to maintain the surfacing of the sidewalks and curbs in good condition and repair, or properly to remove the snow and ice from such sidewalks and curbs; and if the Lessee, at any time or times during the continuance of this lease, shall fail or neglect after thirty days' notice in writing from the Lessor to take such action as may be necessary to place said demised premises, fixtures and facilities in good condition and repair, or to comply with the requirements of the United States or of the State or municipal authorities as aforesaid, or to secure the cancellation of the notice of the violations of said requirements, the Lessor shall have the right and is hereby authorized, on reasonable notice, to enter upon the demised premises and every part thereof, and to make such repairs to said demised premises, fixtures and facilities, or to perform such acts in order to conform to the requirements of the United States or of the State and municipal authorities as aforesaid, as the case may be, as may be reasonably necessary, and the expense of any and all such repairs made by the Lessor as aforesaid, and of the compliance with the requirements of said authorities as aforesaid, shall be considered as additional rental hereunder and shall be added to the Ground Rental payment falling due next after the time of such expenditures, and shall be paid by the Lessee at the time of the payment of said Rental.

That the Lessee shall, however, have the right to contest in good faith by legal proceedings conducted promptly and at its own expense, in the name of the Lessee or Lessor, any such violations alleged in respect of the demised premises or the use thereof or the sidewalks or curbs adjacent to the same, and the pendency of any such legal proceedings, in so far as it shall suspend the effect of such violation, shall suspend the right of the Lessor, as set forth in the paragraph next above, to enter upon the demised premises and to make repairs or to perform other acts, but the Lessor shall be indemnified by the Lessee for any damage to the Lessor resulting from such suspension of Lessor's right, as aforesaid.

That the Lessee, its officers, agents, and servants, shall have the right at such reasonable time or times as will interfere as little as possible with the operation of the railroads of the Railroad Companies, to enter into the excepted space for the purpose of inspecting and repairing, or renewing and replacing, the columns, supports, and foundations constructed within said excepted space for the support of the Building. Before entering into the excepted space for any such purpose the Lessee shall notify the Engineer of the Lessor in writing, specifying the purpose for which entry into said excepted space is desired, and shall make such arrangements with said Engineer as to the appropriate time and the conditions which he deems reasonable for such purpose. All work to be performed by the Lessee in the excepted space in repairing, renewing, or replacing the columns, supports, and foundations of the Building shall be performed in accordance with plans and specifications previously submitted to and approved by the Engineer of the Lessor, and under such rules and regulations as may be required by said Engineer, for the purpose of safeguarding the railroad and terminal structures and improvements within said excepted space and the operation of the railroads of the Railroad Companies within said excepted space. The Lessee shall reimburse the Lessor and the Railroad Companies for the wages of watchmen, flagmen, and inspectors furnished by them, or any of them as shall be required by said Engineer during and in connection with such work. The Lessee shall also, at its own cost and expense, provide such insurance as may be required by said Engineer to protect the Lessor and the Railroad Companies from any and all claims, damages, and liabilities growing out of loss of life or damage or injury to person or property occurring during and in connection with such work.

Assignment, Subletting and Mortgaging. THIRD. That this lease and the leasehold estate hereby created may be assigned from time to time to any one or more persons, firms, or corporations; provided however, that at the time of any such assignment no default is existing or continuing in the performance of any of the covenants, conditions, limitations or agreements of this lease on the part of the Lessee to be performed; and provided, further, that any assignment of this lease as herein permitted shall be made only upon the condition, and such assignment shall expressly provide, that the assignee shall assume and agree to pay the rentals and additional rentals accruing under this lease and to comply with and perform all the other covenants, conditions, limitations and agreements on the part of the Lessee to be complied with and performed under this lease and under the Building Agreement. The assignment of this lease or any interest hereunder or the subletting of the demised premises in whole or in part by the Lessee or by any successor or assign of said Lessee shall not be deemed to release or discharge the assignor from any obligation or liability hereunder. At any time after the commencement of the reconstruction of the existing building and provided the Lessee shall not be in default under the terms of this lease or of the Building Agreement, the Lessee shall have the right to mortgage its leasehold rights under this lease subject in all respects to the terms of this lease and of the Building Agreement; the holder of such mortgage upon the leasehold rights of the Lessee (including the trustee thereunder, if such mortgage be in the form of a deed of trust to a trustee to secure an issue of bonds, notes or other corporate obligations) being referred to in Paragraph Tenth hereof as the Leasehold Mortgagee. Any mortgage or deed of trust upon the leasehold estate hereby created shall by its term be made expressly subject to all the Lessor's rights under the provisions, covenants, conditions, exceptions, and reservations contained in this lease and in the Building Agreement. The Lessee shall have the right, however, at any time after the commencement of the term of this lease, to enter into commitments (a) for such building loan as the Lessee may desire for the purpose of constructing the new building pursuant to the Building Agreement, and (b) for such mortgage as the Lessee may desire for the purpose of mortgaging its leasehold rights under this lease in accordance with the foregoing provisions of this Paragraph Third.

Lessee agrees at any time and from time to time upon not less than ten (10) days' prior written request by Lessor, to execute, acknowledge and deliver to Lessor, and Lessor agrees at any time and from time to time, upon not less than ten (10) days' prior written request by Lessee, to execute, acknowledge and deliver to Lessee a statement in writing, certifying that this lease is unmodified and in full force and effect (or if there have been modifications that the same is in full force and effect, as modified and stating the modifications), and the dates to which the basic rent and other charges have been paid in advance, if any, and whether or not there is any existing default by Lessee with respect to any sums of money required to be paid by Lessee under the terms of this lease, or notice of default served by Lessor. If any such certification by Lessor shall allege nonperformance by Lessee, the nature and extent of such nonperformance shall, in so far as actually known by Lessor, be summarized therein.

Occupancy. FOURTH. That as long as the parcel of land above described shall be occupied by the building at present thereon the Lessee shall use the demised premises only as a high-grade elevator apartment house, with stores and offices on the first floor; and upon the demolition of the existing building and the construction of a new building on said parcel of land as provided in the Building Agreement the Lessee shall use the demised premises only for store and office purposes and in connection with such use, if permitted by law and City ordinances, for the parking of cars of occupants of spaces in the Building, and the Lessee shall not use or permit or allow the Building or any portion thereof to be used for any purpose or purposes other than as above provided without the consent of the Lessor first had and obtained.

That the Lessee, in connection with its use of the demised premises, or the use of said premises by other parties, shall not construct, or allow or permit to be constructed, any advertising signs projecting more than twelve inches beyond the building line of said parcel of land above described (without, in each case, the written consent of the Lessor), or any advertising signs upon any portion of the demised premises of such a character as will offend good taste.

That the Lessee shall also at its own cost and expense, comply with all the regulations, rules and requirements of the Board of Fire Underwriters in respect of the demised premises and shall not knowingly permit any article to be brought upon, or any act to be done upon or about the demised premises that will cause the cancellation of any policy of insurance thereon, or increase the rate for such insurance beyond that usually charged for tenanted buildings of a similar character and construction, used for the purposes herein authorized.

Floor Loads. FIFTH. That the Lessee shall not suffer, allow or permit the loading of any of the floors of the demised premises or any portion or portions thereof beyond the weights permitted by the building ordinances of the City of New York as changed from time to time during the term of this lease by lawful orders of the municipal authorities having jurisdiction in the premises.

Alterations. SIXTH. That except as provided in the Building Agreement the Lessee shall make no structural alterations or changes either in the interior or in the exterior of the Building or in the bearing walls, supports, beams or foundations, or that will increase the loads carried by said walls, supports, beams or foundations, without the written consent of the Lessor first had and obtained, and plans and specifications showing such proposed alterations and changes shall be submitted to the Lessor for approval upon the application for such consent, and all alterations or changes made, with the written consent of the Lessor as aforesaid, shall be made at the sole cost and expense of the Lessee, under the supervision of an architect or engineer satisfactory to the Lessor for such purpose, and shall also be made in accordance with plans and specifications first submitted to and approved by the building department of the City of New York, and the other municipal authorities having charge of such changes and alterations, and in accordance with such rules and regulations as said municipal authorities may, from time to time, make in regard thereto. The Lessee also shall make no change in the mechanical, lighting and sanitary equipment in the demised premises that will make said equipment unsafe, unsanitary or unfit for the purpose for which it was installed.

The Lessee shall have no power to do any act or make any contract which may create or be the foundation for any lien, charge or other encumbrance upon the reversion or estate of the Lessor or of any interest of the Lessor in the demised premises; it being agreed that should the Lessee cause any alterations, rebuildings, replacements, changes, additions, improvements or repairs to be made in the demised premises or labor performed, or material furnished therein, neither the Lessor nor the demised premises shall under any circumstances, be liable for the payment of any expenses incurred or for the value of any work done or material furnished, but all such work, labor and material shall be made, furnished, and performed at the Lessee's expense and the Lessee shall be solely and wholly responsible to all persons furnishing and performing such labor and material. If, because of any act of the Lessee, any mechanic's or other lien, charge or order for the payment of money shall be filed against the demised premises or against the Lessor, the Lessee shall, at its own cost and expense, cause same to be cancelled and discharged of record within ten days after receiving notice of the filing thereof.

Insurance. SEVENTH. That the Lessee shall also, as an additional rental hereunder, pay to the Lessor on the first day of each and every year during the term of this lease such annual sum of lawful money as at the rates chargeable by insurance companies approved by the Lessor in any such year for insurance against loss or damage by fire upon the Building will pay all premiums for insurance in amounts sufficient to prevent the Lessor and Lessee or either of them from becoming a co-insurer within the terms of any policy or policies and in any event in amounts not less than 80% of the reasonable reproduction value of the Building, less depreciation from use, and the Lessor shall, upon receipt of such sums, apply the same for policies of insurance in insurance companies approved by the Lessor as aforesaid, with loss, if any, thereunder, payable to the Lessor, the Lessee, and the Leasehold Mortgagee as their interests may appear. The Lessor shall certify in writing to the Lessee, immediately after the application of such sums, the policies of such insurance so taken out. The sum payable by the Lessee hereunder for insurance premiums may, if the Lessee so desires, be made in such amount as will pay for policies of insurance to the amount and in the companies approved as aforesaid for such number of years in excess of one year as the Lessee may elect, and the amount so paid shall, in that case, be deemed a payment of the annual sum provided for in this paragraph for the years covered by such insurance. The Lessee may, if it so elects, furnish fire insurance policies with premiums paid, to the Lessor, with loss payable as aforesaid, in insurance companies approved by the Lessor, which approval shall not be unreasonably withheld, and to the amount above specified, in lieu of the payment for such insurance herein provided for. In case a mortgage shall be executed by the Lessee covering its leasehold rights in the premises above described, the loss, if any, payable under said insurance policies, during the continuance of such mortgage, shall be to the parties hereto and such mortgagee as their respective interests may appear and the policy or policies of such insurance shall be delivered to the Leasehold Mortgagee and a certificate of such policy or policies shall be delivered to the Lessor; but the insurance moneys payable under said insurance policies, in case of loss or damage, shall be payable as provided in this Paragraph Seventh.

Restoration.   In the event that during the term of this lease, the building upon the parcel of land above described shall be damaged or destroyed by fire or other risk, casualty or hazard covered by insurance furnished by Lessee, as aforesaid, then:

(a) in case the building existing on said parcel of land at the date of this lease shall be partially damaged, but such damage is not so extensive as to render the building untenantable, or as to amount to a total destruction of the building, Lessee shall proceed with reasonable diligence to repair such building at Lessee's own cost and expense, provided, however, that to the extent that Lessor may receive the proceeds of any insurance furnished by Lessee, paid in connection with the loss or damage so occurring, Lessor shall hold such insurance proceeds in trust to apply the same to the extent that such insurance proceeds will permit to Lessee's costs and expenses incurred in repairing said building or damage. Any insurance proceeds remaining in Lessor's hand after full reimbursement of Lessee's costs and expenses, as provided in the preceding sentence shall be and become the sole and absolute property of Lessee.

(b) In case the building existing on said parcel of land at the date of this lease shall be so extensively damaged as to render the said building untenantable or shall amount to a total destruction of the building, or in case the damage to said building shall be so extensive that the Lessee shall decide not to restore the present existing building but to proceed with the reconstruction of the building to be erected upon the said premises in accordance with Building Agreement, then the net proceeds of insurance recovered shall be deposited in a separate account in a bank or trust company approved by the Lessor, to be applied on account of the cost of the reconstruction of such building, as the work of construction progresses, as provided in the Building Agreement. The said payments to be made in the same proportion and at the same time as payments are to be made under the building loan contract to be entered into between the Lessee and the Leasehold Mortgagee.

(c) In case the building to be reconstructed upon the parcel of land above described, pursuant to the Building Agreement, or any building or buildings at any time constructed in place thereof, pursuant to the terms of this lease, shall be so damaged or destroyed, Lessee shall proceed with all reasonable expedition to restore or rebuild, as the case may be, the building so destroyed or rendered untenantable, free from liens of every kind, in substantial accordance with the plans and specifications of the building so destroyed or rendered untenantable (the building so to be rebuilt or restored in respect to its general exterior design, and the mechanical, heating, lighting and sanitary systems therein to be substantially in accord with the building so rendered untenantable), or in case the parties hereto agree in accordance with such other plans and specifications as may be agreed upon by the parties hereto, and in connection with such rebuilding or restoration, the Lessee shall comply with all the rules and requirements of the departments of the City of New York having oversight over such reconstruction or restoration.

(d) If the reconstructed building and improvements or any replacement thereof shall be damaged or destroyed by fire or other risk, casualty or hazard covered by insurance furnished by Lessee as aforesaid and if the proceeds of such insurance policies payable in connection with the loss or damage so occurring shall by the then effective terms of such policies be payable to the holder of a mortgage lien upon this lease, such mortgagee must elect within ten (10) days after receipt of such proceeds to apply the same to the satisfaction of the debt secured by such mortgage or to hold the same in trust to reimburse Lessee, to the extent that such insurance proceeds will permit, for Lessee's costs and expenses in repairing, replacing or rebuilding the building so damaged or destroyed; provided, however, that if such mortgagee shall elect to apply such insurance proceeds to the satisfaction of the debt secured by its mortgage, the balance, if any, of such insurance proceeds remaining after such application shall be paid over by such mortgagee to Lessor to be held in trust for the purposes and upon the terms hereinabove provided in those instances in which such insurance proceeds are payable directly to Lessor, and further provided that if such mortgagee shall elect to hold such insurance proceeds in trust for the purposes aforesaid and if Lessor shall thereafter enter upon the demised premises and complete said repairs, replacement or rebuilding pursuant to the provisions of this lease, such insurance proceeds so held in trust shall also be available as security to Lessor for repayment to Lessor by Lessee of Lessor's cost, damages and expenses in completing such repair, replacement or rebuilding as aforesaid and shall be paid to Lessor upon requisition as provided in this lease. If written notice of election by a mortgagee as hereinafter provided shall not be given to Lessor in the manner provided in this lease, in Paragraph Seventeenth hereof, for the giving of notices to Lessor, within said ten (10) day period, it shall be conclusively presumed that the mortgagee elected to hold such proceeds in trust as aforesaid.

(e) Whenever Lessor or any said mortgagee of this lease and the term hereof shall hold insurance proceeds in trust as aforesaid to be applied upon the cost of repairing, replacing or rebuilding the new building or any replacement thereof Lessor or such mortgagee, as the case may require, shall within five (5) days after presentation by Lessee of properly receipted bills for work done or materials furnished in such repairing, replacement or rebuilding, pay to Lessee a sum, to be computed as hereinafter stated, from such insurance proceeds then remaining in trust, which such sum so to be paid shall be in amount bearing the same proportion to the total insurance proceeds so held in trust as the amount of such receipted bills so presented by Lessee shall bear to the total sum which Lessee shall be obligated to pay for such complete repairing, replacement or rebuilding.

(f) No reduction or diminution shall be made in rentals and additional rentals herein provided for, on account of any loss or damage by fire.

Electric Current. EIGHTH. That the Lessor shall furnish or cause to be furnished to the Lessee, during the existence of the present building, sufficient electric current for lighting and power in the demised premises, and the Lessee shall pay monthly to the Lessor, as an additional rental hereunder, such sum of lawful money as the Lessor may, from time to time, charge for furnishing such electric current at reasonable rates and at rates in no event in excess of the prevailing rates charged for the time being for similar service in the Borough of Manhattan, City of New York, by the Consolidated Edison Company of New York, Inc., or such other large reputable company as shall then be engaged in the business of furnishing electric current for lighting and power to the public in the Borough of Manhattan, City of New York. The service herein provided for, however, covers only the furnishing of electric current from one service switchboard of the standard form of The New York Central Railroad Company unless the Lessor shall otherwise elect, and does not include any connection beyond said switchboard, care of the installation in the demised premises, supply of any electric lamps, the maintenance of the installation in the demised premises, and of the wires, lamps and other lighting and power fixtures and facilities therein, being assumed by the Lessee under Paragraph Second of this lease. The Lessee shall, without charge therefor, furnish to the Lessor a suitable and sufficient room in the basement or ground floor of the Building (free from all pipes or other service facilities) at a location to be designated by the Lessee reasonably appropriate for the purpose, properly lighted and ventilated and with access thereto at all reasonable times, for such service connections, meters and switching and transforming apparatus, as may be reasonably required in furnishing the service herein provided for and also necessary conduits for a direct run of cables from the point of entrance of the conduits into the Building to the room above mentioned. The meters to be provided by the Lessor shall only be such meters as are required by the Lessor to measure the current furnished to said demised premises from one service switchboard as aforesaid; any and all meters desired by the Lessee to measure the current used by the Lessee's tenants shall be provided by the Lessee.

Steam. That the Lessor shall also furnish or cause to be furnished to the Lessee, during the existence of the present building, a supply of steam or hot water sufficient properly to heat the demised premises, when, and as reasonably required by the Lessee, and also a supply of steam for the kitchen, restaurant and laundry facilities, if any, in the demised premises and for heating the water for the plumbing facilities in the demised premises requiring hot water, and the Lessee shall pay monthly to the Lessor, as an additional rental hereunder, such sum of lawful money as the Lessor may, from time to time, charge for furnishing such heating medium, at reasonable rates, and at rates in no event in excess of the prevailing rates charged for the time being for similar service by the Consolidated Edison Company of New York, Inc., or such other large reputable company, as shall then be engaged in the business of furnishing steam to the public in the Borough of Manhattan, City of New York. The service herein provided for, however, covers only the furnishing of such heating medium, and does not include any connection beyond the meter nor care of the pipes, valves, radiators, coils, and the other heating fixtures and facilities in the demised premises, the maintenance of the pipes, radiators and other heating fixtures and facilities therein being assumed by the Lessee under Paragraph Second of this lease. The Lessee shall, without charge therefor, furnish to the Lessor a suitable and sufficient room in the basement or ground floor of the Building, at a location to be designated by the Lessee, reasonably appropriate for the purpose, properly lighted and ventilated and with access thereto at all reasonable times, for such service connections and meters as may be reasonably required in furnishing the service herein provided for, and shall also provide a direct run of pipes from the point of entrance of the pipes into the Building to the rooms above mentioned. The Lessor shall not be required to furnish more than one heating connection. The meters to be provided by the Lessor shall be only such as are required by the Lessor to measure the heating medium furnished to said Building; any and all meters desired by the Lessee to measure the amount of heating medium used by the Lessee's tenants shall be provided by the Lessee.

The Lessee shall make at its own expense all necessary provision for the disposal of condensation from its heating system and devices requiring the use of steam, in a manner approved by the Lessor, or the Lessee may return to the Lessor such condensation under such conditions as may from time to time be agreed upon by the Lessor and the Lessee.

Upon the construction by the Lessee of the new building in place of the existing building on the demised premises in accordance with the Building Agreement, the Lessee shall obtain all electric current and steam required in the demised premises from public utility company or companies furnishing such services in the Borough of Manhattan, City of New York, upon payment by the Lessee of the lawful charges therefor, and the Lessor shall, upon request of the Lessee, permit the company or companies proposing to furnish such services to the Lessee to make connections with the service facilities of the Building at such locations and under such regulations as may be approved by the Lessor.

Right of Entry. NINTH. That the Lessor, its officers, agents and servants, shall have the right at all reasonable hours, and upon reasonable notice, to enter upon the demised premises and every part thereof for the purpose of inspecting and examining the same, and shall also have the right, but at its own cost and expense, to make such changes as may, from time to time, or at any time or times, seem advisable to the Lessor in the supporting structures of the Building below the plane shown on said Plot Plan No. 1, and in the location of said supporting structures, to accommodate the changes desired by the Lessor below said planes, and during the work of making such changes the Lessor shall have the right and is hereby authorized to enter at reasonable hours and upon reasonable notice upon the demised premises above said plane and to place therein such temporary shoring and blocking as may be reasonably required in making said changes, and also to remove all live loads from the particular supports affected by such changes, causing as little inconvenience as possible to the occupants, repairing all injuries done to the demised premises in any such work, and reimbursing the Lessee for all actual loss of use to itself or its tenants (including loss of tenants) of the portions of the demised premises affected by such work during the progress thereof.

Default.   TENTH.   That in case during the term of this lease, default be made in the payment of the Ground Rental or any part thereof when due, and such default shall continue for twenty (20) days, or in case the Lessee shall fail after thirty (30) days' notice to pay the additional rental on account of taxes herein provided, or any of the other additional rentals herein provided, or any part thereof, then the Lessor, its successors and assigns, shall have the right, and is hereby authorized to enter upon and take possession of the demised premises and every part thereof by summary proceedings or other legal proceedings, or by employing necessary force, or otherwise, as to the Lessor shall seem advisable, without being liable in damages therefor, and take and have again the demised premises and every part thereof free, clear and discharged of this lease, and of all the rights of the Lessee hereunder, or the Lessor may, at its option, take such other action or proceeding in the premises as to it shall seem advisable. Interest shall accrue upon any Ground Rental or taxes or other additional rentals unpaid for more than ten days after the same become due.

That in case the demised premises during the term of this lease shall be abandoned by the Lessee, or in case the Lessee shall, for the period of sixty (60) days after the same are payable, fail to pay the Ground Rental or any part thereof, or in case the Lessee shall, for the period of sixty (60) days after the payment thereof is requested by the Lessor, fail to pay the additional rental on account of taxes herein provided, or any of the other additional rentals herein provided, or any ᴿart thereof, or shall fail to make any payment provided for in Para- aphs Fourth or Seventh of the Building Agreement in the manner ᴺd within the time therein provided, or shall fail after ninety (90) days' written notice from the Lessor, to proceed with reasonable diligence to perform or observe any of the other covenants and agreements herein or in the Building Agreement contained when they are to be performed by the Lessee, or in case the Lessee if then the holder of this lease, or successor Lessee if this lease shall have passed by assignment or devolution as in this lease permitted, whichever shall then be the holder of the interest of the Lessee under this lease (respectively hereinafter referred to in this paragraph as the Lessee) shall be declared bankrupt or insolvent according to law, or an application for the reorganization of the Lessee under the Bankruptcy Act shall be filed by or against the Lessee and shall not be dismissed by the Court within ninety (90) days of such filing, or in case the Lessee shall, for the period of sixty (60) days after written notice from the Lessor, permit the demised premises to be used for any purpose other than as herein permitted, or in case this lease shall be assigned or encumbered without the written consent of the Lessor except as in this lease permitted, or in case this lease shall, without the written consent of the Lessor, by operation of law, devolve upon or pass to any corporation, person or persons other than the Lessee (other than the Leasehold Mortgagee or a purchaser on the foreclosure sale in proceedings to foreclose the mortgage to the Leasehold Mortgagee or an assignee of such purchaser, provided that such Mortgagee, purchaser or assignee shall have, within thirty (30) days after acquiring this lease and the leasehold estate hereby created, paid or caused to be paid to the Lessor all sums due from the Lessee to the Lessor under this lease and under the Building Agreement and shall have, by proper instrument in writing, assumed all of the obligations of the Lessee under this lease and under the Building Agreement), or in case the Lessee shall, for the period of ninety (90) days after notice from the Lessor fail to secure the satisfaction and discharge of any mechanics' liens, or any conditional sales or chattel mortgages on any materials, fixtures or articles used in the construction of or appurtenant to the Building upon the parcel of land above described, the Lessor may, in either or any of such events, give written notice by registered mail to the Lessee in the manner provided in this lease and written notice by registered mail to the Leasehold Mortgagee, if any, at the address furnished by such Leasehold Mortgagee to the Lessor for such purpose, specifying the respect or respects in which the Lessee shall be in default under the terms, covenants, conditions, limitations or agreements of this lease and in case at the expiration of thirty (30) days after the service of such notice by the Lessor upon the Lessee and upon the Leasehold Mortgagee as aforesaid, the default specified therein shall not have been cured, then the Lessor may (having previously given thirty (30) days' notice in writing by registered mail to the Leasehold Mortgagee, if there be such, in case the Leasehold Mortgagee shall have furnished to the Lessor an address to which such notice may be mailed), terminate and end this lease and the term hereof by giving to the Lessee notice in writing to the effect that this lease and the term hereof will terminate and end on a day to be named in said notice, which day shall be at least thirty (30) days subsequent to the date of the service of said notice, and in the event of the service of such notice this lease and the term hereof shall terminate and end upon the day named therein. Lessor will accept performance or payment by the Leasehold Mortgagee of any term, covenant, condition, agreement or payment on Lessee's part herein provided to be performed or paid, with the same force and effect as though performed or paid by Lessee. If, upon the termination of this lease as aforesaid, the Lessee or such corporation, person or persons as shall then be in occupancy of the demised premises shall fail immediately to surrender possession of the demised premises to the Lessor, the Lessor may remove the Lessee, its successors, assigns, sub-tenants and under-tenants, if there be such, therefrom by summary proceedings for a holding over and continuance in possession of the demised premises after the expiration of the term of this lease, or may otherwise remove the Lessee therefrom as to the Lessor may seem advisable. The remedies provided in this Paragraph Tenth in case of default shall not be deemed exclusive but shall be in addition to all other remedies at law or in equity in the case of any such default; and no action taken or omitted by the Lessor in case of default shall be deemed a waiver of such default and the waiver of a particular default shall not be deemed the waiver of any other default or a waiver of the same default again occurring.

The Lessee hereby expressly waives any and all rights of redemption granted by or under any present or future laws in the event of the Lessee being evicted or dispossessed for any cause, or in the event of the Lessor obtaining possession of demised premises, by reason of the violation by the Lessee of any of the covenants and conditions of this lease, or otherwise.

In case of the termination of this lease for any default under this lease or under the Building Agreement whereby all rights of the Lessee hereunder shall be terminated and at an end, if at the time of such termination there be a mortgage to the Leasehold Mortgagee upon the leasehold rights of the Lessee under this lease as mentioned in Paragraph Third hereof, written notice to the effect that this lease is so terminated shall be given by registered mail to the Leasehold Mortgagee at the address furnished by such Leasehold Mortgagee to the Lessor for that purpose and the Lessor shall upon request of such Leasehold Mortgagee made within thirty (30) days after the giving to such Leasehold Mortgagee of such notice, upon the Leasehold Mortgagee paying or causing to be paid to the Lessor all sums due from the Lessee to the Lessor under this lease and under the Building Agreement, and upon the assumption by the Leasehold Mortgagee, or by such party as the Leasehold Mortgagee may designate, of all the obligations of the Lessee under this lease and under the Building Agreement, execute a new lease of the demised premises to such Leasehold Mortgagee, or to the said party designated by the Leasehold Mortgagee as aforesaid, for the remainder of the term of this lease subsequent to the date of such termination, at the rentals and additional rentals, subject to the exceptions and reservations, and upon the covenants, conditions, limitations and agreements herein contained, including the covenants in respect of renewal.

End of Term. ELEVENTH. That the Lessee shall peaceably give up and surrender possession of the demised premises and every part thereof unto the Lessor at the expiration or sooner termination of the term of this lease and the last renewal thereof, if there be renewal, together with the Building and all water, gas, electric lighting, power, elevator, heating, sewer, drainage, plumbing and other fixtures and facilities in the Building upon the said demised premises, or forming part thereof, of the character classed as real estate and as part of the Building as between landlord and tenant in as good condition and repair as reasonable use and wear thereof will permit, damage by the elements excepted.

Option to Renew. TWELFTH. That the Lessee, in case it shall not be in default hereunder, shall have the right, not earlier than two (2) years prior to the date of the expiration of the term of this lease, and not later than six (6) months prior to the date of the expiration of the term of this lease, to serve upon the Lessor a notice in writing to the effect that the Lessee elects that this lease shall be renewed for a further term of twenty-one (21) years from the date of the expiration of the term of this lease. In the event that (no default existing) the Lessee shall elect to renew this lease and shall serve notice of such election as aforesaid, then upon the expiration of the term hereof, a renewal lease shall be executed by and between the parties hereto, whereby the Lessor shall let unto the Lessee, and the Lessee shall take and hire from the Lessor, the parcel of land above described with the exceptions and reservations above set forth, for the term of twenty-one (21) years from the date of the expiration of the term hereof, subject to the rights of the Lessor and the Railroad Companies, their and each of their successors and assigns, in and to the use and possession of the portion of the parcel of land above described, excepted from this lease as aforesaid, and in and to the subsurface ....
.... above mentioned, all as herein provided, and at the annual Ground Rental of .... Dollars ($.........), or such larger amount as shall be fixed upon as hereinafter provided in Paragraph Fourteenth, and at the other additional rentals herein contained, and upon the other terms, covenants, conditions, limitations and agreements herein contained, except that said renewal lease shall provide that upon the expiration of said first renewal term the Lessee shall have the right to require a further renewal as provided in Paragraph Thirteenth hereof.

Provided, however, that in case the Lessee shall desire, within the period of six (6) months after the date of completion of the reconstruction of the building as hereinbefore defined, and not then being in default hereunder, to extend the term of this lease to include the first renewal term of twenty-one (21) years herein provided for, then and in such case (no default existing) the Lessee shall have the right, within said period of six (6) months, to serve upon the Lessor a notice in writing to the effect that the Lessee desires to extend the term of this lease to include a further term of twenty-one (21) years from the date of the expiration of the term hereof, and thereupon, within sixty (60) days after the service of such notice, an agreement shall be executed by and between the Lessor and Lessee, whereby the term of this lease shall be extended for the further term of twenty-one (21) years from December 1, 1985, at the annual Ground Rental of . . . . (. . . . .) to November 30, 1985, as herein provided, and thereafter at the annual Ground Rental of . . . . (. . . . .) or such larger amount as shall be fixed upon in the manner and at the time hereinafter provided in Paragraph Fourteenth in respect to fixing the annual Ground Rental to be paid by the Lessee during the first renewal term, and otherwise at the rentals and additional rentals, subject to the exceptions and reservations, and upon the covenants, conditions, limitations and agreements contained in this lease, except that said agreement shall provide that, upon the expiration of the term of this lease as extended as aforesaid, the Lessee shall have the right to require a further renewal of twenty-one (21) years as provided in Paragraph Thirteenth hereof in respect of the second renewal term.

Second Renewal. THIRTEENTH. That if this lease shall be renewed as provided in Paragraph Twelfth hereof (or extended as provided in said Paragraph, such extension being treated, for the purposes of this Paragraph Thirteenth, as a renewal), then the said renewal lease to be executed in that event shall provide that upon the expiration of the term of said renewal lease the Lessee, if it shall not be in default thereunder, shall have the right (unless the Lessor shall elect that this lease shall not be renewed as provided in Paragraph Fifteenth hereof) not earlier than two (2) years prior to the date of the expiration of said renewal term and not later than six (6) months prior to the date of the expiration of said renewal term, to serve upon the Lessor a notice in writing to the effect that the Lessee elects that this lease shall again be renewed for the further term of twenty-one (21) years from the date of the expiration of the first renewal term of this lease. In the event that the Lessee (not being in default) shall elect again to renew this lease and shall serve notice of such election as aforesaid, then upon the expiration of the first renewal term (subject to the provisions of Paragraph Fifteenth hereof) a second renewal lease shall be executed by and between the parties hereto, whereby the Lessor shall let unto the Lessee, and the Lessee shall take and hire from the Lessor the said parcel of land above described, with the exceptions and reservations above set forth, for the term of twenty-one (21) years from the date of the expiration of the first renewal term subject to the rights of the Lessor, its successors and assigns, in and to the use and possession of the portion of the parcel of land above described, excepted and reserved as aforesaid, and in and to the sub-surface of 48th Street, 49th Street and Park Avenue, and the paved way above mentioned, all as herein provided, and at the Ground Rental equal to the annual Ground Rental payable during the first renewal term, or such larger amount as shall be fixed upon as hereinafter provided in Paragraph Fourteenth, and at the other additional rentals herein contained, and upon the other terms, covenants, conditions, limitations and agreements herein contained, except that the second renewal lease shall provide that upon the expiration of the term thereof the Lessee shall have no right to require a further renewal lease.

Renewal Term Rentals. FOURTEENTH. That in case of the renewal of this lease for a first renewal term, as provided in Paragraph Twelfth hereof, if the Lessor shall be of the opinion that the annual Ground Rental of .... (..........) is less than the proper annual Ground Rental to be paid by the Lessee during the first renewal term; or in case of the renewal of this lease for a second renewal term, as provided in Paragraph Thirteenth hereof, if the Lessor shall be of the opinion that the annual Ground Rental payable during the first renewal term is less than the proper annual Ground Rental to be paid by the Lessee during the second renewal term; then the Lessor shall, in either such case, at least four (4) months prior to the expiration date of the term then expiring, notify the Lessee in writing of the annual sum which in the opinion of the Lessor would be the proper annual Ground Rental during the renewal term about to be entered upon. If the Lessee shall not, within twenty (20) days after the service of such notice, advise the Lessor in writing that the annual Ground Rental so named by the Lessor is unsatisfactory, then the annual Ground Rental so named by the Lessor shall be the annual Ground Rental payable during the renewal term about to be entered upon. If the Lessee shall, within twenty (20) days aforesaid, notify the Lessor in writing that the annual Ground Rental so named by the Lessor is unsatisfactory, then the annual Ground Rental payable during the renewal term about to be entered upon shall be determined as hereinafter in this paragraph provided.

If the Lessee shall, within the twenty (20) days aforesaid, notify the Lessor in writing that the annual Ground Rental named by the Lessor is unsatisfactory, then the full and fair value of the parcel of land above described considered as unimproved at the commencement of the renewal term about to be entered upon shall be determined by three arbitrators, one appointed by the Lessor, one appointed by the Lessee and the third by the arbitrators so appointed, or in case of the failure of the arbitrators so appointed to agree upon such third arbitrator within twenty (20) days after their appointment, then such third arbitrator shall be appointed by the person who is then Presiding Justice of the Appellate Division of the Supreme Court of the State of New York for the First Department, or, in case said Appellate Division shall cease to be, by the person who is then the Senior Justice in point of service of the body exercising the functions now exercised by such Appellate Division, upon the application of either of the parties hereto upon reasonable notice to the other party; in case the person who shall be such Presiding Justice (or Senior Justice) shall decline to make such appointment, then such third arbitrator shall be appointed by such one of the other Justices of the Appellate Division (or body exercising the functions thereof) as shall consent to make such appointment, application being made to said Justices as aforesaid in the order of seniority of service in said Court.

In case either of the parties hereto shall fail to appoint an arbitrator as aforesaid for the period of twenty (20) days after written notice from the other party to make such appointment, then the arbitrator appointed by the party not in default shall appoint the second arbitrator, and the two so appointed shall select the third arbitrator.

The arbitrators on their appointment, after having been duly sworn to perform their duties with impartiality and fidelity, shall proceed with all reasonable dispatch to appraise the full and fair value of the parcel of land above described considered as unimproved (in making such appraisal, however, the fact that the excepted portion of said parcel of land is used or is susceptible of use for railroad purposes shall not be deemed to contribute to the value of said parcel of land considered as unimproved), and the amount fixed by said arbitrators or by a majority of them as the value of said parcel of land considered as unimproved as of the time of deciding such arbitration as aforesaid, or the date of the beginning of the renewal term about to be entered upon, whichever occurs first, shall be binding and conclusive upon the parties hereto as the true value of said parcel of land considered as unimproved, for the purpose of determining the annual Ground Rental payable hereunder during the renewal term in question. The Lessor and Lessee shall each pay the expense of the arbitrator appointed by or for such party, and the other necessary expenses and costs of any arbitration hereunder shall be borne equally by the parties hereto.

In case five (5%) per centum of the value of said parcel of land above described, as such value is determined by the arbitrators in respect of the first renewal term, shall be in excess of the sum of ......
.... Dollars ($..........) the annual Ground Rental payable hereunder during the first renewal term shall be such annual sum as will equal five (5%) per centum of the value of said parcel of land as fixed by said arbitrators as aforesaid, and shall be payable in equal monthly installments in advance, and in case five (5%) per centum of the value of said parcel of land as fixed by said arbitrators as aforesaid shall be equal to or less than the sum of ....
.... Dollars ($..........) the annual Ground Rental payable hereunder during the first renewal term shall be the annual sum of .... Dollars ($..........) and shall be payable as above provided.

In case five (5%) per centum of the value of said parcel of land above described, as such value is determined by the arbitrators in respect of the second renewal term, shall be in excess of the annual Ground Rental payable during the first renewal term, the annual Ground Rental payable hereunder during the second renewal term shall be such annual sum as will equal five (5%) per centum of the value of said parcel of land as fixed by said arbitrators as aforesaid, and shall be payable in equal monthly installments in advance, and in case five (5%) per centum of the value of said parcel of land as fixed by said arbitrators as aforesaid shall be equal to or less than the annual Ground

Rental payable during the first renewal term, the annual Ground Rental payable hereunder during the second renewal term shall be such annual sum as will equal the annual Ground Rental payable during the first renewal term and shall be payable as above provided.

Refusal of Second Renewal. FIFTEENTH. That in case this lease shall be renewed for a first renewal term as provided in Paragraph Twelfth hereof, and prior to the expiration of said first renewal term the Lessee shall duly serve notice of its election that this lease be renewed for a second renewal term, as provided in Paragraph Thirteenth hereof, and the Lessor shall be unwilling that this lease be renewed for such second renewal term, then the Lessor shall have the right, notwithstanding the election of the Lessee, that this lease be so renewed, to elect that this lease be not renewed for such second renewal term; and in case the Lessor shall so elect and notify the Lessee in writing of such election within thirty days after service of notice by the Lessee as aforesaid of its election that said lease be renewed, then, upon the expiration of the first renewal term, said lease and the term thereof shall terminate and end without the right of the Lessee to require a further renewal, and the Lessee shall surrender full and free possession of the demised premises and every part thereof to the Lessor.

In case this lease shall terminate without renewal as above provided upon the expiration of the first renewal term hereof, by reason of the service by the Lessor of notice of its election that there be no renewal, and after service by the Lessee of notice of its election that there be renewal, then upon such expiration the Lessor shall pay to the Lessee on the date of expiration of said first renewal term and surrender of possession the then value of the new building which shall have been constructed upon the parcel of land above described (excepting the portion thereof constructed below the plane shown on said Plot Plan No. 1) pursuant to the Building Agreement, and in case the Lessor and Lessee shall be unable to agree upon such value, then such value shall be determined by three arbitrators chosen as provided in Paragraph Fourteenth hereof, and the award of said arbitrators, or of a majority of them, shall be binding and conclusive upon the parties hereto. The expense of any such arbitration shall be borne as provided for in said Paragraph Fourteenth.

Quiet Enjoyment. SIXTEENTH. That the Lessee on paying the Ground Rental and the additional rentals and observing and performing the covenants, conditions, limitations and agreements herein and in the Building Agreement contained on the part of the Lessee to be observed and performed, all as herein and therein provided, shall and may peaceably and quietly have, hold and enjoy the said demised premises for the term aforesaid, subject as hereinbefore provided; and the Lessor covenants and agrees to comply with all the obligations upon it under its grant from The New York Central Railroad Company and The New York and Harlem Railroad Company, and, in case of the exercise of any right of renewal by the Lessee under Paragraphs Twelfth and

Thirteenth hereof, to exercise its right to renewal under said grant from The New York Central Railroad Company and The New York and Harlem Railroad Company.

Notices. SEVENTEENTH. That any notice required to be given by the Lessor under the terms of this lease shall be in writing and shall be sent by registered mail to the Lessee, addressed to the Lessee at the last address of the Lessee furnished by it to the Lessor for that purpose, or in case of the failure of the Lessee to furnish such address, then addressed to the Lessee at ...., New York City, and in all cases a copy of such notice shall be mailed to the Leasehold Mortgagee, if any there be, by registered mail, addressed to such Leasehold Mortgagee at the last address furnished by it to the Lessor for such purpose, or in case of the failure of such Leasehold Mortgagee to furnish such address, then addressed to it at its principal office or place of business, and notice given as aforesaid to the Lessee and to the Leasehold Mortgagee shall be sufficient service to any such notice hereunder.

That any notice required to be given by the Lessee under the terms of this lease shall also be in writing and shall be sent by registered mail to the Lessor, addressed to the Lessor at ...., Borough of Manhattan, City of New York, or at such other address as may be furnished by the Lessor to the Lessee for that purpose and notice so given shall be sufficient service of any such notice hereunder.

Waiver of Jury Trial. EIGHTEENTH. It is mutually agreed by and between the Lessor and the Lessee that the respective parties shall and they hereby do waive trial by jury in any action, proceeding or counterclaim brought by either of the parties against the other on any matters whatsoever arising out of or in any way connected with this lease, the Lessee's use or occupancy of the demised premises and/or any claim of injury or damage.

Successors and Assigns. NINETEENTH. The covenants and agreements herein contained shall be deemed to be covenants running with the land, and shall inure to the benefit of and be binding upon the successors and assigns of the respective parties hereto; provided, however, that no assignment hereof shall be made by the Lessee except upon the conditions hereinabove provided.

IN WITNESS WHEREOF, the parties hereto have caused the execution of this agreement of lease the day and year first above written.

STATE OF NEW YORK } ss.:
COUNTY OF NEW YORK }

On the .... day of ...., 1957, before me personally came ...., to me known, who, being by me duly sworn, did depose and say that he resides at ....; that he is .... President of NEW YORK STATE REALTY AND TERMINAL COMPANY, the corporation described in and which executed the above instrument; that he knows the seal of said Corporation; that the seal affixed to said instrument was such corporate seal; that it was so affixed by authority of the Board of Directors of said Corporation, and that he signed his name thereto by like authority.

STATE OF NEW YORK
COUNTY OF NEW YORK } ss.:

On the .... day of ...., 1957, before me personally came ...., to me known, who, being by me duly sworn, did depose and say that he resides at ....; that he is............ President of ...., the corporation described in and which executed the above instrument; that he knows the seal of said Corporation; that the seal affixed to said instrument was such corporate seal; that it was so affixed by authority of the Board of Directors of said Corporation, and that he signed his name thereto by like authority.

Miscellaneous Leases and Forms

SHORT FORM LEASE, FOR PURPOSE OF RECORDING

(To avoid publicly revealing the terms of a lease, especially that of the rental paid, the following skeletonized lease may be used when it is recorded. Operators of chain stores and others prefer this arrangement in many instances. It also saves recording fees.)

THIS INDENTURE, made in the city of St. Paul, Minn. on June 15, 19...., By the landlord (insert name of landlord here, with address) and the tenant, (insert name of tenant, with address here), witnesseth:

That the landlord, in consideration of the rents reserved, hereinafter referred to, and of the terms, covenants, conditions and agreements on the part of the tenant does hereby demise and lease unto the tenant, and the tenant does hereby take and hire from the landlord the following described property, hereinafter termed the demised premises, to wit (copy in legal and street address in full here) said premises being approximately 50 by 100 feet in size.

TO HAVE AND TO HOLD the demised premises for the term commencing (initial date of lease here) and ending on (termination date here) upon the rents, terms, covenants and conditions contained in a certain collateral agreement or indenture of lease between the parties hereto and bearing even date herewith.

IN WITNESS WHEREOF, the parties hereto have hereunto set their hands and seals, the day and year first above written.

(Signatures, acknowledgments, and so forth.)

EXTENSION OF LEASE

(*A standard form of the Property Management Division, National Association of Real Estate Boards.*)

IN CONSIDERATION of the sum of One Dollar by each of the undersigned parties to the other in hand paid, the receipt whereof is hereby acknowledged, it is hereby mutually understood and agreed that the lease dated ...., 19...., between ....
.... as Lessor, and .... as Lessee, covering rooms Nos. .... on the .... floor of the .... Building, located at ...., expiring (after any existing renewals thereof) on ...., 19...., is hereby extended under the same terms, covenants, and conditions therein expressed and at the same rental, namely, ..., for the further term or period of .... years from ...., 19.....

(Signatures, acknowledgments, and so forth.)

FORM FOR COLLECTING LEASE RENEWALS

(*The following is a brief form which may be used by a broker in making a lease when a renewal is provided for at a later date. It permits the broker to have a continuing interest as the lease becomes subject to renewal.*)

(Brokerage firm here.)
(Street address here.)
(City and state here.)
Inasmuch as you negotiated the lease from The ....
.... Co. to The .... Co., which lease extends for a period of four years and which contains a provision giving to The .... Co. the right to take another term upon the expiration of the first term, it was at the time and is now understood and agreed that if The .... Co. elects to and does take said lease for said term you shall at such time be paid a commission of ......% upon the amount of rental involved.

This letter is written for the purpose of putting in permanent form the understanding between The .... Co. and you at the time.

(Signatures, acknowledgments, and so forth.)

OPTION TO RENT CHAIN STORE PROPERTY

(This is a form used by a southeastern chain store broker.)

To ....:

In consideration of your using your best efforts to obtain a tenant (or tenants) for the property described as follows:

I (or we) hereby grant you the exclusive option to secure a tenant for said property, under the following conditions:

1. The rental shall be:

....

2. The term of the lease shall be:

....

3. The lease shall be on your standard form (copy of which is attached hereto) with the following exceptions:

....

4. The financial responsibility of the tenant shall be such as to warrant the belief that the provisions of the lease will be carried out.

This option shall continue for 30 days after I (or we) give you written notice of my (or our) desire to terminate it.

Upon the termination of this option you shall furnish me (or us) with the names of all prospective tenants with whom you have discussed this lease, and if by any subsequent negotiations I (or we) should consummate a lease on the within described property with any of the aforesaid prospective tenants, you shall receive the same compensation as is provided herein for the period prior to the expiration of this option.

(Signatures, acknowledgments, and so forth.)

METHOD FOR RENEWING INDUSTRIAL LEASE

(This is a clause used by a West Coast broker in industrial leases. It provides that if the principals cannot agree upon renewal terms, the appraisal committee of the local realty board can fix them, Lessor and Lessee agreeing to be bound by the committee's findings.)

IN further consideration thereof, it is mutually covenanted and agreed as follows;

A. THAT if the Lessee shall have kept, observed and performed each and all of its agreements and covenants in this lease contained, it shall have the option to renew this lease (except this paragraph thereof) for another period of .... years beginning at the expiration of the term hereof, provided that, at least .... days before such expiration, the Lessee notifies the Lessor in writing of its intention so to do, all the covenants, conditions, provisions and agreements herein agreed to be paid, kept or performed by the Lessee to continue throughout such extension, except as to the monthly rental, which for the period of such extension shall be such sum as between the date of said notice and .... days before the date of the expiration of the term hereof shall be fixed and determined by the Appraisal Committee of the .... Realty Board, which committee, as a basis for fixing the rental for that period, shall take into consideration the character of the leased premises, its location, other usual factors, and the then general rental value of such property, and the finding of such Committee shall be final and binding upon both the Lessor and Lessee.

WAIVER OF PRIORITY

(At times banks and investors holding mortgages on property under ninety-nine-year lease waive priority to the Lessee, the lease thus becoming first lien on the premises.)

KNOW ALL MEN BY THESE PRESENTS that whereas the undersigned, The .... Trust Company, is the owner and holder of a certain mortgage from .... to The .... Trust Company, dated July 1, 19...., recorded in Volume ...., Page ...., of .... County, ..., records, Document No. ...., securing an indebtedness originally in the amount of Eight Thousand ($8,000.00) Dollars, and

WHEREAS said .... have entered into a ninety-nine (99) year lease agreement with The .... Company, dated October 1, 19...., and recorded with the Recorder of .... County, ..., Document No. ...., and

Whereas the parties to said ninety-nine (99) year lease agreement entered into the same upon the agreement of the undersigned, The .... Trust Company that it would execute a Waiver of Priority of the aforesaid mortgage over the said ninety-nine (99) year lease agreement,

NOW, THEREFORE, in consideration of the premises and the sum of One Dollar ($1.00) paid by the said .... and The .... Company to the undersigned, the undersigned does hereby waive the priority of the above mentioned mortgage over the above mentioned ninety-nine (99) year lease agreement and over the estate of the Lessee, under the said ninety-nine (99) year lease agreement, intending hereby that the rights of the undersigned and its successors and assigns under the aforesaid mortgage shall be as though the aforesaid ninety-nine (99) year lease agreement were executed and recorded prior to the execution and recording of said mortgage without otherwise affecting the lien of the said mortgage.

Executed at . . . . , Ohio, this 29th day of October, 19. . . . .

(Signatures, acknowledgments, and so forth.)

CHATTEL MORTGAGE CLAUSE

(Some states permit the inclusion in short-term leases of a so-called chattel mortgage clause. Where such is permitted, the following form may prove useful.)

And said Lessee does hereby bargain, sell, assign, transfer, convey, set over and deliver unto the said Lessor, his heirs and assigns, all the goods, chattels and personal property of said Lessee which are now, or may be hereafter placed, on said premises, including all

(Detailed description of goods here.)

Provided, however, if said Lessee shall promptly pay all the rent as hereinbefore specified, and shall keep and perform all the covenants and agreements in this instrument contained, on the part of said Lessee to be kept and performed, then this conveyance or mortgage shall be void, otherwise to remain in full force and effect.

And said Lessee hereby covenants and agrees to and with said Lessor, his executors, administrators and assigns, that if default be made in the payment of said rent or any installment thereof, or in the performance of any of the covenants herein contained on the part of said Lessee to be performed, at the time limited therefor, or if said Lessor, his heirs or assigns, at any time before said rent, or any installments thereof, become due, or before the time limited for the performance of the covenants herein contained on the part of said Lessee to be performed, shall deem it necessary for his more perfect and complete security, said Lessor is hereby authorized and empowered to enter said premises, or such other places as the said goods and chattels may be, and take possession of the same and immediately sell the same at public or private sale, without notice, hereby granting unto said Lessor the right to himself become the purchaser thereof at public sale, and out of the proceeds thereof, to retain and pay said rents, with interest and other proper charges, and to pay the expenses of said sale, including expenses incurred in taking possession and keeping said property, with reasonable attorney's fees, and to pay any and all liens that may be thereon having priority over this mortgage, rendering the overplus, if any, to the Lessee, his executors, administrators or assigns. Except as hereinbefore provided, said Lessee shall remain and continue in possession of said goods and chattels and in full enjoyment of the same.

In witness whereof, the said Lessor and Lessee have hereunto set their hands to duplicates hereof on the .... day of ...., 19....

(Signatures, acknowledgments, and so forth.)

ASSIGNMENT OF LEASE AND LEASEHOLD ESTATE

(In assigning a lease, the following form will be found useful, as it is quite complete. If the lease is being assigned by one individual to another individual, it will be necssary to so state, as the form itself indicates that the assignment is made from one corporation to another.)

KNOW ALL MEN BY THESE PRESENTS, That .... an .... corporation, for the consideration of Ten Dollars ($10) and other valuable considerations to it in hand paid by .... an .... corporation, the receipt of which is hereby acknowledged, has sold, assigned, transferred and set over, and by these presents does sell, assign, transfer and set over unto the said .... the instrument of lease and the leasehold estate created by said instrument of lease, dated the .... day of .... A. D. ...., filed for record ...., duly recorded in Volume ...., Pages ...... to ......, inclusive, of the lease records of .... County, ..., made by .... to .... in and to the following described property, to wit:

(Include same description of property here as appears in the lease)

TO HAVE AND TO HOLD THE said instrument of lease, the leasehold estate created thereby, and the buildings and improvements thereon, unto the said ...., its successors and assigns forever, and the said ...., does hereby covenant with the said ...., grantee and assignee, its successors and assigns, that at and until the ensealing of these presents it is the true and lawful owner of said lease and leasehold estate created thereby, and has good right to bargain, sell and transfer the same in manner and form above written; that the said instrument of lease and leasehold estate are free and clear of encumbrances, except taxes and assessments levied thereon for the year 19...., which the assignor herein agrees to pay; except a certain mortgage or deed of trust thereon made by .... to ...., as trustee, dated ...., securing an issue of bonds of the assignor, dated ...., aggregating the sum of .... ($.......) of which there are now outstanding the sum of .... ($........), which bonds together with interest thereon from ...., grantee and assignee assumes and agrees to pay, said mortgage or deed of trust being filed for record ...., and is recorded in Volume ...., page ...., of the mortgage records of .... County, ...; except existing leases on various portions of said leasehold estate, which grantee and assignee assumes; and except such rents as may accrue, under said instrument of lease (it being understood that assignee shall pay the assignor any rentals which shall have been paid by it on account of said instrument of lease beyond), that it will place grantee and assignee in possession of said premises ...., 19....; that there is no default under the terms of said instrument of lease; and that it will forever warrant and defend unto the said grantee and assignee, its successors and assigns, the said instrument of lease, the leasehold estate created thereby, and the buildings and improvements thereon, except as above specified, and subject always to the terms of said instrument of lease.

In consideration of the premises the .... does for itself, its successors and assigns, hereby accept the said assignment and transfer of lease and leasehold estate, and expressly agrees to assume the engagements of .... under the said instrument of lease and agrees to punctually perform all of the same.

IN WITNESS WHEREOF, the said .... and ...., by their respective officers thereunto duly authorized, have affixed their corporate names and seals at ...., ..., all the .... day of ...., this instrument being executed in triplicate.

(Signatures, acknowledgments, and so forth.)

LEASE PERMITTING PURCHASE BY AMORTIZATION PROCESS

(This interesting and unusual lease was made in Baltimore on a theater property. It was for a six-year term at an annual rental of $24,000, payable $600 weekly for a period of forty weeks, beginning with the theatrical season on Sept. 1 of each year. The lessee was required to pay all charges, including insurance, maintenance,

and income taxes, and was even required to maintain a meeting room for the directors of the lessor company. A cash payment of $50,000 was made upon signing the lease and a bond of $50,000 in cash or securities was stipulated, the lessee receiving interest thereon. Beginning with the second year of the lease the lessee was required to proceed with purchasing the premises for a consideration of $500,-000, making yearly payments of $50,000 for five years and two $100,-000 payments in the sixth year. These, with the initial payment of $50,000, made up the total purchase price. As payments were made, interest at 6 per cent was allowed the lessee against the yearly rental and deducted therefrom, gradually extinguishing the lease rental. Title remained in the lessor until all payments were made, when the property was to be conveyed by deed.)

THIS AGREEMENT made and executed in duplicate this 29th day of January, 19...., by .... of .... City, a corporation of the State of ...., party of the first part, hereinafter designated as the party of the first part; and ...., organized under the laws of the State of ...., party of the second part, hereinafter designated as the party of the second part.

WHEREAS, the party of the first part has agreed with the party of the second part to lease to its premises in .... City, hereinafter mentioned and described and known as (description here), for the term of six years, to commence on the .... day of ...., immediately after the expiration of the present existing lease of the same, on the terms of rental and all other terms and provisions hereinafter specially set forth.

AND WHEREAS, the party of the first part has agreed to sell, and the party of the second part has agreed to purchase the fee simple property, and other property leased as above, at the time and upon the conditions hereinafter more fully set forth.

AND WHEREAS, in execution of said agreement said parties hereto have severally united in this agreement, and respectively bound themselves to the performance of all the terms, covenants and agreements, provisions and stipulations herein contained.

NOW, THEREFORE, THIS AGREEMENT WITNESSETH:

First. That the party of the first part hereby leases to the party of the second part, the lot and building on .... Street in .... City, belonging to the party of the first part, commonly known as the .... (said property fronting ...... feet on the west side of .... Street, beginning approximately ...... feet north of .... Street, with a depth of ...... feet, and being more particularly described in a deed for said property from ....

to the said party of the first part, dated the .... day of ....
and duly recorded among the Land Records of City ....)
together with the appurtenances belonging to the party of the first part,
therein contained, for the term of six years, to commence on the termination of the now existing lease, to wit, on the first day of ....,
and to terminate on the first day of ....; in consideration of
the payment by the party of the second part of all the rents and all
other sums of money herein specified to be paid and expended by it, and
the full and faithful performance by the party of the second part of all its
covenants and agreements herein set forth.

Second. The party of the second part, in consideration of this agreement to it, covenants and agrees to pay to the party of the first part the
annual rental of twenty-four thousand dollars ($24,000.00) accounting
from .... and ending .... payable in forty (40)
installments in each year of six hundred dollars ($600.00) each; the first
installment to be paid on the first Saturday of the month of September
in every year during the term, and the following installments on the Saturday of every succeeding week during every such year, until all said installments to the aggregate sum of twenty-four thousand dollars ($24,-
000.00) per annum in all are paid each and every year of said term;
and as additional rental the party of the second part covenants and
agrees to pay to the party of the first part a sum or sums of money which
shall be equivalent to the amount of Federal Income Taxes and/or
Excess Profit Tax, or any and all similar taxes which may be payable to
the United States Government upon the rentals paid to the party of the
first part hereunder, the intent being that the rentals as above provided
and as hereinafter modified by this agreement shall be undiminished by
the necessary subtraction therefrom of such taxes to be paid therefrom
by the party of the first part but the liability hereunder of the party
of the second part for the said additional rental equivalent to the said
taxes shall not be in excess of what part said taxes would be for the particular year computed on the basis of said annual rental being the sole
and only income or profit of the said party of the first part; the first
installment of said additional rental being payable on the first day of
March, 19...., and to be only one-fourth of the amount equivalent to
said taxes so ascertained for the calendar year 19....; and subsequent
installments of said additional rental to be paid on the first days of
March in the years 19...., 19...., 19...., 19.... and 19...., and said
payments to be for an amount equivalent to the whole of said tax so
computed for the preceding calendar year; and the last installment of
said additional rent to be paid on March 1, 19...., and to be limited to
an amount equivalent to three-fourths of said tax as so ascertained for
the preceding calendar year. In the event of any revision or re-deter-
mination by the proper representatives of the United States Government
in the amount of said tax upon review an equitable adjustment shall be
made between the parties hereto, as of the date of final determination.

Third. The party of the first part covenants and agrees to insure, and
keep insured, the building and contents hereby leased, from damage by

fire in the aggregate amount of four hundred thousand dollars ($400,-000.00), and after the party of the second part shall be put in possession of said leased premises, as hereinafter provided, and until the termination of said lease, the party of the second part shall pay to the party of the first part all premiums earned upon said fire insurance policies; but the party of the first part shall use all reasonable efforts to secure the lowest current rate of premium for said insurance, and said premiums shall be paid by the party of the second part for one (1) year in advance on September 1st of each year that this agreement and lease is in force; and return, however, to be adjusted and repaid to the party of the second part as may be equitable.

Fourth. The party of the second part also covenants and agrees to pay to the party of the first part after the party of the second part is put in possession of the premises hereby leased, and thereafter during the continuance of said lease, all City, State and Federal taxes and other public charges whatsoever, including water rents which may be assessed and levied upon the property of the party of the first part herein described, and also that state franchise tax on the capital stock of the party of the first part and also state taxes on the shares of capital stock, and any state income tax on the rental herein arising, if there be any such taxes, and also the Federal Excise Tax upon the capital stock of the party of the first part. All said additional payments shall be made annually on the first day of July in each year for an amount computed or ascertained to be due for the whole of said calendar year, except that the payment to be made July 1, 19...., shall also include one-fourth of said amount accruing for the year 19.... and the amount payable on July 1, 19...., shall be for only three-fourths of the amount accruing for the calendar year 19..... In lieu of computing the amount due, if not exactly ascertained, on the first day of July in each year, as above provided, the party of the first part may, at its option, defer demanding payment therefor until the amount of said taxes shall be actually ascertained thereafter and the party of the second part shall thereafter pay the same within thirty (30) days after demand therefor.

Fifth. The party of the second part also covenants and agrees that it will keep the whole interior and exterior of said building, its contents, fixtures and accessories in the same good order, repair and condition in all respects that it and they are in on September 1, 19...., or when possession thereof is given to the party of the second part; that it will from time to time expend all such sums of money as may be required for repairs, replacements, renovations and betterments upon the request of the said party of the first part, and to the extent that the same may become necessary in order that said building, its contents, fixtures and accessories shall be kept in good condition as hereinbefore provided during the continuance of this agreement.

Sixth. The party of the second part also covenants and agrees that it will on and after September 1, 19...., and during the continuance of this agreement, pay all sums which may be chargeable against said building and other property of the party of the first part herein described, by way of license for their use, provisions for the proper lighting and warming of the same for public entertainments and for all sums whatever which may become due and chargeable by reason of the occupancy of the premises and the use to which it may be put by the party of the second part, or those claiming under, by or from it.

Seventh. The party of the second part also covenants and agrees that the building shall be used for theatrical and operatic performances and other uses not different substantially from those to which it has been heretofore devoted by the lessees, including, however, the right to the party of the second part to use the same for purposes of public entertainment of any character, including motion pictures and vaudeville performances, provided the same shall always be first class only. The party of the second part covenants and agrees to maintain in the building during the theatrical season of every year during this lease, theatrical and operatic performances or public entertainments as aforesaid of the best character only, so as to constitute and keep it at all times a theater of the first class; and also that any and all directors of the party of the first part shall have at all times reasonable free and undisturbed access to all parts of the building except during hours when public performances are in progress, and that said directors shall not be permitted during said performances to have access to the stage without special permission therefor from the party of the second part. The party of the second part also agrees that during the currency of this agreement a proper room in the leased premises shall be reserved for the use of the stockholders and directors of the party of the first part and their executive committee during their regular or special meetings.

Eighth. The party of the second part also covenants and agrees that it will not assign this agreement nor any part of it without the written consent of the party of the first part; nor will it sub-let the whole or said building for any part of the time during said lease without the written consent of the party of the first part; but this shall not preclude the party of the second part at its pleasure from sub-letting parts of the building for stores or offices as has been customary in the past with respect to said premises, nor shall it preclude the party of the second part from sub-letting the theater for limited periods of time to various companies for public performances in the ordinary course of business.

It is further understood and agreed that the party of the second part, after occupancy, shall be at liberty at its own cost and expense to make any alterations that it may desire in any respect in and about the building and to its furniture, scenery, machinery, or decorations or interior arrangement, provided, however, that no such change or alteration, when completed shall in any way decrease or depreciate the value of said building, furniture, machinery, scenery and decorations, and provided further that before the party of the second part shall make any material changes it shall give notice in writing to the party of the first part of its intention with respect thereto, and in reasonable detail state the changes proposed to be made, and if demanded by the party of the first part, the party of the second part shall give immediate and sufficient bond or other satisfactory security to the party of the first part conditioned for the completion of such changes of alterations so that the value of said premises and its contents will not be diminished by said changes.

Ninth. The party of the second part also covenants and agrees that it will, at the time of the execution of these presents, pay to the party of the first part the sum of fifty thousand dollars ($50,000) which shall be the absolute property of the party of the first part as a consideration for entering into this agreement, and that it will also, on the first day of September, 19...., or upon the date of its taking possession of the premises under lease, whichever shall first occur, deposit with the party of the first part, or with the .... Trust Company as depository, an additional sum of fifty thousand dollars ($50,000) in cash or the equivalent thereof in securities approved by the party of the first part, which deposit shall constitute security for the performance by the party of the second part of the terms and conditions of this agreement and shall remain on deposit until the first day of September, 19..... And in the event that the party of the second part shall fail to perform any condition, covenant or agreement herein made binding upon it, during said term, and shall continue in default with respect thereto for the period of thirty days after written notice thereof shall be received by it from the party of the first part, delivered at the address of the party of the second part, No. .... Street, in the City of .... State and County of .... or at such other address for said notice as may hereafter be given in writing by the party of the second part to the party of the first part, then the party of the first part may elect to treat the said deposit sum as its absolute property as liquidated damages for such breach; and the party of the second part hereby authorizes the party of the first part to retain the same and authorizes the said depository to pay over and deliver the said deposit to the party of the first part. Provided, however, that if the party of the second part, after notice thereof, disputes in good faith the existence of said alleged breach, the issue between the parties shall be submitted to arbitration as hereinafter provided in Article Twelfth of this agreement, and if the award is in favor of the party of the second part the controversy shall thereupon terminate, but if in favor of the party of the first part, the party of the second part shall have the period of ten days thereafter to comply with said award, and upon said compliance the breach shall be deemed to have been cured and the party of the first part shall not be entitled to claim said deposit as its property.

Unless and until said deposit shall become payable to the party of the first part as hereinbefore provided, the income from said deposit shall be payable by said depository to the party of the second part and the principal shall be returned to it on September 1, 19.....

Tenth. The party of the second part also covenants and agrees that if any default should be made on its part in the punctual payment when due of any installment of rent or any other sums herein stipulated to be paid by it, the party of the first part, in addition to its rights of distress as herein conceded as one of its optional remedies for the non-payment of any installment or any other sum of money may, at its option at the expiration of thirty days after written notice received by the party of the second part at its address above mentioned, of such default, elect to terminate this agreement unless such default shall have been previously cured by payment. And in the event of any such termination being notified to it in writing the party of the second part covenants and agrees that the party of the first part may re-enter without legal process and take absolute possession of the premises and shall have the right to obtain and possess as liquidated damages the deposit of fifty thousand dollars ($50,000) of its equivalent in securities, hereinbefore mentioned in paragraph Ninth.

Eleventh. The party of the first part covenants and agrees that until September 1, 19...., it will insure or cause to be insured, said buildings and contents in the sum of four hundred thousand dollars ($400,000) without expense to the party of the second part, from damage by fire, and in the event of damage by fire to the building or contents, the proceeds of the insurance policies shall be applied as far as practicable to the restoration of the building premises and contents. But if the cost of restoration or repairs should exceed $400,000, and the existing lease is hereby terminated and the party of the second part is given possession, the additional amount required to repair or restore the buildings and contents shall be provided by the party of the second part, and by such repairs or restoration so made at the expense of the party of the second part shall be made under the direction of the party of the second part and in accordance with its reasonable requirements and plans, provided the value of the property of the party of the first part shall not be thereby impaired. And in the event of a substantial damage by fire which shall not terminate the existing lease on the property, which does not expire until September 1, 19...., the restoration and repair to the building to be made from the proceeds of the insurance as above mentioned shall also be subject to the reasonable plans and requirements of the party of the second part, provided always that the value of the property of the party of the first part shall not be impaired, and provided the rights, if any, of the present tenants shall be duly conserved and protected.

Twelfth. The party of the first part and the party of the second part covenant, each with the other, that if differences should exist, or any question should arise between them as to the true intent or meaning of any of the covenants or provisions of this agreement, or as to anything which either of them is bound to do or not bound to do hereunder, each such difference and question shall be submitted to two arbitrators, one of whom shall be appointed by each of said parties, with the right to such arbitrators to appoint an umpire if necessary, and the award of such arbitrators or their umpire shall be final and conclusive.

Thirteenth. The parties hereto furthermore agree that in the event that possession of the property covered by this agreement cannot be promptly delivered by the party of the first part to the party of the second part by reason of the refusal of the present tenant to vacate the premises on the date fixed for the commencement of the lease herein, to wit, September 1, 19...., then the party of the first part shall take, exercise and diligently prosecute any and all proper legal remedies for the purpose of securing and delivering possession of said premises to the party of the second part as soon as possible thereafter, at the cost and expense of the party of the first part, and for any delay in said delivery of possession, the party of the second part shall be entitled to an equitable and ratable abatement in the amount of the annual rental to be paid for the year ending September 1, 19...., including taxes, insurance and all other charges herein imposed upon the party of the second part. There shall be no liability on the part of the party of the first part if it shall fail to deliver possession of said property covered by this agreement on account of the refusal of the present tenant to surrender at the expiration of its tenancy, provided the party of the first part has adopted and prosecuted all legal remedies as above provided and this agreement shall nevertheless be and remain effective in all its terms and conditions, except as above provided. And if on the other hand the party of the first part is able to deliver possession of the said premises prior to September 1, 19...., then and in that event the party of the second part shall have the right to and shall enter immediately thereupon and into occupancy of said property upon the same terms and conditions as are herein set out as fully as if this agreement had contemplated the beginning of the lease herein provided for as of the date on which possession shall be given by the party of the first part, and all rentals and payments to be made hereunder, including insurance premiums being equitably adjusted or apportioned upon the annual basis hereunder mentioned.

Fourteenth. The parties hereto mutually agree that all the scenery, furniture and chattels in the building shall be scheduled as of the date of this agreement by two persons appointed, one by the party of the first part and one by the party of the second part, and copies of such schedule in duplicate shall be furnished to each of the parties hereto, and that such schedule shall be deemed and taken to be conclusive evidence of the nature and quality of the scenery, furniture and chattels to be delivered by the party of the first part to the party of the second part on the first day of September 19...., or when the party of the first part enters into occupancy of the said building, fire and extraordinary casualty excepted.

Fifteenth. The party of the first part hereby agrees to sell, and the party of the second part hereby agrees to purchase, the property, premises and contents hereinabove described both real and personal, upon the following terms and conditions, to wit:

(1) The party of the second part agrees to pay to the party of the first part as the purchase price of said property, the sum of five hundred thousand dollars ($500,000) as follows:

> On the day of the date hereof, the receipt whereof is hereby acknowledged, being the same sum first referred to in Article Ninth hereof—

September 1, 19...............................	$ 50,000
September 1, 19...............................	50,000
September 1, 19...............................	50,000

March 1, 19..................................... 50,000
September 1, 19................................ 50,000
March 1, 19..................................... 100,000
September 1, 19................................ 100,000

(2) The party of the first part agrees to allow on each installment according and paid on and after September 1, 19...., when and as paid from the date of payment, interest at the rate of six per cent (6%) per annum, which interest shall be allowed and credited in reduction of the annual rental heretofore agreed upon by and between the parties hereto; and no interest shall be charged against or paid by the party of the second part on any deferred installments of the purchase price.

(3) Legal title to the property shall remain in the party of the first part until September 1, 19...., whereupon if all of the said installments have been fully paid, together with all rentals and other charges, as heretofore set out in this agreement, and upon the performance of all other lawful obligations of the party of the second part hereunder, the party of the first part shall convey to the party of the second part by good and sufficient deed, title to said property in fee simple free and unencumbered, and marketable, including land, improvements, scenery, furniture and chattels herein described with covenant of special warranty to be executed by the party of the first part, said deed to be drawn at the expense of the party of the first part, said deed to be drawn at the expense of the party of the second part, the cost of revenue stamps, if any, to be borne equally by the parties hereto.

(4) The party of the first part hereby covenants that it will not nor suffer to be done any act, matter or thing whatsoever to encumber the property above described, except that the same is subject to an outstanding lease thereon expiring September 1, 19.....

(5) The party of the second part hereby covenants to pay when due and payable all of said installments of purchase price, rentals and other charges as hereinbefore set out.

(6) The party of the second part covenants that if default shall occur in the performance by it of any covenant herein binding on it, and such default shall continue for the period of thirty days after notice thereof given by the party of the first part to the party of the second part at its address as hereinbefore provided, the party of the first part shall be entitled forthwith to invoke any remedy or remedies available to it for the enforcement of this agreement, either concurrently or successively and whether legal or equitable, and shall also be entitled, if it so elect, to re-possess the property, provided however, that any proceedings instituted by the party of the first part may be stayed and the status of the party of the second part prior to default may be restored by compliance by the party of the second part with the obligations hereunder within thirty days after proceedings shall have been instituted, which obligations shall include payment of the party of the first part's reasonable court costs, attorney's fees, and other expenses in that behalf paid or incurred; and similarly if the party of the first part fails to perform any of the ob-

ligations herein contained binding, then the party of the second part shall be entitled to have this agreement enforced against the party of the first part by specific performance or other appropriate legal or equitable remedy, the reasonable cost thereof, including court costs and counsel fees, to be paid by the party of the first part.

Provided further that if the party of the first part shall re-possess the property, it shall retain the sums theretofore paid thereunder on account of the purchase price, up to and including $200,000, the initial payment of fifty thousand dollars ($50,000) being considered as a part thereof, in addition to all rentals and other payments, as liquidated damages and not as a penalty, and shall return the balance, if any, of said purchase money to the party of the second part.

And provided further, it is mutually understood and agreed that the title to the property is good and merchantable, in fee simple, as of the date of this agreement, and that the ...... Guarantee & Trust Company of .... will, at the expense of the party of the second part, insure a good and merchantable fee simple title in the party of the first part, for the use and benefit of the party of the second part, as of the date hereof. And if for any cause hereafter arising, the party of the first part shall be unable to convey a good and merchantable title by deed containing all the usual covenants, in fee simple, then this agreement of sale shall be null and void and the party of the first part shall repay to the party of the second part all sums of money which have been paid on account of the principal of the purchase price, including the sum of $50,000, paid at the time of the execution of this agreement, without interest on any of the said principal sums.

(7) It is understood and agreed that the party of the second part shall not be permitted to anticipate any of the payments of the deferred installments on account of the purchase price hereinabove specified, but that the same shall be promptly made as herein specified and that with respect to said payments, time is of the essence of the contract, provided that before the party of the first part shall be entitled to treat the party of the second part as in default with respect to the making of any such payments, thirty days' notice in writing must be given the party of the second part at its address as hereinabove provided, and in the event of payment being made within the period of thirty days or thereafter by the assent of the party of the first part interest at six per cent per annum shall be paid on said delayed payments by the party of the second part for the period of such delay.

IN WITNESS WHEREOF, the party of the first part has caused its corporate name to be signed by its President and its corporate seal to be hereto affixed duly attested by its Secretary, both of said officers acting in pursuance of due authority from the party of the first part, and the party of the second part has also caused these presents to be signed in its corporate name under its corporate seal by its duly authorized officers.

(Signatures, acknowledgments, and so forth.)

AMORTIZED LEASE AGREEMENT

(An interesting way to utilize the principle of leasing has been followed in some cities by use of the amortized lease, with option to purchase. A lease for a certain length of time is made, during which payments on the purchase price of the property are made in the form of rent. At the expiration of the lease, the remainder of the purchase price is paid in cash. Due to tax penalties owners of valuable property often decline to sell, because they cannot spread over a period of years the tax on their profits. Under the plan carried out in this lease, a sale can be made in the form of a lease with an option to purchase at any designated time. The accompanying lease was made in Philadelphia, and is given more or less in detail as to phraseology. This lease was compiled by competent lawyers and is regarded as a very useful form.)

THIS AGREEMENT made the first day of July, A.D. 19...., between (Name of lessor here), of the City of Philadelphia, State of Pennsylvania, hereinafter called the parties of the first part, (Name of lessee here), of the City of Philadelphia, State of Pennsylvania, hereinafter called the party of the second part, and The Land Title and Trust Company, a corporation incorporated under the laws of Pennsylvania, hereinafter called the Trustee, WITNESSETH;

WHEREAS, the parties of the first part have by lease and agreement dated the twenty-seventh day of May, 19...., leased to the party of the second part all that certain property situate at (Description of property here), by lease as follows:

THIS AGREEMENT made this twenty-seventh day of May, A.D. 19...., between (lessor) hereinafter called the lessors, and (lessee) hereinafter called the lessee, WITNESSETH, That the lessors do hereby let and demise unto the lessee All That Certain premises situate: (Here follows a description of the premises, the right of use of railway siding, elevators, etc.) .... for the term of eighteen years, to commence and be computed from the first day of July, 19...., yielding and paying therefor and thereout unto the lessors, their heirs, executors, administrators and assigns, the term rent of Four hundred and ninety thousand ($490,000.00) dollars, payable as follows: Ten thousand ($10,-000.00) dollars at the date of the execution hereof, and thereafter the sum of Ten thousand ($10,000.00) dollars shall be paid on the first days of January and July of each year until One hundred thousand ($100,-000.00) dollars in all has been paid; and thereafter the sum of Fifteen thousand ($15,000.00) dollars shall be paid on the first days of January and July of each year until the remaining Three hundred and ninety thousand ($390,000.00) dollars has been paid; said payments to be made at such place in the City of Philadelphia as the lessors shall from time to time direct.

Upon condition, nevertheless, and it is hereby mutually covenanted and agreed by and between the lessors and lessee, for themselves, their respective heirs, executors, administrators and assigns, in manner following, that is to say, that:

(The next thirteen clauses contain the agreement of lessee to make payment at specified times and places, to pay taxes, water rents, etc.; the right to sub-let; to maintain fire insurance in sum of $240,000.00; to keep premises in good order; to save lessor harmless for damages for injuries to person or property; all goods, etc., on premises to be liable for distress for rent, etc.; right of lessor to visit premises; failure to comply with conditions to void lease, etc.)

14. Lessee may assign his rights or interest in this agreement provided that the assignee shall assume full liability by accepting such assignment, but lessee shall remain primarily liable for the carrying out of all and every the covenants hereof on his part to be performed and kept.

15. If at any time during the continuance of this term the lessee becomes bankrupt or makes an assignment for the benefit of creditors, then the lessors shall have the right to enter upon said premises and repossess the same in the manner hereinabove set forth.

16. If the lessee shall faithfully keep and perform this agreement, and make all payments according to the term hereof, then the lessee may at his option purchase the demised premises at the expiration of this term, by paying to the lessors the sum of One hundred eighty thousand dollars ($180,000.00). At the option of the lessor, said purchase price of One hundred eighty thousand dollars ($180,000.00) shall be payable in cash or by purchase money bond and warrant and mortgage in usual form, payable in instalments of Fifteen thousand ($15,000.00) dollars semi-annually, the first installment to be paid at the execution of the mortgage and semi-annually thereafter on the first days of July and January, together with interest at six (6) per cent, payable semi-annually in advance, with a provision for acceleration of maturity at the mortgagee's option, in event of default in payment of any installment of principal or interest for thirty (30) days after same is due.

17. On or before July 1st, 19...., the demised premises shall be conveyed by the lessors to Land Title and Trust Company as trustee, upon the following trust, that is to say, to re-convey the demised premises to the lessors, or their nominee, upon the expiration of the term or upon the prior termination thereof in the manner and for the cause or causes in this indenture of lease set forth, or in in the event of the exercise by the lessee of his option to purchase in accordance with paragraph No. 16 hereof, to make, execute and deliver the deed for the demised premises to the lessee or his nominee, and receive the purchase money therefor for the account of the lessors; the title so conveyed to the trustees to be clear of incumbrances and such as will be insured by the Real Estate

Title Insurance and Trust Company of the City of Philadelphia, subject as follows:

Taxes and Water Rent for 19.....

Easement of sewer used by property on the North.

Easement of drive and used premises in question and property on the North.

Right to maintain windows West wall overlooking railroads and windows and trimmings East and North walls overlooking property on the East and North and door in North wall off as to mortgagee.

Railroad siding extending into property in question used also by property on the North.

Not fenced parts of North and East lines. For notice only.

Pipes and wires into building from property on North for sprinkler, electric and steam systems. Off as to mortgagee.

The premises in question may be liable for future assessments for the following street improvements, viz: paving (West 16 ft. not paved); curbing (no curb laid for 48' 6" of front) and water pipe (none laid as to West 30' 6⅞"). Off as to mortgagee.

Subject to certain restrictions created by lessor as to the use of the demised premises.

All the expense of the trustee to be paid by the lessee.

18. Lessors covenant to pay the existing mortgage of One hundred twenty-five thousand dollars ($125,000.00) upon the demised premises prior to any conveyance hereunder by virtue of the exercise of the option of purchase, and to assure the lessee against any dispossession hereunder by reason of the prior lien of said mortgage upon the hereby demised premises. In the event of adverse proceedings upon said mortgage, lessee may pay to the holder thereof an amount sufficient to satisfy said mortgage with accrued interest and cost, and the amount so paid by him shall be offset against any moneys then due or thereafter accruing to first parties under this agreement.

19. This agreement shall extend to and bind the heirs, executors, administrators and assigns of the parties hereto.

IN WITNESS WHEREOF the parties hereto have hereunto set their hands and seals the day and year first above written.

(Signatures, acknowledgments, and so forth.)

WHEREAS, the said parties of the first part have conveyed subject to the existing lease and agreement the property described in the foregoing lease by deed in fee simple to the Trustee, said deed of conveyance now about to be lodged for record in Philadelphia and

WHEREAS, The Land Title and Trust Company has no interest, corporate or otherwise, in the said premises and holds title thereto at the request and for the convenience of the parties of the first and second parts, their heirs, executors, administrators or assigns as their interests by said agreement appear.

NOW THE LAND TITLE AND TRUST COMPANY acknowledges and declares that it has no interest in the said premises, but that it holds title to them upon the following terms, conditions and trusts, to wit:

1. That the Trustee shall collect from the party of the second part and forthwith remit to the party of the first part without deduction, on the first days of January and July of each year, the sum of Ten thousand dollars, beginning the first day of January, 19...., and including January 1st, 19...., and thereafter on the first days of January and July of each year the sum of Fifteen thousand dollars until the remaining Three hundred and ninety thousand dollars, under the terms of the lease and agreement heretofore set forth, has been paid.

2. That the said Trustee shall in addition to the rents above enumerated collect from the party of the second part such sum or sums as shall or may be necessary for the payment of all taxes, water rents or assessments, chargeable against the property on or before the twentieth day of August of each year, and shall forthwith apply the said sum or sums so collected for the payment of such taxes, water rents and assessments for and during the continuance of the lease, and shall collect from first parties and forthwith pay all interest on encumbrances on the said premises on or before the dates when such payments shall or may be or become due, from the party liable for the same.

3. That the Trustee is hereby authorized and empowered by the parties of the first part to give to the party of the second part good and sufficient receipts and releases for all moneys paid in accordance with the terms hereof.

4. That the said Trustee shall hold fire insurance policies in the total amount of Two hundred forty thousand dollars in full force and effect marked in accordance with the lease and agreement aforesaid, the premiums thereof to be paid by the party of the second part as and when due.

5. That there shall be paid to the Trustee by the party of the second part an annual fee in the amount of Two hundred dollars in full for all services of the Trustee hereunder.

6. That upon the compliance by second party with all the terms of the lease and agreement aforesaid and payment or securing of purchase money as therein set forth, the Trustee is hereby obligated to grant and convey to the party of the second part, his heirs or assigns the above described property by good and sufficient deed in fee simple to be executed, delivered and recorded after ten days' written notice first being given to the parties of the first part, their heirs, executors, administrators or assigns, such notice to be evidenced by letter registered and sent to the last known address of the parties of the first part.

7. That upon any default by second party in the performance of any of the terms, conditions or stipulations of the lease and agreement aforesaid in the manner as therein particularly recited, the Trustee shall and by the acceptance of this agreement is hereby obligated to forthwith execute and deliver a good and sufficient deed duly acknowledged in fee simple to the above described leased property to Alfred H. Lippincott and F. Hazard Lippincott, their heirs, executors, administrators or assigns.

8. That Land Title and Trust Company shall be under no obligation or liability to defend the described leased premises in any manner whatsoever.

9. By the acceptance of this declaration and their joining in this agreement the said Lessors, parties of the first part, and Lessee, party of the second part, do hereby agree to the terms herein set forth, and the said Joseph J. Greenberg doth further agree for himself, his heirs, executors, administrators or assigns to indemnify and save harmless the said The Land Title and Trust Company, Trustee, of and from all losses or claims whatsoever by reason of the said holding of title provided prompt notice of claim is given second party by registered letter.

The terms of this agreement shall be binding upon the heirs, executors, administrators, successors or assigns of the parties hereto.

IN WITNESS WHEREOF, the parties hereto have set their hands and seals and The Land Title and Trust Company has hereunto caused its corporate seal to be affixed duly attested the day and year first above written.

THE LAND TITLE AND TRUST COMPANY.

(Signatures, acknowledgments, and so forth.)

AGREEMENT TO MAKE A LONG-TERM LEASE

(This agreement has been successfully used by the author on a number of occasions and is reasonably complete. It should be carefully adapted to each property where it is being used.)

THIS MEMORANDUM OF AGREEMENT entered into this . . . . day of . . . ., 19. . . ., BY AND BETWEEN . . . ., Lessor, hereinafter called party of the first part, and . . . ., Lessee, and hereafter referred to as party of the second part, namely: The said party of the first part is the owner of a certain parcel of land situated in the City of . . . . and known as . . . ., having a frontage of . . . . feet of land, and a depth of . . . . feet, on which is located a six-story and basement brick and mill constructed building. Said parties hereby agree to enter into a ninety-nine (99) year lease, renewable forever upon the terms and conditions hereinafter set forth.

First. Rental to be Six Thousand ($6,000) Dollars per annum for the first period of five years. Rental to be Six Thousand Five Hundred ($6,500) Dollars per annum for the second five years. Rental to be Seven Thousand ($7,000) Dollars per annum for succeeding eighty-nine (89) years thereafter. It is agreed that the above rentals are to be paid monthly in advance, and that the initial three months' rental is to be paid at the time this lease is executed.

Second. The lease is to contain a provision entitling the Lessee to purchase the property at any time before the end of the fifth year at One Hundred Thousand ($100,000.00) Dollars; at any time between the sixth and tenth years inclusive at One Hundred and Eight Thousand, Three Hundred and Thirty-three ($108,333.00) Dollars; and at any time between the eleventh and twenty-fifth years inclusive at One Hundred and Sixteen Thousand, Six Hundred and Sixty-six ($116,666.00) Dollars.

Third. The lease is to be for ninety-nine (99) years and is to be renewable forever on the same terms applicable during the ninety-ninth year of the lease.

Fourth. The Lessee is to deposit with a trustee chosen by and acting in behalf of the Lessor, a satisfactory surety bond, or other satisfactory security in the amount of Twelve Thousand Dollars ($12,000.00) to be held for the benefit of the Lessor as security for the performance of the terms of said lease by the Lessee, it being understood that in the event cash is deposited, six per cent (6%) interest is to be paid and in the event securities are deposited, the income from said securities is to be payable to the Lessee during the time said securities are held. In the event that the Lessee deposits security for the faithful performance of said lease then and in that event said securities so deposited are to be returned to the Lessee herein in the event that said Lessee exercises the option to purchase the property.

Fifth. It is agreed that the Lessee is to be permitted to wreck the present building at any time, but will be required under the terms of the lease to erect a new building costing at least Sixty Thousand Dollars ($60,000.00) on the premises, Lessee giving bond for the erection and completion of said building, free and clear of all encumbrances and liens whatsoever, before commencing to wreck the present building now standing on the premises.

Sixth. The Lessee herewith deposits ....
..........., and the receipt of the same is hereby acknowledged by the Lessors, the sum of One Thousand Dollars ($1,000.00) as earnest money, the same to apply towards the rental of the property for the first year. In the event that said lease is not executed then the One Thousand Dollars ($1,000.00) this day deposited with ....
.... shall be returned to the second party.

Seventh. It is agreed that said lease shall be executed and the term of said lease shall begin when the Lessor shall provide an abstract or a certificate of title, showing merchantable title to said premises, free and clear of all encumbrances, clouds and liens whatsoever. The extension of said certificate of title is to be at the instance and request of the Lessee, but at the expense of the Lessor.

Eighth. It is agreed that the Lessee shall pay taxes on the premises from and after the date of execution of the said lease, as it is understood that the taxes are to be pro-rated between parties as of the date of the execution of said lease, Lessors to pay all prior taxes and assessments, including taxes for the year 19.... and any part of the year 19.... which has been consumed and gone by before the execution and delivering of said lease to the parties of the second part.

Ninth. It is agreed by the Lessor that possession of a portion of the premises shall be given to the Lessee not later than March 25, 19..... The Lessor agrees to pay to the Lessee a rent for such portion of said premises as may be retained by Lessor from the date of the execution of said lease to such a time the Lessor agrees to vacate said premises, which shall not be later than September 1, 19..... The rate of rental shall be the same as stipulated to be paid by the Lessee herein. That portion of the premises which Lessor agrees to give possession of to Lessee not later than March 25, 19...., shall consist of all of the second floor of the building herein named, half of the basement under said building and a space at least fifteen feet wide and thirty feet deep on the ground floor, Lessee agreeing to pay the necessary expense for providing access to said ground floor space and for partitioning off said space from that occupied by ....

Tenth. Party of the second part agrees to keep the building now on the premises, or one to be erected and completed hereafter, in constant good condition and repair and insured against loss or damage by fire in insurance companies of general recognized responsibility and credit, satisfactory to a trustee to be named by Lessor, in an amount equal to not less than eighty per cent (80%) of the fair and insurable value thereof, exclusive of foundations.

Eleventh. In the event of the exercise of the option to purchase, the property is to be deeded to the party of the second part, their heirs or assigns, or such persons or corporations as may be designated by them by warranty deed, free and clear from all encumbrances and liens whatsoever, excepting only such as may have been placed on the property by or because of the Lessee, upon payment of the purchase price in cash, or if requested, the deed is to be placed with a responsible abstract company as escrow agent with instructions to deliver upon payment to the abstract company of the purchase price.

Twelfth. Said lease is to be made to the party of the second part herein with the right to transfer or assign the same at any time thereafter to persons or corporations designated by them, their heirs or assigns, with the full privilege of sub-letting all or any part, provided however, that such assignment shall not be made unless party of the second part executes every covenant in said lease.

Thirteenth. Within ten days from the date of the acceptance hereof, the Lessor shall tender to the Lessee a complete draft of a lease of the premises before mentioned, embodying the foregoing terms and provisions and such other provisions consistent therewith as are appropriate and necessary for the setting forth of the rights and obligations of the Lessor and Lessee respectively, and within ten days from the receipt of such draft of lease the Lessee shall either execute the same or tender to the Lessor in writing such amendments, if any, of said draft of lease as he may desire it to contain. In the latter even within ten days from the tender by the Lessee to the Lessor of his amendments to original draft of the lease the parties shall agree upon and execute a lease which shall be and become of full force and effect conditioned only upon both the

Lessor and Lessee carrying out the other covenants of this agreement. In case the parties hereto cannot agree upon the form of the lease within the time above stipulated either one may demand that the arbitrator mentioned herein shall settle the dispute in accordance with the terms of the arbitration agreement.

Fourteenth. In the event the parties hereto are unable to agree on the exact language of any clause, or as to the omission or insertion of any clause or clauses or as to the wording of the complete lease, or if Lessor fails to draw and prepare said lease, then an arbitrator, who shall be .... of The .... Trust Company shall determine said language or shall draw and prepare said lease, which determination and lease so drawn by him shall be binding on both parties. The cost of such arbitration is to be divided equally between the Lessor and Lessee.

Fifteenth. Party of the first part agrees to pay to .... Organization the regular Real Estate Board commission for the execution of said lease, payment to be made at time lease is finally executed.

(Signatures, witnesses, and so forth.)

AGREEMENT TO MAKE A LONG-TERM LEASE

(A form of agreement to execute a lease has been prepared by a number of Cleveland lease brokers and is shown below. It can be reversed if necessary, the lessee signing the contract and the lessor accepting the same.)

................, ..., 19.....
.... (hereinafter referred to as Lessor) hereby authorizes .... to act as agent in LETTING AND LEASING for a period of ninety-nine (99) years, renewable forever thereafter on the same terms and conditions as will be in force in the ninety-ninth (99th) year of the first ninety-nine (99) years of the lease, real estate in the City of ...., known as No. ...., and described as follows, to-wit:
(Description here)

Rental. The rental for same shall be ....
....
payable quarterly in advance.

Possession. ....

Taxes. The Lessor and Lessee shall pay pro-rata, according to their respective occupancies, all taxes, assessments and other public charges, which are or may be payable on said property for the current calendar year 19...., but the Lessee shall pay all subsequent taxes, assessments and public charges which may become a lien, except income, estate or inheritance tax charged against the Lessor's rents or interest. The date of possession shall fix their respective occupancies.

Improvements. The Lessee agrees to improve said property with a new building suitable to its location, within . . . . years from date of said lease of the value of $. . . . ., and contemporaneously with the signing of said lease will furnish the Lessor with satisfactory surety or acceptable securities in the amount of $. . . . . to guarantee the fulfillment of the provisions of such lease up and until such time as the building condition has been complied with, whereupon said surety shall be cancelled or said securities returned, or both.

No building now on said premises shall be removed or razed before Lessee gives Lessor additional satisfactory surety or acceptable securities in the amount of $. . . . ., same to remain with Lessor until building condition has been complied with, whereupon said surety shall be cancelled or said securities returned, or both.

Insurance. The Lessees agree to insure and keep insured at all times any and all buildings on said property in the amount of . . . .% of their full insurable value with policies in possession of The . . . . Trust Company, as Trustee, but with loss available through said Trustee to Lessee for rebuilding.

Purchase. The Lessee shall have the right to purchase said above described property at any time between . . . ., 19. . . ., and . . . ., 19. . . ., for the sum of $. . . . .

Form of lease. Within . . . . days from the date of the acceptance hereof the Lessor shall tender to the Lessee a complete draft of a lease of the premises before mentioned, embodying the foregoing terms and provisions and such other provisions consistent therewith as are appropriate and necessary for the setting forth of the rights and obligations of the Lessor and Lessee, respectively, and within . . . . days from the receipt of such draft of lease the Lessee shall either execute the same or tender to the Lessor in writing such amendments, if any, of said draft of lease as he may desire it to contain. In the latter event within . . . . days from the tender by the Lessee to the Lessor of his amendments to original draft of the lease the parties shall agree upon and execute a lease which shall be and become of full force and effect conditioned only upon both the Lessor and Lessee carrying out the other covenants of this agreement. In case the parties hereto cannot agree upon the form of the lease within the time above stipulated either one may demand that the arbitrator mentioned herein shall settle the dispute in accordance with the terms of the arbitration agreement.

Arbitration. In the event the parties hereto are unable to agree on the exact language of any clause, or as to the omission or insertion of any clause or clauses or as to the wording of the complete lease, or if Lessor fails to draw and prepare said lease, then an arbitrator, who shall be . . . . of The . . . . Trust Company, shall determine said language or shall cause to be drawn and prepared said lease, which determination and lease so drawn by him shall be binding on both parties.

Abstract. The Lessor agrees to furnish to the Lessee a new certificate or an Abstract of Title by The .... Company extended to time of transfer and further guarantees the property to be free and clear from all incumbrances, restrictions and limitations, except ....

....

Time. This instrument expires by limitations at 12 o'clock noon on the .... day of ...., 19...., unless said agent shall have previously secured a responsible party as Lessee who will accept the terms of this instrument and contemporaneously therewith execute a certified check in favor of Lessor in the sum of $............, which shall apply on the first year's rental.

Dower interest. The Lessor hereby agrees that ...., his wife, will sign and execute lease as herein provided for.

(Blank space left here for any special clause)

Commission. For securing the Lessee named below, the Lessor agrees to pay to .... the regular commission as established by The .... Real Estate Board, and in accordance with its rules.

WITNESS: ....

....

ACCEPTANCE

........................, above referred to as the Lessee, hereby accepts and agrees to this contract this .... day of ...., 19...., and deposits with .... $..........., on account of this contract, to apply on first year's rental.

....

WITNESS:

....

AGREEMENT TO SELL A LEASEHOLD INTEREST

(Leases are often sold for bonuses, a cash consideration being paid and the leasehold interests being assigned intact, with the consent of the lessor. This form may be used when necessary.)

This agreement made and concluded at ...., Ohio, this .... day of ...., 19...., by and between D. R. M. of ...., party of the first part, and L. R. S. of ...., party of the second part, witnesseth:

That whereas, one E. E. R., by a certain instrument of lease dated the .... day of ...., 19...., and recorded in the office of the recorder of .... County, Ohio, in Volume .... of leases, Page ...., did demise, let and lease unto said D. R. M. certain premises situated at No. .... Street in the .... of

.............., Ohio, for a term of .... years ending on the
.... day of .... 19...., for the yearly rent of
.... dollars; for a more particular description of said premises, and of said term, and for all the covenants, provisions, terms and conditions of which said lease, reference is hereby made thereto.

Now, therefore said party of the first part in consideration of the sum of .... dollars ($..........) in hand paid the receipt of which is hereby acknowledged and further in consideration of the promises and agreements of said party of the second part herein contained does hereby promise and agree to sell, transfer and assign unto the said party of the second part all the estate and interest of said party of the first part in said premises and in said lease for the residue of the term of said lease subject to all the rents, covenants, conditions, provisions and stipulations in said lease contained on the part of the Lessee to be paid, observed and performed.

Said party of the first part further agrees to execute and deliver to said party of the second part, a good and sufficient instrument of assignment and conveyance of said leasehold interest, with the consent of the said E. E. R. to such assignment endorsed thereon, on or before the .... day of ...., 19....; and to pay all rents, taxes, assessments and charges due and payable by the Lessee under the provisions of said lease up to and including the .... day of ...., 19....; and that said leasehold interest so assigned and conveyed shall be free and clear from all liens or incumbrances, except such as may be created and provided for by said lease due after said .... day of ...., 19.....

Said party of the first part further agrees to give possession of said premises to said party of the second part on or before ...., 19.....

In consideration whereof, said party of the second part hereby promises and agrees to purchase said leasehold interest and to pay therefor the sum of .... dollars ($..........), payable as follows: Said sum of .... dollars ($..........) this day paid to be applied on said purchase price and the balance of .... dollars ($..........) to be paid in cash on the execution and delivery of said instrument of assignment of said lease as hereinbefore provided.

Said party of the second part further promises and agrees to pay the rent, taxes, assessments and other charges, and to perform all the other covenants of said lease on the part of the Lessee to be performed, and to indemnify and save harmless said party of the first part thereupon.

It is mutually agreed by and between the parties hereto that the receipt of the Lessor for the last installment of rent due up to said .... day of ...., 19...., shall be deemed conclusive evidence that the covenants of said lease have been performed by said party of the first part.

In witness whereof the parties have hereunto set their hands to duplicates hereof the day and year first above written.

(Signatures, acknowledgments, and so forth.)

MORTGAGE DEED

(This is the form of mortgage deed used in cases where a bank or bond house issues bonds for the erection of a building on leased land.)

KNOW ALL MEN BY THESE PRESENTS, That I, ..., of the City of ...., ..., the Grantor, for the consideration of .... Dollars ($..........) received to my full satisfaction of The .... Trust Company of ...., ..., a corporation duly organized and existing under the laws of the State of ...., the Grantee, do give, grant, bargain, sell, convey, assign and transfer unto the said Grantee, its successors and assigns, the following described premises and property to-wit:

(Description here)

Said lease is recorded in Volume .... of Leases, Page .... of the records in the office of the Recorder of .... County, ...

To have and to hold the above granted and bargained leasehold estates, premises, property, rights and privileges, with the appurtenances thereunto belonging, or in any wise appertaining unto the said Grantee, its successors and assigns forever. And I, ..., the said Grantor, do for myself and my heirs, executors and administrators covenant with the said Grantee, its successors and assigns, that at and until the ensealing of these presents I am well seized, possessed and entitled of and to the above described leasehold estate, premises, property, rights and privileges with the appurtenances thereunto belonging and have good right, full power and lawful authority to grant, bargain, sell, convey, assign and transfer the same in manner and form as above written; that the same and every part thereof is free and clear from all liens, clouds and incumbrances whatsoever and that I will warrant and defend the same unto the said Grantee, its successors and assigns, against all lawful claims and demands whatsoever.

THE CONDITION OF THIS DEED is such that whereas the said ...., has executed and delivered unto said The .... Trust Company his certain promissory note for .... Dollars ($..........) dated at .... (City) ...., ... (State) ...., ... (Month) ...., 19...., and due one year from date and payable at the office of The .... Trust Co., with interest at the rate of six per cent (6%) per annum, payable quarterly on the 15th days of March, June, September and December in each year until paid; and authorizing any Attorney-at-law to appear in any Court of Record in the State of .... after the above obligation becomes due and waive the issuing and service of process and confess a judgment against him in favor of The ....

Trust Company, or any holder of said note for the amount then appearing due, together with costs of suit and thereupon releasing all errors and waiving all right of appeal.

And the said Grantor agrees that he will pay to the said Grantee or any holder of said note, the principal and interest thereof, promptly as and when the same become due and payable according to the tenor of said note.

And the said Grantor further agrees that so long as said promissory note or any interest thereon or any sums or charges paid or incurred by Grantee for the protection of its lien hereunder shall be and remain unpaid, he will keep the buildings and all other insurable property covered by this mortgage, insured against loss by fire in an amount equal to their full insurable value in fire insurance companies satisfactory to the holder of this mortgage, with loss, if any, payable to such holder as his interest may appear, it being agreed, however, that so much of said insurance as is exacted by the terms of the aforementioned lease, shall be subject to the terms of said lease and payable as therein directed, but the excess over and above the amount so exacted shall be payable directly to the holder of this mortgage, the policies therefor to be left in his possession; and the said Grantor further agrees that during all of the time aforesaid he will keep all rents, issues and profits to be derived from the buildings and improvements on said premises likewise insured to their full gross amount in insurance companies satisfactory to the holder of said note by a policy or policies to be left in the possession of such holder, with loss, if any, payable to such holder as his interest may appear; and all of said fire and rent insurance and any other insurance carried by the said Grantor in respect to the within mortgaged premises, leasehold estate and property (which insurance shall likewise be held by said Grantee) and the proceeds of such policies shall, in case of loss, be further security to the holder of this mortgage for the amount due thereon and may at his election be applied toward the payment thereof.

And said Grantor further agrees that during all the time aforesaid he will also pay, or cause to be paid, punctually, as and when the same become due and payable, all taxes, levies and assessments imposed or assessed, or which may hereafter be imposed or assessed, upon the premises, leasehold estate and property hereby conveyed or intended to be so conveyed, and also all other taxes, assessments, liens, incumbrances, rents and other charges which may lawfully be imposed upon said premises, leasehold estate or property, or any part thereof, or upon the income and profits thereof, the lien whereof might or could be prior to the rights granted by these presents.

And the said Grantor further agrees that during all of the time aforesaid he will comply with all laws, rules and regulations of all legally constituted authorities with respect to the construction, operation and maintenance of his buildings and in respect to the use and occupation of said premises, and that he will, at his own cost and expense, do or cause to be done all things necessary to preserve and keep valid and intact the right and liens of the Grantee hereunder, including the payment of all rents, monies and charges and the performance of, all and singular, the terms, conditions and agreements contained in the lease above referred to; and all monies due or hereafter to be paid by the said Grantor under the terms of said lease aforementioned shall be deposited by the Grantor herein with the Grantee herein for payment to the parties entitled thereto under the terms of said lease, a reasonable time in advance of the time when the same become due and payable according to the terms of said lease.

And the said Grantor further agrees that if any taxes, assessments, rents or other charges on said premises or leasehold estate, or any installments of interest or principal of said note or insurance as above provided, be not paid when due, or if any default be made by the said Grantor in the performance of any of the other stipulations of this mortgage, or if any act be done by him or default committed, which in the opinion of the Grantee, would impair the Grantee's rights or lien hereunder, then the entire principal of said note shall at once become due and payable at the option of the holder of this mortgage; and further that in such event such holder may, and is hereby authorized, to procure such insurance, pay such taxes, assessments, liens, rents and other charges and otherwise cure such defaults, and the amount or amounts so expended by the said holder shall be immediately re-paid to said holder by the said Grantor and unless so paid shall be added to and deemed a part and parcel of the money secured hereby and a lien upon the property hereby conveyed and shall draw interest at the same rate as the principal debt secured hereby.

And the said Grantor, for himself, his heirs, executors, administrators and assigns, agrees with the said Grantee, its successors and assigns, that in the event of the happening of any default of the said Grantor in the performance of the conditions or stipulations of this mortgage, or any of them, it shall be lawful for the said Grantee, its successors and assigns, at any time after said default, to sell, either personally or by attorney, all and singular, the within mortgages, leasehold estate, premises, property, rights and privileges with the appurtenances thereunto belonging, or in any wise appertaining, at public or private sale, at such time and upon such terms as said Grantee may deem advisable, without either advertisement or notice to the said Grantor, the same being hereby expressly waived, and at any such sale said Grantee or any holder of this mortgage, may purchase the whole or any part of the property sold and upon such sale said Grantee is authorized and empowered to execute and deliver to the purchaser or purchasers thereof, good and sufficient deeds or transfers in law for the same; and such sale made as aforesaid shall be a perpetual bar both in law and in equity against said Grantor and all persons or parties lawfully claiming or to claim the said leasehold estate, premises and property with said appurtenances so sold or any part thereof, by, from, through or under the said Grantor; and after deducting from the proceeds of such sale just allowances for all disbursements and expenses of, or incident to such sale, including attorneys and counsellors fees, and all other expenses, advances and liabilities which may have been made or incurred by the said Grantee in respect to said leasehold estate, premises and property, and any and all payments which have been made by it or anyone in its behalf, for taxes, assessments, rents, insurance premiums and charges or liens prior to the lien of these presents on the said premises, leasehold estate and property, or any part thereof, and in doing any other of the things which by the terms of this indenture the said Grantee may do at its election for its own protection, said Grantee shall be entitled to apply the proceeds of such sale toward the payment of its said note and interest; and if, after said note and interest and all other items hereinbefore enumerated are paid in full, a surplus of such proceeds shall remain, such surplus shall be turned over to the said Grantor or to whomsoever may be lawfully or equitably entitled to receive the same, or as any court of competent jurisdiction shall order.

And the said Grantor, for himself, his heirs, executors and administrators, further agrees to and does hereby irrevocably waive the benefit and advantage of any and all valuation, stay appraisement, redemption and extension laws and of all laws requiring mortgages, liens, hypothecations or other securities for money, to be foreclosed by any action now existing or which may hereafter exist under the laws of the State of ...., and which, but for this provision herein, might prevent or postpone the sale of said premises, leasehold estate and property, under the powers and upon compliance with the provisions of these presents; and the said Grantor hereby covenants with the said Grantee that he will not, in any manner, set up, or seek, or take the benefit or advantage of any such valuation, stay, appraisement, redemption or extension law.

And the said Grantor, for himself, his heirs, executors, administrators and assigns, agrees with the said Grantee, its successors and assigns, that in the event of the happening of any default as above set forth, the said Grantee, or its said successors or assigns, by its or their attorneys or agents, may enter into and upon and take and possess, all and singular, the said leasehold estate, premises, property and rights hereinbefore expressed to be conveyed, or any of them, or any part thereof, and have, hold and use the same, and make, from time to time all such repairs, replacements and such useful alterations, additions and improvements thereunto as may seem to it or them to be judicious or convenient, and collect and receive all revenues, incomes, rents, issues and profits of said leasehold estate, premises and property, and of every part thereof; and after deducting and defraying all expenses incurred thereby and the cost of said repairs, replacements, alterations, additions and improvements, and all payments which may be made for rents, taxes, assessments, insurance premiums and charges or liens prior to the lien of these presents, and for the doing of any other of the things which it may do by the terms hereof for its protection, in respect to said leasehold estate, premises, property, or any part thereof, and all other expenses incurred in relation thereto, as well as just compensation for its services and for the services of its agents, attorneys and counsel, the said grantee may apply the monies arising from such collections and receipts as aforesaid, toward the payment of the interest and principal of its said promissory note until the same have been paid in full, or to such lesser extent as it may deem advisable, after which it shall restore said mortgage, leasehold estate, premises and property to the possession of the said Grantor, subject, however, to the covenants and conditions of this indenture, in the same manner and to the same extent as if said entry had not been made, turning over the surplus, if any, to the said Grantor, or as any Court of competent jurisdiction shall order; and the said Grantee, its successors and assigns may avail itself of this remedy as often during the existence of the obligation, or any part thereof, secured hereby, as it may deem necessary.

And the said Grantor further agrees that upon the commencement of any action to foreclose this mortgage, or any time pending such action, or pending any other judicial proceeding in which said Grantee, for its protection, may be required to set up its rights and interests hereunder, the said Grantee shall be entitled, as of right, to the appointment ex parte and without notice to the said Grantor, or to any party claiming any right, title or interest in or to said leasehold estate, premises or property, or any part thereof, of a receiver or receivers of the within mortgaged premises, leasehold estate and property, and of the income, rents, issues and profits thereof, for the benefit of the holder or holders of the indebtedness secured hereby, with full powers to collect the rents, issues and profits of said leasehold estate, premises, property and appurtenances, and to manage the same, during the pendency of such action and apply the same toward the payment of the several obligations hereinabove mentioned and described.

No right or remedy herein conferred upon the said Grantee, its successor or assigns, is intended to be exclusive of any other right or remedy, but each and every such right and remedy shall be cumulative, and shall be in addition to every other remedy given hereunder or existing at law or in equity or by suit; and wherever the word "Grantee" appears in this instrument the same shall be construed and taken to mean "the said Grantee, its successors and assigns."

Now if the said ...., his heirs, executors, administrators or assigns shall well and truly pay the aforesaid note, interest, taxes; assessments, insurance and other charges and punctually keep and comply with all of the above mentioned agreements and stipulations, according to the tenor of said note and the terms of this indenture to and with the said The .... Trust Company, its successors and assigns, or to whomsoever due and payable, then the above deed shall be void; otherwise the same shall remain in full force and virtue in law.

IN WITNESS WHEREOF, I have hereunto set my hand, this .... day of .... in the year of our Lord, One thousand, nine hundred and ....

(Signatures, acknowledgments, and so forth.)

CHECK SHEET CONTAINING ITEMS TO
CONSIDER IN CREATING, SELLING, OR
APPRAISING LONG-TERM LEASES

(This check sheet, containing valuable data and suggestions for consideration in long-term leases, was compiled and issued under the auspices of the National Real Estate Brokers Institute, affiliated with the National Association of Real Estate Boards. It is comprehensive and indicates the many matters which must be investigated in connection with modern leases. To anyone preparing a new lease, it serves as a guide so that important elements may not be overlooked or neglected. It likewise is invaluable to the appraiser in the accumulation of data on which to base his valuation. It is used here with the permission of the Institute.)

LOCATION OF PROPERTY ....
LEGAL DESCRIPTION ....
LESSOR .... ADDRESS ....
LESSEE .... ADDRESS ....
ATTORNEY FOR LESSOR ....
            Broker for Lessor ....
ATTORNEY FOR LESSEE ....
            Broker for Lessee ....

PLAT OF LOCATION
(Space reserved here for detailed plat of premises.)

DESCRIPTION OF PRESENT IMPROVEMENTS, IF ANY: ....
....
IN WHOM IS THE LEGAL TITLE TO THE FEE? ....
....
IN WHOM IS THE LEGAL TITLE TO THE LEASEHOLD? ....
....
WHO IS THE EQUITABLE OWNER OF THE FEE? ....
....
WHO IS THE EQUITABLE OWNER OF THE LEASEHOLD? .....
....

  1.   **DATE:** ....
  2.   **LESSOR** (as Trustee, etc.): ....
           ....
  3.   **LESSEE** (as Trustee, etc.): ....
           ....
            If a corporation, organized under the laws of ....

If a partnership, names of partners: ....

....

4. **PREMISES:**   See legal description on cover ....
Is lease to ⎫
Does lease ⎬ state that no space under, in, upon or above any
street, alley or sidewalk adjoining or adjacent to the premises is
demised, excepting such rights as the Lessor may have and except
at the Lessee's own risk and cost, if any, to the municipality? .....
Will ⎫
Does ⎬ lease state that the premises demised are subject to: Party
walls? .... Building lines? .... Building restrictions? .... Zoning and building ordinances? ....
Existing (sub) leases? ....
Is lease subject to the terms, covenants, provisions, conditions
and limitations of an original lease of the premises in question?
.... If so, make reference to creation of such original lease
(date, parties, term, rental, document number, etc.) ....

....

Are demised premises now subject to a mortgage? ....
If so, who agrees to pay same? .... Is same (to be) subordinate to this lease? ....

....

5. **TERM:** .... years .... months, beginning
.... and ending ....
Is lease a "perpetual" lease, renewable forever? ....

6. **RENTAL:** Total rental for term: $..........................
Payable in annual, semi-annual, quarterly or monthly installments? ....

....

Amount of installments and when payable: ....

....

Where payable? ....
Payable in gold coin of U. S. A., its equivalent; or how? ....
Is lease to ⎫
Does lease ⎬ contain a provision for no abatement of rents except
for inheritance and income tax of Lessor? ....

....

Is lease to ⎫
Does lease ⎬ provide for revaluation of premises to determine
rental for certain periods? ....
If so, for what periods? ....
State conditions of revaluation or reappraisement ....

....

7. **TAXES AND ASSESSMENTS:** Are general real estate taxes to
be paid by Lessee as additional rental? ....
If so, what proportion of the taxes for the first and last years of
the term is to be paid by Lessee? ....

Are special assessments to be paid by Lessee as additional rental?
....

Is Lessee required to pay special assessments existing at the time of the creation of the lease for improvements already completed?
....

Are general tax and/or special assessment receipts to be exhibited to or copies delivered to Lessor? ....

Is Lessee to ⎫
Does Lessee ⎬ have privilege of contesting questionable taxes and

if so upon what indemnity to the Lessor? ....
....

Is lease to ⎫
Does lease ⎬ provide that, if an income tax should in the future

be levied in lieu of or as a substitute for the general real estate tax, Lessee is to be liable for such tax only upon the income derived by the Lessor for the demised premises? ....
....

8. **SALE OF PRESENT BUILDING:** If the demised premises
were ⎫   did ⎫
are ⎬ improved at date of creation of lease, must ⎬ the Lessee pur-

chase the existing building? ....
If so, at what price? ....

9. **MAINTENANCE AND CARE OF BUILDINGS:**

Is lease to ⎫
Does lease ⎬ contain provision that buildings and premises are

to be maintained in accordance with local building, zoning, fire, health and other ordinances? ....

Is lease to ⎫
Does lease ⎬ contain provision that premises are not to be used

for any unlawful purposes? ....

Is lease to ⎫
Does lease ⎬ provide that the Lessee will not use, or suffer or

permit said premises or any part thereof, or any building, at any time situated thereon, or any part of such building, to be used for the sale or manufacture of either spiritous, fermented or intoxicating liquors, except in connection with the bona fide operation of a drug store, and then only in compliance with all laws and ordinances from time to time in force? ....

10. **REPAIRS:** Is Lessee to keep buildings in good order and repair?
....

Is Lessee required to make alterations and repairs upon notice from Lessor or from local or state authorities? ....

Is Lessee to maintain building as of a certain value and if so, to what extent? ....

11. **INSURANCE:** To what extent of value of building is Lessee to maintain fire insurance? ....

Are insurance companies and policies to be first approved by

Lessor and/or by insurance Trustee? ....

To whom is loss under such policies to be made payable? ......

. . . .

Is an insurance Trustee to be designated? If so, name ....

If so, are policies to be deposited with the Trustee? ....

Is lease to ⎫
Does lease ⎬ contain a provision that the Trustee shall not be re-

sponsible for the collection or non-collection of any insurance money, and that it shall be liable only for its own deliberate and wilful default, neglect and/or embezzlement of its employees?

. . . .

Is lease to ⎫
Does lease ⎬ provide that the building must at all times conform

to the Board of Underwriters' rules? ....

Is there (to be) a provision for temporary insurance upon any building under construction by Lessee? ....

What casualty and indemnity insurance is required to be carried by Lessee? Rent? .... Boiler? .... Tornado? .... Workmen's Compensation? .... General Liability? ....

Is Lessee to deliver to Lessor from time to time a schedule of insurance policies if same are to be held by a Trustee? ....

. . . .

Is lease to ⎧
Does lease ⎨ provide that in case Lessee shall encumber or mort-

gage the leasehold estate hereby created and the building standing thereon, the Lessee shall be entitled, so long as any such encumbrance or mortgage shall continue in force, to have a portion of the insurance on the building on the demised premises made payable to the mortgagee or trustee under such mortgage or encumbrance?

. . . .

If so, what amount, or what percentage of the total amount carried on the building? ....

12. **COVENANT AGAINST LIENS:** Is lease to ⎫
Does lease ⎬ contain an ex-

press covenant (1) that nothing in it contained shall authorize the Lessee to do any act which shall in any way encumber the title of the Lessor in and to said premises, (2) that the interest or the estate of the Lessor therein shall be no way subject to any claim by way of lien or encumbrance, whether claimed by operation of law or by virtue of any expressed or implied contract by the said Lessee; and (3) that any claim to a lien upon said demised premises, arising from any act or omission of the Lessee, shall accrue only against the leasehold estate of the Lessee, and shall in all respects be subject to the paramount title and rights of the Lessor in and to said premises? ....

. . . .

Is lease to ⎫
Does lease ⎭ contain an express covenant that the Lessee will not enter into any contract with any person, firm or corporation for labor, services or material in connection with any building to be placed upon said premises or to be rebuilt or remodeled thereon, which contract involves an amount in excess of $........., unless it shall be stipulated in and be a condition of such contract that no lien shall arise or be claimed on account of such contract or on account of any work done or material furnished under said contract as against the title or interest of the Lessor in said premises, or unless such contract provides that the contractor, person, firm or corporation shall waive all rights thereto? ....
....

13. **COVENANT AGAINST WASTE:** Is lease to ⎫
Does lease ⎭ contain a covenant against waste by Lessee? ....

14. **ADVANCES BY LESSOR UPON LESSEE'S DEFAULT:**
Is lease to ⎫
Does lease ⎭ give Lessor the right to make advances upon Lessee's failure to pay taxes, insurance, etc.? ....
Are such advances to be treated as additional rent? ....
What rate of interest is Lessor entitled to upon such advances?
....
Is Lessor excused from making inquiry as to the validity of taxes, insurance, etc. which he may elect to pay? ....

15. **CONSTRUCTION OF NEW BUILDING:** Is a new building to be constructed by Lessee? ....
With what time must construction begin? .... By what time must construction be completed? ....
What is to be the character and type of construction of the building to be erected? ....
....
What is to be the cost of the building to be erected? ....
Height? .... Floor loads? ....
Is lease to ⎫
Does lease ⎭ provide that before the existing building upon the demised premises shall be torn down and in any event, not less than .... days before any work shall be done toward the construction of a new building on said premises and before any contract is let, plans and specifications of the proposed new building shall be furnished by said Lessee to said Lessor, the same to be retained by the said Lessor, to the end that said Lessor may be able to observe and see in advance the intention of the Lessee to comply with the requirements as to such new building? ....
....
Is Lessee to ⎫
Does Lessee ⎭ covenant and agree that said new building shall

be constructed substantially in accordance with the plans and specifications so furnished to the Lessor? ....

Is Lessor to have the right to supervise construction? ....

May building be built so as to connect with adjoining building or buildings? ....

May building be a part of a building to cover demised premises and adjoining premises? ....

If so, what provision is to be made for framing for elevators? ....

For columns and foundations? ....

Along dividing line between leased premises and adjoining premises? ....

Are party columns and foundations to be used? ....

Is Lessee to have the right to enter into party wall agreements or is the consent of Lessor required? ....

What provision is to be made for wrecking existing buildings on premises? ....

If existing buildings are salvaged, is Lessee to be entitled to the moneys therefrom? ....

Is liability insurance and temporary fire insurance to be carried by Lessee during construction? ....

16. **DEPOSIT AND APPLICATION OF SECURITY:** Is deposit of security required of Lessee? ....

If so, when is deposit to be made? .... With whom?......

In what amount shall it be? .... What form shall it take:

Cash? .... First-class bankable securities duly assigned and having a market value of not less than $.................
....?

A bond with a responsible surety company duly authorized to do business in .... as surety thereon in the penal sum of $..................?

Are such deposits to be subject to the approval of Lessor and/or the Trustee? ....

Is Lessee to be entitled to interest on deposits? ....

If so, at what rate? ....

Are moneys to complete building to be on hand before contracts are let? ....

How and when are such moneys to be paid out? (Architects' certificates, etc.) ....

Is lease to ⎫
Does lease ⎰ provide that there shall always be on deposit from time to time sufficient moneys to complete and pay for the proposed new building free and clear of liens of mechanics or material men? ....

If deposit is made with a Trustee, and deposit is made up of securities as above mentioned, shall such Trustee have power to convert securities into cash? ....

If so, under what circumstances? ....

Is Lessee to have right of substitution of securities? ....

Is lease to ⎫
Does lease ⎰ provide that, if at any time the securities so deposited shall depreciate in value, then within .... days after the receipt of notice from the Lessor or the Trustee, Lessee will deposit with the Lessor or the Trustee additional cash and/or securities sufficient to make good such depreciation? ....

What disposition is to be made of deposit in the event of Lessee's default? ....
....

Is lease to ⎫
Does lease ⎰ provide that, until default shall be made by Lessee in the performance of any of the covenants and agreements in the lease contained on the part of the Lessee to be kept, observed and performed, all the net income received from securities or cash deposited (if such be the case), shall be paid over as and when received, to the Lessee upon the Lessee's request, and that if said securities or cash be deposited with a Trustee, that the Trustee's reasonable costs and charges in connection with the deposit hereunder be deducted prior to such payment to the Lessee? ....

In the event of default by Lessee, shall Lessor be entitled to receive from the Trustee out of the deposit on hand an amount equal to such default? ....

In such event shall the Lessee, upon notice from Lessor or Trustee, be required to replace such payment to Lessor with cash and/or good and marketable securities? ....

In the event of default by Lessee in respect to the erection or completion of the new building, may (1) the Lessor complete the building with the deposit on hand if such deposit be sufficient or (2) the Lessor terminate the lease? ....

In the event of termination, shall Lessor be entitled to such cash and/or securities as are on deposit? ....

17. **REBUILDING IN CASE OF INJURY OR DESTRUCTION:**
Under what conditions is Lessee required to rebuild? ....

Within what time must the rebuilding commence and be completed? ....

In case of rebuilding, describe type, size, cost, etc. of building required. ....
....
....

18. **APPLICATION OF INSURANCE MONEY:** What disposition is to be made of insurance moneys in the event of injury or destruction? ....
....

If the Lessee does not build within the specified time, does the Lessor have the right to forfeit securities on deposit and/or to forfeit insurance moneys received by Lessor or held in trust by the insurance Trustee? ....

....

    In the event that the Lessor has and exercises such right of forfeiture shall the lease be thereupon terminated and Lessee released of further liability? ....

....

19. ALTERATIONS AND IMPROVEMENTS (not in case of injury or destruction):
    Does Lessee have the right to make alterations and improvements? (not structural changes) ....
    Must Lessor's consent be obtained? ....
    May Lessor require alterations or improvements? ....
    Is Lessee required to make any deposit prior to making alterations and improvements? ....
    Must waivers of lien be deposited with Lessor? ....
    Are plans and specifications to be submitted to and approved by Lessor? ....
    Are alterations and improvements to become part of the existing building? ....

....

20. FURTHER BUILDING PROVISIONS: Is lease to } Does lease } provide for the erection by the Lessee of any buildings other than the original new building? ....

....

    May the Lessee or Lessee's assigns remove a building placed upon the demised premises by the Lessee for the purpose of erecting a new building in its place? ....
    If so, what shall be the requirements? ....

....

    If so, shall the Lessee be entitled to the proceeds, if any, from the salvage of such removal? ....
    What deposit is required as security for the erection of such future buildings, if any? ....

....

21. BUILDING PART OF REALTY: Is Lessee to agree not to dismantle or remove any building except as specifically allowed? ....

....

    Does building become part of realty? ....
    Are buildings and improvements to vest in Lessor at end of term whether by lapse of time or otherwise, without compensation to the Lessee? ....
    Are buildings and improvements to be purchased by Lessor at end of term? ....
    If so, what provisions are to be made for fixing price? ....

....

    Is an option for extension of the term of this lease to be given Lessee in lieu of the purchase of the improvements by the Lessor

at the end of the term? ....
....

$\left.\begin{array}{l}\text{Does}\\\text{Will}\end{array}\right\}$ lease provide that no building standing upon the demised

premises shall be removed during the last five years of the term?
....

22. **MORTGAGE OF REVERSION BY LESSOR:** Is Lessor required to give Lessee notice of mortgage on leased premises? ....

Is mortgage to prohibit prepayment of rent by Lessee? ....

Is deposit made by Lessee to be applied on mortgage in the event of the termination of the lease? ....

Are insurance moneys to be applied on mortgage in the event of the termination of the lease? ....

Is part of the insurance to be carried for the benefit of mortgagee and if so, to what amount? ....

23. **RE-ENTRY AND FORCIBLE DETAINER:** Does Lessor have right to re-enter upon default by Lessee? ....
....

Does Lessee covenant to surrender possession upon termination of lease? ....

Is demand or notice to Lessee upon termination of lease waived?
....

If Lessee shall fail to deliver up possession of the premises in the event of the termination of the lease in case of default, shall he be deemed guilty of forcible detainer? ....

In such event, shall the Lessee be subject to eviction and removal, forcibly or otherwise, with or without process of law? .....
....

24. **DISTRESS FOR RENT:** In the event of continuing default by Lessee after notices as provided for, may Lessor distrain for rent or any other moneys due Lessor, upon any goods, chattels or property at the time belonging to Lessee? ....
....

25. **LIEN FOR RENT:** Does Lessor have lien for rent? ....

If so, on what? ....

26. **DEFAULT OF LESSEE:** Is notice of default required to be given Lessee? ....

If so, what notice is required? ....

As to rent? (60 days?) .... As to other covenants? (90 days?) ....

Is notice to be served at a designated place personally and/or by mail? ....

What shall constitute proof of service of notice? ....

Does receipt of rent after notice waive prior defaults? ....

$\left.\begin{array}{l}\text{Is lease to}\\\text{Does lease}\end{array}\right\}$ contain provision that no waiver of breach shall

constitute a waiver of succeeding breaches? ....

Is lease to ⎫
Does lease ⎰ provide that upon the written request of the Lessee, addressed to the Lessor in the same manner as a notice would be addressed under the terms of the lease, the Lessor shall be required to furnish to the Lessee a letter stating that the Lessee is not in default under any of the terms, covenants or conditions of the lease, or if the Lessee be in default, stating to what extent such default is existent? . . . .

Is lease to ⎫
Does lease ⎰ provide that in the letter of request from the Lessee, the Lessee must state he desires such letter for the purpose of exhibiting same to a purchaser, a title company, or a trustee under a mortgage or trust deed upon the leasehold estate? . . . .

Is lease to ⎫
Does lease ⎰ provide that if Lessor does not comply with Lessee's request made as above outlined within thirty (30) days after the receipt of same, it may be considered that the Lessee is not in default under the terms of the lease? . . . .

27. **INTEREST:** What rate of interest is to be paid on deferred payments of rent? . . . .%

28. **INDEMNITY OF LESSOR:** Is Lessor to be indemnified against costs, expenses, damages, and reasonable and necessary attorney's fees in litigation to which he is made a party? . . . .

29. **PROVISION FOR RECEIVER:** Is lease to contain a provision for appointment of a receiver? . . . .

30. **REMEDIES CUMULATIVE:** Are all Lessor's remedies cumulative? . . . .

Is lease to ⎫
Does lease ⎰ provide that none of the rights and remedies of the Lessor shall exclude any other rights and remedies allowed by law? . . . .

31. **FRONTAGE CONSENTS:** Are frontage consents required to be executed by both the Lessee and Lessor? . . . .

32. **ASSIGNMENT OF LEASE:** What, if any, conditions exist precedent to the Lessee's right to assign his interest? . . . .

Is lease to ⎫
Does lease ⎰ provide that any assignment thereof, whether by Lessee or subsequent assignees, shall be valid only in case of a bona fide sale of the leasehold estate? . . . .

Is new building to be completed prior to assignment? . . . .

Is assignee to expressly assume liability on lease? . . . .

Is Lessee to be released of liability by any assignment of his interest providing he is not in default under any of the terms of the lease or only if such assignment is effected after the completion of the (first)building required to be built by said Lessee? . . . .

Do above conditions apply to successive assignments? . . . .

Is lessee to ⎱
Does lessee ⎰ have the right to sub-let any part, portion or all of
the said demised premises for any period or periods within the term
hereby demised (subject, however, to all covenants, agreements
and conditions of the lease) with the provision that upon the termination of the lease by lapse of time or otherwise, such sub-lease
or sub-leases shall ipso facto be terminated? ....

33. **MORTGAGE OF LEASEHOLD ESTATE:** Does Lessee have
right at all times to mortgage his leasehold estate? ....
Need notice be given to the Lessor? .... If so, what notice?....
Is mortgagee of leasehold entitled to notice of default of Lessee?
....
If so, what notice? ....
Is lease to contain provision that the mortgagee shall not become
liable as Lessee until seized of title? ....

34. **CONDEMNATION—EMINENT DOMAIN:** Is lease to ⎱ contain
Does lease ⎰
a "condemnation" clause? ....
If lease ⎰ is to ⎰ contain a "condemnation" clause:
⎱ does ⎱
Is lease to ⎱
Does lease ⎰ provide that in case any part of the demised premises less than the whole shall be taken by exercise of the power of
eminent domain, the Lessor shall receive such part of the award
made therefor as represents the value of the land so taken, in the
same manner as if this lease did not exist, but that from and after
the date which
⎰ such taking shall be effected   ⎱
⎱ the Lessor shall receive payment thereof ⎰ , the
yearly rental under the lease shall be abated to the extent of
................% of the amount of the award so paid to the Lessor, but in no event shall the annual rental reserved be less than
$................ per annum? ....
Is lease to ⎱
Does lease ⎰ provide that in case a part of the demised premises
only shall be taken, the balance of the award, representing the
value of the part of the building upon the demised premises so
taken and damages to the remainder, if any, shall be paid to the
Trustee, to be held, applied and disbursed by it, toward the reconstruction of a new or remodeled building? ....
Is lease to ⎱
Does lease ⎰ provide that the Lessee will alter, repair or remodel
the portion of the premises not taken or erect an entirely new
building within .... months? ....
Is lease to ⎱
Does lease ⎰ provide that all costs, expenses and liabilities arising

out of or in any way connected with the making of any alterations, remodeling, repairs, etc. shall be paid by the Lessee? ....

Is lease to ⎱ provide that plans and specifications shall be sub-
Does lease ⎰ mitted to the Lessor in the manner and under the same conditions as in cases of the erection of a new building? ....

Is lease to ⎱ provide for deposits by the Lessee in the same man-
Does lease ⎰ ner? ....

Is lease to ⎱ provide that after the completion of such alterations,
Does lease ⎰ remodeling or repairs, or the completion of such new building, as the case may be, and the payment thereof by said Lessee, that any money or securities remaining on deposit with the Trustee shall be paid by the Trustee to the Lessee if not in default in respect to any of the terms of the lease? ....

Is lease to ⎱ require the Lessee, in case of such partial condem-
Does lease ⎰ nation, to alter, repair or restore any building or to erect a new building, as provided in the lease, if the restoration shall be physically impossible by reason of the size of the area not condemned, or if the same shall be prohibited by the laws and ordinances in force at such time? ....

Is lease to ⎱ provide that in case the whole of the demised prem-
Does lease ⎰ ises shall be taken by exercise of the power of eminent domain, that the lease shall cease and determine upon the taking of possession of the demised premises from the Lessee and that the rights, liens and interests of the Lessor and the Lessee in the award of just compensation which shall be made therefor shall be governed by the law applicable in such cases? ....

Is lease to ⎱ provide that in the event the whole of the demised
Does lease ⎰ premises shall be taken by exercise of the power of eminent domain, while there shall be any money or securities, or proceeds thereof, or proceeds of insurance policies, on deposit with the Trustee thereunder, the same shall be paid or assigned to the Lessee by the Trustee, provided the Lessee shall not be in default in respect of any of the terms of the lease? ....

Is lease to ⎱ provide that in case any part of the demised prem-
Does lease ⎰ ises, less than the whole, shall be taken by exercise of the power of eminent domain, that the Lessor shall receive such pro rata part of the award made therefor as represents the present worth of the leased fee as determined by the proper market rate of capitalization of the rentals agreed to be paid as set forth under the terms of the then existing lease? ....

Is lease to $\Big\{$ provide that in case any part of the demised prem-
Does lease

ises less than the whole, shall be taken by exercise of the power of
eminent domain, that the Lessee shall receive all of the award,
with the exception of the fair market value of the part of the leased
fee so taken in direct proportion to the area of the whole lot?

. . . .

Is lease to $\Big\}$ provide that the Lessee shall be entitled to all of the
Does lease

award and shall be obligated to pay the full agreed rental that was
agreed to be paid for the entire premises, as if no part of the demised premises had been so taken? . . . .

35.   **TITLE OF** $\Big\{$ **LESSOR**   Is Lessor's title in fee simple or a lease-
LESSEE:

hold—in other words, is this an original or a sub-lease? . . . .

Is the Lessor to furnish the Lessee or is Lessee to furnish to purchaser an abstract of title, guarantee policy, or Torrens Certificate
of Title showing good and merchantable title and full right to
execute or sell this lease? . . . .

Is the Lessor to furnish the Lessee or does Lessee furnish to purchaser a survey of premises to be demised? . . . .

. . . .

If survey is to be furnished must it show that the building in
question is within the lot lines and also that there are no encroachments upon the premises in question? . . . .

36.   **SUB-LEASES:**   Are existing sub-leases, if any, to be assigned to
Lessee? . . . .

Does Lessee have unrestricted right to make future sub-leases?

. . . .

Must all sub-leases terminate prior to termination of main lease?

. . . .

37.   **COVENANT FOR QUIET ENJOYMENT:**   Is lease to contain
such a covenant? . . . .

Is the abatement of rent to be the limit of liability of Lessor in
the event of ouster of Lessee by superior title? . . . .

38.   **TRUSTEE AND SUCCESSORS IN TRUST:**   Who is Trustee?

. . . .

Who is first successor in trust? . . . . Who is second
successor in trust? . . . .

Under what circumstances may Trustee be removed and new
Trustee appointed? . . . .

. . . .

Is Lessee to pay Trustee's compensation and expenses? . . . .
What are Trustee's powers to pass on securities? . . . .
Has Trustee any other powers? . . . .

. . . .

39.   **OPTION TO PURCHASE—RENEWAL:**   Has Lessee the op-

tion to purchase leased fee or to renew lease for additional term of years? ....

What notice must be given? ....

Under what conditions may option be exercised? ....

If option to extend is exercised, how is rental for extended term to be determined, or does lease fix rental for extended term? ......

40. JOINT MORTGAGE OF FEE AND LEASEHOLD:

Is lease to $\}$
Does lease $\}$ Contain a provision to the effect that the Lessor

agrees to join with the Lessee in a joint mortgage covering both the fee and the leasehold estate and the improvements thereon, if any? ....

If so, state special conditions under which such joining may be requested of Lessor? ....

....

41. NOTICES: Are notices to be in writing? .... Is mailing of notice conclusive? ....

If so, to what addresses? Lessor: .... Lessee: ....

Are notices sent by mail required to be registered? ....

42. COVENANTS TO RUN WITH LAND: Is lease to $\}$ contain a
Does lease $\}$

provision that all the covenants, conditions, provisions and agreements contained in the lease are to run with the land? ....

43. EXECUTION: Is wife or husband of Lessor to join in lease to release dower and/or homestead? ....

Is lease to be executed in duplicate or triplicate? ....

44. ACKNOWLEDGMENT: Is lease (to be) acknowledged by parties? ....

(RECORDING: Lease $\{$ filed $\}$ Registrar's
recorded .... in the $\}$ Recorder's

Office of .... County .... in Book ....

Page ....)

(Note: The words "Lessor" and "Lessee" wherever used herein shall be construed to mean "Lessors" and "Lessees" in all cases where there is more than one Lessor or Lessee, and the necessary grammatical changes required to make the verbiage hereof apply to corporations or individuals, men or women, are of necessity assumed.)

The following conditions may be regarded as special conditions or clauses which are not covered by the preceding form.

PERCENTAGE LEASE: For example, if the lease is what is commonly known as a "Percentage lease" the following information is important:

Is percentage to be computed on gross sales and/or receipts, which shall include all sales of merchandise and/or performance of any service for any customer or patron for compensation by any salesman or employee working in, out, through, or from the demised premises for cash or on charge basis, paid or unpaid, collected or uncollected, less all credits for returned merchandise, merchandise trade-ins, exchanges, merchandise purchase certificates (due bills), re-possessed merchandise, merchandise cancellations, allowances, discounts, and any and all other credits of similar nature, of the Lessee's business? ....

....

....

Does percentage lease also require a minimum or guaranteed rental? ....

If the latter is the case, what is the amount of the minimum or guaranteed rental? ....

....

What is the rate percent of the gross volume of business which is to be paid? ....

What sales records are to be kept by Lessee? ....

What provisions are to be made for audits? ....

Are copies to be furnished to Lessor? ....

Are periodic statements of the Lessee's business to be furnished to Lessor? ....

What supervision is Lessor to have of accounting methods of Lessee? ....

Are any departments of Lessee's business excluded from operation of percentage provisions? ....

....

AIR RIGHT LEASE: The following conditions may be regarded as special conditions or clauses in the event this is an Air Right lease:

Do the demised premises include certain sub-surface rights to be used for foundations? ....

Above how many feet from .... City Datum are complete rights granted? ....

Must a floor or roof be constructed at such level above .... City Datum? ....

....

What proportion of the general real estate taxes upon the land is the Lessee required to pay? ....

PROPRIETARY LEASE: If lease is a Proprietary lease, the demised premises may be described as:

"Apartment .... on the .... floor in the apartment building of the Lessor known as .... and located at .... on a parcel of real estate in the City of .... County of .... and State of .... known by legal description as: ....

A Proprietary lease should also state those items to which the title of the Lessor in and to the apartment building and the land upon which the same is located is subject, such as mortgage, taxes and special assessments, other proprietary leases, etc. and should also state the proportionate liability of the Lessee as to cash requirements, including maintenance and operating costs ....

Before Closing a Transaction, Check this List to Avoid Omissions, Errors and Other Misunderstandings

Have $\begin{Bmatrix} \text{lessor and lessee} \\ \text{seller and purchaser} \end{Bmatrix}$ and/or their respective attorneys or agents approve settlement sheet.

In connection with cash and/or securities under lease which are turned over to the $\begin{Bmatrix} \text{lessees} \\ \text{purchasers} \end{Bmatrix}$ an indemnification from the $\begin{Bmatrix} \text{lessees} \\ \text{purchasers} \end{Bmatrix}$ and/or from other responsible person should be obtained, as the original $\begin{Bmatrix} \text{seller} \\ \text{lessor} \end{Bmatrix}$ becomes liable in the event of the non-application of the cash and/or securities as provided in the lease.

A letter should be obtained from the Mortgage or Financial Institution and/or Bond House, showing the exact status of the mortgage or trust deed, particularly with respect to Monthly Deposits, Federal Income Taxes, State Taxes, etc. Such letters should also state that the mortgage is not in default, and if so in what respect.

All mortgages or trust deeds should be examined to ascertain whether the mortgage or trust deed gives to any person, company or corporation the right to take possession of and to operate the premises, during the extension of the mortgage indebtedness.

Does the trust deed or mortgage contain any provisions with reference to amortization, sinking fund or any other unusual provisions?

Ascertain if the $\begin{Bmatrix} \text{lessor} \\ \text{seller} \end{Bmatrix}$ or any preceding owner has given out any contract or management or has become obligated in any way to any person, firm or corporation for any commission accrued or to accrue on account of the management, leasing, and/or care of the property being sold.

Purchase money mortgage or trust deed should contain this expression: "This Trust Deed or Mortgage and the notes secured thereby are given as part purchase price of the premises herein described."

In the event the title of the property is under the Torrens System or Land Registration Act, see that an Owner's Duplicate Certificate of Title, issued by the Registrar of Titles, or a certified copy thereof showing title in the Grantor in said deed, together with a search made by the Registrar to the date thereof, has been made.

If the property has been recently improved, bear that in mind in connection with the pro-rating of taxes, because the previous year's taxes used as a basis for pro-rating may have been assessed on vacant property, while the current year's taxes may be on the property as improved.

Papers to Be Secured

Leases (assigned) or occupancy agreement.

Paid principal notes—First Mortgage.
Paid interest notes—First Mortgage.
Paid principal notes—Second Mortgage.
Paid interest notes—Second Mortgage.
Paid principal notes—Third Mortgage.
Paid interest notes—Third Mortgage.
Guarantee policies (assigned).
Abstracts.

Insurance policies (assigned).
Receipt for insurance policies.
Acceptance of assignment of insurance polices.

General tax bills.
Special assessment bills.
Survey.
Receipt for abstract, title papers, etc.
Advertising contracts.
Muniments of title.
Receipt for cash and/or securities.
Roof guarantee.
Sidewalk guarantee.

Plumbing, heating and other guarantees.
Statement of renting agent.
Service contracts, such as Exterminator, Elevator, etc.

Orders to all tenants to pay $\left\{\begin{array}{l}\text{purchaser}\\\text{lessee}\end{array}\right\}$ rent to

Miscellaneous contracts.
Letter to loan or mortgage houses.
Water, light and power bills.
Affidavit as to mechanics' liens and repairs.
Affidavits as to judgments, bankruptcy, divorce and pending proceedings.
Affidavit or letter from seller as to any outstanding promises or obligations to tenants for decorating and/or repairs.
Extension agreements of existing loans.
Agreements as to possession.
Cancel original contract after formal closing.
Record necessary papers.
Brokers' commission should be paid and receipt for same obtained.

Some Points to Consider in Closing

Original lease should be assigned and delivered.

Letter from proper parties showing lease not in default.

Security, if any, on deposit should be properly assigned.

The ground rent should be apportioned to date of the transfer.

What is the area of the lot?

What is the exact location?

What are the zoning restrictions and privileges?

Is the building built in conformity with the restrictions and in conformity with building ordinances?

Have any street lights been installed by private contractor which are unpaid for?

Are there any unpaid bills for planting or shrubbery?

Is there a definite understanding as to what fixtures go with the building? Such as: Hall carpets, ice boxes, refrigeration equipment, gas ranges, bath room fixtures, lighting fixtures, vacuum cleaners, lawn mowers, basement tools, scrubbing machinery, ladders and other equipment in use in the operation of the building, garden hose, storm doors, storm windows and screens.

Is there an agreement with the $\left\{\begin{array}{l}\text{lessor}\\\text{seller}\end{array}\right\}$ as to when he shall surrender possession and as to payment of rent during occupancy?

Who holds the loans on the premises?

Is there a portable garage on the premises?

Is there an understanding as to who pays for the owner's policy and who pays for the mortgage policy and for later date continuations?

Will the person ordering the guarantee policy pay the title company after the closing of the deal?

Are there any easements?

Ascertain rights or claims of parties in possession not shown of record. Ascertain if there are mechanics' lien claims where no notice appears of record.

Index

A

Access, right of, 16
Accounts, settling of, 52-55
Adaptability, of standard leases, 144-45
Additional rent, 14, 152
Advance rentals, income tax and, 136
Advertising:
    concessions and, 68-69
    direct mail, 62
    tenant, 59-60
Air rights, lease of, *specimen:*
    alterations, 368-69
    assessments, other charges, 363-64
    completion, date of, 359-61
    default, 374-76
    demised premises, 357-58
    electric current, 372
    entry, right of, 373-74
    floor loads, 368
    heirs, binding of, 382
    insurance, 369-70
    notices, 382
    occupancy, 367-68
    option to renew, 377-78
    quiet enjoyment, 381-82
    refusal, of second renewal, 381
    renewal term rentals, 379-81
    rent, 358-59
    repairs, 364-66
    restoration, 370-72
    second renewal, 378-79
    steam, 372-73
    subleasing, 366-67
    taxes, 361-63
    term, 358, 376-77

water and sewer rents, 361
Allowance, capital improvements, 63
Alterations, cost of, 18
America, origin of leasing in, 3-5
American chain stores, history, 86
Amortization lease, *specimen:*
    arbitration, 393
    default, 395-96
    delivery of premises, 396-97
    fire damage, 396
    insurance, 392-93
    premises, description of, 391-92
    purchase clause, 395
    rent, 392
    repairs, 393
    scheduling of chattels, etc., 397
    subleasing, 394-95
    taxes, 393
    use of premises, 394
Amortized lease agreement, *specimen:*
    assignment of rights, 401
    heirs, binding of, 402
    payment of existing mortgage, 402
    purchase clause, 401
Annuity, 118-19
Apartment lease, *specimen:*
    default, 268
    fire damage, 264
    possession, delivery of, 264
    repairs, 263
    subleasing, 265
    utilities, 264
Apartments:
    owner's obligation, 28
    tenant's obligation, 27

Assignment:
  definition, 9
  right of, 16
  short-term leases, 23
Attica, 1

B

Bacon, Matthew, 4
Bankruptcy, 14
  amortized lease agreement, 401
  Chicago percentage lease, 164
  concession lease, 216
  loft lease, 287
  new office building lease, 246
  sale-leaseback transaction, 318-19
  shopping center lease, 202
Baronical system, 2
Billboard and sign lease, *specimen:*
  rent, 298-99
  termination, 299
Bills, 14
Binding of heirs:
  air rights lease, 382
  amortized lease agreement, 402
  chain store lease, 178
  drilling for oil and gas, lease for, 305-6
  farm lease, 294
  furnished house or apartment lease,
    274
  in Knoxville percentage lease, 171
  manufacturing space lease, 281
  ninety-nine-year lease, 337
  in percentage store lease, 155
Bohack, 87
Bonuses:
  definition, 9
  income tax and, 136
Brownlow Realty, 44-45, 49, 168
Building agreement, *specimen:*
  abandonment, 353-55
  construction, 350-51
  disputes, 355
  engineering, 351
  liens, 351-52
  occupancy, 352
  planning, 348-49
  security, 352-53
Building Managers Association of
    Chicago, 62
Building services, 16
Business:
  manner of conducting, 58-59
  name of, 56-57

C

Canada, Dominion of, 86
Cancellation clause, 63-64
Capital improvements allowance, 63
Carter, H. W., 86
Casinghead gas, gasoline, 305
Chain stores:
  definition, 84
  extent of operations, 85
  history of, 85-88
  lease forms, 145
  leases, 91
  mail order houses, 87
  methods of operation, 88-89
  option to rent property for, 386
  percentage lease, *specimen:*
    alterations, 175
    damage or destruction, 175-76
    default, 176-77
    heat, 178
    heirs, binding of, 178
    laws, compliance with, 175
    lessor, inspection by, 178
    possession, delivery of, 177
    quiet possession, 177
    renewal, 178
    rentals, 173-74
    repair, 174-75
    subleasing, 175
    utilities, 178
  postwar development, 84-85
  in real estate field, 89-90
Charities, sale-leaseback and, 106
Chattel mortgage clause, *specimen*, 388-
    89
Check sheet, for long-term lease (*see*
    Long-term lease, check sheet)
Chicago percentage lease, *specimen:*
  additional charges, 160-61
  completion of premises, 161-62
  condemnation of premises, 162-63
  conduct, restriction of, 165
  damage by fire, 162
  default, 164
  description of premises, 158
  exclusives, 167
  fixtures, installation of, 167
  laws, compliance with, 165
  lessee, alteration rights of, 158-59
  lessor, examination by, 163
  liability insurance, 164
  maintenance, 159
  name, no change of, 159

Chicago percentage lease (*Cont.*)
  premises, surrender of, 168
  proper notices, 167
  rental, 160
  repairs, 163
  sales, definition of, 160
  subleasing, 163-64
  subordination of lease, 161
  tenant, alterations by, 165
  trade fixtures, removal of, 163
  use, restriction of, 164-65
  violations, 165-67
  warranty to tenant, 163
China, chain store in, 85
Clauses, recapture, 63-64
Coke, Lord, 3
Collecting lease renewals, form for, 385
Commissions, on concessions, 67
Common law, English, 4
Compliance with laws:
  chain store lease, 175
  Chicago percentage lease, 165
  concession lease, 218
  in Knoxville percentage lease, 170
  loft lease, 286
  mortgage deed, 412-13
  new office building lease, 238-39
  office lease, 226, 230
  sale-leaseback transaction, 314
  theater lease, 275-76
Compulsory advertising, 59-60
Concessions:
  advertising, 68-69
  default, 70
  definition, 9
  delivery service, 69
  employees, 69
  fixtures, 69
  lease for, *specimen:*
    advertising, 221-22
    bankruptcy, 216
    books and records, 221
    default, 219-20
    fire damage, 216-17
    fixtures and signs, 217
    insurance, 217-18
    labor unions, 221
    laws, compliance with, 218
    notices, 216
    property damage, 215-16
    rent, 211
    repairs, 219
    rules and regulations, 214-15
    sales records, 212-13
    services, 213-14

    taxes, 215
    term, 211
  location, 67-68
  management policy and, 66
  as mercantile transactions, 66
  most commonly leased, 66
  nature of operation, 68
  promotion, 68-69
  reasons for leasing, 65-66
  rental, 67
  sales receipts, 70
  store customs, 69
  store name, 68-69
  taxes and insurance, 70
  term of lease, 68
Continued occupancy, 58
Controllers Congress of the National Retail Dry Goods Association, 66
Controllers Institute, 67
Corporations, leases made by, 11
Corporations, subsidiary, 56-57
Covenants:
  definition, 6, 10, 13
  leasehold value and, 116-17

D

Damage, to property, 16
Declining balance depreciation, 138-39
Default, 14
  air rights lease, 374-76
  amortization lease, 395-96
  apartment lease, 268
  chain store lease, 176-77
  Chicago percentage lease, 164
  concession lease, 219-220
  drilling for oil and gas, lease for, 307
  farm lease, 294
  furnished house or apartment lease, 273-74
  house lease (short form), 308
  in Knoxville percentage lease, 170-71
  manufacturing space lease, 278, 280-81
  mortgage deed, 413
  new office building lease, 247
  news stand lease, 223-24
  ninety-nine-year lease, 334
  office lease, 227-28
  percentage store lease, 155
  sale-leaseback transaction, 318-19
  shopping center lease, 202-3
  theater lease, 276
  Woolworth Company lease, 326

Demise, definition, 10, 11
Department, Treasury, 113
Department stores, 88
Depreciation, income tax and, 138-39
Depression, leases and, 4
Differential:
    percentage, 62
    between wholesale and retail sales, 61-
        62
Direct mail sales, 62
Discount theory, of leasehold valuation,
    118-19
Diversification, portfolio, 109
Domain, eminent (*see* Eminent domain)
Drilling for oil and gas, lease for, *speci-
        men:*
    default, 307
    dry hole, 306
    heirs, binding of, 305-6
    operations, commencement of, 305
    rent, 304-5
    term, 305
Drive-ins, 85
Dwellings:
    owner's obligaticn, 26
    reasons for renting of, 25
    tenant's obligaticns, 25-26

                            E

Elizabeth I (England), 3
Eminent domain, 17
    new office building lease, 243
    shopping center lease, 200-201
Emphyteusis, 2
England, origin of leasing in, 2-3
Errors, checklist for, 431
Escalation clause:
    definition, 8
    in office building lease, 31
    in short-term leases, 22
Estate, leasehold, 115
Exclusive rights, 60-61
Extension, definition, 9

                            F

Farm lease, *specimen:*
    rent, 293
    repairs, 294-95
    subleasing, 294
Federal Housing Administration, 94, 98
Feudal system, 2

Financing, defined, 126
Financing leaseholds:
    investment by lessee, 130-31
    mortgaging the fee, 127-28
    value and, 129
Fire damage:
    amortization lease, 396
    apartment lease, 270
    Chicago percentage lease, 162
    concession lease, 216-17
    in Knoxville percentage lease, 169
    loft lease, 289
    news stand lease, 223
    ninety-nine-year lease, 333
    office lease, 230
    sale-leaseback transaction, 316-17·
Fire insurance, 15
Fixed rental, 41-42
Flat lease, 95
Forms, lease, 23
Fraternities, sale-leaseback and, 106
Furnished house or apartment lease,
        specimen:
    default, 273-74
    heirs, binding of, 274
    rent, 273

                            G

Gas station lease, *specimen:*
    permanent improvements, 298
    rent, 297
Gilman, George, 86-87
Ginter Company, 88
Graded lease, 95
Great Atlantic & Pacific Tea Company,
        86-87
Greece, origin of leasing in, 1
Gross lease, definition, 8
Gross receipts, 50
Gross sales, 49-50
Ground leases:
    advantages, 96-97
    dangers of high ground rentals, 100-
        101
    defaults, 103
    fixing rent on, 99-100
    inflation and, 101
    special users of, 102
    termination of, 103
    types of lessees in, 95-96
    types of property:
        commercial, 97
        industrial, 98-99
        residential, 97-98

H

Habendum, definition, 10, 12
Heirs, binding of (*see* Binding of heirs)
Henry VIII (England), 3
House lease (short form), *specimen:*
    rent, 307
    subleasing, 308
Hudson's Bay Company, 86

I

Income tax:
    basic principles:
        lessee, 134-35
        owner-lessor, 134
    changes in laws and regulations, 133-34
    considerations of lessee, 139-42
    considerations of lessor, 136-37
    cost of operation and maintenance, 137-38
    depreciation, 138-39
    income and expense in computation of, 136
    on lease cancellation payments, 137
    operating expenses of lessee, 140
    on property improvements, 137
    property improvements, 141
    real estate taxes, 140
    renewal options, 141-42
    rent as deduction, 139-40
    sale-leaseback transactions, 142
Industrial lease, method of renewing, 386-87
Insane, leases made by, 11
Institute of Real Estate Brokers, 157
Insurance, 14
    air rights lease, 369-70
    amortization lease, 392-93
    Chicago percentage lease, 164
    concession lease, 70, 217-18
    mortgage deed, 412
    ninety-nine-year lease, 331
    sale and leaseback transaction, 107, 313
    shopping center lease, 198
    short-term leases and, 22
Insured pension funds, 107
Intent, letter of, 146
Interest, leasehold, 115
Intermediate shopping center, 72
Intermediate-term leases, 7
Internal Revenue Code, 134
Internal Revenue Service, 133

J

Japan, chain store in, 86

K

Kinney, 88
Knoxville percentage lease, *specimen:*
    additional rental, 172
    agent, naming of, 171
    conduct, limitation of, 171
    default, 170-71
    extended occupancy, 170
    exterior sign, 170
    fire damage, 169
    fixtures, ownership of, 171
    heat, 169-70
    heirs, binding of, 171
    laws, compliance with, 170
    lessor, examination by, 170
    new front, installation of, 172
    privileges, waiver of, 171
    proper notice, 171
    quiet possession, 172
    repair, 169, 171
    utilities, 170
Kresge, 88
Kress, 88
Kroger Grocery Company, 87

L

Landlord (*see* Lessor)
Landlord leases, 144
Landscaping, in shopping center, 74
Laurium, 1
Laws, compliance with (*see* Compliance with laws)
Lawyer, need for, 145-46
Lease and leasehold estate, assignment of, 389-90
Leaseback, sale and (*see* Sale and leaseback)
Leased departments (*see* Concessions)
Lease forms, 23
    book of, 144-45
Lease forms:
    for chain stores, 145
Leasehold:
    agreement to sell:
        premises, delivery of, 410
        purchase clause, 410
        rent, 409-10
    definition, 6, 115

Leasehold (*Cont.*)
  financing of (*see* Financing lease-
    holds)
  and lessor-lessee relationship, 21-22
  when mortgagable, 129
  as mortgagable risk, 130
  selling of, 131
  valuation (*see* Valuation of lease-
    holds)
Leasehold estate, 115
Leases:
  adaptability of standard, 144-45
  agreements to make, 146
  of apartments, 27-28
  and bankruptcy, 14
  cancellation payments, tax on, 137
  for chain stores, 91
  characteristics, 10-19
  definition, 6, 10, 115
  drawing of, 143-47
  of dwellings, 24-28
  eminent domain, 17
  extensions of, *specimen*, 385
  Income Tax Laws and (*see* Income
    tax)
  infants, by or to, 11
  influence of shopping center character-
    istics on, 77-83
  landlord, 144
  and legal counsel, 23
  long-term (*see* Long-term leases)
  on office buildings, 29-31
  percentage (*see* Percentage leases)
  re-negotiation of, 146-47
  shopping center (*see* Shopping center
    leases)
  short-term (*see* Short-term lease)
  standardized, 143-44
  of stores, 28-29
  termination of, 19
  utility charges, 14
Leasing:
  during depression, 4
  lack of uniformity in, 3
  methods, 1
  origin, 1-5
Lessee, 1
  ability to pay, 43-45
  advertising by, 59-60
  capital improvements allowance, 63
  of chain store, 90-91
  compliance with statutes, 15
  as concessionaire, 65-70
  condemnation award, 17

credit rating of, 108
  deductions of, 134-35
  definition, 6
  in early England, 3
  exclusive rights of, 60-61
  gross sales and, 50
  inspecting books of, 51-52
  leasehold mortgagee and, 126-27
  legal counsel for, 144
  long-term building leases, 4
  in long-term ground lease, 95-96
  manner of conducting business of, 58-
    59
  obligations concerning care of property,
    18-19
  recapture clause and, 63-64
  rent deductible by, 139-40
  restriction against other outlets of, 59
  sale-leaseback and, 108
  security of, 9
  subletting by, 12, 60
  tax considerations of, 135, 139-42
  trade name, 56-57
Lessor, 1
  allowable expenses of, 134
  amortization, payments required for,
    table, 114
  concessions and, 65-70
  definition, 6
  exclusive rights given by, 60-61
  expenses of, 139
  lessee's books inspected by, 51-52
  lessee's trade name, 56-57
  ninety-nine-year lease and, 4
  recapture clauses and, 63-64
  restriction against other outlets by, 59
  right of access of, 16
  sale-leaseback and, 106-8
  security and, 14-15, 102-3
  subleasing and, 60
  tax computation of, 135
  tenant's business methods, 58-59
Lewis, Clarence M., 128
Location, importance of, 33
Loft buildings, 31
Loft lease, *specimen:*
  abandonment, 287-88
  additions and alterations, 285-86
  bankruptcy, 287
  charter of occupancy, 286
  fire damage, 289
  lessor, indemnification of, 292
  property damage, 288
  quiet possession, 291

Loft lease (*Cont.*)
  rent, 284
  rules and regulations, 290
  services, 284-85
  subleasing, 286-87
Long-term lease:
  agreement, *specimen:*
    lessee, rent paid to, 406
    purchase clause, 404-5
    rent, 404
    security, 405
  as aid to rental housing, 94
  of buildings, 4
  capital value of land, 100
  check sheet:
    air right lease, 430
    alterations and improvements, 423
    assignment, 425-26
    condemnation, 426-28
    construction of new building, 420-21
    default, 420, 424-25
    distress for rent, 424
    eminent domain, 426-28
    execution, 429
    fee, legal title to, 416
    frontage consents, 425
    further building provisions, 423
    indemnity of lessor, 425
    insurance, 418-19, 422-23
    interest, 425
    joint mortgage of fee and leasehold, 429
    leasehold, legal title to, 416
    lessor, mortgage of reversion by, 424
    lien for rent, 424
    liens, covenant against, 419-20
    maintenance of buildings, 418
    mortgage of leasehold estate, 426
    percentage lease, 429-30
    premises, 417
    present improvements, 416
    proprietary lease, 430-31
    purchase, option to, 428-29
    quiet enjoyment, 428
    realty, building part of, 423-24
    rebuilding, 422
    receiver, provision for, 425
    recording, 429
    re-entry, 424
    remedies cumulative, 425
    renewal, 428-29
    rental, 417
    repairs, 418
    run with land, covenants to, 429
    sale of present building, 418
    security, 421-22
    subleases, 428
    taxes and assessments, 417-18
    term, 417
    trustee, successors, 428
    waste, covenant against, 420
  classification:
    as to lease term and renewal provisions, 95
  classifications:
    as to type of property, 94
  definition, 7, 92-93
  on land, 95-103 (*see also* Ground leases)
  lessor and, 21
  tax consideration, 93-94
  twenty-one year standard, 93
  utilization of, 93-94
Los Angeles percentage lease, *specimen:*
  abandonment, 181-82
  alterations, 180
  casualty, restoration, 182-83
  condemnation, 183
  construction of lease, 186-87
  damages and claims, 182
  holding over, 186
  insolvency, 185-86
  lessor, inspection by, 181
  mechanics' liens, 184-85
  notices, 186
  percentage rent, 183-84
  possession, delivery of, 179-80
  premises, 179
  rent, 179
  repairs, 180-81
  subordination, 185
  taxes and charges, 182
  term, 179
  use of premises, 180

M

McAleer, E. F., 323
McCrory, 87
Magazine advertising, 59-60
Mail order houses, 87
Maintenance:
  Chicago percentage lease, 159
  loft lease, 291
  shopping center lease, 196-97
Manufacturing buildings, 31

Manufacturing space lease, *specimen:*
　　alterations, 279
　　default, 278, 280-81
　　heirs, binding of, 281
　　lessor, examination by, 279-80
　　rent, 277-78
　　rules and regulations, 281-83
　　use of premises, 278-79
　　utilities, 280
Massachusetts Institute of Technology,
　　323
Media, visual, 59-60
Melville Shoes, 88
Minimum rental, 40-42
Misunderstandings, checklist for, 431
Mitsui, Takatoshi, 86
Mortgage, self-liquidating, 110
Mortgage, deed, *specimen:*
　　default, 413
　　foreclosure, 415
　　insurance, 412
　　laws, compliance with, 412-13
　　promissory note, 411-12
　　sale, 413-14
Mortgage financing, sale-leaseback and,
　　109-11
Mortgaging the fee, benefits of, 127-28

N

National Institute of Real Estate Brokers,
　　46
Neighborhood shopping center, 72
Net lease:
　　definition, 8
　　insurance, 14
　　taxes, 14
　　usual duration of, 22
Net rental, definition, 8
New office building lease, *specimen:*
　　alterations, 238
　　bankruptcy, 246
　　certificate of occupancy, 245
　　default, 249
　　definitions, 253
　　end of term, 249
　　fees and expenses, 249
　　heat, 252
　　landlord, remedies of, 248
　　laws, compliance with, 240
　　lessor, examination by, 244-45
　　proper notice, 252
　　property damage, 240-41

　　quiet enjoyment, 250
　　rent, 237
　　repair, 239
　　rules and regulations, 254
　　waiver of redemption, 248
　　water charges, 252
Newspaper advertising, 59-60, 68-69
News stand lease, *specimen:*
　　default, 223-24
　　heirs, binding of, 224
　　rent, 223
New York State Rent Commission, 28
Ninety-nine-year lease, *specimen:*
　　appropriations, 336-37
　　arbitrators, 334-35
　　binding of heirs, 337
　　default, 334
　　fire damage, 333
　　insurance, 331
　　quiet possession, 338
　　rent, 329
　　short form, 339-46
　　strikes, 332
　　taxes, 330
Northwest Company, 86
Notices, 14

O

Occupancy, continued, 58
Office building:
　　escalator clause, 31
　　owner's obligation, 30
　　rent, 29-30
　　tenant's work, 30-31
Office lease, *specimen:*
　　default, 227-28
　　double rent, 229
　　fire damage, 230
　　laws, compliance with, 226, 230
　　proper notice, 231
　　rent, 225
　　rules and regulations, 232-35
　　subleasing, 226
　　termination, 228-29
　　utilities, 229
Off premises sales, 62-63
Oil well lease (long form), *specimen:*
　　assigning of, 304
　　lessor, percentage of oil to, 302
　　rent, 303

Oil well lease (short form), *specimen:*
  pipe lines, depth of, 301
  rent, 300
  well, completion of, 300-301
Omissions, checklist for, 431
One family house lease, *specimen*, 295-96
Options, renewal, 141-42
Other outlets, restriction against, 59
Owl Drug, 88

P

Papers, to be secured, *list*, 432
Parking, at shopping center, 73-74
Pension funds, sale-leaseback and, 107
Percentage differentials, 61-62
Percentage lease:
  accounting provisions, 48-55
  advantages, 36
  of Chicago (*see* Chicago percentage
    lease, *specimen)*
  definition, 8, 32
  development, 32-33
  disadvantages, 36
  kinds of, 34-35
  kinds of businesses under, 37-38
  of Knoxville (*see* Knoxville percentage
    lease, *specimen*)
  of Los Angeles (*see* Los Angeles per-
    centage lease, *specimen*)
  main use of, 5
  minimum rental, 40-42
  for news stand (*see* News stand lease)
  percentage rates, 42-47
  special provisions:
    capital improvements allowance, 63
    continued occupancy, 58
    differential between wholesale and
      retail sales, 61-62
    exclusive rights, 60-61
    manner of conducting business, 58-
      59
    name of business, 56-57
    off premises sales, 62-63
    percentage differentials for varying
      types of merchandise, 62
    prior possession, 57-58
    recapture clause, 63-64
    subleasing, 60
  tenant qualifications, 38-39

term of, 34
Percentage rates:
  list, 46-47
  tenant's ability to pay, 43-45
Philadelphia Retail Controllers Association,
  66
Planning element, in shopping centers, 75-76
Portfolio diversification, 109
Possession:
  lessor's failure to give, 17-18
  prior, 57-58
  tenant's right to, 15-18
Present value, *tables*, 120-23
Present value theory, of leasehold valuation,
  119-25
Primary rental, definition, 8
Prime rating, 108
Prime tenant, definition, 7
Priority, waiver of, *specimen*, 387-88
Prior possession, 57-58
Privileges, waiver of (*see* Waiver of
  privileges)
Property:
  condemnation of, 17
  loss of, 16
  tenant's obligation, 18-19
Public areas, care of, 19

R

Real Estate Board of New York, 13, 14
Reappraisal lease, 95
Recapture clauses, 63-64
Receipts, gross, 50
Recitals, definition, 10, 11-12
Reddendum, definition, 10, 12
Regional shopping center, 72
Reimbursables, 81-83
Religious organizations, sale-leaseback and,
  106
Re-negotiation, 146-47
Renewal options, 141-42
Renewal option, definition, 9
Rent:
  additional, 14
  air rights, 358-59
  amortization lease, 392
  chain store lease, 173-74
  Chicago percentage lease, 160
  computation of, 29-30

Rent (*Cont.*)
   concession lease, 211
   default in payment of, 14
   definition, 6
   drilling for oil and gas, lease for, 304-5
   farm lease, 293
   fixed, 41-42
   furnished house or apartment lease, 273
   gas station lease, 297
   house lease (short form), 307
   income tax and, 136
   inflation and, 101
   leasehold value and, 116
   loft lease, 284
   long-term lease agreement, 404
   long-term leases and, 94
   Los Angeles percentage lease, 179, 183-84
   manufacturing space lease, 277-78
   minimum guaranteed, 40-42
      continued occupancy, 58
      prior possession, 57-58
   mortgage deed, 413
   new office building lease, 235-36
   news stand lease, 223
   ninety-nine-year lease, 329
   office lease, 225
   oil well lease, 303
   one family house lease, 295
   percentage store lease, 151-52
   sale and leaseback transaction, 312
   shopping center lease, 189-90
   as tax deduction, 139-40
   tenant's obligation to pay, 13-15
   theater lease, 275
   Woolworth Company lease, 324
Renting agent, 144
Repair:
   air rights lease, 364-66
   amortization lease, 393
   apartment lease, 271
   chain store lease, 174-75
   Chicago percentage lease, 163
   concession lease, 219
   farm lease, 294-95
   good state of, 18-19
   house lease (short form), 308
   Knoxville percentage lease, 169, 171
   Los Angeles percentage lease, 180-81
   new office building lease, 237-38
   sale-leaseback transaction, 314-15
Revaluation lease, 95
Rights:
   concession, 65-70
   exclusive, 60-61

Roads, in shopping center, 73-74
Roaring Twenties, 4
Rome, origin of leasing in, 1-2

S

Sale and leaseback:
   basic interest rate, 111-12
   commitment to purchase, 309-10
   definition, 105
   income tax and, 142
   initial lease term, 111
   lease for, *specimen:*
      buy, options to, 321-22
      condemnation of premises, 316-18
      default, 318-20
      fire insurance, 313
      landlord's investment, 314
      laws, compliance with, 314
      miscellaneous, 322
      options to renew, 320-21
      premises, description of, 310-11
      rent, 312
      repairs and alterations, 314-15
      subleasing, 318
      taxes, 312-13
      term, 311-12
   lessee in, 108
   lessor in, 106-8
   option to repurchase, 113
   pension funds, 107-8
   pros and cons, 108-9
   rental, 111
   sales price, 111
   type of property, 113-14
   versus mortgage financing, 109-11
Sales:
   daily reporting of, 53
   definition, 50-51
Sales:
   differential between wholesale and retail, 61-62
   direct mail, 62
   gross, 49-50
   off premises, 62-63
   reporting of, 52-55
Sales checks, separate, 53
Sandwich lease, definition, 7
Satisfactory rating, 108
Sears, Roebuck & Company, 87
Secondary rental, definition, 8
Security, 9, 14-15
Security deposits, income tax and, 136-37
Self-administered pension funds, 107-8
Self-liquidating mortgage 110

Services, building, 16
Shopping centers:
  characteristics, 72-73
  completion of buildings, 76
  definition, 71
  general administration, 73-74
  lease for, *specimen:*
    access to premises, 199-200
    assignment, 199
    bankruptcy, 202
    books and records, 191
    care of premises, 193-94
    commencement date, 188
    construction standards, 209-10
    covenant to hold harmless, 197
    damage, 201-2
    default, 202-3
    delayed possession, 188
    eminent domain, 200-201
    gross sales, 190
    heating, 207-8
    insurance, 198
    lease consideration, 189
    maintenance of building, 196-97
    new building, construction of, 187
    non-liability, 204
    occupancy, ready for, 189
    operation and maintenance, 191-93
    possession, delivery of, 187-88
    receiving, delivery, parking, 199
    rent, 189-90
    sales reports, 190-91
    signs and alterations, 197
    subordination, 203
    use of premises, 193
    utilities, 194-96, 206-7
  planning element, 75-76
  speculative element, 74-75
  types, 71-72
Shopping center leases:
  central administration, 77-79
  completion of buildings, 80-83
  planning element, 79-80
  speculative element, 79
Short-form lease:
  definition, 8-9
Short form lease:
  for recording purposes, 384
Short-term leases:
  commonest types of, 5
  definition, 7
  domination of market by, 20-21
  on dwellings, 24-28
  general rules for, 22-23
  improvements by tenant, 23

lack of partnership element in, 21
leasehold value and, 129-30
mortgage on, 16
oral, 21
recitals, 11-12
standardized, 143-44
subletting, 23
Singer Sewing Machine Company, 88
Speculative element, in shopping centers, 74-75
Split percentage lease, 168
Standardized leases, 143-44
Statutes, compliance with, 15
Step-up lease, 95
Storage space, 31
Store Leasing Committee of the Building Managers Association of Chicago, 59
Stores:
  percentage lease for, *specimen:*
    additional rent, 152
    business records, 152-53
    character of business, 154
    default, 155
    gross sales, definition, 152
    heirs, binding of, 155
    new store front, 153
    rent, 151-52
    rules and regulations, 156-57
    subleasing, 153-54
    termination, 155
    utilities, 154-55
  restrictions on tenants, 28-29
  structural improvements, 29
Straight lease, 95
Straight line depreciation, 138-39
Streets, in shopping center, 73-74
Subleasing:
  air rights, 366-67
  amortization lease, 394-95
  apartment lease, 265
  chain store lease, 175
  Chicago percentage lease, 163-64
  definition, 6
  farm lease, 294
  house lease (short form), 308
  loft lease, 286-87
  new office building lease, 246
  ninety-nine-year lease, 332
  office lease, 226
  percentage store lease, 153-54
  sale-leaseback transaction, 318
  theater lease, 276
  Woolworth Company lease, 325
Subordinate lease interests, sale of, 131-32
Subsidiary corporations, 56-57

Sum of digits, depreciation computed by, 138-39
Super markets, 88
Supra, 7-8

T

Taxes, 14
    air rights, 361-63
    amortization lease, 393
    concessions and, 70, 215
    and long-term leases, 93-94
    Los Angeles percentage lease, 182
    mortgage deed, 413
    ninety-nine-year lease, 330
    sale-leaseback transaction, 109-110
    sale and leaseback transaction, 312-13
    short-term leases and, 22
    Woolworth Company lease, 324
Television advertising, 59-60
Tenancy at will, definition, 7
Tenant (*see* Lessee)
Tenant advertising, 59-60
Term:
    definition, 6
    end of, 19
    leasehold valuation and, 117
Thasos, 1
Theater lease, *specimen:*
    default, 276
    laws, compliance with, 275-76
    proper notice, 277
    rent, 275
    subleasing, 276
    utilities, 275
Thompson, John R., 87-88
Thorn, George R., 87
Trade name, 56-57
Trading posts, 86
Treasury Department, 113
"Treatise on Leases and Terms for Years, A," 4
Trusted pension funds, 107

U

Ungraded lease, 95
United States Tax Court, 134
Universities, sale-leaseback and, 106
Use, of premises, 15
Utilities:
    apartment lease, 270-71
    chain store lease, 178
    in Knoxville percentage lease, 170
    loft lease, 284-85
    manufacturing space lease, 280
    office lease, 229
    percentage store lease, 154-55
    shopping center lease, 194-96, 206-7
    theater lease, 275
Utility charges, 13

V

Valuation of leaseholds:
    complexity, 115
    creation, 116-17
    limitations, 116-17
    open market concept, 115-16
    term of lease and, 117
    theory of, 117-25
Variety stores, 87-88
Visual media, 59-60

W

Waiver of priority, *specimen,* 387-88
Ward, Montgomery, 87
Westminster, Duke of, 2-3
William the Conqueror, 3
Willing buyer-willing seller theory, 115-16
Wolfson, Major Henry, 173
Woolworth, Frank W., 87
Woolworth Company lease, *specimen:*
    condemnation, 325-26
    default, 326
    fixtures, 324-25
    rent, 324
    subleasing, 325